Women in Management Worldwide

Women in Management Worldwide

Progress and Prospects

Second Edition

Edited by

MARILYN J. DAVIDSON
University of Manchester, UK

and

RONALD J. BURKE
York University, Toronto, Canada

GOWER

Gower Applied Business Research
Our programme provides leaders, practitioners, scholars and researchers with thought provoking, cutting edge books that combine conceptual insights, interdisciplinary rigour and practical relevance in key areas of business and management.

Published by
Gower Publishing Limited
Wey Court East
Union Road
Farnham
Surrey, GU9 7PT
England

Gower Publishing Company
Suite 420
101 Cherry Street
Burlington,
VT 05401-4405
USA

www.gowerpublishing.com

British Library Cataloguing in Publication Data
Women in management worldwide : progress and prospects. – 2nd ed.
   1. Women executives –Cross-cultural studies.
   I. Davidson, Marilyn. II. Burke, Ronald J.
   658.4'0082-dc22

Library of Congress Cataloging-in-Publication Data
Women in management worldwide : progress and prospects / Marilyn J. Davidson and Ronald J. Burke.
     p. cm.
   Includes index.
   ISBN 978-0-566-08916-9 (hardback : alk. paper) – ISBN 978-0-566-08917-6 (ebook)
  1. Women executives – Cross-cultural studies. I. Davidson, Marilyn. II. Burke, Ronald J.

   HD6054.3.W66 2011
   331.4'81658–dc22

          2011003097
ISBN 9780566089169 (hbk)
ISBN 9780566089176 (ebk)

MIX
Paper from
responsible sources
FSC
www.fsc.org
FSC® C018575

Printed and bound in Great Britain by the
MPG Books Group, UK

Contents

List of Figures

List of Tables

List of Contributors

Editors

Marilyn J. Davidson is Professor Emerita, Manchester Business School, University of Manchester, UK and Co-Director of Davidson and Wood Consultants. Her current research interests include minority entrepreneurs; lesbian, gay and transsexuals in the workplace; women in management; gender pay gaps; occupational stress and gender differences; and diversity and equality in the workplace.

Ronald J. Burke is Professor Emeritus, Schulich School of Business, York University, Toronto, Canada. His current research interests include work and health; crime and corruption in organizations; occupational health and safety; corporate reputation; and human resource management in small businesses, non profit organizations and the public sector.

Contributors

Zeynep Aycan is Professor of Industrial and Organizational Psychology, Koc University, Department of Psychology, Istanbul, Turkey.

Carlos Cabral-Cardoso is Professor of Management, Faculty of Economics, University of Porto, Portugal.

Nuria Chinchilla is Professor of Managing People in Organizations, IESE Business School, University of Navarra, Barcelona, Spain.

Fang Lee Cooke is Professor of Human Resource Management and Chinese Studies, Department of Management, Monash University, Melbourne, Australia.

Sarah E. Crozier is a Senior Lecturer at the MMU Business School, Manchester Metropolitan University, Manchester, UK.

Mireia las Heras is Assistant Professor of Managing People in Organizations, IESE Business School, University of Navarra, Barcelona, Spain.

Carianne M. Hunt is a Research Associate, Quality Improvement Directorate, Salford Royal NHS Foundation Trust, Salford, UK.

Hayat Kabasakal is Professor of Organization Studies, Bogazici University, Management Department, Istanbul, Turkey.

Fahri Karakaş is Research Fellow at Open University Business School, at International Management Practice, Education, and Learning (IMPEL) Initiative, Milton Keynes, UK.

Rekha Karambayya is Associate Professor in Organizational Studies, Schulich School of Business, York University, Toronto, Canada.

Ronit Kark is a Senior Lecturer in the Department of Psychology, Bar-Ilan University, Israel and currently heads the Social-Organizational Section (Department of Psychology) and the "Gender in The Field" Program (Graduate Program for Gender Studies).

Saleema Kauser is Lecturer in Strategy and Director of Mbus Global, Manchester Business School, University of Manchester, Manchester, UK.

Roberto Kertész is Professor and President of the Flores University of Buenos Aires and Director of the Iberoamerican Institute of Family Businesses, University of Buenos Aires, Argentina.

Athena Petraki-Kottis is Professor Emeritus (Economics) of the Athens University of Economics and Business, Athens, Greece.

Haydée Kravetz is Dean of the School of Administration, University of Flores, Buenos Aires, Argentina.

Jacqueline Laufer is Emeritus Professor in Management and Human Resources, HEC School of Management, Paris, France.

Consuelo León is a Researcher at the International Centre for Work and Family, IESE, University of Navarra, Barcelona, Spain.

Ceyda Maden is a part-time instructor at the Management Department of Fatih University and Department of International Trade of Bogazici University, Istanbul, Turkey.

Kimberly Mathe is a doctoral student in the School of Hotel Restaurant Administration at Oklahoma State University, Oklahoma, USA.

Babita Mathur-Helm is Senior Lecturer of Business Administration in Organizational Development and Transformation and Gender Development, University of Stellenbosch Business School, University of Stellenbosch, Cape Town, South Africa.

Judy McGregor is Equal Employment Opportunities Commissioner of the Human Rights Commission, Wellington, New Zealand.

Susan Michie is a Visiting Professor of Management at the University of New Mexico, Albuquerque, Mexico, USA.

Debra L. Nelson is the Spears School of Business Associates' Distinguished Professor of Management at Oklahoma State University, Oklahoma, USA.

Astrid M. Richardsen is Head of Department of Leadership and Organizational Behaviour and Professor at BI Norwegian Business School, Oslo, Norway.

Golchehreh Sohrab is a Doctoral Candidate in Business Administration/ Organizational Studies, Schulich School of Business, York University, Toronto, Canada.

Kea G. Tijdens is Research Coordinator, Amsterdam Institute for Advanced Labour Studies (AIAS), University of Amsterdam, The Netherlands.

Hayfaa Tlaiss is an assistant professor at the faculty of business, University of New Brunswick, Saint John, Canada.

Laura E. M. Traavik is Associate Professor at BI Norwegian Business School, Oslo, Norway.

Zoe Ventoura-Neokosmidi is Assistant Professor (Economics) of the Athens University of Economics and Business, Athens, Greece.

Ronit Waismel-Manor is a Lecturer in the School of Behavioral Sciences, Netanya Academic College, Netanya, Israel.

Fiona M. Wilson is currently Professor of Organizational Behavior and Head of Management, University of Glasgow Business School, Glasgow, Scotland.

Glenice J. Wood is former Deputy Head of School, Learning and Teaching, Ballarat Business School, University of Ballarat, Ballarat, Australia and presently Co-Director of Davidson and Wood, Equality and Diversity Consultants.

Gina Zabludovsky is Professor and Researcher of Sociology, Facultad de Ciencias Politicas y Sociales, Universidad Nacional Autonoma de Mexico (UNAM), Mexico City, Mexico.

Acknowledgements

We have known and worked together for over 20 years. This is our fourth collaboration and we would like to acknowledge our colleagues in earlier women in management research and writing: Tamara Weir, Carol McKeen, Esther Greenglass, Lisa Fiksenbaum, Mary Mattis, Rekha Karambayya, Debra Nelson, Cary Cooper, Andrew Gale, Mary Barrett, Glenice Wood, and Sandra Fielden.

We also thank our international contributors. Our participation in this collection was supported in part by York University and the Manchester Business School (special thanks to Jackie Kan and Arqam Mir).

Finally, thanks to our courageous daughters – Fern Eyre-Morgan, Sharon Burke and Rachel Burke.

Marilyn J. Davidson   Ronald J. Burke

Women in Management Worldwide: Progress and Prospects – An Overview

Marilyn J. Davidson and Ronald J. Burke

> *Women are the most underutilized natural resource in the world.*
> *CARE, USA.*

Introduction

Women continue to enter the workplace in increasing numbers in all developed countries. Several factors account for this trend. An increasing number of economies have become industrialized, the service sector has grown opening up positions for women, and growth in public and not-for profit sectors have created new opportunities for women. Finally, attitudes towards working women, particularly women with children, as well as political and legal initiatives, have supported this trend.

However, the pace of advancement for women mangers and professions continues to be slow and uneven in different countries and cultures (Barreto, Ryan and Schmitt, 2009; Burke, 2009; Burke and Mattis, 2007; Helfat, Harris and Wolfson, 2006; Tarr-Whelan, 2009). In many cases, these women have invested in preparation for careers by undertaking higher education, with the proportion of women in university now equal to or greater than that of men. Women tend to enter the workplace at levels similar to men, with similar credentials and expectations, but their career paths quickly begin to diverge (Burke and Mattis, 2005; Burke and Nelson, 2002). Furthermore, women are obtaining the necessary experience for advancement but still fall short, a finding observed in all developed countries (Adler and Izraeli, 1988; Davidson and Burke, 2004; Wirth, 2001).Women continue to be paid less than men doing similar types of work (Blau and Kahn, 2007). It should also be noted there are indications that the worldwide economic recession may be facilitating an increasing number of women's employment into part-time jobs in some countries (for example, UK and USA), it may also be having a more determined impact on full-time female employment. In the UK for example, during the third quarter of 2009, women suffered a greater loss of full-time jobs (68,000) compared to men (12,000) (Office for National Statistics, 2009).

Why should organizations be interested in developing and using the talents of women? Schwartz (1992) offered several reasons why supporting the aspirations of talented women makes sound business sense. Organizations that do this get the best people for leadership positions, providing senior-level male executives experience in working with successful women. Supporting capable women signals to women employees, and both male and female clients and customers, that women will be treated similarly to men, and role models for junior women managers will be available. Finally, supporting qualified and talented women ensures that all managerial jobs will be filled with strong individuals. These benefits are particularly important given the acknowledged shortage of effective managerial talent (Burke and Cooper, 2006), the failure of at least half the current managerial incumbents in performing their jobs successfully (Hogan and Hogan, 2001), the self-acknowledged failures of organizations to develop managerial talent (Fulmer and Conger, 2004), and the current "war for talent" (Michaels, Handfield-Jones and Axelrod, 2001). It makes no sense to ignore the talents of half the population.

In Japan for example, only 0.8 percent of CEOs are women versus 10 percent in the UK. Less than 10 percent of Japanese managers are women versus 43 percent in the US and Japan is currently having a severe shortage of talent and does not encourage immigration (Catalyst, 2007). The only viable solution to this talent shortfall is for Japan to do a much better job of developing and advancing qualified women.

Shriver (2009), based on the fact that half the US workforce is now female, used the phrase "female nation" to highlight the fact that this body of employed women is going to bring about changes to men, women, families, organizations and society as a whole. More working women now have children. An increasing number of women are earning more salary than their husbands/ partners do. These facts are changing the nature of families, and the roles that men and women play. Children want both their mothers and fathers to come home from work less tired and less stressed. More men are now shouldering home and family responsibilities. Dual earner families need to negotiate who is responsible for what and flexibly respond to changes as they arise. Both women and men are increasingly desirous of workplace flexibility and lower workloads and job demands (Shriver, 2009).

In addition, it is clear that women are becoming an increasing economic force in terms of their purchasing influence and power (Silverstein and Sayre, 2009a; 2009b). Silverstein and Sayre indicate that women in the USA control $20 trillion in consumer spending and this figure is expected to increase. In addition, women earn about $11 trillion in total yearly income and this figure will also rise. Women make the major purchasing decisions in several areas (for example, home furnishings, vacations, automobiles). Women represent the largest market opportunity in the world (Wittenberg-Cox and Maitland, 2008). Yet women get little help at home (Jones, Burke and Westman, 2006) and are too often ignored by manufacturers and service providers. Tapping into these women represents a unique organizational competitive advantage, more likely to be realized if more women influence organizational decision making.

Tarr-Whelan (2009) makes a strong case for increasing the numbers of women in senior executive and key decision-making roles in organizations. The key point is using the talents of half the population that previously have been ignored. She suggests that having 30 percent of these leadership positions filled by qualified women represents a "tipping point" that puts the influence on business issues and off gender. Konrad, Kramer and Erkut (2008) also suggest that having three or more women on a corporate board of directors serves as a similar critical mass or tipping point.

What do women bring to the table? Tarr-Whelan (2009) identifies five benefits organizations realize from having more women in senior jobs:

- Higher profits, more risk awareness, less hypercompetitive and a greater ability to survive financial downturns.

- Policies that contribute to individual and societal health – education, families, entrepreneurship.

- A stronger integration of work and family leading to higher productivity and quality of life.

- Increased commitment to both personal and corporate responsibility and broader and more long-term planning.

- Management that reflects the twenty-first century –teamwork, participative decision making.

But why are there still so few women in top management? Suggestions that address this question have been offered by Catalyst (2002; 2007). In 2002, Catalyst's survey on 20 European countries and the USA, found stereotypes and preconceptions of women's roles ranked the top barrier to women's advancement (Catalyst, 2002). Indeed, these findings were once again replicated more recently when analyzing data from 110 US corporations' Talent Management Systems and Catalyst (2007) found gender biases and stereotypes existed particularly in succession planning processes. Other career development barriers which particularly affected women and minorities included the lack of 360 degree performance appraisal.

Over a decade ago, Powell (1999) observed that men continued to dominate senior-level positions and it was difficult to eliminate bias and discrimination in the workplace. Men are likely to be more comfortable with other men – the "old boy network". Hiring and promotion decisions are often unstructured and open to bias. More recently, the Harvard Business Review (Silverstein and Sayre, 2009a; 2009b), reported on a survey of 500 companies which found that candidates for senior executive positions typically went through only one to five interviews (32 percent) and half relied on the hiring manager's "gut feeling" (a feeling that the candidate had what it takes to be successful in any job). So much for objective selection procedures and acknowledgement of "similarity–attraction" theories! Research continues to indicate that talented women at lower levels may not receive the necessary development opportunities compared to their male counterparts (Powell, 2010). Furthermore, some women may not go after higher-level jobs because of their family responsibilities and the lack of family-friendly and flexible working environments and/or an unwillingness to make the sacrifices necessary to succeed in them (Davidson and Fielden, 2003).

Morrison, White and Van Velsor (1987) reported that women had difficulties fitting into their organization's culture, were seen by men as wanting too much for themselves or for other women, or had performance difficulties. Managerial women had to walk a fine line, they had to be tough but not too tough, they had to stand on their own two feet yet ask for help when needed, and they had to take career and job risks but still perform at a high level. More than 20 years later, male-defined views of work and career success still represent the norm (O'Neil, Hopkins and Bilimoria, 2008). One consequence of these barriers is a tendency for women to leave large organizations and pursue entrepreneurial and/or small business careers (Belkin, 2003; Fielden and Davidson, 2005; 2010; Mattis, 2004; Moore, 2000; Moore and Buttner, 1997)

Women in Management Worldwide (2004)

Women in management research and consultancy has been undertaken in several countries, over two decades or more. We decided in 2003 that it was time to take stock on initiatives being undertaken in various countries and develop some common metrics to determine the status of women at work and women in management in these countries. We (Davidson and Burke, 2004) asked authors from 21 countries to describe the status of women in management in each of their countries in common areas (for example, women in education, country legislation supporting women's advancement). These data would permit an examination of changes over time, comparisons across countries and provide baseline information to benchmark changes in the status of women over time. These data might also shed light on the role of country culture on women's work experiences and career progress.

We solicited chapters from countries in all major regions of the world, both developed and developing. It is interesting to note that some invited contributors declined as their countries did not systematically collect information of the kind we wanted to include. This resulted in our previous publication of the highly successful and award winning book *Women in Management Worldwide* (Davidson and Burke, 2004).

Women in Management Worldwide (2011)

Six years later in 2009, we decided to update our first book and asked some of the original contributing authors to update their chapters in describing the current status of women at work and in management and reflecting whatever had changed in the intervening six or seven years. In addition, we also invited a number of new cultures and included some new countries. Our objectives for this book were similar to those underlying the 2004 edition:

- Understand more about the status of women at work and women in management in a number of countries around the world.

- Continue the process of collecting common information to capture both trends over time and support comparisons across countries.

- Facilitate more cross-cultural research in these areas.

- Encourage more collaborative research across countries in these areas.

- Continue to raise the issue of utilizing the best talent available.

This book is divided into seven parts. These are: European Union countries (France, Greece, the Netherlands, Portugal, Spain and the United Kingdom); Europe (Norway and Russia); North and Central America (Canada, Mexico and the United States); Australasia (Australia and New Zealand); Asia (China, Israel, Lebanon and Turkey); South America (Argentina); and Africa (South Africa). Chapters consider labour force characteristics, numbers of women pursuing education, numbers of women in management, women entrepreneurs, legislation and initiatives supporting women in the workforce, and thoughts on what the future might hold. Below we summarize some of the similarities and differences which have emerged in this book in relation to the above objectives.

Similarities and Differences between Countries

LABOUR FORCE CHARACTERISTICS

The proportion of women in the paid workforces in all but two countries (China and Turkey) increased, particularly among married women with children; the proportion of women in the US workforce increased only marginally and has remained stable over the past few years.

WOMEN PURSUING EDUCATION

The proportion of women entering higher education, and education in business and the professions (law, accounting, management) continues to rise in most countries with women now also comprising a higher percentage of university students than men. Figures in both the US and New Zealand have remained stable, however, with women still comprising a higher percentage of university students than men. Considering university education in general, men and women still study different specializations. Men are more often found in engineering, mathematics and the sciences; women more often in the languages and social sciences. Countries differed in the percentages of women studying business with some having more women than men (for example,

Australia, Canada. France, Greece and Norway) and others, considerably more men than women (for example, South Africa, although white women still dominate management positions).

WOMEN IN MANAGEMENT

Women have increased their participation rates in managerial and professional jobs in most countries; the rates were fairly stable in Argentina. Women generally made progress at lower-management positions but are still woefully under-represented at senior levels of management. Women in all countries still get paid less than men, often working in the same jobs. There is also continued gender segregation with more men working in engineering, construction, mining and manufacturing and more women working in human resources, marketing and public relations. There was also considerable country variation: China reported the lowest percentage of female managers and professionals (16 percent) with Australia, Canada, the UK and the US the highest, at over 30 percent.

However, it should be noted that there is still a dearth of statistics and research on certain minority groups within the female management populations in many of the 20 countries, for example, indigenous women managers, black and minority ethnic women managers, disabled women managers, lesbian and bisexual women managers, one parent women managers, women managers from different religious denominations and so on.

WOMEN ENTREPRENEURS

There was an increasing proportion of women entrepreneurs and small business owners in almost all countries but in some countries the growth was slow (for example, Argentina) and in most countries these proportions were low (for example, Israel and Turkey). Women's entrepreneurial and small business ventures were typically very small in dollar volume and employee size, and though often working long hours, offered them employment flexibility. As well, women's entrepreneurial and small business ventures were also more likely to be in the service sector.

COUNTRY LEGISLATION

All countries had legislation in place supporting women at work, some countries more encompassing than others. There was a sense in some countries that more "teeth" needed to be in place to follow through on existing legislation (for example, Canada, Mexico and New Zealand). Moreover, there seemed to be great variability across countries in the interest and support of organizational employers in developing policies and programmes to support women's career advancement. Organizations in Canada, the UK and the US seemed to be the most proactive whereas employers in Argentina, South Africa, and Turkey seemed to be the least proactive in support of their women managers and professionals. On the other hand, more countries had efforts by government units, non-governmental organizations and women's organization/professional associations to support women's advancement.

THE FUTURE

Despite the current global economic recession, chapter authors were, in general, cautiously optimistic about the future of their women managers and professionals. As the countries represented in this collection started at different places, issues that the contributors thought needed addressing in the future also varied. These included closing the education gap (for example, Turkey), putting more teeth in country legislation (for example, Australia and China) and getting more organizations to proactively support women's development (for example, New Zealand). There is no question that progress has been made and continues to be realized but some of our authors have described it as glacial. While some writers have attempted to project when true equality would be achieved (half the board members women, half the senior executive jobs held by women) – estimated at 100 to 200 years down the road – many thought this was unlikely to ever be realized.

Putting it All Together

When we summarize some of the overall findings of the material representing 20 countries included in this book, certain and common themes emerge. First, women's participation rates in the workforce have increased in almost all countries, but occupational segregation still exists. Childcare was an important concern for women in almost all countries. Second, women had increased their participation rates in university education, equaling or exceeding that of men in most cases. Third, the proportion of women in management has increased but still remained very low at the higher levels of organizations particularly at board level. There was also considerable variability among countries in the percentage of women in management. Fourth, women increasingly moved into small business and entrepreneurship in most countries to earn income. Female entrepreneurs tended to develop small businesses and earn less income from them than did men. Fifth, an increasing number of countries developed legislation to support women at work and women in management. Unfortunately it seemed as if these initiatives lacked teeth in many cases. Legislation did have the desired effect of increasing women's representation in the workforce and working toward creating a more equal workplace experience (for example, Norway and Spain). Sixth, there were only a few countries in which employing organizations developed initiatives to specifically support the development and advancement of women (for example, Canada, UK and US). .Seventh, the data indicated some positive developments in several countries (for example, more women in education, higher levels of country support for women in the workplace, changing family roles and responsibilities, improved employment (Jones, Burke and Westman, 2006) and labour market conditions), but several aspects seemed to be slow to change (few women in senior management, women paid less than men, bias and discrimination).

These chapters represented countries most likely to be active in supporting managerial and professional women, and collecting data on the status of their women in the workforce. As we found in the 2004 volume, there was considerable variation among these countries in this volume on such indicators as the percentage of the labour force that is female, percentage of managers and professionals that are women, legislation supporting women's advancement and organizational efforts to develop and advance women.

Certainly, there were some positive aspects in the 20 countries. These included: more women in management and in the professions; more supportive government practices; changing family roles and responsibilities; changes in demographic characteristics offering more opportunities for women; and improved economic and labour market conditions for women. Nevertheless, there were also several disheartening aspects across the 20 countries. These included: a slow pace of change and improvement; women still faced discrimination and gender, ethnic, cultural and religious stereotyping; continuing male domination at senior-management and corporate board levels; and some plateauing in societal and legislative support for women's advancement (for example, Canada).

This left us with the question of whether the cup was "half full" or "half empty". These countries included in this book were among the "best" countries as far as women's progress was concerned. But whether one uses the metaphors of a glass ceiling (Barreto, Ryan and Schmitt, 2009), concrete walls, sticky floors or a labyrinth (Eagly and Carli, 2007), women's advancement and progress had fallen short of expectations. The International Labor Organization updated the Wirth (2001) report in 2004 (ILO, 2004), and provides yearly reviews on the status of women at work, and came to similar conclusions.

Adopting a Broader Lens to Women's Advancement

Since we both teach in schools of management and business, we have usually focused our work on women in the private sector. Our chapter authors, however, also examined women in the public sector, women in the voluntary sector and women in government. There was a higher percentage of women in management in the government and voluntary sectors in some countries. It was sometimes difficult to combine percentages of women in these sectors since we did not know the total number of managers. Catalyst (2007) (a New York City-based women's advisory and research group), has provided these figures for 13 of the 20 countries included in this collection. These figures, representing the percentage of women legislators, senior government officials and managers, are shown in Table 1.1.

Table 1.1   **Percentage of women legislators, senior government officials and managers – 2007**

Country	%
Argentina	23.2
Australia	37.6
Canada	36.2
China	16.5
France	36.9
Israel	28.9
Mexico	27.3
New Zealand	39.6
Norway	32.9
Russia	38.9
Spain	31.7
United Kingdom	34.5
United States	41.8

Source: Adapted from Catalyst (2007) Women in Management, Global Comparison

These range from a high of 41.8 percent in the US and 39.6 percent in New Zealand to a low of 16.5 percent in China and 23.2 percent in Argentina, and are generally consistent with the picture conveyed in these chapters.

The Bigger Picture

As this chapter was being written, stories about the experiences and progress of women worldwide appeared in the media. These stories, as often as not, referred to women in the workforce other than managers and professionals, and from a variety of countries, most not included in this collection, that seemed relevant to understanding the findings in this collection. These stories place this volume on managerial and professional women into a broader context and seemed to shed some light on the limited gains we observed in the 2004 and 2010 collections.

We would like to get behind the numbers and focus on the tangible "flesh and blood" experiences of women, and men, in several countries through events and stories reported in various media. It should be clearly noted that our sample of stories and events is non-random and likely non-representative of the experiences of women and men, in the workplace worldwide.

THE GOOD NEWS

Considerable "firsts" were reported

- A Canadian woman, Stacey Allister, replaced a man, Larry Scott, as CEO of the Women's Tennis Association.

- The first woman was awarded a Nobel prize in Economics in 2009. In addition a total of five women received Nobel prizes in 2009, the highest total ever awarded in any one year.

- In June 2009, Venice appointed its first female gondolier, Giorgia Boscoli, their first female gondolier in 900 years.

- The appointment by President Barack Obama and later senate confirmation of Judge Sonia Sotomayor, a Latina woman, for the US Supreme Court. Of the 111 Supreme Court Justices, 108 have been white males. She is the third woman and first Hispanic Justice.

- Hilary Clinton was appointed Secretary of State by President Obama, succeeding another woman, Condoleeza Rice, and the earlier Madeleine Albright.

- Ursula Burns became the first African American woman to lead a major US corporation (Xerox, June 2009) succeeding another women, Anne Mulcahy.

- Anne Giardini became the first female president of Weyerhauser, the large US forest product company in 2008.

- India (June 2009) elected its first female speaker of their parliament. (Meira Kumar); described as a tribute to the women of India for the contributions they have made to their country.

- Lithuania elected its first female president in May 2009, Dalia Grybavskavite.

- The first woman was elected to the Kuwait parliament in 2009.

- Saudi Arabia appointed its first woman minister, Nora bind Abdulla Hal-Fayuiz, as Deputy Education Minister of a new department for female students.

- Women were active in Iran's resistance movement in the recent election results controversy (June 2009).

- The Iranian leadership appointed three women ministers in August 2009, the first women appointments since the Islamic Revolution in 1979.

- Women are making great progress on the boards of not-for-profit organizations in Canada, with a representation about equal to mens, based on a study of 240 boards.

- The Egyptian parliament passed a law giving women a 64 seat quota in their lower chamber, one-eighth of the total.

- Muslim women in Indonesia are making significant gains as both managers and entrepreneurs.

- Women were just as ambitious as men and desirous of more job responsibilities as men in a US study reported by the New York City-based Families and Work Institute.

- The United Nations voted (October 2009) to create a higher-level agency to promote women's rights. This new agency will put four under-staffed and under-funded women's units under one roof. It is obviously too early to tell if this new agency will get the funding and support it needs to be effective.

- There is some evidence that having more women on boards of directors and in senior management jobs may be associated with better organizational performance but the reasons for this are open to debate. A study recently conducted in France showed that companies having 38 percent or more women in executive jobs had their stock fall less in 2008 than companies with a smaller percentage of women executives.

- Having more women in senior corporate jobs and on boards of directors is a possible solution to the economic mess that advanced countries found themselves in 2008/2009. According to the Chicago-based Hedge Fund Research in 2009, hedge funds run by women have fallen only half as much during the financial crisis as those managed by men.

- Several highly rated schools of business have developed courses for women interested in learning more about themselves and their careers (for example, Rotman School of Management at the University of Toronto, the Stanford University school of business and INSEAD) and the Center for Creative Leadership has offered such courses for several years.

Taken together, these examples of "good news" add some optimism to the sense of progress that women have made at work and in their careers.

Implications

There were some tangible signs of progress, though uneven, and indications of stalling and back-sliding. More women are now in the workforce. More women are getting the necessary education and experience to equip them for success in the workforce. There continue to be many "firsts".

However, the fact that we are still celebrating "firsts" is disheartening. The bad news includes evidence showing little and slow progress in women's career advancement to senior-level position, some back-sliding in terms of enforcing supportive legislation, lots of rhetoric but little action or follow through, many countries in which organizations seem to not be doing anything specifically to develop and support their women managers and professionals, along with a series of worldwide events revealing some deeply rooted societal biases towards women (International Labor Organization, 2004).

There seemed to be only modest change in our findings from our Davidson and Burke *Women in Management Worldwide* 2004 volume. It is likely that the six to seven year interval was not long enough to bring about large improvements.

This volume also identified many of the difficulties in undertaking international comparisons. First, some countries did not have data in some categories even though we invited contributors from "developed" nations. Second, the definitions and categories used to classify features of their workforces differed as well.

Our focus on managerial and professional women reflected, in part, our affiliation with leading schools of business and management, and the undergraduate and MBA students that we teach. Undoubtedly, many of our female students become successful professionals and managers. In addition, we both live in developed industrialized, advanced countries (Canada and the UK). Women in our home countries, while facing unique challenges because of their gender, are also supported in several important ways. This legitimate emphasis, however, may have blinded us to the reality of a significantly larger number of women in the workplace. In addition, appreciating the reality and experiences of these women in a wider range of countries, highlighted the huge challenges these women face and why addressing these obstacles is also likely to advance the cause of their more educated and privileged "sisters".

The work and life experiences of women in several countries in the developing world indicated many distressing features (for example, bias, hostility towards women, huge restrictions on women's choices). Sadly, women worldwide still lack basic rights such as education, freedom from violence, opportunities to pursue what many of us see as taken-for-granted life options, and justice in the workplace and in their societies. We hope, in time, that the circumstances in these countries will change to provide a higher quality of life and access to more equality of opportunity among women and girls.

We believe that efforts must be made along at least two inter-related tracks simultaneously if greater progress is to be realized. One track, consistent with the purpose of this collection, involves a continuation of efforts to support the education and advancement of women into professional and managerial jobs and create organizational climates that embrace diversity and equality in the workplace (Davidson and Fielden, 2003; Powell, 2010). Having more women in decision-making roles will help change the character of these decisions and more decisions will take women's needs into account and improve not only their lot in life but organizational and societal performance. There is emerging evidence that enacting country legislation to equalize/improve the proportions of women serving on corporate boards of directors or at higher-level managerial jobs does work, though not as well as expected (see the experiences of Norway and Spain). More organizations need to be convinced that supporting and developing the talents of their female employees makes good business sense. Women's associations need to continue their pioneering efforts. The second track is to tackle the pervasive negative attitudes, behaviours and experiences that face women worldwide .Clearly, the evidence presented from the 20 countries represented in this book indicated that while a country's political, economic and legislative context does appear to have some impact on women's participation in managerial roles (particularly at senior levels), the greatest influences are more often driven by deeply rooted socio-cultural traditions and values. Efforts need to be made at the societal (macro) level before significant progress will be seen at the levels of individual women (micro). Political and business leaders need to speak up for the human rights of women in many countries around the world through umbrella groups such as the United Nations (UN), the International Labour Organisation (ILO), the G20 and the G7 associations.

There is also an important role for members of the academic and research communities. We need to continue to collect information on the status of women at work (including frequently ignored and "invisible" minority groups) and their experiences in the workplace. Communication of the benefits of utilizing the talents of all employees must continue. Assistance must be provided to organizations interested and willing to support the development and progress of their women employees. More efforts must be made to help women re-enter the workforce after time away (Hewlett and Luce, 2005; Hewlet, Luce,

Shiller and Southwell, 2004). Business programmes need to become more "friendly" to women students and business schools need to include diversity and gender issues as part of their curriculum. In addition, some curriculum issues seem particularly critical in order to fully understand the barriers to women's advancement and benchmarks for progress. These include women in science, technology, engineering and mathematics (Cacace, 2009; Burke and Mattis, 2007; Ceci and Williams, 2004) and women serving on corporate boards of directors (Burke and Mattis, 2000; Vinnicombe, Singh, Burke, Bilimoria and Huse, 2008). As Konrad, Dramer and Erkut (2008) have shown, a small increase in numbers of women serving on a corporate board of directors makes a huge difference.

In the words of Kristof and WuDunn (2009):

> *The world is awakening to a powerful truth: women and girls aren't the problem; they're the solution.*

References

Adler, N. J. and Izraeli, D. N. (1988) *Women in Management Worldwide* (Armonk, NY: M. E. Sharpe).

Barreto, M, Ryan, M. K. and Schmitt, M. T. (2009) *The Glass Ceiling in the 21st century: Understanding Barriers to Gender Equality* (Washington, DC: American Psychological Association).

Belkin, L. (2003) The opt-out revolution, *New York Times Magazine*, October 26, 42.

Blau, F. D. and Kahn, L. M. (2007) The gender pay gap: Have women gone as far as they can? *Academy of Management Perspectives*, 21, 7–23.

Burke, R. J. (2009) Cultural values and women's work and career experiences. In R. S. Bhagat and R. M. Steers (eds) *Culture, Organizations, and Work* (Cambridge: Cambridge University Press. pp. 442–461).

Burke, R. J. and Cooper, C. L. (2006) *Inspiring Leaders* (London: Routledge).

Burke, R. J. and Mattis, M. C. (2000) *Women on Corporate Boards of Directors: International Challenges and Opportunities* (Dordrecht: Kluwer).

Burke, R. J. and Mattis, M. C. (2005) *Supporting Women's Career Advancement: Challenges and Opportunities* (Cheltenham: Edward Elgar).

Burke, R. J. and Mattis, M. C. (2007) *Women and Minorities in Science, Technology, Engineering and Mathematics: Upping the Numbers* (Cheltenham: Edward Elgar).

Burke, R. J. and Nelson, D. L. (2002) *Advancing Women's Careers: Research and Practice* (London: Blackwell).

Cacace, M. (2009) *Guidelines for Gender Equality Programmes in Science* (Rome: Prages).

Catalyst (2002) *Women in Leadership – European Business Imperative* (New York, NY: Catalyst).

Catalyst (2007) *Expanding Opportunities for Women and Business – Women in Management Global Comparison* http://ww.catalyst.org/publications/215/women-in-management-global-comparison, accessed 9 October, 2008.

Ceci, S. J. and Williams, W. M. (2000) *Why Aren't More Women in Science? Top Researchers Debate the Evidence* (Washington, DC: American Psychological Association).

Davidson, M. J. and Burke, R. J (2004) *Women in Management Worldwide: Facts, Figures and Analysis* (Aldershot: Gower Publishing).

Davidson, M. J. and Fielden, S. (eds.) (2003) *Individual Diversity and Psychology in Organizations* (Chichester: John Wiley).

Eagly, A. H. and Carli, L. L. (2007) *Through the Labyrinth: The Truth About How Women Become Leaders* (Boston, MA: Harvard Business School Press).

Fielden, S. L. and Davidson, M. J. (eds) (2005) *International Handbook of Women and Small Business Entreprenuership* (Cheltenham: Edward Elgar).

Fielden, S. L. and Davidson, M. J. (eds) (2010) *International Research Handbook on Successful Women Entreprenuers* (Cheltenham: Edward Elgar).

Fulmer, R. M. and Conger, J. A. (2004) *Growing your Company's Leaders* (New York, NY: AMACOM).

Helfat, C. E., Harris, D. and Wolfson, P. J. (2006) *The Pipeline to the Top: Women and Men in the Top Executive Ranks of U.S. Corporations, Academy of Management Perspectives*, 20, 43–64).

Hewlet, S. A., Luce, C. B. Shiller, P. and Southwell S (2004) *The Hidden Brain Drain: Off-Ramps and On-Ramps in Women's Careers* (Harvard University: Harvard Business on Line).

Hewlett, S. A. and Luce, C. B. (2005) Off-ramps and on–ramps: Keeping talented women and the road to success. *Harvard Business Review*, March, 10.

Hogan, R. and Hogan, J. (2001) Assessing leadership: A view of the dark side, *International Journal of Evaluation and Assessment*, 9, 40–51.

International Labor Office (2004) *Breaking Through the Glass Ceiling: Women in Management* (Geneva: International Labor Office).

Jones, F., Burke, R. and Westman, M. (2006) *Work-life Balance: A Psychological Perspective* (Hove: Psychology Press).

Konrad, A., Kramer, V. and Erkut, S. (2008) The impact of three or more women on corporate boards, *Organizational Dynamics*, 37, 145–164.

Kristoff, N. D. and WuDunn, S. (2009) *Half the Sky: Turning Oppression into Opportunities for Women Worldwide* (New York, NY: Knopf).

Mattis, M. C. (2004) Women entrepreneurs: Out from under the glass ceiling, *Women in Management Review*, 19, 154–163.

Michaels, E., Handfield-Jones, H. and Axelrod, B. (2001) *The War for Talent* (Boston, MA: Harvard Business School Press).

Moore, D. P. (2000) *Careerpreneurs* (Palo Alto, CA: Davies-Black Publishing).

Moore, D. P. and Buttner, E. (1997) *Women Entrepreneurs: Moving Beyond the Glass Ceiling* (Thousand Oaks, CA: Sage Publications).

Morrison, A. M., White, R. and Van Velsor, E. (1987) *Breaking the Glass Ceiling* (Reading, MA: Addison-Wesley).

Office for National Statistics (2009) *Unemployment Statistics* (London: HMSO).

O'Neil, D. A., Hopkins, M. M. and Bilimoria, D. (2008) Women's Careers at the Start of the 21st century: Patterns and Paradoxes, *Journal of Business Ethics*, 80, 727–743.

Powell, G. N. (1999) *Handbook of Gender and Work* (Thousand Oaks, CA: Sage Publications).

Powell, G. N. (2010) *Women and Men in Management (Fourth Edition)* (London: Sage).

Schwartz, F. N. (1992) *Breaking with Tradition: Women and Work: The New Facts of Life* (New York, NY: Warner).

Shriver, M. (2009) *The Shriver Report: A Women's Nation Changes Everything* (Washington, DC: The Center for American Progress).

Silverstein, M. J. and Sayre, T. K. (2009a) The female economy, *Harvard Business Review*, 87, 46–53.

Silverstein, M. J. and Sayre, T. K. (2009b) *Women Want More: How to Capture Your Share of the World's Largest Market* (New York, NY: HarperCollins).

Tarr-Whelan, L. (2009) *Women Lead the Way: Your Guide to Stepping up to Leadership and Changing the World* (San Francisco, CA: Berrett-Koehler).

Vinnicombe, S., Singh, V., Burke, R., Bilimoria, D. and Huse, M. (2008) *Women on Corporate Boards of Directors: International Research and Practice* (Cheltenham, UK: Edward Elgar).

Wittenberg-Cox, A. and Maitland, S. (2008) *Why Women Mean Business: Understanding the Emergence of Our Next Economic Revolution* (Chichester: John Wiley).

Wirth, L. (2001) *Breaking through the Glass Ceiling – Women in Management* (Geneva: International Labor Office).

PART I

Women in Management – European Union Countries

2

Women in Management in France

Jacqueline Laufer

Introduction

In France as elsewhere, the sheer number of women entering higher education has not eliminated gender inequalities in terms of careers for women in management and accessibility to the highest ranks in business and organizational hierarchies. This chapter reports on the situation of women in management in the French context and the glass ceiling they come up against. After a review of statistics illustrating the main characteristics of the situation of women in the French labour force, certain education-related issues are presented before analyzing the situation of women in management and women entrepreneurs, and the principal conclusions of research in France on the topic of the glass ceiling in business organizations. The legal and institutional framework of equal opportunities in the professional sphere in France are then outlined, followed by the social partners' and companies' initiatives concerning the situation of women in management. Finally, certain aspects of the action strategies designed to erase career inequalities and break the glass ceiling are highlighted.

Labour Force Characteristics

In 2008, nearly half of the working population in France were women (47.6 percent), with 82.9 percent of women aged between 25 and 49 in work, a rise of 23 percent since 1976. While women are more often "salaried" than men (92.7 percent against 86 percent), they are also more often employed in the public sector. Women represent 59.1 percent of public sector employees and 42 percent of private sector employees (women, are more likely to be on short-term contracts (10.8) percent, against 6.0 percent of men) and they constitute 82 percent of part-time workers. Among women working part time, 29.2 percent (compared to 36.1 percent of men) would like to have a full-time job, especially manual and administrative workers (Service des Droits des Femmes et de l'Egalité, 2008).

Economically active women are more often employees or clerks (47.4 percent) while economically active men are more often manual workers (35.4 percent). French women's employment is gender segregated and half of the jobs occupied by women are concentrated in 12 of 86 identified jobs and professions (Maruani, 2003). Women's jobs are concentrated in sectors such as domestic and administrative services, sales, care, education and health: women represent 99.1 percent of child-caring jobs ,66.4 percent of social workers, 86.8 percent of nurses and they also make up the majority of teachers (65.0 percent) (Secrétariat d'Etat Chargé de la Famille et de la Solidarité, 2009).

Furthermore, pay differentials between men and women persist and in 2007, the mean net annual salary for women working full time in the private and semi-public sectors was 19.1 percent lower than for men. In the public service, and especially in the State administration, differences are smaller and amount to 13.3 percent. It is among managers that pay differentials are the highest, with female managers earning 23.6 percent less than male managers in the private or semi-public sector, 18.4 percent less in the central civil service and 17.1 percent less in the decentralized civil service (Secrétariat d'Etat Chargé de la Famille et de la Solidarité, 2009).

Women Pursuing Education

In terms of education, in 2007 the baccalaureate pass rate was 84.6 percent for girls and 82.1 percent for boys. However, gender differences remain in the field of studies: while 63.8 percent of boys opt for a scientific baccalaureate, that choice is only made by 40.6 percent of girls, who also remain under-represented (42.6 percent) in the more selective "classes préparatoires" (intensive two-year courses preparing candidates for competitive entrance exams to France's most prestigious higher educational institutions). In those "classes préparatoires" girls represent 75.6 percent of the literary section, 55 percent of the economic section and 30.4 percent of the scientific section. Indeed, even though women now represent half of business school students, they constitute only 26.8 percent in engineering schools. In universities, women made up 56.9 percent of students in 2007–2008, but here again they are unevenly represented among the various fields. They represent 73.4 percent of students in literature, 58.9 percent in economics and 45.5 percent in scientific sections, with only 27.8 percent studying "fundamental sciences and applications" (Service des Droits des Femmes et de l'Egalité, 2008).

Women in Management and Women Entrepreneurs

In administrative, managerial and professional occupations, feminization has increased. Women now account for 56.4 percent of the professions and scientific professions, 43.1 percent of executives and managers in the public sector, 42.4 percent of firms' business administration and sales executives and 21.7 percent of engineers and technical executives in business firms (INSEE, 2009). Nevertheless, in 2007, only 19.9 percent of CEOs of firms with 10 employees or more were women, with variations between different sectors (13.1 percent in industry, 21.2 percent in commerce and 20.3 percent in services) and firm sizes (18.9 percent for firms with under ten employees, 15.1 percent for firms with between 100 and 249 employees and 8.6 percent for firms with 250 or more employees) (Secrétariat d'Etat Chargé de la Famille et de la Solidarité, 2009)). In companies belonging to France's CAC 40 stock index, 7.6 percent of CEOs, 8.5 percent of directors and 6 percent of executive committee members are women (CapitalCom, 2008). According to a recent study by the European Professional Women's Network (2008), women occupy only 9.7 percent (8.5 percent in 2006) of the seats on the boards of directors of Europe's 300 largest companies and France lies only in twelfth position, with 7.6 percent of women directors (up from 6.5 percent in 2004).

The situation is similar in the French public administration and civil service: although women make up the majority of the workforce in this sector (59.1 percent) in 2006, they accounted for only 16 percent of the 6,782 senior staff. Slowly but surely, this percentage is rising. It was 12 percent in 2001 and 14 percent in 2003. In universities and research institutes, women represent 11.3 percent of the directors and presidents and in hospitals, where women represent 87.8 percent of the administrative staff, only 17 percent of hospital directors are female (Service des Droits des Femmes et de l'Egalité, 2008).

Among entrepreneurs, in 2006, 29 percent of firms in industry and services were created by women (an increase of 2 percent since 2002). Women who become entrepreneurs tend to have higher educational qualifications than their male counterparts and 64.7 percent have the baccalaureate compared to 50 percent of men. Even so, the women have less previous work experience and only 42.2 percent were economically active before creating their business compared to 53.3 percent of men. Women entrepreneurs are also more likely to choose service and commercial entrepreneurial activities, and five years after starting up, the firms created by women are proportionately less likely to be still active compared to male-founded counterparts, that is, 49 percent against 52 percent respectively (Service des Droits des Femmes et de l'Egalité, 2008).

In addition to vertical segregation, horizontal segregation is also observed among women managers who are concentrated in a much smaller number of occupational sectors: health, education and the social services and are more often found in administration, communications and human resources functions. A 1997 analysis of the Carnet du Nouvel Economiste (1996) reporting on the top management teams of France's "5,000 leading companies" showed that women executives were most often to be found in communication and advertising (15 percent) (in firms with over 500 employees, one female executive in four was director of communication), human resources (13 percent), general administration (13 percent), finance, control and accounting (12 percent). Very few women were directors of research (2 percent) or information technology (2 percent) and almost none headed strategy or international affairs (Laufer and Fouquet, 2001).

A study of the Eurolist firms (772 French firms and 118 foreign firms listed on the Paris stock exchange) found that women general managers were distributed as follows in the various sectors: 12.3 percent in services, 11 percent in technology, 16 percent in health, 3.7 percent in industry, 4.3 percent in consumer goods and 9 percent in real estate (Conseil Economique et Social, 2007). Also, a recent study has shown that the 136 female top executives of Eurolist firms were distributed as follows: 27 percent in general management; 20 percent in communications and marketing, 13 percent in human resources, 10 percent in finance, 8 percent in legal affairs, 5 percent in information systems and 5 percent in sales (Conseil Economique et Social, 2007). Of the 6 percent female executive committee members in CAC 40 firms, only 14 percent had line management responsibilities at divisional or regional level (CapitalCom, 2008).

Women remain underrepresented in operational functions and management of large teams. This situation is reflected in the significant pay differences for men and women in the upper echelons of business: female CEOs earn an average one-third less than their male counterparts, and the difference remains at the level of 20 percent even when sector, firm size, legal structure and age of the manager are comparable (Brouillet, 2004).

In France, women's studies and gender studies initially focused on the situation of the least qualified female workers (manual workers and clerks). More recently, research has also concentrated on the gender issues related to more skilled professional groups (Boigeol, 2003; Cacouault-Bitaud, 2001; Lapeyre, 2006; Le Feuvre, 1999; Marry, 2004).

The law on "parity" (Mossu-Lavau, 2005) brought greater attention in France to the small numbers of women holding positions of power in the political sphere, and more generally to the difficulties related to "women's access to decision making" in the worlds of politics, economics, civil service and trade unions (Colmou, 1999; Conseil Economique et Social, 2007; Laufer, 1997; Laufer and Fouquet, 1997; Le Pors and Milewski, 2003).

Although the horizontal and vertical segregation that is characteristic of women's experiences in professions and organizations have been highlighted, less attention has been paid to the organizational processes, particularly within firms, which could account for the "reproduction of rarity" of women at the top of organizational hierarchies, in contrast with the development of research into "gender and organizations" in the US and in the UK (Angeloff and Laufer, 2007). Indeed, in France, most empirical analyses of the obstacles encountered by women within organizations, preventing greater numbers from reaching positions of power, are relatively recent (see Belghiti-Mahut, 2004; Dambrin and Lambert, 2008; Fortino, 2002; Guillaume and Pochic, 2007; Landrieux-Katorchian, 2005; Laufer, 1982; Laufer, 2005; Laufer and Fouquet, 1997; Pigeyre, 2001).

The complexity of the glass ceiling phenomenon relates to the cross-disciplinary approach required for its interpretation, and also to the fact that it involves several levels of analysis: society and the various types of policies implemented both to promote gender equality and a good work-life balance, organizations (firms, the civil service, universities, unions and so on) and the strategies of the individuals themselves, both male and female (Belghiti-Mahut, 2004; Guillaume and Pochic, 2007; Laufer, 2003). At the level of society, in France in particular, several authors (EPHESIA, 1995) have documented that women were long kept out of and considered non-legitimate in the spheres of political power, and also in firms (Laufer, 1982), although French sociology of organizations only too rarely considers (not to say neglects) the gender factor in analyses of power relations within organizations (Angeloff and Laufer, 2007).

It is also well known that while girls' educational success has been a determinant for gender equality, in France as in many countries, girls' and boys' educational choices are marked by a traditional representation of male and female roles and skills, especially in regard to technical disciplines. This process is all the more important in France, where formal qualifications and diplomas are determinants for career development.

Analysis of the glass ceiling must also take into consideration the influence of stereotypical representation of social roles, which still subject women at any level of responsibility to an unequal division of household and family work. In France, since the 1970s and then under the influence of the European Union, family policies have seen a range of measures designed to help women combine work and family responsibility more satisfactorily (Fagnani and Letablier, 2005; Laufer, 1998). Despite this, women executives still have to cope with more conflict between work and family roles than their spouses or partners, and with working in environments that are not conducive to restoring the work-family gender balance, particularly through rules and practices associated with long working hours which put women executives at a serious disadvantage (Conseil Economique et Social, 2007). Dambrin and Lambert (2008) analyzed the relationship between the glass ceiling and motherhood in France in public accounting firms, stressing the contradiction between the country's broad social acceptance of women returning to work shortly after childbirth and the lack of childcare structures for mothers with children under three.

At the organizational level, the roles of organizational cultures and norms and career development policies in constructing gender inequalities have been also highlighted (Guillaume and Pochic, 2007; Laufer, 1982; Laufer, 2005; Laufer and Fouquet, 2001). According to the GEF[1]/Accenture survey (2003) of the 300 top French companies, 93 percent of managers acknowledge that "there are obstacles to women's careers in the world of business".

Organizational rules and career development policies that claim to be neutral have in fact been historically based on masculine models – for example the male model of self-investment in work or long working hours – and consequently detrimental to women in practice, contributing to the ongoing scarcity of women at the top of organizations. These "neutral" and "impersonal" rules which define the requirements for hiring, promotion and appointment to top positions, such as age, seniority or "merit" do not have the same significance for men and

---

1   The *"Grandes Ecoles au Féminin"* network, whose members are women graduates of the French "Grandes Ecoles", the country's most prestigious higher education establishments.

women, and may in practice be discriminatory against women who do not "fit" the model (Laufer and Fouquet, 2001; Pigeyre, 2001).

For a long time, women executives had "women's careers" in more routine posts or administrative positions, or as expert advisors; these positions, peripheral to decision making and power, were supposedly better suited to the constraints and aspirations of women, while men were expected to occupy more mobile positions offering more decision power and opening up access to genuine management positions (Laufer, 1982). Women continue to work more frequently in specialized functions such as communication and human resources. However, the fact that women are reaching higher education in increasing numbers now justifies the integration of new female graduates into career development policies similar to those aimed at men. The shifting gender balance in education is also changing the attitudes and expectations of women graduates, who have greater aspirations for leadership positions.

Career development policies are thus becoming more "gender-neutral" and more likely to foster equal opportunities for men and women by providing more objective bases for decisions on compensation and promotion. However, the principle of gender-neutrality in early-stage career management is not sufficient to eliminate the influence of "male" organizational norms, which lead to the scarcity of women in the upper echelons of organizations (Laufer and Fouquet, 2001).

Analysis of the causes of the glass ceiling thus raises the questions of women's career profiles, the necessary alternation between functional and operational positions in order to move up through the hierarchy, and also the development of team leadership capacities. The survey on a sample of 12,739 managers published by the French executive employment association APEC (Association pour l'emploi des Cadres, 2010) observed that women are less likely to reach top management or general management jobs and to manage large teams: among managers aged 45–49, 14 percent of women managers occupy such jobs versuus 30 percent of male managers.

Additional issues relate to the importance of practices in respect of mobility and promotion, the pace of career advancement and the "total availability" model, which do not have the same impact for men and women, and the role networks and mentors play in career development. French women who break through the glass ceiling do have mentors and have benefited from the various networks they have been able to develop throughout their career (Laufer, 2005).

A further factor to consider, meanwhile, is the way women executives' attitudes and behaviours develop in response to these organizational environments, and the diversity of those responses, taking into consideration the trade-offs women have to make due to the gender division of labour in the home. The situation of dual-career couples, conjugal negotiations and men's and women's strategies to achieve a good work–family balance are clearly essential considerations in this context. Regarding work–life balance, much research has shown that in most organizations the dominant pattern of executive careers in France and elsewhere emphasizes employee availability and a willingness to accept geographical mobility. While some women are willing and able to pursue a typically male pattern, have supporting husbands, and may often employ domestic help, most women managers in fact pursue career development but withdraw from the competition for power when it comes to reaching the top executive jobs, therefore leaving the dominant organizational norms unchanged (Guillaume and Pochic, 2009; Laufer, 2005; Le Feuvre, 1999).

Country Legislation

The measures taken by firms to support women's careers and access to top executive jobs are part of the overall corporate policies for equality and diversity in the workplace that are now being introduced in an increasing number of French firms, particularly large firms (Laufer, 2007). The French laws on gender equality in the workplace enacted on July 13, 1983 and May 9, 2001 impose a three-fold obligation on businesses:

- They must implement equal treatment between men and women, and take the necessary steps to eliminate direct and indirect discrimination against women.

- They must carry out a diagnosis of the comparative employment situation of women and men (based on a comparative report required by the 1983 law) in order to better identify workplace inequalities.

- They must open negotiations with the social partners and if necessary set up measures to rectify the inequalities observed. Such negotiations were optional in the 1983 law, but became mandatory under the May 2001 law.

French firms are thus required to take action to remedy any discriminatory human resource management practices, and have to demonstrate their ability to implement corrective action for equality in the workplace (Laufer, 2008).

Legislation introduced in March 2006 required firms to negotiate measures to eliminate differences in compensation by the end of 2010, using an indicator-based diagnosis carried out internally. It also supported reconciliation of work and parenthood by introducing a mechanism to offset the effect of maternity on employee pay. The law grants employees on maternity or adoption leave pay rises equal to the general rise plus the average individual pay rise awarded during the leave period to employees in the same professional category, or if this is not possible, the average of all individual pay rises awarded.

The French financial security law of 2006 introduced a new type of parental leave, to be "shorter" (one year) but better compensated, open to working parents after the birth of a third (or subsequent) child. To qualify for this leave, the parent must have worked for at least two years in the five years preceding the birth.

Last but not least, the law of December 21, 2001 introduced paternity leave of 11 successive days (18 for multiple births), open to fathers (working or unemployed, whether employees or self-employed) in the four months following the birth or adoption of a child. In 2010, two-thirds of new fathers have benefited from this paid leave, full pay being now more frequent in several large firms.

Initiatives Supporting Women in the Workforce

In parallel to advances in research on the glass ceiling, the question arises of what measures should be taken, by organizations in general and business organizations in particular, to bring about greater gender equality in access to positions of power. There is nothing new about the scarcity of women with formal power and decision-making positions in organizations but, as in the US, the situation is looking increasingly unjustifiable in Europe given the growing proportion of women graduates and women managers. The publicly adopted stances of international and European Union organizations (European Commission DGV, 1995) have advanced debate on the issue, and fostered the development of legislation on gender equality at work and a growing corporate concern to integrate gender equality and diversity policies into strategic business objectives. In France as elsewhere, the development of a "business case" for gender equality and diversity has been largely driven by the realization that the recruitment, hiring and development of managerial women is a bottom-line issue related to corporate success (Landrieux-Kartochian, 2005; Meda and Wierinck, 2005).

The measures set forth in the company agreements negotiated in application of France's 1983 law mainly concerned training for low-skilled female workers and clerks (Laufer, 1992). The new agreements negotiated under the May 9, 2001 law concern all human resource management policies: hiring, career opportunities, training, compensation and work–life balance; they also place greater emphasis on the question of career development and women's access to top positions (Laufer and Silvera, 2006). The introduction of qualitative and quantitative diagnostics for a better analysis and understanding of inequalities and the impact of existing human resource policies, training raising management awareness of stereotypes, and career development policies with special emphasis on women and actions to "help female candidates overcome any personal blocks", are all initiatives that are likely to raise general awareness of the glass ceiling among all employees in the firm (Laufer, 2008).

Also, in addition to the laws on working conditions for pregnant women, many workplace equality agreements include measures intended to "neutralize" maternity leave effects on compensation and careers, to encourage more equitable treatment of female employees notwithstanding the fact that they have children and take maternity leave. These measures may take the form of supportive interviews and training for the women concerned when they leave, or return from, maternity leave. Another approach is to consider maternity leave as time effectively worked, and include it when calculating seniority. A general pay rise is granted to women who have been on maternity leave, equal to the average for the employee's category plus a variable performance-related portion. Other special measures also address the issue of career advancement and promotion for women on maternity leave (Laufer and Silvera, 2006).

Similarly, the "diversity" policies set up by several international and French firms focus particularly on the question of women's place in management. They include several measures designed to better assess merits and skills, and raise management consciousness of stereotypes and discriminations: review the age criteria in management of "high-potential" executives (which put women at a disadvantage); review the criteria for identifying "potential" and "merit" (which in practice are often coded in male terms); consider the impact of mobility policies and possibly question them if they are detrimental to women; and develop action and services intended not only for mothers but for both parents, deliberately encompassing men, with a view to enhancing the "work–life balance" (ANVIE, 2002; Bender, 2004).

The Future

Although accurate measurement of the impact of corporate measures to remove the glass ceiling is difficult since they are not systematically assessed, significant developments are visible in the consideration given by all actors to addressing the question. However, the limitations of the policies adopted can also be observed.

First, the development of agreements on equality in the workplace (though in 2004, 72 percent of firms had not yet begun negotiations on the subject (Laufer and Silvera, 2006) and the number of firms that have initiated diversity policies, indicate that a greater number of firms now want to develop commitments to professional equality and gender diversity. Several also support initiatives (prizes, raising young women's awareness of scientific careers, forums, support for existing networks, help for women with low qualifications, programmes to keep girls in school in developing countries, and so on) or release statements on their own in-house initiatives. However, there is room for legitimate concern that some firms are better at making declarations of intent than actually taking action. A 2007 study of corporate communication by CAC of 40 firms on the subject of equality in the workplace (including the documents available to the public), showed that only a minority of firms disclose any detailed information on their policy for equality in the workplace, and only four firms stated that they had set up a body dedicated to the question (equality officers or an equality commission). The vast majority of firms simply reported the percentage of women in the workforce, and 60 percent compared this indicator with the percentage of women in management. Furthermore, 38 percent of firms stated the proportion of women hired and in top management, and only 25 percent reported an indicator of the pay differential between men and women in the group (CapitalCom, 2008).

Regarding equality and diversity, in 2006 France's equality and anti-discrimination authority HALDE (Haute Autorité de Lutte Contre les Discriminations et pour l'Égalité) presented a report on a survey of 173 firms. Three-quarters of respondent firms said they were actively engaged in promotion of non-discrimination and diversity, including gender diversity and also ethnic diversity, age, sexual orientation and so on, in compliance with the law of November 17, 2001 which lists all cases of discrimination prohibited in employment. However, only 72 of them had signed specific agreements and just 55 had set up concrete implementation measures (Halde, 2006).

Another well-known phenomenon is the emergence of a large number of intra-firm and interfirm women's networks, reflecting female executives' determination to break out of the "era of invisibility" that characterized the past. Although concerns have been voiced over the development of women-only networks, the initiatives, newsletters, debates, studies and reports produced by these networks now make up a force to be reckoned with.

Finally, analysis of corporate policies to deal with the glass ceiling raises questions over the strategies that should be deployed. There is a general consensus that it is necessary to apply an equal treatment principle in hiring, training, and promotion, which means that management must change their attitudes and behaviours, and be made more conscious of the existence of stereotypes. There is also growing awareness of the need to identify and remedy "indirect discrimination" (Lanquetin, 2003), that is, the "neutral" practices that have negative consequences for women, for example career development policies that are in fact based on male models.

However, setting numerical targets for the promotion of women in top-level jobs is not a widely adopted strategy. Only one agreement negotiated under the 2001 law states that in respect of access to leadership, target figures will be set for each function and division. Few firms set targets for hiring or training or for the proportion of women in management, but the application of a "proportionality principle" is more common. More firms are seeking to ensure that the proportion of women promoted is the same as the proportion of men promoted, or that the list of candidates for promotion puts forward equal numbers of men and women (Laufer and Silvera, 2006). Many actors in fact argue that this type of "positive action" based on numerical targets, may be the only solution able to overcome enduring resistance to a more balanced gender mix in boards and in management (Lanquetin, 2006). This has led to the vote of a law in January 2011 which imposes large firms (those employing over 500 persons, listed companies or firms with a turnover of 50 million Euros) to have reached in 2017 a 40 percent quota of women on their boards. While the law does not apply to top managerial jobs, it could lead to a positive evolution concerning the setting of quantitative targets for women in the top managerial roles.

In France as in most countries, women executives in private and public companies must overcome a range of obstacles and difficulties to reach the highest positions. Both in and outside France, two apparently contradictory phenomena co-exist: women's progress in higher education and qualified professions, and their increasingly unbroken career paths; and the continuing inequalities in careers and access to positions of formal power, reflected in women's minority position in organizational hierarchies, to give just one illustration. The factors determining access to the upper echelons of organizational power do not appear to be the same as the factors that have positively influenced the rise in the proportion of women in business, and among managers. In particular, simply rewarding objective criteria of merit such as those conferred by the very qualifications that have brought more women into the workplace, is no longer enough (Powell, 1999).

In the case of France, several steps could be taken to bring about more decisive progress in breaking through the glass ceiling. Some examples of such necessary changes are: measures to raise the proportion of female students in the top engineering schools (where only 22 percent are women); the development of (more) proactive policies within firms to gradually increase the share of women executives on the basis of numerical targets; the introduction of family-friendly policies for all to meet fathers' expectations and change organizational cultures in this respect.

References

Angeloff, T. and Laufer, J. (coordinators) (2007) Genre et organisations [Gender and organizations], *Travail Genre et Société*, 17. 21–105

ANVIE (Agence Nationale pour la Valorisation de la Recherche auprès des Entreprises) (2002) *Comment Promouvoir la Mixité de l'Encadrement et l'Accès aux Responsabilités par les Femmes [How to Promote a Mix of Managers and Access to Women's Leadership]*, J. Laufer and C. Belotti.

APEC (Association pour l'Emploi des Cadres) (2011) *Femmes Cadres et Hommes Cadres: des Inégalités Professionnelles qui Persistent [Women Managers and Men Managers: Continuing Professional Inequality]*, APEC.

Belghiti-Mahut, S. (2004) Les déterminants de l'avancement hiérarchique des femmes cadres [Determinants of hierarchical advancement of women managers], *Revue Française de Gestion*, 30(151), 145–160.

Bender, A. (2004) Egalité professionnelle ou gestion de la diversité, Quels enjeux pour l'égalité des chances? [Equal professional or management of diversity, what challenges for equality of opportunity?], *Revue Française de Gestion*, 30(151), 205–218.

Boigeol, A. (2003) Male strategies in the face of feminisation of a profession: The case of the french Judiciary. In U. Schultz and G. Shaw (eds) *Women in the World's Legal Professions* (Oxford: Hart Publishing, pp. 401–418).

Brouillet, F. (2004) Une dirigeante de société gagne un tiers de moins que son homologue masculin – Les salaires des dirigeantes de société en 2001 [A female company director earns a third less than her male counterpart – The salaries of corporate executives in 2001], *Insee Première*, 951(March), 10–14.

Cacouault-Bitaud, M. (2001) La féminisation d'une profession est-elle le signe d'une baisse de prestige? [The feminization of a profession – a sign of a decline in prestige?], *Travail, Genre et Sociétés*, 5, 93–116.

Capitalcom (2008) La Place des Femmes dans la Communication des Sociétés du CAC 4,0, www.capitalcom.fr.

Colmou, A. (1999) *L'encadrement Supérieur de la Fonction Publique: Vers L'égalité entre les Hommes et les Femmes [The Senior Civil Service: Towards Equality Between Men and Women]* (Paris: La Documentation Française).

Conseil Economique et Social (2007) *La Place des Femmes dans les Lieux de Décision [The Status of Women]*, Promouvoir la Mixité, Paris.

Dambrin, C. and Lambert, C. (2008) Mothering or auditing? The case of two big firms in France. *Accounting, Auditing and Accountability Journal*, 21(4), 474–506.

EPHESIA (1995) *La Place des Femmes. Les Enjeux de l'Identité et de l'Égalité au Regard des Sciences Sociales [The Status of Women. Challenges of Identity and Equality in a Social Sciences Context]*, La Découverte.

EPWN (European Professional Women Network) (2008) *Women in Boards; Moving Mountains*, M. Visser and A. Gigante.

European Commission, DGV (1995) V/7139/93-EN, Réseau, Femmes dans la Prise de Décision, Bruxelles.

Fagnani, J. and Letablier, M. T. (2005) La politique familiale française [French family policy]. In M. Maruani (ed.) *Femmes, Genre et Sociétés, L'état des Savoirs [Women, Gender and Society, The State of Knowledge]* (Paris: La Découverte, pp. 167–175).

Fortino, S. (2002) *La Mixité au Travail [The Mix at Work]*, La Dispute.

GEF (Grandes Ecoles au Féminin)/Accenture (2003) *Etude sur la Situation des Femmes Cadres dans Les Grandes Entreprises en France [Study on the Status of Women Managers in Large Companies in France]* (GEF/Accenture).

Guillaume, C. and Pochic, S. (2007) La fabrication organisationnelle des dirigeants. Un regard sur le plafond de verre [Manufacturing organizational leaders. A look at the glass ceiling], *Travail, Genre et Sociétés*, 17, 79–103.

Guillaume, C. and Pochic, S. (2009) What would you sacrifice? Access to top management and the work/life balance, *Gender, Work and Organization*, 16(1), 14–36.

HALDE (Haute Autorité de Lutte contre les Discriminations et pour l'Egalité) (2006) *Rapport Annuel [Annual Report]*.

INSEE (Institut National de la Statistique et des Etudes Economiques) (2009) *Enquète Emploi 2009, Insee. Fr.*

Junter, A. (2006) Les mesures proactives; une méthode au service de l'égalité [Proactive measures, a method for equality], *Revue de droit du travail*, Juillet/ Août, 18–23

Landrieux-Kartochian, S. (2005) Femmes et performance des entreprises, émergence d'une nouvelle problématique [Women and business performance, the emergence of a new problem], *Travail et Emploi*, 102 (Avril– Juin), 11–20.

Lanquetin, M. (2003) Un autre droit pour la femme [Another woman's right]. In J. Laufer, C. Marry and M. Maruani (eds) *Le travail du genre. Les Sciences Sociales du Travail à L'épreuve de la Différence des Sexes [The Work of the Genre. Social Sciences Labour Test of Gender Difference]* (Paris: La Decouverte, pp. 315– 344).

Lanquetin, M. (2006) Les quotas: une étape dans la réalisation d'une égalité effective [Quotas: a step in the achievement of effective equality], *Revue de Droit du Travail*, Juillet/Août, 1, 10–20.

Lapeyre, N. (2006) *Les Professions Face aux Enjeux de la Féminisation [Professions Facing the Challenges of Feminization]* (Toulouse: Octares).

Laufer, J. (1982) *La Féminité Neutralisée? Les Femmes Cadres dans l'Entreprise [Femininity Neutralized? Women Executives in Business]* (Paris: Flammarion).

Laufer, J. (1992) *L'Entreprise et l'égalité des Chances, Enjeux et Démarches [The Company and Equal Opportunities, Challenges and Approaches]* (Paris: Documentation Française).

Laufer, J. (1997) L'accès des femmes à la décision dans la sphère économique [Women's access to decision making in the economic sphere]. In F. Gaspard (ed.) *Les Femmes Dans la Prise de Décision en France et en Europe [Women in Decision-Making in France and Europe]* (Paris: L'Harmattan, pp. 158–167).

Laufer, J. (1998) Equal opportunity between men and women: the case of France, *Feminist Economics*, 4(1), 53–69.

Laufer, J. (2003) Entre égalité et inégalités: les droits des femmes dans la sphère professionnelle [Between equality and inequality: the rights of women in the professional sphere], *L'Année Sociologique*, 53(1), 143–173.

Laufer, J. (2005) La construction du plafond de verre [The construction of the glass ceiling], *Travail et Emploi*, 102(Avril/Juin), 31–44.

Laufer, J. (2007) L'égalité professionnelle hommes femmes, une mise en perspective [Professional equality between men and women, put in perspective]. In I. Barth and C. Falcoz (eds) *Le Management de la Diversité. Les Enjeux, Fondements et Pratiques [The Management of Diversity. The Challenges, Foundations and Practices]* (Paris: L'Harmattan, pp. 25–49).

Laufer, J. (2008) *GRH et Genre. Les Défis de l'égalité Hommes-Femmes [HRM and Gender. Challenges of Gender Equality]* Collection (AGRH, Edition Vuibert).

Laufer, J. and Fouquet, A. (1997) *Effet de Plafonnement de Carrière des Femmes Cadres et Accès des Femmes à la Décision dans la Sphère Économique [Effect of Capping Career Women Executives and Access of Women to the Decision in Economic Sphere]*. Groupe HEC. Centre d'Études de l'Emploi; Service des Droits des Femmes.

Laufer, J. and Fouquet, A. (2001) Les cadres à l'épreuve de la féminisation [Managers to test feminization]. In P. Bouffartigue (ed.) *La Grande Rupture [The Great Rift]* (Paris: La Découverte, pp. 249–268).

Laufer, J. and Silvera, R. (2006) L'égalité des femmes et des hommes en entreprise: de nouvelles avancées dans la négociation? [Equality between women and men in business: new advances in the negotiation?], *Revue de l'OFCE*, 97(Avril), 245–271.

Le Feuvre, N. (1999) Gender, occupational feminisation and reflexibility. In R. Crompton (ed.) *Restructuring Gender Relations and Employment: the Decline of the Male Breadwinner* (Oxford: Oxford University Press, pp. 150–178).

Le Pors, A. and Milewski, F. (2003) *Promouvoir la Logique Paritaire [Promoting Parity Logic]*, Rapport au ministre de la Fonction publique de la réforme de l'état et de l'aménagement du territoire, La Documentation Française.

Marry, C. (2004) *Les Femmes Ingénieurs, Une Révolution Respectueuse [Women Engineers, A Respectful Revolution* (Paris: Belin).

Maruani, M. (2003) *Travail et Emploi des Femmes [Labour and Employment of Women]* (Paris: La Découverte).

Meda, D. and Wierinck, M. (2005) Mixité professionnelle et performance des entreprises, un levier pour l'égalité [Mixed professional and business performance, a lever for equality], *Travail et Emploi*, 102(Avril–Juin), 7–46.

Mossu-Lavau, J. (2005) Parité, la nouvelle "exception" française [Parity, the new French "exception"]. In M. Maruani (ed.) *Femmes, Genre et Société [Women, Gender and Society]* (Paris: La Découverte, pp. 307–314).

Nouvel Economiste (1996) *Le Carnet du Nouvel Economiste. Les 5,000 Sociétés Leaders en France et Leurs 30,000 Dirigeants [The Book of the New Economist. The 5,000 leading companies in France and Their 30,000 Leaders]*, (Annuaire) Paris.

Pigeyre, F. (2001) Les femmes dirigeantes, les chemins du pouvoir [Women leaders, the paths of power]. In P. Bouffartigue (ed.) *Cadres: Cadres,*

La Grande Rupture [Managers: Managers, The Great Breakdown] (Paris: La Découverte, pp. 269–280).

Powell, G. N. (1999) *Handbook of Gender at Work* (Thousand Oaks, CA: Sage).

Secrétariat d'Etat Chargé de la Famille et de la Solidarité (2009) *L'Égalité Entre les Femmes et les Hommes Chiffres Clés [Equality Between Women and Men Key Figures]*.

Service des Droits des Femmes et de l'Egalité (2008) *L'Égalité Entre les Femmes et les Hommes Chiffres Clés [Equality Between Women and Men Key Figures]*.

3

Women in Management in Greece

Athena Petraki-Kottis and Zoe Ventoura-Neokosmidi

Introduction

Despite their achievements in recent decades, women in Greece still lag considerably behind men in relation to their position in the workplace and at home. When it comes to higher managerial positions men still call the shots since women's participation is nominal or non-existent. Being in a transitional stage, the country is characterized by a mixture of traditional and modern attitudes and this is reflected in relative position of women.

In this chapter we present information concerning women's situation in employment and management and discuss related issues. In defiance of the importance of this subject, and contrary to what has happened in other developed countries, there is a dearth of related statistical information, research and bibliography. This restricts the possibilities for a more in-depth analysis in this chapter.

Labour Force Characteristics

In Greece, the employment of women has increased in recent decades and has improved regarding its occupational and industrial composition but the country is still among the EU members with the lowest women's employment rate (EC, 2009a) and less than half of working-age women are in employment (EC, 2010a). Moreover, the proportion of women in traditional occupations and industries is still relatively large and there has been a deterioration in their relative position regarding unemployment (NSSG, 2000; 2008). The regional variations within the country observed in the past (Petraki-Kottis, 1990) continue to be significant and the reduction of the gender inequality has moved at a relatively slow pace.

In 2008, women constituted 39.4 percent of employed individuals aged 15 to 64 years, which was an improvement compared to the past. Besides other factors, women's opportunities to participate in the labour market are restrained by the limited availability of childcare services which are well below the Barcelona target (EC, 2009b). In 2006, only 10 percent of children up to three years and 60 percent of those aged between three years and mandatory school age were cared for by formal arrangements (EC, 2009b).

The unemployment rate for women fell during 2000–2008 in line with a general reduction of unemployment in Greece, but in 2008 it was almost three times the men's rate, raising the proportion of women among the unemployed to 62 percent. (NSSG, 2000; 2008). Nevertheless, the decrease in employed women working as unpaid assistants in family businesses (from 17.2 percent in 2000 to 9.7 percent in 2008, NSSG, 2000; 2008) was a definite improvement, given that this type of employment is usually disadvantageous, making women dependent upon other family members, usually men.

Women in the Greek labour force have traditionally achieved higher educational qualifications compared to men, and there has been a constant improvement in this regard. The proportion of women in the labour force with a tertiary education degree increased from 32.4 percent in 2000 to 42.3 percent in 2008 (NSSG, 2000; 2008).

Table 3.1 presents information[1] concerning women's position in the labour market in the years 2000 and 2008. On the basis of this and other statistical information the following observations can be made about changes during that period:

- Women's employment rates have shown a substantial increase, tending to come closer to those in other developed countries.

- Women are constantly gaining a larger share in employment growth compared to men. During 2000–2008, 56 percent of the newly created jobs went to women.

---

1   The data refers to women aged 15 to 64 and differ from similar data referring to women 15 years old and over.

- There was a rise in the proportion of women employed in the tertiary sector and a fall in the proportions employed in the primary and secondary sectors.

- There was a considerable reduction in the proportion of women working as unpaid assistants in family businesses.

- Women's unemployment rates were much higher than men's and their share in unemployment and in long-term unemployment showed a steep rise.

- There has been a constant improvement in the educational qualifications of women in the labour force.

Table 3.1   **Women's labour market situation, 2000–2008**

	2000 (%)	2008 (%)
Employment rate	41.8	49.0
Share in employment	37.3	39.4
Share in the labour force	38.2	41.0
Unemployment rate	17.3	11.1
Share in unemployment	50.4	61.9
Share in long-term unemployment	64.7	66.6
Ratio of women's to men's unemployment rate	2.3	2.9
Percent of employed women working as unpaid assistants	17.2	9.7

Source: NSSG, LFS, B Quarter, 2000; 2008

The data concerning women's occupational composition in 2000 and 2008 (Table 3.2) indicate that their proportion in the group of legislators, senior officials and managers increased but was much smaller than their share in employment overall. Women's participation in scientific, artistic and technical occupations was similar to men's but they had a disproportionate presence in the groups requiring little or no skills.

Table 3.2   Women's share in one-digit occupational groups

	2000 (%)	2008 (%)	Change of share 2000–2008 (%)
Legislators, senior officials and managers	25.1	28.3	+3.2
Scientific and artistic occupations	46.9	49.0	+2.1
Technicians and associate professionals	47.4	49.3	+1.2
Office clerks	57.1	60.1	+3.0
Service and sale workers	50.3	55.0	+4.7
Skilled agricultural and fishery workers	42.0	41.3	-0.7
Craft and related trade workers	13.3	7.4	-5.9
Plant and machine operators and assemblers	9.2	8.8	-0.4
Non-specialized workers	51.3	54.2	+2.9
Unclassified workers	7.3	9.4	+2.1
Total employment	37.3	39.4	+2.1

Source: NSSG, LFS, B Quarter, 2000; 2008

In recent decades, women's employment in the public sector increased by more than men's and there was a substantial improvement in their educational qualifications. Their proportion increased from 32.1 percent in 2000 to 36.9 percent in 2008. In 2008, 58.6 percent of women in this sector had a tertiary education degree compared to 50.6 percent of men (NSSG, 2000; 2008). Women continued to cluster in lower positions but their presence in higher positions increased and their situation was better than in the private sector.

It is interesting to note that there has been a rapid increase in the number of women employed in new technology in both the public and the private sector. However, women cluster mostly in lower-level tasks such as key-punching and have small participation in higher-level positions (NSSG, 2008). Furthermore, women's presence in engineering professions is relatively small and varies among different specializations. According to one survey, women constituted 22 percent of all engineers with a university degree but their participation ranged from 2.3 percent among electrical engineers to 40.7 percent among architects (Technical Chamber of Greece, 2003). It was also found that women in engineering had lower incomes and their unemployment rate was double compared to men.

Historically, women's average earnings were much below men's (Petraki-Kottis, 1987). There has been a gradual improvement but in 2008 the gender pay gap was 22 percent, well above the EU average (EC, 2010a) and the pay gap is more acute for highly educated women (Papapetrou, 2007).

Women Pursuing Education

Women in Greece have made significant advances in the area of education. Their participation in higher education has shown a steep rise while girl's participation at the secondary and primary levels is similar to those of boys. In 2007, women constituted 59 percent of regular university students and 58 percent of university graduates (MoE, 2007). Girls turn more to areas such as literature and social sciences and less to engineering, information technology and medicine. However, the pattern is constantly changing. For instance, in the largest technical university in 2007 women constituted 32 percent of all students but 35 percent of first-year students (MoE, 2007).

There has also been a steady increase in the number of women taking up business studies. In 2007, among the regular students in the undergraduate programmes of the three largest universities offering education in business and economics, 54 percent were women. Women constituted 48 percent and 34 percent of students of master's degree and doctorate programmes respectively and 48 percent and 39 percent of respective graduates (MoE, 2007).

Women's presence among persons employed in teaching is considerable and increasing. Their proportion increased from 60.8 percent in 2000 to 63.5 percent in 2007. However, most of them were in primary and secondary education. In recent years, more women started taking university teaching positions but the majority are clustered in the lower ranks of the hierarchy. In 2007, women constituted 33 percent of university teaching staff but they made up 40 percent of lecturers and only 18 percent of full professors (MoE, 2007).

Women in Management

There has been a constant increase of women in management but most of them remain in the lower and middle ranks of the hierarchy. Very few women succeed in breaking the glass ceiling and reaching the top (EC, 2010a; EC, 2010b). As a result of the high numbers of university graduates, women with business degrees are often obliged to accept clerical jobs that do not relate to their qualifications, while most of those who get managerial positions enter and stay at the lower end of the ladder.

Data and research concerning the position of women in management in Greece are scant but whatever evidence exists indicates that, due to visible and invisible barriers, the top positions are held mostly by men (EC, 2010a). Few women are found in top managerial positions and most of those in such positions are related to major shareholders. Prejudices and traditional attitudes concerning gender roles, formal and informal power structures and the unequal division of household responsibilities prevent women from advancing to higher levels (Ventura and Neokosmidi, 2007).

According to the Fourth European Working Conditions Survey (Parent-Thirion, 2007), the proportion of women among managers in Greece was around 22 percent, which was one of the lowest figures in the EU, placing Greece 24th among the 27 EU members. Fewer than 20 percent of all subordinates declared that their immediate boss was a woman. There was a greater likelihood of an employee reporting to a woman in the wholesale and retail trade.

Women's exclusion from the inner circle of top corporate management can be easily seen by examining the composition of the boards of companies listed in the Athens Stock Exchange. In most cases the presence of women on boards is non-existent or nominal and only in exceptional cases does a company have a woman president or general director (Athens Stock Exchange, 2009). For instance, in 2009, all heads of commercial banks listed in the Athens Stock Exchange were men and, of their 167 board members, there were only 15 women (constituting less than 9 percent). In the Central Bank the Governor was, as always, a man and among the 11 board members there was only one woman, despite the fact that appointments were made by the Government which is supposed to pursue policies aiming at the extinction of gender inequalities. In three large commercial banks, in which the state had ownership rights and the top management were nominated by the Government, the heads were men. In two of these banks there was no woman on the boards, while in the third there was only one.

On the basis of a European Professional Women's Network study of the largest European companies, among the 116 board members of the participating Greek corporations only seven were women. On average there was 0.8 women per corporation, which means that some firms did not have even a token woman on their boards. Among the 17 countries covered by the survey, Greece was ranked 15th (EPWN, 2008; Visser, 2009).

According to a European Community (EC) database, in 18 of the largest publicly quoted companies in Greece, 26 percent of individuals in managerial positions were women but all of the companies were headed by men and only 6 percent of their board members were women. In these companies, all employee representatives in the highest employee decision-making body were men (EC, 2008).

It is interesting to examine the findings from an in-depth survey conducted in the mid-1990s among 107 of the largest companies in the country. Ninety-five percent of the companies were headed up by a man, while in 43 percent there was no woman on the board, and in 36 percent there was only one woman. In most cases where a woman was at the top of a company or on its board, she was a close relative of major shareholders. The most striking finding was that most male top executives, in trying to explain women's absence from higher managerial positions, gave reasons revealing explicitly negative preconceptions and biases against women (Petraki-Kottis, 1996). Since then women's presence in top managerial positions has not changed substantially, but there has been a significant improvement in one aspect. At present, the prevailing corporate culture is such that male executives are not likely to express openly outdated views concerning gender roles. Indeed, surveys show that attitudes towards women managers have improved considerably in recent years (Papalexandris et al., 2007). However, it is questionable whether convictions have actually changed given that the improvement in attitudes has not been reflected in women's proportion in managerial positions, particularly at the higher levels.

Distance between words and deeds is also revealed by the findings of a survey concerning firms' practices for promoting equal opportunities for women. It was found that company representatives were sufficiently informed and sensitized about existing gender inequalities and declared that promoting equal opportunities was among their goals and strategic objectives. However, an examination of respective practices indicated that the actual situation was far from what was being proclaimed (Epitropaki, 2007).

To better understand the gender gap in management, it is useful to look at women's participation in decision making in Greece. Women's presence in higher political positions has always been minimal. The country has always had male presidents and prime ministers, while women's participation in the government has been nominal or non-existent. In March 2009 there were only three women among the 41 ministers and deputy ministers, while the national parliament was chaired by a man and only 16 percent of its 300 members were women. Furthermore, in 2008, among representatives in regional assemblies only 17.5 percent were women (EC, 2009c).

The position of women is better in the public sector compared to the private sector. In 2008, the head of the Supreme Audit Organization was, as always, male, but women constituted 29 percent of public sector employees at the top level and 39 percent of those at the level below (EC, 2008). Women's presence in higher positions in the public sector is considerable but is not analogous to the proportion of female employees overall (Vaxevanidou, 2007).

In the judiciary domain, the general prosecutor and the presidents of the supreme and the highest administrative courts have been always men. In 2008, women's participation as members of these courts was only 17 percent (EC, 2008). In the judiciary and also the diplomatic corps, women are under-represented at the higher levels partly because, up to few decades ago, women were excluded by law.

Women Entrepreneurs

Entrepreneurial activity has always been an attractive employment option for women given their relatively high unemployment rates, their problems in moving up the managerial ladder and the fact that this activity offers greater work schedule flexibility, enabling women to better reconcile work with family responsibilities (Petraki-Kottis, 1998). Nevertheless, there are many obstacles facing female entrepreneurs. Finding the capital to start and operate a business has commonly been found to be problematic. Indeed, financial considerations were always the most serious factor limiting the survival and growth prospects of women's enterprises in Greece. Lack of experience and business connections is another impediment. Furthermore, negative male preconceptions and attitudes towards female entrepreneurs have often been found to create additional problems (Haratsis and Petraki-Kottis, 1993; Hassid, 2000; Katsanevas 2007).

In 2008, 21.2 percent of women in work were self-employed but only 4.3 percent were employing other people, while the remaining 16.9 percent were working on their own (NSSG, 2000; 2008). Women's self-employment rates lagged considerably behind those for men, particularly in the case of self-employed women with employees, whose rates were less than half of those for men. During 2000–2008 there was a small increase in the percentage of self-employed women with employees and a corresponding decrease in the percentage of those working on their own but their overall rate did not change significantly.

According to a European survey (Ioannidis, 2007), 12 percent of women in Greece had a business or were in the process of starting a new one and this was the highest percentage among the countries surveyed. About 30 percent of new entrepreneurs and 50 percent of established entrepreneurs were women. One-quarter of women entrepreneurs did not employ any personnel and close to 40 percent were engaged in this activity because they did not have other options. Women's participation in entrepreneurial activity was found to be relatively high, but in many cases women's enterprises actually belonged to men, mainly husbands, who for various reasons had not registered their enterprises under their names (Ionnidis, 2007).

The problem with women's entrepreneurial activity in Greece is not its size but its qualitative aspects. Most of women's enterprises are very small with low turnover and profits, are mainly in activities which offer services to final consumers, and are associated with intense competition and limited growth potential (Katsanevas, 2007; Theofilou and Ventura, 2007).

In the past, a relatively large number of women became self-employed because of their low levels of education and incomes and their inability to find dependent employment (Petraki-Kottis, 1998). In recent years the situation seems to be changing. According to Ioannidis (2007) about 53 percent of women entrepreneurs engaged in entrepreneurial activity because they wanted to take advantage of a good business opportunity and only 39 percent because they did not have another alternative. At least 42 percent of female new entrepreneurs had graduate or postgraduate degrees and about 36 percent declared that their products were considered innovative by customers.

Country Legislation

The existing legislation for promoting gender equality is based on the State Constitution of 1975 and its 2001 revision. Since 1975, several important pieces of legislation have been introduced while the country ratified the International

Treaty entitled "Equal Pay between Men and Women for Work of Equal Value", the 1979 UN "Convention for the Elimination of Discrimination Against Women" and the "Optional Protocol to the Convention on the Elimination of all forms of Discrimination Against Women". It has also signed several other related treaties (GSGE, 2005; 2008).

As a result of the country's accession to the EC in 1981, all Community rules and regulations for the promotion of gender equality became part of the Greek Law. The Community Guidelines led to various types of legislative and other action (Petraki-Kottis. 1991). The modernization of the Family Law in 1983 brought significant changes in the position of women in society. In 2001, the Government established quotas that at least one-third of positions in various bodies of public and local administration organizations and in the electoral lists for local and regional governments should be held by women (GSGE, 2005).

From 1975 onwards, the Greek legislation for gender equality has made significant steps forward. As a matter of fact the obstacles to women's advancement and the persistence of the glass ceiling cannot be attributed to inadequate legislation. Problems arise because many cases of unfair treatment cannot be taken to the courts due to their indirect or covert nature and women's inability to assemble the required legal evidence. Furthermore, in many cases, women cannot seek legal help because they do not have sufficient information, lack financial resources or, most importantly, are afraid of social disapproval or punitive action on the part of their employers.

Initiatives Supporting Women in the Workforce

Several institutions have been established and various types of action have been taken for promoting equal opportunities for women. In 1985, the Government founded the General Secretariat for Gender Equality (GSGE) for disseminating information, proposing corrective measures and intervening at all levels for the promotion of gender equality. It also established Committees for Equality in all prefecture offices and "Offices for Equality" in all ministries and public organizations. In 1994, the "Research Centre for Gender Equality" was created, under the auspices of the GSGE, with the task of undertaking research and other activities for improving the position of women (GSGE, 2005; 2008).

Up to 2004, Greece annually prepared Action Plans for Employment which included chapters on measures and policies for promoting equal opportunities for women. In 2004, the Government adopted a four-year action plan focusing on combating the equality deficit in the labour market, eliminating stereotypes and negative perceptions, preventing violence against women and promoting women's participation in decision-making centers. Furthermore, gender equality was integrated as an important element of the operational programmes in the National Strategic Development Plan 2007–2013 (GSGE, 2008).

The reconciliation of work and family life has received special attention in all Government plans. Several measures have been introduced for extending the availability of childcare services and for better leave arrangements, particularly for fathers, but a great deal of work remains to be done in that area.

In all Greek Manpower Organisation programmes, priority is given to the participation of women by at least 60 percent (GSGE, 2008). In 2006, a national committee for equality between women and men was established as a permanent mechanism for social dialogue. The GSGE has undertaken several projects to assist unemployed women to receive training and find employment, help working women in middle-sized and large enterprises to acquire additional skills, combat gender stereotypes and promote equal opportunities for women in the workplace and in the education process (GSGE, 2008). Special action has been taken by the Ministry of Education to remove discriminatory attitudes and practices from educational materials.

To encourage women's entrepreneurship, the Government has introduced several programmes for providing assistance in the form of subsidies and technical expertise for starting a new enterprise. Among others, the Research Centre for Gender Equality operates a programme under which individualized support in the form of mentoring and technical assistance is provided to women aspiring to become entrepreneurs (GSGE, 2008).

To sensitize teachers about gender equality, the Ministry of Education, in collaboration with the GSGE, organized optional training programmes for primary and secondary school teachers but participation was very limited. Before political elections, the GSGE, in collaboration with women's groups, organize meetings to assist women candidates in their campaigns.

Women's organizations have played an important role for promoting gender equality. Most of them are members of the European Women's Lobby. The Greek Association for Business Management has established the Institute for the Development of Women Managers and Entrepreneurs to undertake activities promoting the status and image of women managers and entrepreneurs and increasing their numbers (IAGME, Women's Organisation of Managers and Entrepreneurs, http://www.eede.gr).

To improve the position of women in the workforce, the National Confederation of Labour Unions, representing workers in the private sector, has established a secretariat for women and a network of women syndicalists in labour centres and federations (http://www.gsee.gr). A similar secretariat has also been established by the confederation of unions representing public sector employees (http://www.adedy.gr).

The Future

To assess future prospects it is useful to start with an overview of the situation at present. As outlined in this chapter, women's participation in the higher levels of the managerial ladder and in all top positions in Greece is relatively small and often minimal or non-existent. Women can reach the lower and middle hierarchical levels, but very few can break the glass ceiling. Their advancement is inhibited by preconceptions, outdated stereotypes and institutional and social structures inherited from the past. Some of these factors are also indirectly reinforced by advertising and the mass media (Petraki-Kottis and Ventura-Neokosmidi, 2004).

Although there is concern about women's under-representation in higher managerial and other positions, there has been very little in-depth research in this regard. Gender inequality prevails in the higher ranks in all areas of economic, social and political life and there is need for monitoring and analyzing the problem. Greek society is under-utilizing women's talents and abilities and this is wasteful and absurd, particularly in a period when the country and firms have to perform in a highly competitive world.

One basic factor contributing to gender inequality in the country is the unequal distribution of household responsibilities which, due to tradition, fall mostly on women. The situation is aggravated because of the inadequacy of public and enterprise arrangements for supporting the work/family reconciliation (EC, 2010a; 2009b). As a result, working women with families carry an excessive burden and this limits the time and energy needed to advance their careers. Moreover, because of various obstacles to their promotion, some women retire early, a practice encouraged in the past by special provisions in the social security legislation. While such arrangements were viewed as favouring women, in essence they worked against them. The mere knowledge that women may retire early discouraged employers from providing training for them and assigning them to jobs of higher responsibility. Recently, due to changes in legislation, this possibility has been drastically reduced.

Looking at future prospects, there are several reasons for optimism. First of all, mentalities and attitudes have started to change, particularly among younger people. The institutional and legislative framework established in recent decades, the increasing sensitization surrounding issues related to gender equality and the gradual strengthening of women's presence in decision making are creating an environment more favourable to women's advancement. Moreover, the constant increase in women's participation in all fields of higher education is bound to create a strong impetus for them to move higher. The dissemination of information about the need for a more equal division of household responsibilities between men and women and the gradual establishment of facilities enabling individuals to reconcile a better work and family balance, could also have a strong impact on women's prospects for advancement.

We believe that the future of women depends also upon women themselves. It is important that women strengthen their determination to fight for what they deserve and discard any remains of old mentalities and attitudes and any feelings of victimization and despair. The notion that in a male-dominated environment women do not advance to top positions may become a self-fulfilling prophesy. Furthermore, although views and attitudes creating obstacles to women's advancement are unfounded, they should not be entirely written off by them. Women aspiring to higher positions must undertake a careful examination of their priorities and attitudes to ensure that nothing feeds or sustains existing biases or stereotypes, and it is imperative that they address arrangements at home in order to reduce their home/work conflicts.

The Government, universities and all interested organizations can play a key role in speeding up the extinction of the gender equality deficit. Among other actions, more attention should be paid to encouraging and supporting in-depth research concerning the obstacles that impede women's advancement, the consequences for private and public organizations and society from women's under-utilization and the policies and measures to be used to rectify the situation. It is important to produce evidence showing society the absurdness of devoting valuable resources to educate women and then letting a large part of this investment go to waste. It is also important that all policies and initiatives introduced to promote gender equality are carefully evaluated. The evaluation of projects and programmes for gender equality is an area that has not received the attention it deserves.

Concluding this chapter, it is worth mentioning a contradiction regarding Government policies towards gender equality in Greece. In recent decades, all Governments introduced legislation and initiatives aimed at reducing the gender gap but when it came to nominating individuals for appointments at higher-level positions, they systematically ignored well-qualified women. This inconsistency raises doubts about sincere interest on the part of top-level decision-makers to promote gender equality at all levels and indicates that Greek women have a long way to go until they actually achieve equal opportunities with men.

References

Athens Stock Exchange (2009) http://ase.gr/companies, accessed 10 February, 2009.

EC (European Community) (2008) *Women and Men in Decision-Making* http://ec.europa.eu/employment_social/women_men_stats/out/en037/htm, accessed 5 February, 2009.

EC (European Community) (2009a) *Employment in Europe* (Luxembourg: Office for Official Publications of the European Communities).

EC (European Community) (2009b) *The Provision of Childcare Services* (Luxembourg: Office for Official Publications of the European Communities).

EC (European Community) (2009c) *Women in European Politics – Time for Action* (Luxembourg: Office for Official Publications of the European Communities).

EC (European Community) (2010a) *Report on Equality Between Women and Men* (Luxembourg: Office for Official Publications of the European Communities).

EC (European Community) (2010b) *More Women in Senior Positions* (Luxembourg: Office for Official Publications of the European Communities).

Epitropaki, O. (2007) Corporate practices for the promotion of equal opportunities within firms in Greece. In M. Vakola and E. Apospori (eds) *Women and Management* (Athens: Sideris Publishers, pp. 266–229) (in Greek).

EPWN (European Professional Women's Network) (2008) Milan Press Release, www.europeanpwn.net, accessed 3 April, 2009.

GSGE (General Secretariat for Gender Equality) (2005) *Sixth National Report of Greece to the United Nations* (Athens: General Secretariat for Equality).

GSGE (General Secretariat for Equality) (2008) *Recent Policies and Actions on Gender Equality, 2004–2008*, Athens, www.isotita.gr, accessed 6 March, 2009.

Haratsis, E. and Petraki-Kottis, A. et al. (1993) *Self-employment in Greece* (Athens: Manpower Employment Organisation of Greece) (in Greek).

Hassid, I. (2000) Greek women entrepreneurs, *The Greek Economy*, EPILOGI, pp. 202–206 (in Greek).

Ioannidis, S. (2007) *Women Entrepreneurs in Greece 2006–2007*, GEM, IOBE, www.iobe.gr, accessed 10 March, 2009 (in Greek).

Katsanevas, T. (2007) *Women's Entrepreneurship, Research Project for Archimed*, Interreg, www.wbc-net.org, accessed 16 March, 2009.

MoE (Ministry of Education) (2007) *Education Statistics*, www.ypepth.gr, accessed 25 February, 2009.

NSSG (National Statistical Service of Greece) (2008) (and 2000) *Labour Force Survey*, B Quarter, www.statistics.gr, accessed 16 March, 2009.

Papalexandris N., Galanaki, E. and Bourantas, D. (2007) Acceptance and leadership style of women managers in Greece. In M. Vakola and E. Apospori (eds) *Women and Management* (Athens: Sideris, pp. 164–188) (in Greek).

Papapetrou, E. (2007) Education, labour market and wage differentials in Greece, *Economic Bulletin*, 28 (Athens: Bank of Greece).

Parent-Thirion, A. (2007) *Fourth European Working Conditions Survey*, Dublin: European Foundation for the Improvement of Living and Working Conditions.

Petraki-Kottis, A. (1987) Earnings differentials in manufacturing in Greece, *International Journal of Manpower*, 8(4), 26–32.

Petraki-Kottis, A, (1988) Sources of growth of female employment in Greece: a shift-share analysis, *International Journal of Manpower*, 9(1), 18–20.

Petraki-Kottis, A. and Petraki-Kottis, Z. (1990) Shifts over time and regional variation in women's labour force participation rates in a developing economy, *Journal of Development Economics*, 33, 117–132.

Petraki-Kottis, A. (1991) Single European labour market: equality between women and men, *International Journal of Manpower*, 12(3), 3–8.

Petraki-Kottis, A. (1996) Women in management and the glass ceiling in Greece, *Women in Management*, 11(2), 30–38.

Petraki-Kottis, A. (1998) Self-employment in Greece, *TRENDS*, No 31, European Employment Observatory, EC, 22–26.

Petraki-Kottis, A. and Ventoura-Neokosmidi, Z. (2004) Women in management in Greece. In M. J. Davidson and R. J. Burke (eds) *Women in Management Worldwide: Facts, Figures and Analysis* (Aldershot: Gower, pp. 19–31).

Technical Chamber of Greece, (2003) *Employment and Professional Situation of Engineers University Graduates*, www.tee.gr, accessed 15 March, 2009.

Theofilou, A. and Ventura, Z. (2007) Women's Entrepreneurship. In M. Vakola and E. Apospori (eds) *Women and Management* (Athens: Sideris, pp. 242–263) (in Greek).

Vaxevanidou, M. (2007) Women managers in Public Administration. In M. Vakola and E. Apospori (eds) *Women and Management* (Athens: Sideris, pp. 139–161) (in Greek).

Ventura, Z. and Neokosmidi, A. (2007) Women in management: The case of Greece. In M. Vakola and E. Apospori (eds) *Women and Management* (Athens: Sideris, pp. 84–101) (in Greek).

Visser, M. (2009) *Women on Boards Moving Mountains*. Paper presented at the American Hellenic Chamber of Commerce, Athens, January 28.

4

Women in Management in the Netherlands

Kea G. Tijdens

Introduction

This chapter highlights the current labour force characteristics in the Netherlands, including an overview of the changes over the past ten to 20 years. It extends the conclusions of a similar chapter for the 1970s and 1980s and for the 1990s (Tijdens, 1993; 2004). First, this chapter details the labour force characteristics of women followed by a review of women pursuing education, and the focus then changes to women in management. This broad category is sub-divided into women in managerial occupations, women in supervisory jobs, women on corporate boards of directors, and women holding elected offices in local and national government. The following section draws attention to women entrepreneurs, notably self-employed women, assisting members of the family, and professional women. The final sections highlight the legislation in the Netherlands, the initiatives to support the advancement of women and predictions about the future.

Labour Force Characteristics

During the post-war period, Dutch women were supposed to contribute to the rebuilding of society by starting a family. Many of them did, as the baby boom in the late 1940s and early 1950s shows. Women overwhelmingly left the labour market on the day of their marriage to become full-time, permanent housewives. The breadwinner system was firmly established in industrial relations, in wage policies as well as in general attitudes towards gender roles. Male workers were supposed to earn a family wage in a 48-hour working week, and nearly all men were able to do so, thanks to a non-dispersed wage distribution. Women spent on average far more than a 48-hour week on their household chores. In this period, women's work was predominantly girls' labour (Pott-Buter and Tijdens, 1998).

Due to a steady decline in household time, increasing education levels, and the growth of the service sector at the cost of the agricultural and manufacturing industry, women's participation rates have grown, particularly since the 1970s (Tijdens, 2006). Prime age women became predominantly the core of the female labour force. Female participation rates in the age group 15–64 grew from 34 percent in 1982 to 48 percent in 2008.[1]

The Netherlands is well known for the highest part-time rate of female workers in the European Union (Portegijs and. Keuzenkamp, 2008). In 1992, almost 38 percent of women had a job requiring them to work 20–34 hours per week. Sixteen years later, in 2008, this had increased to 52 percent. Similarly, the share of women working 12–29 hours per week has grown from 15 to 18 percent, whereas the share of women in jobs of 35 hours and over has declined from 47 to 30 percent. When taking also into account the women with a job requiring them to work 1–12 hours per week, almost three-quarters of working women are not employed full time. The more children working women have, the more likely they are to work in a small part-time job (CBS, 2009a).

Part-time jobs facilitate the reconciliation of work and family life, once women have started or anticipate starting a family of their own. In the past decades, the Netherlands has opted for regulating and equalising part-time employment as a main strategy for policies concerning reconciliation of work and family life (Pott-Buter and Tijdens, 1998). These policies have influenced employers, as they tend to set the starting and finishing times of work and they have transferred the prerogative of the number of working hours to the employee. Taken into account the very high percentages of part-timers, the Netherlands is unique in Europe, both with respect to women's and to men's labour.

The part-time employment policies consist of three options. First, employees' right to adjust their own working hours. Second, working hours can be adjusted in one's own job, and therefore do not imply any job changes. Third, all discriminatory clauses based on working hours have been removed.

---

1   See www.cbs.nl/statline, Centraal Bureau voor de Statistiek, Den Haag/Heerlen, accessed
    1 October, 2009.

These policies are integrated in both national legislation and regulation, and collective bargaining (Pott-Buter and Tijdens, 1998). Over the years, these policies have largely prevented part-time jobs from marginalization and in general, part-time jobs of more than 12 hours per week do not differ greatly from full-time jobs. For the large majority of households, an income based on one full-time and one part-time working partner is sufficient for a decent living. Moreover, the large majority of Dutch working couples fit this profile (CBS, 2009d).

Although husband's and wife's working hours are not equal, their leisure time is. According to Merens and Hermans (2008) women's total working and household hours are converging over time, and were, in 2005, one hour less than that of men's. The Netherlands is the only country in the European Union where women have as much leisure time as men. In all other European countries, men have more leisure time than women (Breedveld and Van den Broek, 2001). In addition, partly because of the opportunities to adjust working hours, women have increasingly, a continuous working career (Portegijs and Keuzekamp, 2008).

Women Pursuing Education

During the twentieth century, participation rates in education grew steadily, the boys mostly a step ahead of the girls (Pott-Buter and Tijdens, 1998). In 1950, almost 70 percent of boys aged 14 and 15 were in full-time education, as opposed to 60 percent of girls. It was not until 1975 that girls closed this gap with almost 100 percent of the boys and girls in this age group being in full-time education (Pott-Buter and Tijdens, 1998). Similar patterns can be seen for older girls and boys and by 1985, 17-year-old girls had closed the gap with participation rates of nearly 90 percent. By 2006, girls' overall education attainments were generally better than those of boys.[2]

In the 1960s, the gender-separated educational systems in the Netherlands were abolished and were integrated into co-education. Nevertheless, although more females are opting for subjects and disciplines which have traditionally been a male preserve, gender-based differences in subject choices still remain (Pott-Buter and Tijdens, 1998). In particular, very few males choose traditionally female educational courses (CBS, 2009b). In secondary education, boys are

---

2   See www.cbs.nl/statline, Centraal Bureau voor de Statistiek, Den Haag/Heerlen, accessed 1 October, 2009.

much more likely to opt for subjects in science, chemistry and advanced maths, whereas girls are still more likely to choose French language, German language and biology. With regard to subjects such as economics or introductory maths, the gender gap is small. In universities, most studies have kept constant their sex typing over time, but some faculties have not and it is interesting to note that subject areas such as medicine, law and psychology have faced a feminization.[3]

In the 25–44 years age-group men and women have virtually the same level of education with the females in the workforce being on average a little more highly educated than their male counterparts.[4] Perhaps not surprisingly, compared to higher-educated women, lower-educated women are more likely to choose being a homemaker as a career (Portegijs and Keuzekamp, 2008). As well, non-western ethnic minorities are clearly less educated than indigenous persons, and this gap rises with age. However, among those aged under 35, Moroccan women in particular, and to a somewhat lesser extent Turkish women, are comparatively better educated than women over 35 years of age (Merens and Hermans, 2008). Generally speaking the labour market prospects for training courses predominantly taken by girls are good, although many of these courses offer few career opportunities and are generally not as well paid. More men than women take part in education at a later age. Furthermore, the men are more often concerned with obtaining professional qualifications (Merens and Hermans, 2008).

Women in Management

In this section, the focus is firstly on women in managerial positions. Table 4.1 reveals that both the number of men and the number of women in managerial positions has increased from 1992 to 2008. Here, managerial positions are defined as occupational groups at higher vocational training level and at university level with predominantly managerial tasks.[5] Expressed in a percentage of the male and female workforce employed 12 hours and more, the share in managerial positions has remained stable over time at around 2 percent for the males and 1 percent for the females. In line with their increase in the labour force, women's share in managerial positions has steadily increased from 15 percent in 1992

---

3   See www.vsnu.nl/Universiteiten/Feiten-Cijfers/Onderwijs/Downloadbare-tabellen-onderwijs. htm, accessed 1 October, 2009.

4   See www.cbs.nl/statline, Centraal Bureau voor de Statistiek, Den Haag/Heerlen, accessed 1 October, 2009.

5   These are codes 788 respectively 988 in the occupational classification scheme of Statistics Netherlands.

to 27 percent in 2008.[6] The managerial positions include both women in wage employment and the self-employed women, though this growth must primarily be attributed to women's substantial increase in managerial positions in wage employment and only slightly to the minor growth of women's share in self-employment.[7] In some professions such as lawyers and other legal professions, as well as doctors and other medical professions, the percentages of women are quickly rising. Not surprisingly, the demand for part-time jobs in these occupations is also increasing (Bouma, 2007).

Table 4.1 **Labour force and managerial positions for men and women, 1996–2008**

	Labour force: men (000s)	Labour force: women (000s)	Labour force: total (000s)	% Women	Managerial positions: men (000s)	Managerial positions: women (000s)	% Managers in labour force: men	% Managers in labour force: women
1996	3870	2315	6185	37	103	18	2.7%	0.8
1997	3940	2444	6384	38	113	25	2.9%	1.0
1998	4036	2551	6587	39	118	29	2.9%	1.1
1999	4105	2663	6768	39	113	28	2.8%	1.1
2000	4162	2755	6917	40	127	41	3.1%	1.5
2001	4202	2818	7020	40	121	38	2.9%	1.3
2002	4178	2857	7035	41	120	41	2.9%	1.4
2003	4127	2874	7001	41	124	39	3.0%	1.4
2004	4068	2851	6919	41	85	23	2.1%	0.8
2005	4045	2873	6918	42	82	24	2.0%	0.8
2006	4085	2989	7074	42	90	30	2.2%	1.0
2007	4146	3114	7260	43	92	32	2.2%	1.0
2008	4191	3220	7411	43	88	33	2.1%	1.0

Source: Statistics Netherlands, www.cbs.nl/statline, accessed 29 April, 2009

Having a closer look at the characteristics of women in supervisory positions compared to men, the 2008 data of the WageIndicator web-survey present a detailed comparison of male and female supervisors, using multivariate analyses.[8] Regarding job characteristics, the two groups differed with respect

---

6 See www.cbs.nl/statline, Centraal Bureau voor de Statistiek, Den Haag/Heerlen, accessed 29 April, 2009.
7 See www.cbs.nl/statline, Centraal Bureau voor de Statistiek, Den Haag/Heerlen, accessed 29 April, 2009.
8 Author's analyses on the dataset of www.wageindicator.org (English) or www.loonwijzer.nl (Dutch).

to personal and household characteristics. The female supervisors were less likely to be living with a partner or having one or more children, compared to their male counterparts. Age hardly differed across the two groups. The female supervisors were less likely to work full time and, even though they had on average a higher education level than the male supervisors, were more likely to report they felt underqualified for the job. In terms of pay, females' hourly earnings were almost a quarter less than males, they supervised fewer employees and they worked in smaller companies. The largest differences, however, were found with regard to segregation by gender. The supervisors in female-dominated firms (80–100 percent females) were very likely to be women, and the supervisors in male-dominated firms (0–20 percent females) were even more likely to be men. Compared to their female counterparts, male supervisors were twice as likely to be in work environments where most of their colleagues in similar positions were men. Therefore, these data point to the continued existence of gendered structures in organizations in relation to supervisory positions.

Turning our attention to the elite network of the stock exchange, it still firmly remains an "old boys network", with the only major changes relating to substituting the "oldest boys" by "boys" of a younger age. Women are almost wholly absent, and there has been no progress over the past 15 years (Merens and Hermans, 2008). Furthermore, the proportion of women on boards in the top companies has hardly changed in the past few decades. In 1992, there no women on the board of executive directors of the 25 largest companies quoted at the stock exchange, and this was still the case in 2007 (although in between one or two women made it on to the board and then left). However, the gender composition of the board of governors in these companies increased from 2.8 percent to 8.9 percent during this time period (Merens and Hermans, 2008).

When it comes to women holding elected offices in National Government, women's share in Parliament grew steadily up from one-quarter in the 1980s, through to one-third in the 1990s increasing to 41 percent in 2008 (Merens and Hermans, 2008). The percentage of female mayors also shows an upward movement since the 1980s, rising steadily from 4 percent in 1984 to 19 percent 25 years later (Merens and Hermans, 2008).

A recent European study explaining the share of women in managerial, higher academic and elected positions showed a strong relationship between women's labour force participation rates and their share in elected positions in 15 European countries (De Wilde, 2007). Nevertheless, hardly any correlation was shown regarding women's participation rates and their share in managerial and higher academic positions. Presumably, more factors than women's participation rates only are at stake when explaining women's advancement in management across countries (De Wilde, 2007).

Although the Netherlands has no legislation on quotas, and contract compliance is rarely included in equal opportunities programmes, during the 1990s there was definitely increasing Government pressure and policies towards stimulating women's participation in decision-making bodies. However, this pressure became less intense in the 2000s. Also, there appears to be a growing awareness in the electorate for supporting female candidates and the majority of the political parties are aware of the importance of having women on their list of candidates (Leyenaar, 2007).

Women Entrepreneurs

The category of female entrepreneurs ranges from freelancers, who have no employees, to managers or owners of large companies, employing tens of thousands of employees. In our review of women entrepreneurs, we have utilized data from the Statistics Netherlands.[9] In 1992, the self-employed working at least 12 hours a week in their business, totalled 627,000 individuals, of which 28 percent were female. In 2008, the number had increased to 982,000, and the share of women amounted to 31 percent.[10]

Self-employment among women reveals a clear age-related pattern. In the female labour force aged 50–64 years, self-employment is the most prominent, followed by those aged 25–49, with only few women being self-employed under 24 years of age.[11] However, between 1992 and 2008, the share of self-employment among the oldest group of women has shown a decline, compared to an increase among the youngest group. In 2008, approximately 3 percent of the female labour force aged 15–24 were self-employed, compared to 9 percent for those aged 25–49 and 14 percent for those over 50 years of age.[12]

Increasingly, women are being considered as good successors in family-owned businesses. For example, in a family-based publishing and printing

---

9   See www.cbs.nl.
10 See www.cbs.nl.
11 See www.cbs.nl, accessed 1 October, 2009.
12 See www.cbs.nl, accessed 1 October, 2009.

company, established in 1836, it was not until the fourth generation that daughters were deemed possible successors.[13] The current male director has four daughters, and the oldest is working in the company with a view to taking over the family business. Indeed, this example is typical for many family-owned companies in the last decades of the twentieth century.

When it comes to the female assisting members of the family in running their own business, focus is primarily on the agricultural sector (Pott-Buter and Tijdens, 1998). However, in the 2000s, their numbers have shown a sharp decline due to the decline in the number of agricultural businesses. However, the decline was steeper among the heads of businesses compared to that of the female assisting members, and as a consequence, women's contribution to agricultural businesses has increased with women now constituting more than 95 percent of all assisting spouse family members.[14] Even so, it should be emphasized that this also is a product of the economic advantages in terms of both tax and legal reasons for women to be registered as co-entrepreneurs with their husband. Presumably most of all, it reflects the growing self-confidence of women.

Country Legislation

The feminist and women's movement in the late 1960s and early 1970s made it very clear that Government needed to respond to changes in society, particularly women's demands not to spend their whole adult life as housewives and to attain equal rights. In 1974, an Equal Opportunities Commission was set up as an advisory body and since 1978 the Government made funds available to stimulate equal rights policy throughout society. Subsequently other measures were to follow, which increasingly aimed at women in paid employment.[15] In legislation, the issue of reconciling work and family life has received substantial attention throughout the 1980s, 1990s and 2000s. A few of the major policies will be summarized here.

In the Netherlands, maternity leave is 16 weeks and a 100 percent replacement rate applies, paid according to the Sickness Benefits Act. Self-employed women are entitled to paid maternity leave, though here conditions

---

13 'Waanders Uitgevers, Drukkers en Boekverkopers (1836) ['Waanders Publishers, Printers and booksellers (1836)'] , in *Forum*, March 7, 2002.
14 See www.cbs.nl, accessed 1 October, 2009.
15 Stimuleringsregeling Positieve Actie [Policy towards positive action, House of Representatives], Tweede Kamer, 1987–1988, 20 343, nr. 1.

of insurance apply. The Parental Leave Act entitles both women and men in wage employment to unpaid parental leave of one year in total for at most half of their working hours, though in some Collective Agreements clauses for payment during leave apply. The leave arrangements are not transferable between parents.[16]

Women's rising participation rates in paid employment, particularly of women with young children, caused a growing demand for day care (Pott-Buter and Tijdens, 1998). From the 1970s onwards, the State used to finance playgrounds for children aged from 2–4 years, where they could play for a few hours a day. During the 1980s, regardless of the severe pressure from women's organizations, trade unions, tripartite bodies and others, Government kept its view that the care for children was solely the parents' responsibility. It was expected that private day care centres would come into being, because the demand for childcare was estimated to be high. However, this did not happen as only a small minority of couples could afford the high childcare costs (Tijdens and Lieon, 1993). It was not until 1989 that the Government changed views and decided to subsidize childcare, under the condition that both employers and parents took part in the costs. A substantial increase in day care facilities followed. The capacity of childcare facilities, and especially out-of-school childcare, increased further in the 2000s although it is still the more highly educated women who predominantly use formal childcare, with the middle- and less-educated women relying on informal childcare such as relatives (CBS, 2009c).

As far back as 1951, the International Labour Organisation (ILO) agreed on equal pay for equal work for male and female employees. Typical of the Netherlands, the Government did not take action until the social partners had agreed upon the principle, which took more than two decades. In 1971, when all wage inequality had been removed from collective agreements, Government ratified the ILO convention and in 1975 the Parliament passed the Equal Pay Act. In 1976 and 1980, the Equal Pay Act was followed by two acts prescribing equal treatment at work in the public and private sector. According to these laws, women as well as men, be it individually or as a group, can submit complaints to the Equal Treatment Commission if they believe they have been treated unfairly at work or paid unequally. The 1975 legislation on equal pay and the 1980 legislation on equality were integrated into the 1994

---

16 See http://home.szw.nl/index.cfm?fuseaction=app.document&link_id=72370, accessed 1 October, 2009.

legislation on equal treatment.[17] However, in the 2000s, it became clear that equal pay legislation would not solve the gender wage gap, by 2005 it was still 18.3 percent according to Statistics Netherlands, and the Government changed its policy towards raising awareness rather than improving legislation (Van Klaveren, Sprenger and Tijdens, 2007).

Initiatives Supporting Women in the Workforce

In this section, attention is drawn to three initiatives to support the advancement of women in employment. By 1995, the Ministry of Home Affairs established a national information centre on positive action to consult the municipalities, provinces and water control boards for advice. By then, 30 percent of all employees in central Government had to be female. The centre developed into E-Quality, a knowledge centre for gender, family and diversity issues. It collects and analyses facts, figures, research data and practical examples for advising governments, politicians and public organizations. E-Quality aims at stimulating equal treatment, individual growth and equal development of all people.[18]

In 1983, female teachers and students of polytechnic schools set up a foundation to promote the advancements of women in technical studies. Only 1.7 percent of students were female. It was awarded a start-up subsidy to support counselling of these female students, in addition to promoting girls into choosing technical educations. VHTO also set up a network of women engineers. Over the years the foundation has become a centre of expertise in the field of girls/women and science/technology/IT, focusing on the schooling system as well as on the labour market and the Foundation has taken a wide range of initiatives to promote their aims.[19]

In 1996 Opportunity in Bedrijf[20] was established. It was shaped after the UK's Opportunity 2000 that in 1991 was launched by a business association and backed by the Prime Minister. Although originally initiated by the Ministry of Social Affairs and Employment, from the very beginning Opportunity in Bedrijf was meant to become an independent consultancy, predominantly financed by the members' fees. An increasing number of firms, particularly

---

17 See www.eiro.eurofound.eu.int/2002/01/word/NL0110103s.doc.
18 See http://www.e-quality.nl/.
19 See http://www.vhto.nl/.
20 Bedrijf is Dutch for Business.

large firms, joined Opportunity in Bedrijf. Its consultants support members in analyzing the workforce with regard to the gender characteristics, setting goals and targets for the proportion of women in higher grades, and introducing a plan of action.[21] Furthermore, the consultancy maintains a relationship with recruitment agencies for women, with management consultants and others. The signatories agree upon the goals they want to reach with regard to the recruitment, turnover and career steps in their female workforce. Reducing recruitment and training costs and improved customers service are both stated as being major goals. Nevertheless, in 2009 Opportunity in Bedrijf concluded that the percentage of women managers had increased only very slowly.[22]

The Future

This chapter on women in management in the Netherlands has shown the dynamics in the female workforce over the past 10 to 20 years. Prominent findings include the rapid increase in female participation rates in the workforce, the decrease of homemaker careers among young women, the huge increase and acceptance of part-time employment (the highest in Europe), and the slowly rising share of women in managerial and entrepreneurial positions. Nevertheless, the chapter also highlights that when it comes to the highest hierarchical levels and to senior decision-making positions, women's progress has been very slow and there is still a long way to go.

It is also evident that, in the Netherlands, there is still massive gender segregation in the workplace. Both, self-selection by potential employees and selection by the organization play a role in continuation of a masculine organization culture, particularly in senior managerial positions. As regards to future developments, women's increased participation in the labour force and women's increasing purchasing power may force male-dominated organizational levels with predominantly masculine organizational culture to adopt feminine values.

In general, segregation by gender is assumed to have a large impact on women's careers. Even in female-dominated occupations, proportionally, men still dominate senior positions and the majority of female supervisors are supervised by males. In the future it is more likely that this hierarchical

---

21 See http://www.opportunity.nl/, accessed 1 October, 2009.
22 See http://www.opportunity.nl/2009/09/toptelling-vm-stringente-maatregelen-nodig-om-versnelling-te-forceren/, accessed 1 October, 2009.

gender balance will be changed more in female-dominated organizations than in male-dominated ones. This may lead to better career possibilities for women in these female-dominated organizations. However, breaking through the thick walls in male-dominated organizations will definitely require more time, and more effort. To conclude, gendered organizational structures and career structures are quite likely mutually interlocked. Further research is necessary on how gendered organizational structures coincide with unequal attribution of power, including, for example, the allocation of budgets, internal career opportunities, managerial commitment, authority, and contacts within and outside the organization.

References

Bouma, H. (2007) Nieuwe generatie wil parttime werk [New generation wants part-time jobs], *Het Financieele Dagblad*, 19 Feb, 2007.

CBS (Central Bureau voor de Statistiek) (2009a), *Steeds meer Moeders met Grotere Deeltijdbaan [Growing Number of Mothers with Large Part-time Jobs]* (The Hague,: Statistics Netherlands, Webmagazine).

Breedveld, K. and Van den Broek, A. (2001) *Trends in de Tijd [Trends over Time]* (The Hague: Social Cultural Planning Office).

CBS (Central Bureau voor de Statistiek) (2009b), *Vrouwen Volgen in het mbo Hogere Opleidingen dan Mannen [Women Pursue Higher Levels of Education in Vocational Training than Men]* (The Hague: Statistics Netherlands, Webmagazine).

CBS (Central Bureau voor de Statistiek) (2009c), *Hoogopgeleide Moeders Maken meer Gebruik van Kinderopvang dan Laagopgeleide Moeders [More Highly Educated Mothers use Childcare Facilities More Often than Less Educated Mothers]* (The Hague: Statistics Netherlands, Webmagazine).

CBS (Central Bureau voor de Statistiek) (2009d), *Partners Meest te Spreken over Combinatie Voltijd – en Deeltijdbaan [Partners Prefer the Combination of Full-time and Part-time Jobs Most]* (The Hague: Centraal Bureau voor de Statistiek, Webmagazine).

De Wilde, L. (2007) *De Weg Naar de Top! Een Onderzoek naar Vrouwen in Topposities in EU15 [The Road to the Top! A Study on Women in Higher Level Jobs in 15 Countries of the European Eunion]*, Rotterdam: Master Thesis Sociology, Erasmus University, Rotterdam.

Leyenaar, M. (2007). *De Last van Ruggespraak [The Trouble with Feedback]*, Inaugural lecture, Nijmegen: Radboud Universiteit.

Merens, A. and Herman, B. (2008), *Emancipatiemonitor [Monitoring Women's Progress]* (The Hague: Social Cultural Planning Office and Statistics Netherlands).

Portegijs, W. and Keuzenkamp, S. (2008) *Nederland Deeltijdland. Vrouwen en Deeltijdwerk [The Netherlands is a Part-time Country. Women and Part-time Jobs]* (The Hague: Social Cultural Planning Office).

Pott-Buter, H. A. and Tijdens, K. G. (1998) *Vrouwen, Leven en Werk in de Twintigste Eeuw [Women, Their Lives and Work in the Twentieth Century]* (Amsterdam: Amsterdam University Press).

Tijdens, K. G. (1993) Women in business and management – The Netherlands. In M. J. Davidson and C. L. Cooper (eds) *European Women in Business and Management* (London: Paul Chapman Publishing, pp. 79–92).

Tijdens, K. G. (2004) Women in Management – The Netherlands. In M. J. Davidson and Burke, R. J. (eds) *Women in Management Worldwide: Facts, Figures and Analysis* (Aldershot: Gower Publishing, pp. 68–82).

Tijdens, K. G. (2006) *Een Wereld van Verschil: Arbeidsparticipatie van Vrouwen 1945–2005 [A World of Differences: Women's Labour Participation Rates 1945–2005]*, Inaugural lecture, Erasmus University, Rotterdam.

Tijdens, K. G. and Lieon, S. (1993). *Kinderopvang in Nederland. Organisatie en Financiering [Chikdcare in the Netherlands Organisation and Finances]* (Utrecht: Uitgeverij Jan van Arkel).

Van Klaveren, M., Sprenger, W. and Tijdens, K. G. (2007). *Dicht de Loonkloof! Verslag van het CLOSE (Correctie LOonkloof in SEctoren) Onderzoek voor de FNV, ABVAKABO FNV en FNV Bondgenoten [Close the Gender Pay Gap. Report of the CLOSE Project. Research fot the FNV, ABVAKABO FNV and FNV Bondgenoten]* (Eindhoven/Amsterdam: STZ Advies & Onderzoek/Universiteit van Amsterdam).

5

Women in Management in Portugal

Carlos Cabral-Cardoso

Introduction

Women in Portugal are the best-educated segment of the labour force and, slowly but steadily, they occupy an increasing proportion of managerial jobs. However, women's access to the very top management positions remains nearly residual. This chapter describes the situation of women in the labour force and reflects on recent developments and challenges facing women managers in Portugal.

Two major statistical sources were used to describe the characteristics of the Portuguese labour force: Official statistics from the Ministry of Employment and Social Security (MTSS), and the Office for National Statistics (INE). Figures of the MTSS were extracted from the 2006 dataset. This dataset ("Quadros de Pessoal") is based on a compulsory survey of all establishments with at least one employee. 2008 figures were already available in the case of the INE database. The two datasets also differ in scope. The INE dataset covers a broader spectrum of the working population including public administration, armed forces and self-employed individuals. Besides these two major sources, Eurostat data were also taken into account. Annual reports and other documents published by the Commission for Equality in Labour and Employment (CITE), provided very useful information about the situation of men and women in the Portuguese labour market. Different coding and methodology adopted by the various sources does not always make the comparison meaningful but, taken together, they contribute to depict a general picture of the situation in Portugal.

Labour Force Characteristics

In 2008, the population in Portugal aged 15 or more was about nine million, 52.1 percent of whom were women (INE, 2009). The foreign population with legal status of residence was, in 2007, slightly over 400,000 individuals and 45.3 percent were women. In general, official statistics in Portugal do not consider diversity dimensions such as the ethnic group or religious faith and, therefore, it is difficult to find any reliable statistics on minority groups in the labour force.

Female employment in Portugal has increased in the last decades at a rate consistently higher than male employment. With an overall activity rate of 56.2 percent in 2008, female employment is now close to the Lisbon objective of 60 percent, though Eurostat figures place the employment rate of Portuguese women in 2007 already above that at 61.9 percent (EU, 2009). Official employment statistics show that the proportion of women in the labour force has increased steadily since the mid-1980s, rising from 32.5 percent in 1985 to 41.8 percent in 1999 and reaching 43.5 percent in 2006 (MTSS, 2006 dataset). Furthermore, recent 2008 data reveal women make up about 46.2 percent of the employed population (INE, 2009). The participation rate of women in the employed population is relatively close in all age groups, varying from 43.4 percent in the under 25 years of age group to 47.2 percent in the 35 to 44 years of age group (INE, 2009).

It is interesting to note that, differences between age groups in terms of gender participation rates that were still apparent a decade ago (Cabral-Cardoso, 2004) are no longer significant. Currently, the dominant pattern is for women to join the labour market in their mid-twenties and remain active during their entire working life. Eurostat figures indicate that the employment rate of older women (over 55 years old) is one of the highest in Europe (EU, 2009). Moreover, 2008 data show that the highest participation rate – about 87 percent – was found in the 25 to 34 age group (INE, 2009). In other words, 87 out of 100 women from that age group were in work or seeking work. Bearing in mind that the mean age of women at the birth of their first child was 28.4 in that same year (INE, 2009), these figures mean that women reach the highest activity rate in the labour market at the age when they are most likely to become mothers. Women's activity rate remains very high – about 85 percent in 2008, in the 35 to 44 years old age cohort, leaving only a small fraction of women outside the labour market. It is, therefore, apparent that the number of women leaving the labour market for maternity or childcare reasons is negligible.

Eurostat figures confirm that, in terms of employment of women aged 25 to 49 in the EU, Portugese women are the second least affected by parenthood (EU, 2009). In other words, the difference in employment rates between Portuguese women with a child under 12 and without children is only -0.8, the second lowest percentage in the EU (EU average: -12.4).

Furthermore, unlike other countries in Northern Europe, the proportion of women working part time in 2008 was very limited, only about 17 percent of the female employed population (INE, 2009). That figure represents only a tiny increase from the one found a decade before (about 15 percent in 1997), according to INE (2009). These figures are very low when compared to the percentage of women employees in the EU working part time – 31.2 percent on average in 2007 (EU, 2009). The data indicate that women in Portugal tend to stay active in the labour market despite maternity and they do so working full time in most cases. Moreover, Portuguese women have a considerable participation in other less family-friendly work arrangements such as shift work (46.2 percent) and night work (32.8 percent) (CITE, 2009).

Therefore, the overall picture that emerges from the employment figures suggests a significant participation of women in the labour market, despite the family and caring responsibilities that largely remain in the women's sphere. That participation represents an important challenge to work–family relations and takes place against a background of unfriendly work–family cultures prevailing in the majority of organizations, a limited provision of childcare support and the preservation of traditional gender roles in the family (Santos and Cabral-Cardoso, 2008). The growing divorce rate and the proportion of single parent households – six times more likely to be a single mother than a single father families (INE, 2009), provide further evidence of the difficulties faced by Portuguese women when it comes to reconciling work and family. Despite the progress in recent years, the Portuguese Government has yet to fulfil the so-called "Barcelona objectives" according to which member states were invited to provide affordable and quality childcare facilities as part of the policies for a better reconciliation of work and private life (EU, 2009). In this context, the fertility rate of Portuguese women (1.37 in 2008, according to INE, 2009), one of the lowest in Europe, is a foreseeable outcome and an illustration of the current social malaise felt in Portuguese society.

As pointed out above, unlike other countries in Europe where the unequal share of domestic and family responsibilities has led many women to work part time or to leave the labour market, Portuguese women tend to remain in the labour market despite maternity and in full-time jobs in most cases. Besides tradition, low income may explain the limited use of part-time jobs. The average monthly base salary of Portuguese workers in 2007 was only about 808.5 euros or 965.3 euros when the overall earnings are taken into account. The wider sex differences in terms of overall earnings, when compared to base salaries, are explained by the duration of the work journey and availability to work overtime. In 1999, the daily average duration of paid work was longer in the case of men (7.9 hours) than women (7.0 hours) (INE, 2009). However, most recent 2005 figures relating to the "paid work week" show that men work on average 43h30min per week while women worked 41h06min. In 2007, women's base salary was on average 81.2 percent of men's, and women's overall earnings were about 77.6 percent of men's (CITE, 2009). And yet, the gender pay gap in Portugal was the fourth lowest in Europe in 2007, according to the Eurostat and it was slightly narrower than two years before (CITE, 2009; EU, 2009). Nevertheless, the pay gap tends to become wider in the categories of employment that require a higher-education degree. In this group, women had a base salary that was only 71.1 percent of men's whereas women in non-qualified jobs got 93.9 percent of men's base salary in that period (CITE, 2009).

The gender segregation of the labour market remains largely unchallenged. The participation of women in the labour market is strongest in the service sector, in which they made up about 55.3 percent of the overall employed population in 2008 (INE, 2009). A closer look at the figures (INE, 2009) for the different segments indicate that, in 2008, women were the majority among "professionals and scientists" (55.9 percent), "clerks and related workers" (61.1 percent), "service workers and shop and market sales workers" (67.6 percent), "hotels and restaurants" (59.9 percent), "education" (76.7 percent), and "health and social work" (83.5 percent), according to official statistics (INE, 2009; CITE, 2009).

The feminization of the service sector is not new, but gender segregation in this sector is now wider than a decade ago with the representation of women growing consistently in most segments of the service sector since then. In 1997, for example, women were already the majority of the employees in the service sector, about 52.0 percent (INE, 2009) and constituted "only" 50.7 percent of the "professionals" and 59.8 percent of the "clerks and secretaries". In general, segments in which women were already the majority a decade ago, have witnessed a further increase in the proportion of women in that segment. Where women were the minority, slight progress has been made towards parity but women still remain the minority. That is the case in "manufacturing" (41.1 percent), "construction" (4.3 percent), "agriculture, forestry and fishing" (48.3 percent), and "electricity, gas and water supply" (19.3 percent) (CITE, 2009). In sum, data show a consistent increase in the participation of women in most occupations, but gender occupational segregation by gender remains significant and has even got wider in the sectors and segments in which women were already the majority of the labour force.

Taking into account the average monthly base salary of men and women in the various sectors and segments, some differences are apparent that reflect the level of occupational gender segregation and the job status of men and women in that sector. In general, it appears that the women's base salary compares poorly with men's in sectors with a larger participation rate of women. That is the case in "education" in which women made 76 percent of the workforce in 2006 and received an average monthly base salary that was only 78.1 percent of men's, and also in "health and social work" in which women made 86.5 percent of the workforce and got an average base salary of just 71.4 percent of men's. These figures (INE, 2009) seem to suggest that in highly feminized sectors women tend to occupy the lower ranks while men are possibly better represented at the top.

In contrast, in male-dominated sectors women seem to do better in terms of average income. For example, this is the case in sectors such as "construction" in which women received in 2006 an average monthly base salary that was 110.7 percent of men's or 106.4 percent if average monthly overall earnings are taken into account. Another example is provided by the "transport, storage and communication" sector in which women only constituted about 22 percent of the workforce but got an average monthly base salary that was 115.2 percent, or 106.4 percent of the overall earnings of their male counterparts. These figures (INE, 2009) seem to portray a picture that is the reverse of the one described above. In male-dominated sectors, demographically speaking, men seem to perform the lower manual tasks while women take on the better paid clerical and managerial jobs.

In less gender-segregated sectors, salary differences tend to be narrower. For instance, the "public administration and defence" sector, one of the most demographically balanced sectors in Portugal, women made up about 48 percent of the workforce in 2006 (INE, 2009) and received an average monthly base salary that was 104.7 percent of their male colleagues, or 101 percent when the average overall earnings were taken into account. Thus, more demographically gender-balanced sectors seem to be associated with income figures closer to parity.

When examining the 2008 unemployment figures (INE, 2009), they show that women made up about 56.6 percent of the registered unemployment. In that year, women's unemployment rates were higher than men's in all age groups except in the above 55 years of age cohort. Taking into account the educational level, women's unemployment rate in 2008 was higher than men's in all groups with the widest difference among the higher-educated graduates. In this group, women constituted about 68.5 percent of the registered unemployed in 2008. The full impact of the financial crisis in the gender composition of the unemployed population is not yet clear but women seem to have been more affected than men. While keeping the highest unemployment rate (9.6 percent against 8.6 percent for men) in August 2009, according to Eurostat (EU, 2009), the gap has got closer when the figures are compared to the previous year (8.8 percent for women and 6.5 percent for men in 2008).

The progress of women in Portugal in terms of education is quite remarkable on all accounts. The proportion of women in the most educated segment of the labour force – individuals holding a higher-education degree – has consistently grown since the 1970s. In 1995, women represented about 38.6 percent of the labour force holding a university degree and in 1999, that percentage had risen to 43.8 percent. In 2006, women already represented about 51 percent of the best-educated segment of the workforce. Furthermore, taking into account that the proportion of women holding a higher-education degree in the overall population is 58.6 percent (2008 data), there is still room for further increase in the proportion of women in the most educated segment of the labour force.

Differences between men and women in the workplace can be attributed, to a large extent, to the different roles they play in the family and in society in general. Domestic tasks remain a major responsibility of women. Data from 1999 (INE, 2009) show that women spent on average about five hours a day in so-called "unpaid work", which includes housekeeping, childcare and other caring activities. According to the same source, childcare took a daily average of 1.5 hours, and care and assistance to adults in the family another hour a day. Men, on the other hand spent on average less than two hours a day performing "unpaid work". More recent data reveal that the sex distribution of "unpaid work" has not changed. Figures from a 2005 survey indicate that women spend more than 25 hours per week in "unpaid work" against less than ten hours per week in the case of men (CITE, 2009).

Survey results indicate that the level of gender segregation in domestic tasks was still very strong in 1999, with domestic tasks remaining primarily women's jobs (INE, 2009). The data showed that women were "always" involved in the preparation of meals (62.5 percent), house cleaning (59.1 percent), washing and ironing (60.6 percent), and shopping (49.2 percent). More often than not, men were "never" involved in the preparation of meals (48.3 percent), house cleaning (69.3 percent), washing and ironing (81.2 percent), and even shopping (36 percent). Unlike housekeeping activities, administrative tasks were mainly conducted by men ("always" by 31.4 percent of men against 23.1 percent of women), though 28.3 percent men revealed they "never" engaged in that type of work (against 35.9 percent women). Gardening appears to be the only activity conducted in relatively similar proportions by men and women. In sum, despite the considerable changes that have taken place in the last decades in Portuguese society, the role of men and women in the family has not been significantly challenged. That being the case, it is unlikely that equality between men and women is achieved in the labour market.

Women Pursuing Education

The sex composition of the resident population in Portugal, in terms of level of education, shows that women are the dominant group at the two extremes of the spectrum – the least educated and the best educated segments of the population. Using 2008 data (INE, 2009), women accounted for 68.7 percent of the population with no formal education (about 15.5 percent of the overall female population in Portugal). On the other hand, however, women were also the dominant group at the best-educated end of the spectrum, representing 60.4 percent of the population with a higher-education degree. In lower education levels, the population is more gender balanced. Men are the slight majority of the population with basic education (52.1 percent) and the population with secondary education is close to parity (50.8 percent female).

In higher education, women represented 55.7 percent of the students enrolled in 2005 (INE, 2009), a proportion that has remained relatively stable since the early 1990s. In 1960/61, women were only 24.5 percent of the student enrolment in public universities. Official statistics indicate that, although the participation rate of women in higher education started to grow in the 1960s, the figures climbed during the 1980s when the criteria for accessing higher education were changed to take into account the students' marks during their secondary education.

A similar trend emerges in terms of graduation, though in this case with more dramatic figures. The proportion of female student graduates in the last decade varied from 59.6 percent in 2007/08 to an all time high of 67.2 percent in the 2001/02 and 2002/03 academic years (GPEARI, 2008). Since 1995/96 and with the exception of the year 2007/08 pointed out above, the proportion of women in the population of student graduates in higher education, has consistently been above 60 percent (GPEARI, 2008). The gender gap is therefore wider in Portugal than in Europe in general, where 56.7 percent of the students who graduated in 2004 were women (EU, 2009). On the other hand, the fact that the gap is wider in actual graduates than in enrolled students, seems to suggest a higher rate of male students dropping out of the system.

In postgraduate studies, the prevalence of women remains at the master's level, though increasing at a lower rate. In 2004, 56.6 percent of master's degrees were awarded to women, according to INE (2009), up from 50.1 percent in 1997. At the PhD level, the figures are close to parity – 48.2 percent of PhDs were awarded to women in 2004 (INE, 2009), up from 44.4 percent in 1997.

Even though women were a slight minority in terms of the number of researchers in higher education – 45.9 of the individual researchers or 47.6 percent of full-time equivalent researchers in higher education in 2003 – they represented 54.3 percent of beneficiaries of research funds in that same year (INE, 2009). Indeed, women's prevalence among beneficiaries of research funds is a consistent pattern since the turn of the century, according to official statistics.

Sex segregation in education remains very strong with a clear dominance of women in most fields. The number of students enrolled in higher education in 2005 (INE, 2009) indicates a growing number of highly feminized fields with women representing more than two-thirds of the students enrolled: social services (89.1 percent), education (84.0 percent), medicine and health sciences (74.5 percent), journalism (69.6 percent), humanities (67.5 percent), life sciences (67.0 percent), and veterinary sciences (66.6 percent). It is only in a tiny number of technological fields that women remain a clear minority: computer sciences (23.8 percent), engineering (17.7 percent), military and security services (22.6 percent). Even in traditionally male-dominated fields like law (58.9 percent) and business (55.4 percent) women already represent the majority of students enrolled. In sum, the persistent supply of highly qualified women will inevitably have an impact on the sex distribution of management jobs. What is not clear yet is whether women will finally find their way to the top positions or remain stuck in the middle-management levels.

Women in Management

Official statistics from the Ministry of Employment show that the proportion of women holding positions at the director level was about 27 percent in 2006. That proportion reached 30.2 percent in small and medium-sized enterprises (SMEs) (MTSS, 2006 dataset). Overall, the proportion of women in executive and managerial jobs was about 29.0 percent in that year, according to those sources. Figures from the same database indicate that, slowly but steadily, the proportion of women in executive and managerial jobs has been increasing from 24.5 percent in 1995 and 26.7 percent in 1999. The progress of women is apparent in most sectors but it appears more significant in sectors having the highest proportion of women in the labour force, and in smaller and Portuguese-owned firms (MTSS, 2002 dataset). In public administration, the percentage of women in managerial positions was already 37.7 in 2001 (Lisboa et al., 2006).

Other sources, such as the CITE, present slightly different figures in their annual reports and indicate the proportion of women at the managerial level to have reached 33.9 percent in 2005 (CITE, 2007). The different descriptions of who are classified as "managers" possibly explains the gap between the different sources. Moreover, Eurostat indicates Portuguese women represent 32.1 percent of the leaders of business in 2007, thus placing the proportion of Portuguese women leaders of business very close to the European average of 32.3 percent (EU, 2009).

On the other hand, similar to what has been depicted for the overall workforce, differences between men and women managers can be detected in terms of education, basic salary and total earnings. Women managers are the best-educated segment of the management population, but 2003 salary figures show that women managers only earned, on average, about 71 percent of the amount obtained by men (CITE, 2007).

A less optimistic picture emerges when the most senior positions are taken into account. Here again, different understandings of what a senior position means makes it hard to compare the figures, but some conclusions can still be drawn. Eurostat figures for the highest decision-making bodies of the largest publicly quoted companies, indicates the proportion of women to be only 3 percent, the lowest proportion in Europe (EU, 2009). A list of the top 2,500 corporate directors and top managers in 1999 indicated that 6.9 percent were women (Exame, 1999). Other studies estimate the number of women on the board of PSI20 companies (companies included in the Lisbon stock market index) to be about 5.7 percent of all board members (Almeida, 2008), and a 2005 survey detected a proportion of 8.7 percent women on the board of a sample of large companies (Lisboa et al., 2006). Two conclusions seem to emerge from these data. Firstly, regardless of the sources used, it is clear that there is a considerable gap between the proportions of women in management in general, and in top positions of the largest companies in particular. Secondly, although some progress has been made in terms of managerial positions, access for women to the very top executive positions remains problematic.

Women are also largely outnumbered in the political system, particularly at the top level. In 2005, women represented 21.3 percent of members of Parliament and 11.3 percent of members of central Government, ministers and State secretaries (INE, 2009). In 2008, the percentage of women members of Parliament had risen to 29 percent while the women senior ministers in national Government had remained around 12 percent (EU, 2009). However, women have no representation at the board of the Portuguese central bank and in local authorities, only about 6.1 percent of the council leaders were female (INE, 2009). The recent introduction of a quota system in Parliamentary elections (imposing a 33 percent quota for women, according to 2006 legislation) has not produced considerable changes yet, in terms of the gender composition of political leaders. In other words, despite the legislative efforts, the political system has failed to match even the low progress already made by the private business sector.

Women Entrepreneurs

Although it is generally assumed that the proportion of self-employed individuals is rising, official statistics fail to show a significant increase in that category of the working population. Stability is also the trend in terms of the gender composition of the self-employed. Women represented 42.2 percent of the self-employed population in 1997 and 42.5 percent in 2008 (INE, 2009). Hence, the proportion of self-employed women has remained stable in the last decade, whether measured in terms of "self-employed with employees"

(27.7 percent of the 2008 population in this category) or "self-employed without employees" (47.1 percent of the 2008 population in this category).

Portuguese women have traditionally been less likely to be involved in entrepreneurial activity than men (GEM, 2002) and are driven by different motivational factors such as need for achievement when starting a business (Pereira, 2001). Nevertheless, in recent years, the gender gap in entrepreneurial activity has been narrowing and starting a business has become a socially accepted option for women (GEM, 2007).

However, the main problems hindering the development of entrepreneurship in Portugal, a highly risk-averse culture (Hofstede, 1991) have long been identified: "The prevailing social attitude in Portugal is one of dependence upon established corporations and the public sector for jobs and security. Entrepreneurship is neither an expected nor respected career choice, and failure is deemed unacceptable" (GEM, 2002: 92). The current National Plan for Equality, Citizenship and Gender (CIG, 2007) includes the development of entrepreneurialism among women as one of the objectives for the period 2007–2010 as a means to mobilize women towards active economic lives and to promote self-employment among women. Such a mobilization is mainly conducted through training programmes, the dissemination of success stories of women entrepreneurs and financial support schemes specifically designed for female entrepreneurs. Furthermore, the support of structures such as the Association of Women Entrepreneurs is also instrumental to achieve the stated objective.

Country Legislation

Since the 1970s, substantial changes in legislation have granted equal rights for men and women. The 1976 Constitution was very progressive in social matters and civil liberties and held the State responsible for the promotion of equal opportunities in the access to work and for the prevention of whatever might hinder equal access on the grounds of sex. The Constitution states that work compensation must respect the basic principle of "equal pay for equal work" and provides women with special protection during pregnancy and after maternity, namely a leave of absence with no pay loss during a certain period of time. Subsequent legislation, such as the Equal Opportunities between Men and Women Act of 1979 and the Equal Treatment in Work and Employment Act of 1997 incorporated the concept of indirect discrimination and moved forward the principle of non-discrimination on the grounds of sex. Moreover, European Directives and rulings of the European Court of Justice have forced the national legislation to refine the prevention of discrimination in employment on the grounds of sex and further regulate equality in employment relations.

More recently, the 2003 Labour Code included specific sections on equality and non-discrimination on the grounds of sex and the protection of maternity and paternity. In some circumstances the Code reversed the burden of proof in discrimination processes and typified sexual harassment for the first time in Portuguese legislation. In this new legal framework, positive discrimination might be permitted as long as it is regarded as a temporary measure and targets certain disadvantaged groups. In sum, if inequality persists in Portuguese work settings, legislation cannot be solely to blame. However, the country has a reputation regarding difficulties in law enforcement, and the judicial system is often accused of being too slow and ineffective.

Initiatives Supporting Women in the Workforce

The mainstreaming of gender equality in employment was adopted as a general policy framework by the Portuguese Government. This policy involved the development of national equality plans that are cross-cutting strategic and coordination instruments aiming to go beyond the traditional labour market integration and vocational training issues. Currently, the III National Plan for Equality, Citizenship and Gender (2007–2010) defines five strategic intervention areas, 32 objectives and 155 measures, as well as the indicators and entities responsible for their implementation (CIG, 2007). The 2005–2008 National Employment Plan defined the promotion of equal opportunities between men and women in the labour market, and the reduction of gender gaps in employment, unemployment, pay and occupational segregation, as well as the promotion of the reconciliation between of work and family life as national priorities (CITE, 2007).

The Commission for Equality in Work and in Employment (CITE) was established in 1979 and since then it has played a considerable role in promoting equal opportunities for men and women in the work context and in translating workers' rights and legal principles into common language. The Commission handles complaints of unfair discrimination at work in cooperation with other public institutions, and provides legal recommendations and interpretations of the legislation. Most complaints (nearly 90 percent in some years) are related to the enforcement of pregnancy and maternity legislation while other sex discrimination issues and sexual harassment complaints are seldom received by the Commission (CITE, 2009).

The Future

The evidence presented related to the participation of women in the labour market and in managerial activities indicates that, broadly speaking, Portugal follows the European pattern. About one in three managers is a woman but only one in 20 top managers is female and, although progress is apparent for women managers in general, little changes are detected when it comes to women occupying very senior positions. Furthermore, the high proportion of women graduating from higher education seems to be supplying the labour market with women with the appropriate skills and knowledge to fulfil general management positions. Slowly but surely the participation rate of women in management is increasing and women are being awarded for the enhancement of their academic credentials.

A different picture emerges regarding the top senior positions in which the participation of women remains almost residual. Changing this state-of-affairs seems to require other more radical transformations in Portuguese society. Entrenched gender stereotypes and social values and, above all, the gender roles in the family have to be challenged before significant changes can be expected in relation to the proportion of women reaching positions at the very top of organizations. In fact, the growing numbers of women that now populate the business school environment have so far been unable to challenge the traditional gender stereotypes in management. Studies conducted among Portuguese management students of both sexes found that, although the social stereotypes of the female manager and the male manager are relatively close and reflect the dimensions of instrumentality and rationality associated with the management contexts (Fernandes and Cabral-Cardoso, 2006), the image of the manager remains closer to the masculine stereotype than to the feminine stereotype (Fernandes and Cabral-Cardoso, 2003) leaving the masculine sub-category as the reference to describe the female manager. Having to play the masculine card will ultimately disadvantage women in their management careers.

Moreover, gender roles in the family seem to be the key barrier to real progress in changing the workplace (Loureiro and Cabral-Cardoso, 2008). The cumulative effects of the prevailing full commitment, long hours worked and family-unfriendly organizational cultures and the normative ideology of gender roles in the family (Santos and Cabral-Cardoso, 2008), seem to be powerful obstacles holding women back and preventing them from reaching the highly demanding jobs in the senior ranks. No doubt a considerable challenge for the next generation.

References

Almeida, S. J. (2008) Mulheres são raras na gestão executiva [Few women at the executive level], (*Público-Economia*, 28 March, http://economia.publico.clix. pt/noticia.aspx?id=1323939, accessed 28 March, 2008.

Cabral-Cardoso, C. (2004) Women in management in Portugal. In M. J. Davidson and R. J. Burke (eds) *Women in Management Worldwide: Facts, Figures and Analysis* (Aldershot: Gower Publishing, pp. 83–98).

CIG (Comissão para a Cidadania e Igualdade de Género) (2007) *III National Plan for Equality, Citizenship and Gender (2007–2010)* (Lisboa, Portugal: Comissão para a Cidadania e Igualdade de Género, Presidência do Conselho de Ministros [Commission for Citizenship and Gender Equality, Prime Minister's Office])

CITE (Comissão para a Igualdade no Trabalho e no Emprego) (2007) *Annual Progress Report on Equal Opportunities for Men and Women at Work, in Employment and Vocational Training (2005)* (Lisboa: Comissão para a Igualdade no Trabalho e no Emprego [Comission for Equality in Work and Employment]).

CITE (Comissão para a Igualdade no Trabalho e no Emprego) (2009) *Relatório Sobre o Progresso da Igualdade de Oportunidades Entre Mulheres e Homens no Trabalho, no Emprego e na Formação Profissional [Progress Report on Equal Opportunities for Men and Women at Work, in Employment and Vocational Training] (2006/2008)* (Lisboa: Comissão para a Igualdade no Trabalho e no Emprego [Comission for Equality in Work and Employment]).

EU (European Union) (2009) *Report from the Commission to the Council, the European Parliament, the European Economic and Social Committee and the Committee of the Regions: Equality between women and men – 2009* (Brussels: Commission of the European Communities), http://epp.eurostat.ec.europa.eu/cache/ITY_PUBLIC/3-01102009-AP/EN/3-01102009-AP-EN.PDF, accessed 12 October, 2009.

Exame (1999) Who's Who: The 2500 executives that lead Portugal, *Exame*, July/ August.

Fernandes, E. and Cabral-Cardoso, C. (2003) Gender asymmetries and the manager stereotype among management students, *Women in Management Review*, 18(1/2), 77–87.

Fernandes, E. and Cabral-Cardoso, C. (2006) The social stereotypes of the Portuguese female and male manager, *Women in Management Review*, 21(2), 99–112.

GEM (Global Entrepreneurship Monitor) (2002) *2001 Portugal Executive Report* (London, UK: The Global Entrepreneurship Monitor), http://www. gemconsortium.org/document.aspx?id=189, accessed 3 November, 2009.

GEM (Global Entrepreneurship Monitor) (2007) *Projecto GEM Portugal 2007*. The Global Entrepreneurship Monitor, http://www.dgae.min-economia.pt/ aaaDefault.aspx?f=1&back=1&codigono=76207859AAAAAAAAAAAAAA AA, accessed 3 November, 2009.

GPEARI (Gabinete de Planeamento, Estratégia, Avaliação e Relações Internacionais) (2008) *Número de diplomados no Ensino Superior: 1997–1998 a 2005–2006* (Lisboa: Gabinete de Planeamento, Estratégia, Avaliação e Relações Internacionais – Ministério da Ciência, Tecnologia e Ensino Superior), http:// www.gpeari.mctes.pt/?idc=21&idi=213464, accessed 12 October, 2009)

Hofstede, G. (1991) *Cultures and Organizations: Software of the Mind* (London: McGraw-Hill).

INE (Instituto Nacional de Estatística) (2009) Portuguese Official Statistics (Lisboa, Portugal: Instituto Nacional de Estatística), http://www.ine.pt/ xportal/xmain?xpid=INE&xpgid=ine_perfgenero&contexto=pgi&menuBO UI=13707294&perfil=1464373&selTab=tab0&xlang=en, accessed 15 October, 2009.

Lisboa, M., Frias, G., Roque, A and Cerejo, D. (2006) Participação das mulheres nas elites políticas e económicas no Portugal democratic [Women's participation in political and business elites in democratic Portugal] (25 de Abril de 1974 a 2004), *Revista da Faculdade de Ciências Sociais e Humanas*, (18), 163–187.

Loureiro, P. and Cabral-Cardoso, C. (2008) O género e os estereótipos na gestão [Gender and stereotypes in management], *Tékhne, Revista de Estudos*, 6(10), 221–238.

MTSS (2002) *Quadros de Pessoal*. Lisboa, Portugal: Ministério do Trabalho e da Solidariedade Social (Ministry of Employment and Solidarity) (Data in magnetic media).

MTSS (2006) *Quadros de Pessoal*. Lisboa, Portugal: Ministério do Trabalho e da Solidariedade Social (Ministry of Employment and Solidarity) (Data in magnetic media).

Pereira, F.C. (2001) *Representação Social do Empresário [Social Representation of Business People]* (Lisboa: Edições Sílabo).

Santos, G. G. and Cabral-Cardoso, C. (2008) Work–family culture in academia: a gendered view of work–family conflict and coping strategies, *Gender in Management: An International Journal*, 23(6), 442–457.

6

Women in Management in Spain

Mireia las Heras, Nuria Chinchilla and Consuelo León

Introduction

Politically, economically and socially, Spain is a rich and varied country that has transformed dramatically in the recent past. Up until 1975, Spain had been ruled by a dictatorship for 36 years and the transition into a democratic monarchy was marked by the Spanish Constitution of 1978. In 1986, Spain and Portugal became the 11th and 12th countries to join the European Community. The ascension into the European Community has been conducive for the economic well-being of the country: over the last three decades, Spain's gross domestic product has grown by more than 200 percent (INE, 2009a). With four official languages, numerous distinct cultures and a very long history, Spain has been endowed with a diverse and intense heritage. Yet, in almost every aspect of society, family plays a vital and central feature in everyday life where wives and mothers often retain their conventional roles as caregivers. Nonetheless, the status of women may have transformed more in Spain than perhaps in any other country within western Europe in the past 50 years.

Up until its abolishment in 1975, Article 57 of the Civil Code, also known as *permiso marital*, forbade women from employment, owning property and travelling without the consent of their husband. Women typically held the traditional role of mother and housewife. At the end of the 1970s, only 22 percent of women were present in the workforce (Solsten and Meditz, 1998). Since then, Spanish society has undergone major shifts in social demographics. The percentage of women in the workforce has steadily grown and the rate of employed females has more than doubled. Women have become much more educated than previous generations and, by 2007, for every one male graduate in higher education, there were 1.40 females (Eurostat, 2009d). Women also currently make up roughly half of the entrepreneurial enterprises in Spain. Yet, their presence is scarce in decision-making positions in both politics and business. Additionally, the number of births per Spanish woman has declined significantly within the past three decades. The birth rate is currently one of the lowest in Europe and has declined from 1.94 children per woman in 1982 to 1.46 in 2008 (Eurostat, 2009c).

This chapter is divided into a number of sections. We first present labour force characteristics on women in Spain, followed by the progress of Spanish women pursuing education. We then address the presence of women in decision-making roles in politics and corporate management, as well as data on female entrepreneurs and women's involvement in small and medium enterprises (SMEs) in Spain. We analyze existing challenges for professional women in Spain and we describe some recent legislative improvements as well as listing the organizations in Spain that facilitate and encourage entrepreneurship for women. Finally, we propose a few recommendations on how companies and the Spanish Government can become more accommodating to employees to create a more harmonized work–life balance.

Labor Force Characteristics

Almost 25 years ago, women were barely present in the workforce. In the last few decades, women have become greatly integrated into the workforce and almost 9 million women have been incorporated into the labour market (Instituto de la Mujer, 2008). The rate of employment for men was 64.4 percent and the rate of female employment was 26.6 percent in 1987. These rates have increased by the end of 2008 to 45 percent for women and 62 for men (Eurostat, 2009f) (see Figure 6.1).

Although the rate of employed women in the workforce has grown closer and closer to the rate of male employment, Spain currently has one of the lowest rates of employed females within the European Union (see Figure 6.2 below) (Eurostat, 2009f). The average rate for women in the European Union is 59 percent (Eurostat, 2009f).

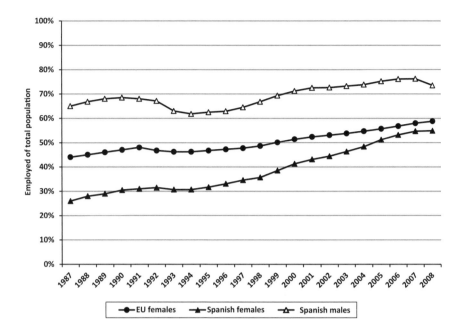

Figure 6.1   Active workforce

Source: Elaborated from Eurostat (tsiem010) – Employment by gender – %). Employment rate was calculated by dividing the number of persons by gender aged 15 to 64 in employment by the total population of that same age group and gender

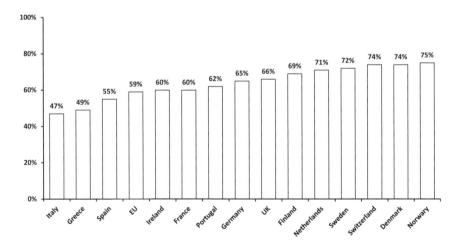

Figure 6.2   Comparison of female employment rates across Europe in 2008

Source: Elaborated from Eurostat (tsiem010) – Employment rate by gender – %). Employment rate was calculated by dividing the number of females aged 16 to 64 in employment by the total population of females in this same age group

Of the 45 percent of employed women in 2008, almost half (23 percent) worked part time (Eurostat, 2009b). This is a substantial contrast to men where, of the 62 percent of actively working men, only 4.2 percent worked part time (Eurostat, 2009b). The higher rate of women compared to men in part-time positions is possibly due to the fact that Spanish women are more likely than men to slow down their careers in order to combine work and family life (see Table 6.1).

Partly due to the economic crisis of 2008, known in Spain as "*La Crisis*", unemployment has dramatically spiraled upwards from 2008 throughout 2009. By the end of 2008, the *total* rate of unemployment in Spain was the highest within Europe at almost 15 percent, which is twice as high as the EU average of 7.6 percent (Eurostat, 2009e). The rise in unemployment has affected both men and women equally. Throughout 2009, the rate continued to rise and by October 2009, the *total* rate had soared to 18.9 percent, which was on a par with unemployed males during this time (Eurostat, 2009e).

Table 6.1   **Comparison of employment status with Spain and the European Union (averages for 2008)**

	Spanish women (%)	Spanish men (%)	EU-25 average women (%)	EU-25 average men (%)
Employment rate	43.40	46.70	61.50	61.70
Part-time employment rate	22.70	4.20	32.40	7.90
Monthly unemployment rate (Dec 2008)	15.80	14.30	7.90	7.60

Source: Elaborated from Eurostat, 2009e

Even before *La Crisis*, Spain's economic progress over the past several years has led the country towards a demographic–economic paradox – the inverse correlation between wealth and fertility. As women in Spain are becoming more educated, staying in education longer and are more prominent in the workforce, they are having children later in life and having fewer children.

Almost two decades ago, 68 percent of women bore children under 30 years of age; however, this rate had drastically declined to 37 percent by 2006 (Instituto de la Mujer, 2008). The current birth rate in Spain is 1.46 children per woman (Eurostat, 2009c). These rates are lower than what is recommended by the European Commission, who states birth rates must be at least 2.1 births per woman in order to maintain the population constant (Eurostat, 2008).

There are about four major sectors in Spain, which include agriculture, industry, construction and services (see Table 6.2 below). Women are much more present in the services sector than in any other area by over 53 percent (Instituto de la Mujer, 2008). Within each of these four major sectors, women are least present in the construction industry and only represent about 5.7 percent (Instituto de la Mujer, 2008).

Table 6.2   Breakdown of female percentages in occupations between
             1987 and 2007

	1987 (%)	2007 (%)
Agriculture and fishing	26	22
Armed forces	0	10
Artists and industrial manufacturing, construction and mining	15	6
Hospitality and sales	55	64
Installation and machine operators	2	13
Management of companies and public administration	32	32
Non-qualified workers	14	56
Professional and technical support	39	45
Professionals in science	42	53

Source: Elaborated Mujeres en Cifras 1983–2008

Within occupational positions, women play a much larger role in hospitality and sales. This higher percentage of women in hospitality and sales has remained constant and has continued to increase in the past 20 years. The reason that more women are prominent in this sector may be due to the fact that this industry is comprised of small, local, family-owned or entrepreneurial businesses. However, the rate of women in managerial roles is still less than mediocre due to barriers Spanish women encounter in their professional careers.

Not only are women less represented in the workforce in Spain, particularly in decision-making roles, work in different sectors than men, and are under-represented in managerial positions, but they also tend to make less money within the same job description, that is, managerial positions versus staff or non-managerial roles. In 2007, the average annual salary gap between men and women was 17 percent less for women than for men (Eurostat, 2009a). In perspective, for every 50,000 euros a man made, a woman would earn 41,450 euros. The average for the European Union in 2007 was almost 18 percent (Eurostat, 2009a). The largest gap reaches 35 percent among directors with ten salaried subordinates; that is, for a male director with a minimum of 10 salaried subordinates that makes 50,000 euros a year, a female director with the same characteristics would earn only 32,500 euros (Instituto de la Mujer, 2009d).

Because of its close geographic proximity, it is noteworthy to compare the gender pay gap of Spain with that of France and Italy. In their 2008 study, ICSA (Investigación, Consultoria, Sistemas y Aplicaciones), a consulting firm, discovered that the salary gap changes depend on one's position within the organization. In France, for instance, the salaries are alike at lower-level positions where they tend to be highly regulated by unions (ICSA, 2008). In Italy, women in positions of middle management in several occupations earn more than men in the same roles. More specifically, when men and women do not have a degree and work as analysts, software developers, environmentalists or safety specialists, the percentage point pay gap is in favour of women: between 3 percent to 4 percent (ICSA, 2008). Table 6.4 shows the pay differences between job levels in these three countries. The lack of childcare provisions may partly account for the gender pay gap in Spain, as well as in other countries (Arulampalam, Booth and Bryan, 2007). Arulampalam, Booth and Bryan (2007) found that countries with more "generous" work–family policies have a lower wage gap at the bottom of wage distribution, and a wider gap at the top.

Table 6.3   Pay differences between job levels in Italy, France, and Spain

	Executives and managers .(%)	Middle managers (%)	White collar employees (%)	Blue collar workers (%)
Italy	5	4	11	7
France	10	5	2	1
Spain	11	10	15	13

Source: Elaborated with data from ICSA (2008)

Women Pursuing Education

The university degree structure in Spain is significantly different from the Anglo-Saxon model and is currently in the process of changing. *Diplomaturas* are typically three-year university degrees and are most comparable to a four-year Bachelor's degree (BA/BSc). *Licenciaturas* are five or six-year university degrees that are most equivalent to a six-year master's degree (MA/MSc) or degrees from professional schools, such as medicine, business or law. The university degree structure is currently changing due to the Bologna process and will be complete in the years 2010–2011.[1]

By the mid-1980s, the rate of women in university education was almost on a par with men, and today, women are more present in tertiary studies and have higher graduation rates than men. In 2007, females accounted for 76 percent of graduates of *Diplomaturas* and 65 percent of *Licenciaturas* (Instituto de la Mujer, 2009c). And although there are more females present overall in higher education, the rate of women who graduate with a doctoral degree is only 38 percent (Instituto de la Mujer, 2009g).

In comparing European Union averages in major academic fields, the percentage of European females enrolled in tertiary studies is more or less even with averages of Spanish females across most fields of study. However, female participation rates in both Spain and the European Union compared to men are much lower in quantitative fields such as computing, engineering, manufacturing, and construction, and mathematics and statistics (see Table 6.4 below).

---

1   The resolutions may be viewed at: http://www.boe.es/boe/dias/2007/10/30/pdfs/A44037-44048.pdf (in Spanish. Accessed: September 15, 2009).

Table 6.4   Percentage of female students in ISCED 5 & 6 tertiary studies
              between European Union countries and Spain in 2007

	EU-27 (%)	Spain (%)
Business administration	55.3	58.1
Computing	17.3	17.6
Engineering, manufacturing and construction	24.7	28.1
Health and welfare	73.5	74.5
Humanities and arts	66.1	60.3
Journalism and information	64.7	66.8
Law	58.0	55.0
Life science	62.3	65.1
Mathematics and statistics	24.0	18.1
Physical science	41.0	51.4
Social science	58.2	58.8
Teacher training and education science	75.5	78.1

Source: Elaborated from Eurostat – Tertiary Students (ISCED 5–6) by field of education and sex

In all levels of education, the dropout rate for Spanish females is lower than for men. Women equal 44 percent of total dropouts; however, only 6.5 percent of total female students abandon a higher level of education than previously obtained (INE, 2009b). Within tertiary studies, the dropout rate of women and men is 5.2 percent and 5.8 percent, respectively (INE, 2009b).

Women in Management

Although progress is slow, women in Spain are becoming more present in positions of power within government, business and management roles. Over the course of ten years, women in management positions supervising more than ten employees in both the public and private sectors have jumped from 14 percent in 1998 to more than 23 percent in 2008 (see Table 6.5).

Table 6.5   Percentage comparison of women in positions of leadership

	1998 (%)	2008 (%)
Total percentage of leadership in public administration and companies	31.1	32.5
Management of public administration and companies with more than 10 salaried employees	14.3	23.5
Executive and legislative power of public administrations, management of organizations	25.0	32.0
Management of companies with more than 10 salaried employees	13.7	22.9
Management of companies with less than 10 employees	23.6	29.1
Retail	28.5	34.3
Hospitality	27.6	36.4
Other companies	16.9	22.5
Management of companies without salareid employees	46.8	47.2
Retail	54.1	54.3
Hospitality	34.1	48.0
Other companies	31.0	29.2

Source: Data elaborated from the survey on active population, INE

In their annual corporate governance report by the Comisión Nacional del Mercado de Valores (CNMV), the supervisory board of the Spanish financial markets, the rate of female board directors has increased between 2007 and 2008. In 2007, there were 30 female directors in board rooms and by 2008 this rate increased to 44. However, the percentage of female boardroom directors is significantly low compared to Spain's European counterparts (see Figure 6.3 below). Within the IBEX-35 index, the rate of female boardroom directors was 8.7 percent and their roles fell in the following manner: 64.6 percent independent, 29.6 percent shareholders, 4.5 percent executives and 2.3 percent in other categories (Mujeres and CIA, 2009).

According to annual reports, by the end of 2008, there were 39 female directors in Spain, of which four were vice presidents and one was a president of a company within the IBEX-35 index. Of these women, only one woman had a title of president of the board: Ana Patricia Botín-Sanz de Sautuola O'Shea of Banco Español de Crédito, S.A. (Banesto), a large credit bank based in Madrid. The four female vice presidents of the board were Esther Koplowitz Romero de Juseu and Esther Alcocer Koplowitz, both of Fomento de Construcciones y

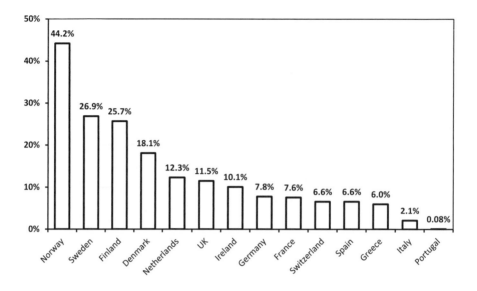

Figure 6.3   Percentages of women in boardrooms in Europe 2008
Source: Catalyst, 2008

Contratas, S.A. (FCC), a construction company based in Barcelona; Carmen Godia Bull of Abertis Infraestructuras S.A., which is also a construction company; and Margarita Prat Rodrigo of Bolsas y Mercados Espanoles (BME), the holding company for the Spanish financial markets. Only Margarita Prat Rodrigo of BME has reached her position through her own professional trajectory. The other three have gained these positions though shareholder majority from family inheritance.

According to data from *General Administración de Estado* (General State Administration), women represented only 8.5 percent in the European Parliament in 1984 and their presence has increased to 36 percent by 2009 (Instituto de la Mujer, 2009k). Women in Spain in this regard have fared reasonably well. In comparison to other countries within Europe in 2009, Sweden and Finland have well over 50 percent of female delegates in the European Parliament (Instituto de la Mujer, 2009k). Yet, large countries such as Italy, United Kingdom and Germany have smaller percentages of female delegates representing 22 percent, 32 percent and 37 percent, respectively (Instituto de la Mujer, 2009k).

Female participation in the main political parties has risen from 5.3 percent in 1981 of the party *Unión de Centro Democrático* (UCD) to over 50 percent by

2009 in the party *Partido Socialista Obrero Español* (PSOE) (Instituto de la Mujer, 2009f). A more striking figure has been the increase of women in legislation. Within the *Congreso de los Diputados* (Lower House) of the Spanish Parliament, the percentage of women rose from less than 5 percent in 1982–1986 to more than 36 percent after the last elections in March 2008 (Instituto de la Mujer, 2009e). Within the *Senado* (Upper House), the proportion increased from 4.4 percent to more than 28 percent (Instituto de la Mujer, 2009h).

At the regional level, the presence of women within the parliaments of the 17 autonomous communities has increased as well. In 1983, less than 6 percent of women held positions in the regional political offices; however, this rate was almost 42 percent in 2009 (Instituto de la Mujer, 2009i). The effect of a legislation, the *Men and Women Equality Law* (LOIEMH), has also reached senior posts in the *Administración General del Estado* (General State Administration), where the percentage of women nominated for political positions has risen from 14 percent in 1995 to more than 36 percent in the last elections in 2008 (Insituto Mujer, 2009d). The only area where female political power has not grown is within local, mayoral offices where there has only been a growth of 6 percent since 1982 (Instituto de la Mujer, 2009b).

Female presence in management in public finances is not as considerable as in national politics. Within the *Banco de España* (Bank of Spain), there is currently only one female advisor, Ana María Sánchez Trujillo, within the team of six on the Governing Council of the Bank. Women account for 30 percent of the governing body of the *Ministerio de Economía y Hacienda* (Ministry of Economy and Treasury); there are neither female ministers nor secretaries of state – the positions with the highest level of power in the Ministry (Instituto de la Mujer, 2009j).

Barriers are defined as events or conditions, either within the person or within his or her environment, that make career progress difficult (Swanson, Daniels and Tokar, 1996). The reasons for the under-representation of women in management in Spain are varied yet socially and culturally ingrained. Based on studies by IESE, a business school in Spain, the five main obstacles that impede advancement in managerial positions include:

- *Difficulties in reconciling family and working life.* The main barrier that hinders women from advancing is the double burden they experience between work and family life. In 2007, 95 percent of Spanish women left their conventional careers for family reasons (Instituto de la Mujer, 2009a).

These burdens lead women to have lower professional ambitions. Lower ambitions do not reflect their inability or unwillingness to achieve, but their desire to take care of other personal commitments. Such double burdens eventually lead women to voluntary discontinue their careers in order to care for other responsibilities. Women in Spain still take primary responsibility for their children and for the care of elderly parents as well as household chores – regardless of their work hours.

- *Concrete ceiling*. This is a self-imposed ceiling that women often place on themselves because they know that the more responsibility they take on in their careers, the more hours they will need to spend at work – which will jeopardize family life (Chinchilla et al., 2006). Women often avoid promotions also because they know that they will still need to be the primary caregivers.

- *Work or family dilemma*. Data on time spent with children, which has been collected from 14 European Union countries, show that women actually spend much more time than their male counterparts with children and on household chores (HETUS, 2003). Spanish married females spend on average 2 hours and 21 minutes a day performing basic tasks such as bathing, feeding and accompanying their children. Married fathers spend 51 minutes, on average, performing those tasks (HETUS, 2003). On average, female mothers spend over 2.5 times more time caring for their children than the children's fathers (HETUS, 2003). Working women feel guilty when they dedicate more time to their work than their family but they also feel guilty when they neglect their career to care for their family.

- *Discrimination*. Supervisors and colleagues are not inclined to be very understanding of women who are committed and involved with their family responsibilities. A study in Spain developed by *Adecco* in collaboration with IESE researchers revealed that women are discriminated against in their careers when they are young and have children (Adecco, 2003). This research illustrates that when decision makers were presented with hypothetic cases to hire new employees, they tended to avoid hiring mothers. This might be because child rearing and family responsibilities are regarded as obstacles to a women's availability to work – instead of seeing those responsibilities as enriching the person's competencies (Chinchilla and

Leon, 2004). Additionally, face-time is still regarded as a requirement for effectiveness within the organization.

- *Stereotypes*. Many Spaniards still hold traditional views regarding how men and women should fulfil their roles in society and how to be good managers, citizens and family members. There is a perception that women should be responsible for the education and care of young children, while managers should be assertive – typically thought of as a more masculine trait. Women tend to also fall into stereotypical views when considering the necessary competencies that leadership requires and what it takes to be an effective manager.

Women Entrepreneurs

Women are most present in the management of small and medium-sized companies (SMEs or PYMEs in Spanish).[2] According to a survey from 2008 performed by Axesor, a consulting group, women made up two out of every three administrative positions, out of the total number of roles within SMEs (Axesor, 2009). Moreover, of the total positions in management in SMEs, 18 percent were women and the majority of the SMEs were service-based (Axesor, 2009).

According to the annual report *Global Entrepreneurship Monitor* (GEM), 42 percent of the enterprises that were created in 2008, were established by women (GEM, 2008). This is a significant increase from prior years. The rise in female entrepreneurship may be due to a symptom of the economic crises that began in 2008 or to the increase of political support in regards to micro-financing. Since the majority of enterprises created by women are customer service-oriented, businesses in this sector are, in general, more cost effective to maintain. Female entrepreneurs develop companies that are in the sales and hospitality sectors; whereas Spanish male entrepreneurs are concentrated mostly within the agriculture, manufacturing, building and transport/communication sectors (Díaz and Jiménez, 2006).

---

2   In order to be qualified as SME by the European Union, a company must be: 1) one that engages in economic activity; 2) have less than 250 employees; 3) have either an annual sales turnover of less than 50 million euros or a balance sheet total of 43 million euros; 4) be autonomous, in which there are restrictions on the percentage of shares of other enterprises that the SME may own.

Country Legislation

Traditionally, women have four months of paid maternity leave. After maternity leave expires, females legally have the right to negotiate their working hours with proportionally reduced salaries. In 1999, the Government passed the *Ley Conciliación Vida Familiar y Laboral* (the Law of Family Life and Work) to initiate more work–life balance for working parents. According to the *Ley Conciliación*, men were entitled to two paid days off and were able to trade off part of the maternity leave with the child's mother. For instance, if the father decided to take off two weeks from work, the mother would have three and a half months of maternity leave. Yet, this was not very effective. Only around 5,000 men annually opted for this benefit (Instituto de la Mujer, 2008).

The *Ley de Igualdad* or Gender Equality Act in English, was established in March 2007 with three main objectives: 1) to facilitate leave of absence from work for maternity and family obligations and to protect parents from unfair dismissal; 2) to initiate equal treatment and opportunities in all areas of public policies including labour, social, educational, housing, and so on; and 3) to promote a more balanced participation between men and women in public offices and boardrooms of public companies. The new law added an additional 13 days paid leave for fathers to the initial two. The rate for both parents is augmented whenever a child is born into a large or single-parent family, as well as for multiple births. After maternity or paternity leave expires, parents have the right to negotiate an unpaid full-time leave of absence until the child's third birthday or reduced working hours up to half time, with a proportionally reduced salary, until the child turns six years old. This may account for the large proportion of women in part-time positions.

A year after the establishment of the *Ley de Igualdad*, the *Ministerio de Igualdad* (Ministry of Equality) performed a study to calibrate the success of the new legislation. The number of parents that benefited from the law in one year was around 175,000. Comparing the two figures, from 5,000 fathers to 175,000, suggests that the new legislation has been a success (INE, 2009a).

Because so many women are incorporated in SMEs, micro-companies and entrepreneurship enterprises, the *Ministerio de Igualdad* has collaborated with the *Ministerio de Industria, Turismo y Comercio* (Ministry of Industry, Tourism, and Commerce), the *Dirección General de la Pequeña y Mediana Empresa* (DGPYME – Director's Office of Small and Medium-Sized Enterprises) and the *Confederación Española de Cajas de Ahorros*, which is composed of several other federations and organizations, to assist female entrepreneurs in financing. There are also several public and private organizations in Spain that encourage and support female entrepreneurs. These organizations provide potential female entrepreneurs with consulting services on business planning and marketing as well as information on laws, regulations and news about changing policies. Two organizations, *El Instituto de la Mujer* and *Banco Mundial de La Mujer* facilitate access to loans with favorable financing costs in collaboration with the Spanish department of small and medium enterprises (SMEs or PYMEs in Spanish), the *Ministerio de Industria, Turismo y Comercio* (Ministry of Industry, Tourism and Trade) and *La Caixa*, a regional bank in Spain. Other organizations that provide similar support and networking opportunities include; *Federación Española de Mujeres Empresarias de Negocios y Profesionales* (FEMENP), *Organización de Mujeres Empresarias y Gerencia Active* (OMEGA) and the *Association of Organization of Mediterranean Business Women*.

Initiatives Supporting Women in the Workforce

PROPOSED GOVERNMENT INITIATIVES TO SUPPORT THE ADVANCEMENT OF WOMEN

Spanish women often opt out of having more children because of the imbalance that additional children will bring between work and family. Considering Spain's low birth rate and the growth rate of women active in the workforce, it is a public concern for the Spanish social system to facilitate working women and families to have as many children as a family desires. Additionally, the number of inactive people that are not looking for work has increased for women. Of the 62 percent of women that remain inactive in the workforce, 97 percent of the time it is due to caring for children or elderly relatives (Instituto Mujer, 2009l). It is unreasonable that women carry these burdens. And the law, as it currently stands, is not enough to pass more family responsibilities to the father. Further recommendations to the Spanish Government include the following:

- Implement work–family policies that facilitate balance for those families that have children. For instance, Spanish Government measures could resemble those of the French Borloo Plan[3] such as the Universal Work Service Cheque. This cheque is a payment voucher that is financed partially or wholly by the company that can be used

---

3   The Borloo plan was a plan named after its creator Jean-Louis Borloo, Minister of Work and Social Cohesion 2004–2007.

to pay for more than 20 types of services, for example, care for elderly relatives, childcare, and so on. The Universal Work Service Cheque is funded by the employee's company, public administrations or insurance groups. Each beneficiary can receive up to 1.830 euros a year, tax free, and as of January 2008, the public budget for the cheque was approximately 100 million euros. By implementing this kind of policy, the Government would help create social and human capital and guarantee a sustainable society in Spain.

The graph in Figure 6.4 shows the average number of children that a family had at the beginning of 2006 and the average monthly allowance per child that a family received by the end of 2006. The graph has been constructed with data from Eurostat and the European Commission's Mutual Information System on Social Protection (MISSOC). This graph could illustrate a linear relationship between how much a government gives to families and the birth rate. Compared to other major EU countries, Spain has one of the lowest monthly allowances and lowest percentages of children per family.

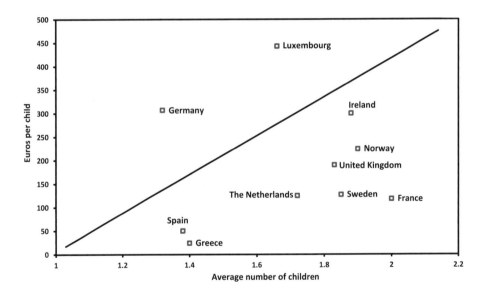

Figure 6.4   **Relationship between average number of children and average monthly allowance per child provided by the government in 2006**

Source: Eurostat & MISSOC

- The Certification of Family Responsible Companies is one of the pioneering initiatives in Europe carried out by the research effort of IESE Business School in this field within the corporate world and also from the support of the Ministry of Labor and Social Affairs and the +Family Foundation. The Family Responsible Company Certificate is awarded based on the social responsibility of an organization, which has rights and obligations that it must harmonize with its specific mission of creating wealth. There are currently more than 100 business certificates that have been issued. The Government could incentivize companies to be certified through preferences in concessionary contract proposals and fiscal advantages.

- Seek to implement more effective policies and legislation that solve the uneven share of women's responsibilities in family life. Due to the *Ley de Igualdad*, the current status of paternity leave is of special interest for future research. The resolution grants the father 15 days of paid leave for each child and these days are not transferable from the father to the mother. The purpose of this measure is to raise men's awareness of the difficulty and challenges of caring for a baby, as well as to initiate and facilitate involvement in the daily care of children. However, 15 days is not enough to level the playing field between men and women and advancement in their professional careers.

PROPOSED CORPORATE INITIATIVES

The Government should not be alone in assisting working women and families. There are a number of way companies can palliate barriers for women in the workforce and these include:

- *Detecting problems.* Companies should detect the most salient problems that deter women from thriving in their environments and from being promoted to positions of power. First of all, companies should avoid informal practices, such as late meetings as well as weekend or excessive travel that hinder women from taking care of other commitments, such as caring for their own children, spouses or parents. Second, companies should facilitate flexible arrangements that allow women as well as men to be efficient in their work and care for their families. In these cases, special attention should be given to promotion and evaluation processes to ensure that women and men, that have less face-time or face-to-face interaction with their supervisors, are not punished or neglected, but rather evaluated for their performance while being considered for promotion.

- *Reviewing the current evaluation processes*. In a time where work is done collectively, evaluations still tend to over-emphasize individual performance. Companies that want to promote women should find out which contributions are crucial to facilitate performance and those that are traditionally regarded as female competencies, such as team building, which are mostly neglected in work evaluations.

- *Providing necessary training*. Companies should encourage talented women to move up by making sure they receive the necessary training and are included in succession plans.

- *Identifying alternative career practices*. By identifying alternative career practices to those that expect linear and continuous involvement in the job market. There should be viable options that facilitate women as well as men to take time out of their careers, if necessary, and return to the workplace when they are able to.

The Future

Even though there are more women now in the Spanish workforce than ever before, women still opt out of their careers to care for family members (Instituto de la Mujer, 2009a). The gap between men and women in the workforce in Spain is still quite significant and is a concern for several reasons. Firstly, this difference could often indicate discrimination, directly or indirectly, towards women, inflexibility in companies, as well as rigidity in the legislations. Secondly, this gap may create further problems in the future as the labour force in Spain shrinks due to an aging population, which might cause considerable strain to its social support system. Finally, this difference is a concern because it means that, in Spain, there are highly educated women who are not entering or remaining in the workforce.

It is acceptable when women remain out of the workforce when they do so due to personal reasons, individual priorities or family constraints. However, it is a waste of human capital and an unfair situation when women remain out of the workforce due to a lack of infrastructure (such as kindergartens or elder daycare), flexibility (such as telecommuting arrangements or alternative arrangements) and domestic equity (such as sharing household chores with their spouses). Although attitudes and the way of life for most Spaniards have changed radically in the last three decades, the family is still a vital and core feature of Spanish life. Companies and Government need to do more to facilitate women the advance of their professional trajectory.

Despite the progressive rates of women pursuing education, their presence is still less than men's at the doctoral level. However, it is difficult to know whether this is a cause or an effect of the choice of subjects that women study at the undergraduate or graduate level. Women are concentrated more within the lower or intermediate levels of company hierarchies, and are represented significantly less than men at senior management levels. There is a decrease of the percentage of women from one stage to another: the higher the educational and hierarchical stage, the more restrictive the barriers are for women entering them. This vertical segregation in the workplace is what has been often called the glass ceiling. Differences in salary, as well as in entrepreneurial activity and achievement between men and women, are often a result of the combined effect of this double segregation.

Several issues need to be tackled to enable women to gain access to all levels of managerial work, entrepreneurial activities and governmental bodies. Most of the barriers and challenges that women in Spain face in professional advancement do not seem to be deliberate attempts to discourage women from managerial positions, but subtle reminiscences of workplaces that were designed in an era when the breadwinner–homemaker pattern was considered mainstream. This was also a time when jobs used to require daily face-to-face interaction. However, this is not the case anymore. The technology to work remotely, easily and effectively is already available, and it is continuously advancing. The challenge that lies ahead for the Spanish Government, companies and individuals is to enable a more effective work–life infrastructure, that includes a more effectual legal framework coupled company cultures which make the workplace more welcoming to men and women. Thus, that everyone will be able to achieve their full potential.

References

Adecco (2003) *Criterios de Decisión en los Procesos de Selección en España [Decision criteria in selection proceses in Spain]* (Fundación Adecco).

Arulampalam, W., Booth, A. L. and Bryan, M. L. (2007) Is there a glass ceiling over Europe? Exploring the gender pay gap across the wage distribution, *Industrial and Labor Relations Review*, 60(2), 163–186.

Axesor (2009) *Study for BORME* (Boletín Oficial del Registro Mercantil). http://www.axesor.es/.

Chinchilla, N. and Leon, C. (2004) *The Female Ambition: How to Reconcile Work and Family* (Basingstoke: Palgrave Macmillan).

Chinchilla, N., León, C., Torres, I. and Canela, M. A. (2006) *Career Inhibitors and Career Enablers for Executive Women*, Working Paper No. 632. IESE Business School.

Díaz, C. and Jiménez, J. J. (eds) (2006) *Spain – The Gender Gap in Small Firms' Resources and Performance* (Cheltenham: Edward Elgar Publishing Limited).

Eurostat (2008) *The Life of Women and Men in Europe – A Statistical Portrait*, p. 21, http://epp.eurostat.ec.europa.eu/cache/ITY_OFFPUB/KS-80-07-135/EN/KS-80-07-135-EN.PDF, accessed 11 December, 2009.

Eurostat (2009a) *Gender Pay Gap in Unadjusted Form*, http://epp.eurostat.ec.europa.eu/tgm/table.do?tab=table&init=1&language=en&pcode=tsiem040&plugin=1, accessed 24 December, 2009.

Eurostat (2009b) *Persons Employed Part-Time* (% of total employment), http://epp.eurostat.ec.europa.eu/tgm/refreshTableAction.do?tab=table&plugin=1&pcode=tps00159&language=en, accessed 24 December, 2009.

Eurostat (2009c) *Total Fertility Rate – Number of Children per Woman*, http://epp.eurostat.ec.europa.eu/tgm/table.do?tab=table&init=1&language=en&pcode=tsdde220&plugin=1, accessed 23 December, 2009.

Eurostat (2009d) *Tertiary Students (ISCED 5-6) by Field of Education and Sex*, http://epp.eurostat.ec.europa.eu/portal/page/portal/eurostat/home/, accessed 23 December, 2009.

Eurostat (2009e) *Unemployment Rates – Monthly Data by Sex and Age Group (%)*, http://epp.eurostat.ec.europa.eu/portal/page/portal/eurostat/home/, accessed 23 December, 2009.

Eurostat (2009f) *Population by Sex, Age Groups, Nationality and Labour Status (1000)*, http://epp.eurostat.ec.europa.eu/portal/page/portal/eurostat/home/, accessed 22 December, 2009.

GEM Global Entrepreneurship Monitor (2008) *GEM National Report – Spain*, p. 59.

HETUS (2003) *Harmonised European Time Use Survey*, https://www.testh2.scb.se/tus/tus/default.htm, accessed 23 May, 2009.

ICSA (Investigación, Consultoría, Sistemas y Aplicaciones) (2008). *Retribuciones Hombre–Mujer Puestos Directivos en España [Men–Women Retributions*

Management Positions in Spain] (Informe Privado). Observatorio Salarial de ICSA.

ICWF (International Center for Work and Family) (2009) *IESE Family-Responsible Employer Index* (IFREI), http://www.iese.edu/en/Research/CentersandChairs/Centers/ICWF/Home/Home.asp, accessed 11 December, 2009.

INE (Instituto Nacional de Estadística) (2009a) *Producto Interior Bruto [Gross Domestic Product]* (PIB), http://www.ine.es/prensa/pib_tabla_cne.htm, accessed 24 December, 2009.

INE (2009b) *Survey on Adult Population Involvement in Learning Activities (Year 2007)* Persons began to study an educational level higher than that achieved, and dropped out, by sex and age group, http://www.ine.es/jaxi/menu.do?type=pcaxis&path=/t13/p459&file=inebase&L=1, accessed 24 December, 2009.

Instituto de la Mujer (2008) *Las Mujeres en Cifras [Women in Numbers]* 1983–2008.

Instituto de la Mujer (2009a) *Abandono del Mercado de Trabajo por Razones Familiares [Men–Women Retributions Management Positions in Spain]*, http://www.inmujer.migualdad.es/MUJER/mujeres/cifras/tablas/w844.xls, accessed 23 December, 2009

Instituto de la Mujer (2009b) *Alcaldías, Según CCAA [Female Mayors, According to the Autonomous Communities]*, http://www.inmujer.migualdad.es/mujer/mujeres/cifras/tablas/W94.XLS, accessed 24 December, 2009.

Instituto de la Mujer (2009c) *Alumnado Que Terminó Estudios Universitarios [Students Who Completed University Studies]*, http://www.inmujer.migualdad.es/mujer/mujeres/cifras/tablas/W620.XLS, accessed 23 December, 2009.

Instituto de la Mujer (2009d) *Ganancia Media Anual, en Euros, por Trabajador/a y Ocupación Según CNO [Annual Average Earnings, in Euros, by Employee and Occupation According to National Classification of Occupations]*, http://www.inmujer.migualdad.es/mujer/mujeres/cifras/tablas/WE73.XLS, accessed 24 December, 2009.

Instituto de la Mujer (2009e) *Mujeres en el Congreso, por Grupo Parlamentario [Women in Congress by Parliamentary Group]*, http://www.inmujer.migualdad.es/mujer/mujeres/cifras/tablas/W91.XLS, accessed 24 December, 2009.

Instituto de la Mujer (2009f) *Mujeres en el Gobierno [Women in Government]*, http://www.inmujer.migualdad.es/mujer/mujeres/cifras/tablas/W747.XLS, accessed 23 December, 2009.

Instituto de la Mujer (2009g) *Población de 16 y Más Años, Según Nivel de Estudios Terminados [Population of 16 Years of Age and Above, According to Completed Level of Studies]*, http://www.migualdad.es/mujer/mujeres/cifras/tablas/W19bis.XLS, accessed 23 December, 2009.

Instituto de la Mujer (2009h) *Mujeres en el Senado, por Grupo Parlamentario [Women in the Upper House, by Parliamentary Group]*, http://www.inmujer. migualdad.es/mujer/mujeres/cifras/tablas/W92.XLS, accessed 24 December, 2009.

Instituto de la Mujer (2009i) *Parlamentos Autonómicos Según CCAA [Autonomous Parliaments according to the Autonomous Communities]*, http://www.inmujer. migualdad.es/mujer/mujeres/cifras/tablas/W93.XLS, accessed 24 December, 2009.

Instituto de la Mujer (2009j) *Participación en Cargos de los Ministerios de Economía y Hacienda [Participation in positions in the Ministry of Economy and Treasury]*, http://www.inmujer.migualdad.es/mujer/mujeres/cifras/tablas/W772.XLS, accessed 24 December, 2009.

Instituto de la Mujer (2009k) *Participación de las Mujeres en el Parlamento Europeo [Participation of Women in the European Parliament]*, http://www.migualdad. es/mujer/mujeres/cifras/tablas/W90.XLS, accessed 23 December, 2009.

Instituto de la Mujer (2009l) *Personas Inactivas que no Buscan Empleo por Razones Familiares [Inactive Persons Who do not Seek Employment for Family-related Reasons]*, http://www.inmujer.migualdad.es/mujer/mujeres/cifras/tablas/W987. xls, accessed 24 December, 2009.

Mujeres y CIA (2009) *Bies: 46% más de Consejeras Mujeres [Ibex: 46% More Women in Management]*, http://www.mujeresycia.com/?x=nota/9719/1/ibex-46-mas-de-consejeras-mujeres-, accessed 17 July, 2009.

Solsten, E. and Meditz, S.W. (1998) *Spain: A Country Study*, http://countrystudies. us/spain/43.htm, accessed 11 December, 2009.

Swanson, J., Daniels, K. and Tokar, D. (1996) Assessing Perceptions of Career-Related Barriers: the Career Barriers Inventory, *Journal of Career Assessment*, 4, 219–244.

7

Women in Management in the UK

Fiona M. Wilson

Introduction

The number of women in management in the UK has grown and continues to grow (Chartered Management Institute, 2009). However the lack of equality that women managers face is quite striking; there is particularly a lack of female managers in the most senior positions. A good deal of concern has been expressed about women's seeming inability or lack of success in breaking through the "glass ceiling" (Cornelius and Skinner, 2008). Equal pay is an issue as are attitudes towards women in management. The slow progress towards equality is also an area for concern. For example, at the current rate of progress it will take another 73 years to achieve an equal number of female directors of FTSE companies and another 27 years to achieve equality in Civil Service top management (EHRC, 2008). Before we look in more detail at women in management, let's look at the labour force characteristics to tease out whether there are fundamental differences between men and women's employment.

Labour Force Characteristics

There are now more women at work in the UK; more women are either seeking work or in work than was the case in the past. A vast amount of literature has charted the rise in women's employment, particularly that of mothers, in the last 40 years. While only a half of women were in or seeking any sort of work in 1971, currently around 70 percent of women are working (Li, Devine and Heath, 2008; Office for National Statistics, 2009). The number of men and women in jobs is almost equal with men performing 12.8 million jobs and women 12.7 million, although almost half of these are part time (Office for National Statistics, 2009). Marriage and children now makes little difference to whether or not women work; there is little difference in the percentage of married women versus non-married women in employment outside the home, and almost 70 percent of mothers with dependent children are working (Scott, Dex and Joshi, 2008). Furthermore, women continue to return to work after childbirth at faster rates (Dex, Ward and Joshi, 2008). However females continue to be segregated into certain jobs and sectors. For example, in the UK, 25 percent of employees in manufacturing are female but 80 percent in both health and social care (Ogden, McTavish and McKean, 2006). Women are also more likely to work in the public sector than men. About a quarter of female employees do administrative or secretarial work, while men are more likely to be managers, senior officials or in skilled trades (Office for National Statistics, 2009). Indeed, it has been estimated that increasing women's participation in the labour market and reducing gender segregation could be worth between £15 billion and £23 billion to the UK economy (Opportunity Now, 2009).

Women in the labour force face inequality and it is still women, rather than men who take time out of paid work when they have children and who then suffer the "parenthood penalty" on their return to work (Scott, Dex and Joshi, 2008). However, highly educated women are more likely to return to full-time paid work earlier, often to the same employer, and do not suffer the parenthood penalty as much as less educated women (Li, Devine and Heath, 2008).

One may presume that because women have a higher share of childcare responsibilities, research might show that their work commitment is less than that of men. On the contrary, recent research has indicated that women's work commitment is typically stronger than men's and that work commitment is stronger among the more highly educated and higher social classes (Esser, 2009). Employment commitment is also highest for those in the higher-status jobs, where both the financial and intrinsic rewards are generally high compared to other occupations (Gallie et al., 1998).

Despite women's higher commitment, women in the UK face the highest gender pay gap of the 15 countries of the European Union (Grimshaw, 2007). Instead of the pay gap narrowing and the situation improving, the gender pay gap (as measured by the median hourly pay excluding overtime of full-time employees) widened between 2007 and 2008. The gap between women's median hourly pay and men's was 12.8 percent compared with a gap of 12.5 percent recorded in April 2007, when it was at its lowest since records began. Median earnings of full-time male employees were £512 per week in April 2008; for women it was £412. The increase in the gender pay gap can be explained by a significant number of women moving into full-time jobs with low rates of hourly pay (Annual Survey of Hours and Earnings, 2009). The gender gap in earnings also varies with age, beginning to appear in the early-20s and reaching a maximum in the mid-40s (Purcell and Elias, 2008). Even highly educated women graduates do not enjoy the same rates of pay on entering the labour market and in fact the gender pay gap grows over time (Purcell et al., 2005). Female managers earned an average of £43,521 in the year to January 2006, which was £5,147 less than the male equivalent and represents an 11.8 percent difference. It is estimated that women across the UK will have to wait 187 years before their take home pay outpaces men (Chartered Management Institute, 2009). Certainly there are good reasons for women to pursue higher education, to try to avoid the lower-paid, lower-status jobs.

Women Pursuing Education

Participation in higher education is expanding. There has been a significant change in the percentage of females in higher education in the last three decades (Scott, Dex and Joshi, 2008). Women now outnumber men as registered students in the UK, constituting 57 percent of students in England and 58 percent in Scotland (HESA, 2009). Both older and younger women have higher participation rates than men in higher education and there are more full-time women as well as part time (HEPI, 2009).

While women outnumber men in the majority of university subjects studied (including law and medicine), similar to other countries, there are some subjects where men are more numerous. These include the physical sciences, computer science and engineering (HEPI, 2009). According to HEPI, (2009:2): "Once at university women continue to outperform men. They are more likely to obtain good degrees whilst men are more likely to drop out. If they do graduate, men are more likely to be unemployed or in non-graduate jobs. However, if they are employed male graduates are, on average, better paid." However, what is evident is that both male and female graduates work in a wider range of occupations than they used to with a high proportion of these occupations involving the production, management or transfer of knowledge or information (HESA, 2009).

Women in Management

The number of women occupying management positions is greater than it has ever been. However, as Table 7.1 below shows, of the managers in the UK, there are more men than women (Labour Force Survey, 2006).

Table 7.1   Percentage of managers in the UK, Winter 2005/6

	All in employment	Women	Men
Managers and senior officials	15.1%	11.2%	18.4%
All persons	28,812,000	13,288,000	15,524,000

Source: Labour Force Survey, August 2006

Table 7.2 shows the percentage of female managers at different levels of management. It illustrates that the number of female managers has grown over the past decade and the percentage of women in management roles more than trebled in between 1994 and 2005 (Chartered Management Institute, 2009; www.managers.org.uk). In 2005, women also accounted for 14.4 percent of directors (a figure that has more than tripled since 1998) and at section leader level, women represented more than one-third (36.9 percent). However, it also shows that there was a slightly higher percentage of women at director level in 2002 than in 2005. More recently it has been found that the proportion of women in senior management posts in FTSE 350 companies has fallen from 38 percent to 22 percent since 2002 (EHRC, 2009).

Table 7.2   Percentage of managers who are women at different levels of responsibility in the UK

	2005	2004	2002	2000	1998	1994
Director	14.4	13.2	14.8	9.6	3.6	2.8
Function head	—	17.4	20.1	15.0	10.7	6.1
Department head	—	26.2	24.1	19.0	16.2	8.7
Section leader	36.9	38.2	34.5	26.5	21.9	12.0
All females	33.1	31.1	29.2	22.1	18.0	9.5

Source: National Management Salary Survey, Chartered Management Institute/ Remuneration Economics, 2009 (a survey of 20,989 individuals)

Table 7.3 highlights the percentage of women by function group between 2000 and 2004 and shows a very uneven distribution of women across the different kinds of managerial jobs with certain functions such as HR/Personnel becoming even more feminized (Chartered Management Institute, 2009; www.managers.org.uk). It is interesting to note that there appear to be some improvement in percentages of women in most of the groups, but some groups show decline in percentages of women in them (actuarial, insurance and pensions, management services/IT, and general management and administration).

Table 7.3   Percentage of women managers in the UK by function group

Function Group	2004	2002	2000
HR/Personnel	68.8	61.4	60.5
Marketing	*N/A	48.0	43.1
Services	24.0	32.9	22.2
Financial	38.1	33.6	26.9
Actuarial, insurance and pensions	47.3	50.9	53.9
Sales, marketing and retail	35.0	24.3	18.6
Management services/IT	12.0	15.8	15.6
General management and administration	11.1	13.4	11.4
Purchasing and contracting	14.7	13.9	11.0
Physical distribution	*N/A	7.9	5.1
Research and development	8.2	15.4	7.7
Manufacturing and production	5.0	6.1	3.2
Whole sample (managers only)	31.4	29.6	22.5

Source: Chartered Management Institute 2009; www.managers.org.uk

*   Physical distribution was combined with purchasing and contracting in 2003; marketing was combined with sales, marketing and retail in 2004.

There is further evidence from the Labour Force Survey of women's mixed progress in managerial jobs. For example, an increase in female banking managers from 31 percent to 36 percent during the period 2001–2005 and in the 1990s human resource managers from 46 percent to 59 percent. However, this latter trend in the increase in female human resource managers was partially reversed during 2001–2005 with a drop of 6 percentage points (Grimshaw and Rubery, 2007).

With women making up only 14.4 percent of directors of companies, it is interesting to review what happens when women are appointed to these most senior positions. In 2003, a newspaper report questioned whether women on the board were a help or a hindrance. There was a correlation between the number of women on UK company boards and lower company share price performance. Women had "wreaked havoc on companies'" performance and share prices (Judge, 2003:21). The article went on to argue that companies with no women on their boards tended to outperform the FTSE average and that "corporate Britain may be better off without women on the board" (2003:21). Ryan and Haslam (2005) questioned this finding, suggesting in fact that it was the drop in share price and company fortunes more generally that had led to women being appointed to leadership positions. It was noted that women managers, at board level, were prone to find themselves on "glass cliffs", to find that their leadership positions were more precarious than those occupied by men and associated with greater risk of failure and criticism (Ryan and Haslam, 2005). Ryan and Haslam have recently offered more words of caution for women leaders arguing that glass cliffs are not easy to scale and there is no level playing field for men and women (Ryan and Haslam, 2009). This then, can be the reality that the female board member faces. Women may, however, be heartened by the news that the boards of Britain's Most Admired Companies are more female than they were ten years before; the proportion of women had more than doubled, but it still only stands at 11 percent (*Management Today*, 2008).

All the studies show a continuing problem for women who aspire to top management positions. The glass ceiling (a term coined in 1986 to describe the invisible barrier preventing women moving the corporate ladder) continues to be firmly in place (Weyer, 2007). Women are not seen to have the necessary characteristics for leadership in senior or middle management positions compared to men. Successful middle managers are perceived to possess those characteristics attitudes and temperament more commonly ascribed to men than to women (Harris, 2001; Schein, 1973). Schein's (1973) adage "think manager, think male" appears to still apply well in the UK. Not only are the characteristics held by a manager seen as similar to the conceptions of men, but also those who select managers are likely to see men as more plausible candidates for managerial jobs (Harris 2002; Schein et al., 1998). The type of behaviour deemed appropriate coincides with images of masculinity and centres around rationality, measurement, objectivity, control and competitiveness (Kerfoot and Knights, 1996). Women are associated with "feminine" characteristics like caring, nurturing and sharing. Gender role stereotypes have a major impact not only on selection but also on promotion and evaluation of managerial performance (Vinkenburg, Jansen and Koopman, 2000). Gender stereotypes have shown little change over the last 50 years; there may even be an increase in sex typing, especially regarding the stereotypes and self-concepts focusing upon the personality traits of women (Lueptow, Garovich-Szabo and Leuptow, 2001). Further, women themselves may experience "role conflict" in thinking of themselves as managers (Liff and Ward, 2001).

What other explanations are there as to why the proportion of women in top management has remained so small? Powell (2000) goes as far as to argue that women's presence at top levels of management violates the norm of male superiority. This is one explanation as to why women are likely to be sexually harassed; men are hostile to women who compete with them for jobs and can demonstrate that hostility in the form of sexual harassment (Wilson and Thompson, 2001). Women as a minority encounter difficulties in adjusting to and fitting into male managerial cultures (Kanter, 1977). They become "tokens", their behaviour taken as an example of "women's" behaviour and always in the spotlight. They face an unsupportive environment, the "old boys" network, an unwillingness by those in power to confront and eliminate sexism and being assigned less influential projects (Nelson and Burke, 2000).

How do women in management perceive their situation? A survey by the Institute of Management (2001) found that only around a third of the women managers who responded believed their organization discriminated against them in terms of pay policy while 47 percent thought women suffer discrimination when their company makes decisions affecting their career progression. Twenty seven percent pointed to family commitments as a career block and the old boy network was seen by over a third (35 percent) as a major barrier. Similarly, an Opportunity Now UK survey (2002) found that a third of their women respondents believed they were discriminated against at the point of promotion. The obstacles were greater for older women and those from ethnic minorities – 49 percent of women from ethnic minorities cited direct discrimination. More than half the 1000 women surveyed thought they had to put their career before family to win promotion in their organization. When the statistics show such inequity in numbers, one might expect to see far more women managers perceiving discrimination in their organizations.

Managerial styles are not a fixed and unchanging function of an individual's sex. It may be that organizational traits, rather than personality traits, determine management style (Wajcman, 1998). It is interesting to note that Wahl (1998) studied a women-dominated company and found that style depended on the functional position of the manager.

There is some suggestion from the research in Britain that women are rejecting the way in which managerial work is organized. Marshall (1995), in her study of women who left senior management jobs, found that these women no longer wanted to work in masculine work cultures. Liff and Ward (2001) in a study of a UK bank, found that management in general, and senior management in particular, was a predominately male preserve where women represented only 2 percent of senior managers and 10 percent of middle managers. Only 5 percent of applicants for a set of new, relatively senior posts were women. Liff and Ward (2001) discovered that women perceived senior managers in the bank as part super human workaholics, willing and able to accommodate enormous workloads and prepared to devote themselves entirely to the bank. In addition, they viewed these senior managers as being able to impress the right people and be in the right place at the right time. The women believed that showing an interest in flexible working was risking being seen as a non-career person. Women who attempted to have a career were either seen as aberrant women (in the sense they put work before a family) or as having second-class careers which advanced more slowly or disjointedly than men's. The situation could be described as "think female manager, think childless superwoman" (Liff and Ward, 2001).

Formal provisions such as career breaks may not be taken up if women feel that it will be construed as evidence that they are not able to compete on the same terms as men (Liff and Ward, 2001) Many organizations have an ambivalence about employees family commitments. For example, an Industrial Society report showed that while 55 percent of managers said that enabling employees to balance home and work life was essential to ethical management, only 30 percent said it was true in their organization (IRS, 1996). Balancing the demands of home and work is important for both men and women. However, the total workload (including domestic as well as paid work) tends to be higher for women, and increases with the number of children in the family (Nelson and Burke, 2000).

While part-time work is increasing, paradoxically, excessively long working hours for managers have become the norm. This is due in part to work intensification and partly because long working hours have come to be an indicator of commitment. Work intensification has come about, in part, due to restructuring and downsizing (Simpson and Holley, 2001) and more recently due to the economic recession. Evidence of increasing managerial workloads is widespread. Recently, research has shown an alarmingly high level of concern amongst managers about how their health is being negatively affected by the long hours they work. Around half the managers surveyed by Worrall, Lindorff and Cooper (2008) linked personal health problems to the long hours they worked. Forty five percent believed their productivity at work was disadvantaged by the long hours spent at work; it also impacted on social lives and personal relationships. As a result of long working hours, men and women have to make a stark choice between work and families. In order to counter this, they may feel motivated to set up their own businesses at home.

What about managers from ethnic backgrounds? How do they fare in management? There may still be a colour bar to management jobs in the UK. While 11 percent of white British women are senior managers or officials, there are just 9 percent Black Caribbean and Pakistani and only 6 percent Bangladeshi women (EOC, 2007; Race for Opportunity, 2008; Brittan et al., 2005). While fewer than 1 percent of white managers indicate that racial discrimination had been a barrier to their progression, one-third of Asian and 20 percent of black managers indicate that this is a barrier for them (Wilton, 2008).

Women Entrepreneurs

A number of researchers in the UK have suggested that women's entrepreneurship can be seen as a means of escaping the persistent inequalities and the occupational confines of the labour market (for example, Marlow, 1997). Developing women's enterprise and encouraging that wealth-creating potential is seen to be important for our economy (SBS, 2006). There are, however, fewer women defined as entrepreneurs than men. While 8.9 percent of men are classed as entrepreneurs in the UK, the figure stands at just 3.8 percent for women (Startups, 2006). Nevertheless, there are signs of progress and the number of self-employed women has increased by around 10 percent over the years 2002–2006 (SBS, 2006). Statistical reports show that the UK is becoming increasingly entrepreneurial with higher rates of entrepreneurship than every other major economy outside the USA (Work Foundation, 2006). However, there is also evidence to show no progress. For example, the female share of self-employment has been more or less static at around 26–27 percent for the past 20 years (SBS, 2006).

Female entrepreneurs find they are judged by and evaluated against a norm established by a self-evident majority group standard (Lewis, 2006). In focusing on sex as a variable, certain differences have been highlighted and others obscured. Female entrepreneurs are portrayed as lacking or "lesser". For example, the GEM report says that women "are less likely to know an entrepreneur, less likely to be thinking of starting a business, less likely to think they have the skills to start a business, less likely to see business opportunities and more likely to fear failure than their male counterparts"(Harding, 2007:37). However, these trait-based approaches do not accurately represent the social locations of women (Mirchandani, 2005). Women entering self-employment are more likely to be younger than men, their businesses are more likely to be newer, located in the home and operated on a part-time basis (Carter and Shaw, 2006) and may be less concerned with financial rewards. When the effect of industry is controlled for, the difference between male and female failure rates has been found not to be significant (Watson, 2003); there are also few differences in performance (Watson, 2002). It is the values attached to gender characterizations of feminine and masculine stereotypes that are the cause (Marlow and Patton, 2005).

Country Legislation

In Britain there are two major complementary pieces of legislation to deal with sex discrimination. These are the Equal Pay Act 1970 and the Sex Discrimination Act 1975. (Both laws have been amended – by the 1983 Equal Value Regulations, the Sex Discrimination Act, 1986 and Sex Discrimination (Gender reassignment) Regulations, 1999). This domestic framework of legislation enacts various requirements in European law and continues to be profoundly influenced by rulings of the European Court of Justice.

The Equal Pay Act did not come into effect until 1975. It has had some, but limited effect. In 1971 women earned only 63 percent of the average hourly earnings of full-time male employees, leaving a pay gap of 37 percent. The pay gap currently stands at 17.2 percent for full-time workers (ONS, 2008).

The act asserts the principle that men and women should receive equal pay for equal work, including redundancy pay, pensions, severance pay, sick pay and paid leave. The legislation requires a comparator that can be "like work", "work rated as equivalent" and "work of equal value". The Sex Discrimination Act covers discrimination on grounds of gender, marital status and gender reassignment. The provisions of the act apply to women, men and married persons.

Positive discrimination is not permitted under British sex discrimination law but positive action is allowed. Under-represented groups can be encouraged to apply for posts, and an organization can set targets for the number of women to be recruited. Family-friendly measures like career breaks, flexible working time and assistance with childcare help individuals carry the double load of paid work and domestic commitments (Dex and Smith, 2002). Access to single-sex training can allow women to overcome earlier educational and training disadvantage and encourage them to move up the management hierarchy.

Further legislation, has strengthened the existing legislation to extend women's rights. For example, there have been extensions of the maternity leave period, with a widening of coverage to more women as well as increases in the paid maternity leave entitlement and the introduction of paid paternity leave to fathers. The Equalities and Human Rights Commission have proposed radical reforms to maternity leave legislation (Guardian, 30 March, 2009). In addition, the British Government have introduced a new Equality Bill (2010) which among other changes bans "secrecy clauses" regarding pay and makes public authorities report on gender pay.

Initiatives Supporting Women in the Workforce

A nationwide voluntary business campaign, established in 1991, called Opportunity Now, set key goals for tackling inequality through a broad-based business-driven policy approach. (www.opportunitynow.org.uk). Senior managers are asked to drive change from the top, be seen as role models in leading equal opportunities, develop and address the issues as part of their business strategy. They are asked to make an investment, change behaviour, communicate and share ownership in developing new working methods to enhance business performance. Members of Opportunity Now are required annually to demonstrate how they have met their goals. Opportunity Now currently boasts a membership of 350 employers from the UK's largest organizations in the private, public and education sectors "who

wish to transform their workplaces by insuring inclusiveness for women"
(www.opportunitynow.org.uk).

Equal opportunities polices have been part of employment policy and
business practice since the early 1980s. To further enhance these policies, the
gender equality duty came into force in April 2007; this duty requires all public
sector bodies to eliminate discrimination and harassment and to promote
equality of opportunity between women and men (www.equalityhumanrights.
com). It was introduced in recognition of the need for a radical new approach to
equality – one which places more responsibility with service providers to think
strategically about gender equality, rather than leaving it to individuals to
challenge poor practice. The public sector has been regarded as leading the way
in the development of equal opportunities policy. Results in both the private
and public sector have been very mixed. Research has found that line managers
play an important role in either challenging or reproducing inequality (Kirton
and Greene, 2000).

The Future

The model of the successful manager is male and while these stereotypes remain,
they succeed in perpetuating the dominant place for men in management.
Management cultures are described as masculine, characterized by long work
hours, bullying and harassment and lacking in family-friendly policies. While
the traditional male career model of a full-time career is the norm and some
women and very few men step off the fast track to meet family responsibilities,
women will continue to be at a competitive disadvantage. Organizational
initiatives relating to family-friendly policies should be directed at both men
and women in organizations to facilitate a change but this change alone will
not bring about equality for women in management in Britain.

References

Annual Survey of Hours and Earnings (2009) *National Statistics Online*, www.
    statistics.gov.uk, accessed 3 March, 2011.
Brittan, E., Dustin, H., Pearce, C., Rake, K., Siyunyi-Siluwe, M. and Sullivan,
    F. (2005) *Black Minority Ethnic Women in the UL*, The Fawcett Society, http://
    www.fawcettsociety.org.uk/?PageID=767, accessed 3 March, 2011.

Carter, S. and Shaw, E. (2006) *Women's Business Ownership: Recent Research and Policy Developments*, Report to the Small Business Service, London, http://www.berr.gov.uk/files/file38330.pdf, accessed 3 March, 2011.

Chartered Management Institute (2009) *Managers Pay in the UK*, Figures from the National Management Salary Survey, www.managers.org.uk, accessed 3 March, 2011.

Cornelius, N. and Skinner, D. (2008) The Careers of Senior Men and Women – a capabilities theory perspective, *British Journal of Management*, 19, S141–S149.

Dex, S. and Smith, C. (2002) *The Nature and Pattern of Family Friendly Employment in Britain* (Bristol: Policy Press and Joseph Rowntree Foundation).

Dex, S., Ward, K. and Joshi, H. (2008) Changes in women' occupations and occupational mobility over 25 years, Chapter 2. In J. Scott, S. Dex and H. Joshi (eds) *Women and Employment: Changing Lives and New Challenges* (London: Edward Elgar, pp. 54–80).

Eagly, A. H. and Johnson, B. T. (1990) Gender and leadership style: a meta-analysis, *Psychological Bulletin*, 80(5), 389–407.

EHRC (Equality and Human Rights Commission) (2008) *Sex and Power*, equalityhumanrights.com, accessed 3 March, 2011.

EHRC (Equality and Human rights Commission) (2009) *Equal Pay Position Paper*, March equalityhumanrights.com, accessed 3 March, 2011.

EOC (Equal Opportunities Commission) (2007) *Black and Asian women are "missing from almost a third of workplaces in areas with significant ethnic minority populations*, Press release, 15 March.

Esser, I. (2009) *Has Welfare Made us Lazy? Employment Commitment in Different Welfare States, British Social Attitudes, the 25th Report* (London: Sage).

Ferrario, M. and Davidson, M. J. (1991) Gender and management style: a comparative study. In M. J. Davidson and C. L. Cooper (eds) *Shattering the Glass Ceiling* (London: Paul Chapman).

Gallie, D., White, M., Cheng, Y and Tomlinson, M. (1998) *Restructuring the Employment Relationship* (Oxford: Oxford University Press).

Gardiner, M. and Tiggemann, M. (1999) Gender differences in leadership style, job stress and mental health in male and female dominated industries, *Journal of Occupational and Organizational Psychology*, 72(3), 301–315.

Grimshaw, D. (2007) *The Gender Pay Gap in the UK: Key Issues*, Women's Budget Group seminar given at HM Treasury, January.

Grimshaw, D. and Rubery, J. (2007) *Undervaluing Women's Work*, Working Paper series No. 53. Equal Opportunities Commission, Manchester.

The Guardian (2009) Parental leave: fathers to get months of paid leave in paternity rights shakeup, 30 March.

Harding, R. (2007) *State of Women's Enterprise in the UK* (Norwich: Prowess Ltd).

Harris, H. (2001) Researching discrimination in selection for international management, *Women in Management Review*, 16(3), 118–125.

Harris, H. (2002) Think international managers, think male: why are women not selected for international management assignments? *Thunderbird International Business Review*, 44(2), 175–203.

HEPI (Higher Education Policy Institute) (2009) *Gender and Higher Education*, Press Release, 7 June, 1–2.

HESA (Higher Education Statistical Agency) (2009) *Students in Higher Education Institutions 2007/8* (Cheltenham: HESA).

Institute of Management (2001) *A Woman's Place? A Survey of Female Managers' Changing Professional and Personal Roles* (London: Institute of Management).

IRS (1996) Hypocrisy rife in company ethics, *Employment Trends*, 619(November), 2.

Judge, E. (2003) Women on the board: help or hindrance? *The Times*, 11 November, 21.

Kanter, R. M. (1977) *Men, Women and the Corporation* (New York, NY: Basic Books).

Kerfoot, D. and Knights, D. (1996) The best is yet to come: searching for embodiment in managerial work. In D. Collinson and J. Hearn (eds) *Men as Managers, Managers as Men: Critical Perspectives on Men, Masculinities and Management* (London: Sage, pp. 78–98).

Kirton, G. and Green, A. M. (2000) *The Dynamics of Managing Diversity* (Oxford: Butterworth-Heinemann).

Labour Force Survey (2006) www.managers.org.uk or www.statistics.gov.uk, accessed 3 March, 2011.

Lewis, P. (2006) The Quest for Invisibility: female entrepreneurs and the masculine norm of entrepreneurship, *Gender, Work and Organization*, 13(5), 453–469.

Li, Y., Devine, F. and Heath, A. (2008) *Equality Group Inequalities in Education, Employment and Earnings*, EHRC Research Report 10, Manchester.

Liff, S. and Ward. K. (2001) Distorted views through the glass ceiling: the construction of women's understandings of promotion and senior management positions, *Gender Work and Organization*, 8(1), 19–36.

Lueptow, L.B., Garovich-Szabo, L. and Lueptow, M.B. (2001) Social change and the persistence of sex typing, 1974–1997, *Social Forces*, 80(1), 1–32.

Management Today (2008) How Britain's most admired boards have changed in a decade, *Management Today*, 16 December.

Marlow, S (1997) Self employed women – do they mean business? *Entrepreneurship and Regional Development*, 9(3), 199–210.

Marlow, S. and D. Patton (2005) The financing of small business – female experiences and strategies, Chapter 6. In S. L. Fielden and M. J. Davidson (eds) *International Handbook of Women and Small Business Entrepreneurship* (Cheltenham: Edward Elgar).

Marshall, J. (1995) *Women Managers Moving On: Exploring Career and Life Choices* (London: Routledge).

Mirchandani, K. (2005) Women's entrepreneurship: exploring new avenues, Chapter 19. In S. L. Fielden and M. J. Davidson (eds) *International Handbook of Women and Small Business Entrepreneurship* (Cheltenham: Edward Elgar, pp. 253–263).

Nelson, D. L. and Burke, R. J. (2000) Women, work stress and health, Chapter 12. In M. J. Davidson and R. J. Burke (eds) *Women in Management: Current Research Issues Vol.II* (London: Sage).

Ogden, S. M., McTavish, D. and McKean, L. (2006) Clearing the way for gender balance in the management of the UK financial services industry, *Women in Management Review*, 21(1), 40–53.

ONS (Office for National Statistics) (2008) London.

ONS (Office for National Statistics) (2009) *Labour Market: The Jobs People Do, National Statistics* www.statistics.gov.uk, accessed 3 March, 2011.

Opportunity Now (2002) *Sticky Floors and Cement Ceilings*, Report discussed in *Financial Times*, 5 March, Women held back by bullying, harassment and discrimination and *Personnel Today*, 5 March Putting family first holds back career women.

Opportunity Now (2009) www.opportunitynow.org.uk, accessed 3 March, 2011.

Powell, G. N. (2000) The Glass Ceiling: explaining the good and bad news, Chapter 16. In M. J. Davidson and R. J. Burke (eds) *Women in Management: Current Research Issues Vol. II*, (London: Sage).

Purcell, K. and Elias, P. (2008) Achieving equality in the knowledge economy, Chapter 1. In J. Scott, S. Dex and H. Joshi (eds) *Women and Employment: Changing Lives and New Challenges* (London: Edward Elgar).

Purcell, K., Elias, P., Davies, R. and Wilton, N. (2005) *The Class of '99: A Study of the Early Labour Market Experiences of Recent Graduates*, DfES Research Report No. 691 (Nottingham: DfES Publications).

Race for Opportunity (2008) www.bitc.org.uk, accessed 3 March, 2011.

Rutherford, S. (2001) Any Difference? An analysis of gender and divisional management styles in a large airline, *Gender, Work and Organization*, 8(3), 326–345.

Ryan, M. and Haslam, S. A. (2005) The glass cliff: evidence that women are overrepresented in precarious leadership positions, *British Journal of Management*, 16(2), 81–90.

Ryan, M. K. and Haslam, S. A. (2009) Glass cliffs are not so easily scaled: on the precariousness of female CEO's positions, *British Journal of Management*, 20(1), 13–16.

SBS (Small Business Service) (2006) *Women's Business Ownership: Recent Research and Policy Developments* (London: Small Business Service).

Schein, V. (1973) The relationship between sex role stereotypes and requisite management characteristics, *Journal of Applied Psychology*, 57(2), 95–100.

Schein, V., Mueller, R., Lituchy, T. and Liu, J. (1998) Think managers – think male: a global phenomenon? *Journal of Organizational Behaviour*, 17(1), 33–41.

Scott, J., Dex, S. and Joshi, H. (2008) *Women and Employment: Changing Lives and New Challenges* (London: Edward Elgar).

Simpson, R. and Holley, D. (2001) Can restructuring fracture the glass ceiling? The case of women transport and logistics managers, *Women in Management Review*, 16(4), 174–182.

Startups (2006) www.startups.co.uk, accessed 3 March, 2011.

Vinkenburg, C. J., Jansen, P. G. and Koopman, P. L. (2000) Feminine leadership – a review of gender differences in managerial behaviour and effectiveness, Chapter 9. In M. J. Davidson and R. J. Burke (eds) *Women in Management: Current Research Issues Vol.II* (London: Sage).

Wahl, A. (1998) *Surplus Femininity*, Paper presented at Gender Work and Organization Conference, 9–10 January, Manchester. (Cited in Rutherford, 2001.)

Wajcman, J. (1998) *Managing Like a Man: Women and Men in Corporate Management* (Cambridge: Polity Press).

Watson, J. (2002) Comparing the performance of male-and-female-controlled businesses: relating outputs to inputs, *Entrepreneurship Theory and Practice*, 26(3), 91–100.

Watson, J. (2003) Failure rates for female-controlled businesses: are they any different? *Journal of Small Business Management*, 41(3), 62–277.

Weyer, B. (2007) Twenty years later: explaining the persistence of the glass ceiling for women leaders, *Women in Management Review*, 22(6), 482–496.

Wilson, F. and Thompson, P. (2001) Sexual harassment as an exercise of power, *Gender, Work and Organization*, 8(1), 61–83.

Wilton, P. (2008) *Management Recruitment: Understanding Routes to Greater Diversity*, June, Report for Chartered Management Institute, London.

Work Foundation (2006) *UK Increasingly a Nation of Entrepreneurs*, News Release, 9 January, www.prnewswire.co.uk, accessed 3 March, 2011.

Worrell, L., Lindorff, M. and Cooper, C. (2008) *Quality of Working Life 2008: A Survey of Organizational Health and Employee Well-being* (London: Chartered Institute of Management).

PART II

Women in Management – European Countries

8

Women in Management in Norway

Laura E. M. Traavik and Astrid M. Richardsen

Introduction

In 2008 Norway ranked as the number one country in the Global Gender Gap report on gender equality (Hausmann, Tyson and Zahidi, 2008). Norway was also the first country to legislate in 2003 that corporate boards of directors should contain at least 40 percent women for both public and private sector companies and continues to have one of the highest female workforce participation rates in Europe (Eurostat, 2007). With these amazing achievements Norway is often viewed as a country in which women have reached equality, yet unfortunately, this is not the case. Norway represents a country with groundbreaking legislation and unsurpassed gender equality yet inequities, discrimination and gender segregation in both education and the labour market still exist.

Norway has a population of almost 4.8 million people, and life expectancy in 2008 was 78 years for men and 83 years for women (Statistics Norway, 2009). The average number of children per woman is approaching two, which is one of the highest fertility rates in Europe, and 84 percent of children between the ages of one and five have either day-care, pre-school or kindergarten places (Statistics Norway, 2009). Nine percent of the population is foreign born and in the last two years Norway has experienced one of the highest immigration flows in the OECD (Liebig, 2009). The largest number of immigrants come from Poland, Pakistan, Sweden, Iraq and Somalia (IMDi, 2009). Although Norway is a relatively homogeneous country the pattern is changing.

Single parents are eligible for substantial government support until their child reaches three years of age (NAV, 2009), and Norway has laws that ensure women's right to have an abortion on demand. Norwegian culture prioritizes family life and children, which is reflected in working hours and national holidays. The overall standard of living is one of the highest in the world, having recently ranked second in the UN human development index (UNHD, 2008). In this country of high living standards and equality, we examine the current situation for women in management and present both where Norway is leading and where inequalities remain.

Labour Force Characteristics

Norway has a long history of female participation in the workforce, yet occupational segregation and wage disparity continue. Between 1980 and 1998 the percentage of women in the workforce increased in all age groups. In the 1970s female participation was below 50 percent and today the latest statistics show that 78 percent of women are active in the labour market compared to 85 percent of men (Statistics Norway, 2009). In 2007, 79 percent of women with children between ages nought to two, and 84 percent with children between ages three and six were active in the workforce[1] (Statistics Norway, 2008). In the year 2007 women made up almost 50 percent of the Norwegian workforce (Statistics Norway, 2009).

Although women have increased their overall participation in the Norwegian labour market the degree of their participation is very different from men. Eighty-seven percent of employed men compared to 57 percent of employed women are working full time (The Equality and Anti-discrimination Ombud, 2008). In fact, Norway has a high rate of women working part time in comparison to both European and OECD countries (OECD, 2007). On average, women work seven hours less per week in paid work compared to men. However, trends indicate that the degree of participation among women is increasing. In 1990, 48 percent of women were working part time, whereas in 2007 this had been reduced to 43 percent (Statistics Norway, 2009). The number of men working part time has increased from 9 percent in 1990 to 13 percent in 2007 (Statistics Norway, 2009). Women's participation in the labour market has been shown to increase as their children get older, although it is the number rather than the age of the children that has the largest impact. Women often work part time when they have more than one child. Norway does not have statistics on minority women, however data is available on immigrants and their descendants. In this group, labour market participation is often lower and

---

1   It should be noted that women are counted as employed even when they are on maternity leave.

varies greatly depending on country of origin, length of time in Norway and reason for immigration (IMDi, 2009). For example, women from the Nordic countries have a higher employment rate than native Norwegian women, but women from Africa have a much lower rate (62 percent). Overall, the statistics show that women have a strong presence in the Norwegian workforce, however they continue to work less than men and their participation in the labour market is strongly influenced by their family situation and their country of origin.

When we examine *where* these women work, stark gender differences emerge. Norway has one of the most gender-segregated labour markets within the OECD regions (The Equality and Anti-discrimination Ombud, 2008). Many professions are either dominated by men or by women. In 2007, a mere 11 percent of workers in the building and construction industry were women, yet women made up 88 percent of the nurses and care workers and 97 percent of pre-school teachers (Statistics Norway, 2009). Men continue to dominate the engineering profession (88 percent) and women make up an overwhelming majority of cleaning personnel (84 percent). A disturbing fact is that these figures from 2007 have not changed more than 1–3 percent in the last 20 years. Another obvious difference between men and women is in which sector they work. In 2009, 69 percent of those employed in the public sector are women compared to 37 percent in the private sector (Statistics Norway, 2009). The data clearly demonstrate that gender segregation continues to be pronounced, and when we review the statistics on educational choices later in the chapter, the future continues to look bleak.

Perhaps the most unexpected labour force characteristic found in Norway, given its ranking on gender equality, is the persistent difference between men and women's salaries. Women continue to have salaries 16 percent below that of their male counterpart (SALDO, 2008). When we look more closely at the Global Gender Gap Index (Hausmann, Tyson and Zahidi, 2008) Norway falls to 23rd place on the wage disparity sub-scale, and is placed 16th among the EU countries (SALDO, 2008). Men have higher salaries than women in *all* professions and types of work, both in the public and private sector. Another finding shows that the discrepancy in wages increases with education (SALDO, 2008). Some of the reasons identified as to why men continue to earn more than women have been related back to the gender segregation in the labour market. Although there have been many policy initiatives and political discussions, this difference has been stable for 20 years.

The overall picture of the Norwegian labour market is that women are participating in increasing numbers, however they work less than men; they are not obtaining the same salary levels as men; they are not entering into traditionally male-dominated professions or jobs; and they are not increasing their numbers in the private sector. The Norwegian woman continues to face challenges.

Women Pursuing Education

Trends in higher education in Norway send a mixed message. The good news is that women have entered higher education in droves. In 2007, women accounted for 63 percent of university and college graduates, and 50 percent of doctoral candidates. The bad news is that the gender segregation found in the labour market is clearly observed in the educational choices of both Norwegian men and women. These gender differences have remained relatively constant during the last ten years. Technical studies and the sciences continue to be dominated by men (77 percent in both 1995 and 2005), whereas women make up the overwhelming majority in health and welfare studies (85 percent in both 1995 and 2005). There are positive exceptions, such as in the study of medicine. In this field the number of women has risen from 12 percent in 1970 (NOU 2008:6) to approximately 65 percent in 2008 (Den norske legeforening, 2009). Also in economics and administration, women have increased their representation from 25 percent in 1980 to over 50 percent today (SALDO, 2008). Another positive trend is that in 2007 the number of women applying to study engineering showed a 25 percent increase from 2006, and there was a general increase in the percentage of women applying to study technology and the sciences (NOU, 2008:3). When we examine the immigrant population, Norwegian-born women with foreign parents have a rate of participation in higher education of 40 percent which is substantially more than the Norwegian national average of 30 percent (IMDi, 2009).

The proportion of women among academic and research staff continues to be low, although signs are that it is slowly improving. In Norway, postgraduate education is often funded through scholarships. Even though more women are taking postgraduate studies and qualifying for academic careers in record numbers (almost 47 percent of all doctorates completed in 2008), in 2007 only 18 percent of professors and 36 percent of associate professors in Norway were women (SALDO, 2008; Norwegian Social Science Data Services, 2009). Seventy percent of research funds go to male-dominated research areas (such as technology) and only 24 percent of research project leaders are women (Norwegian Research Council, 2009).

The data show that while women are making great progress in many fields, as well as in the sheer percentages actually obtaining higher education, there continues to be dramatic differences in choices of study, indicating that women and men continue to choose gender-stereotyped fields.

Women in Management

Statistics on women in management positions are usually reported separately for the political, public, and private sectors. We begin with an overview of Norwegian political leaders, where women have made the greatest inroads.

In 2008, women made up 34 percent of the members of the national Parliament, and 47 percent of the cabinet. At the municipal level, women represented 38 percent of the councils and at the city level 23 percent of the mayors (SALDO, 2008). The number of women in politics had a sharp increase from the 1970s into the 1990s but in the last few years these numbers have stabilized between 34–36 percent (Statistics Norway, 2006). The increase in the number of women was a result of a proactive strategy from the Socialist left party and the Liberal party. These political parties initiated voluntary gender quotas in the 1970s, and today almost all parties use gender quotas to ensure female nominees (Norwegian Ministry of Children and Equality, 2009). However, gender segregation also appears in the areas of political leadership. For example, Norway has never had a female Minister of Foreign Affairs and in 2008 the three powerful ministerial committees (control and constitution, finance and defence) comprised almost 90 percent men (SALDO, 2008). In the less powerful and more stereotypically female committees, such as family affairs and culture, women made up a comfortable majority of almost 60 percent (SALDO, 2008).

Within the administrative division of the public sector itself, there has been a law since 1981 (Lovdata, 2009) that all public governing boards, working groups and councils should comprise at least 40 percent of each gender. In 2007, these groups included 47 percent women (SALDO, 2008) and it is only the defence department which has not fulfilled the law, having only 32 percent female representation (up from 26 percent in 2006). Examining the management and leadership level, we find that the percentage of female managers in the public sector increased from 44 percent in 2004 to 51 percent in 2007, although only 27 percent were found in top management, and 38 percent were leaders of government departments (SALDO, 2008). Within the public sector we also observe gender segregation in terms of female leadership in the different departments. In the Prime Minister's Office and the Defence Department, only 21 percent were women, and in the Oil and Energy Department 27 percent were women. In the Department for Children and Equality, women made up 62 percent of the management (SALDO, 2008). In the public sector, as with the labour market in general and in education, we observe a positive trend of female involvement and participation, however, obtaining a top leadership position and entering male-dominated sectors remain a considerable challenge for Norwegian women.

When we investigate the private sector, the percentage of women in management positions at all levels was 24 percent in 2007, and only 18 percent of senior managers in private companies were women (Statistics Norway, 2009). The percentage of women who hold a position as director of the board in joint stock companies was 7 percent in 2008 (SALDO, 2008). However, after Government legislation in 2003 and 2006 and accompanying threat of Government action, joint stock companies now have boards comprising 40 percent women, up from 18 percent in 2006 (Statistics Norway, 2009).

Small business in Norway, that is, companies with less than 50 employees, represent 96 percent of all firms, and employ 40 percent of the private sector workforce (Spilling, 1998). The Central Registry of Firms and Establishments indicates that not all registered companies provide data on leadership and gender. However, of the firms with records on the company manager and gender, general managers consist of 16 percent women and 84 percent men (Spilling and Berg, 2000). A recent study showed similar findings. Skalpe (2006) investigated almost 18,000 small and medium-sized private sector companies in 2005 and found that women represented only 10 percent of the managing directors and were most often leaders of small companies in sectors with low profits and poor salary levels (Skalpe, 2006). No salary differences were uncovered for women and men who run their own companies, but the wage gap was most pronounced among leaders with no ownership (Skalpe, 2006). The study found that even the largest companies in female-dominated arenas were led by men. Once more we find gender segregation, with women representing 35 percent of the top leaders in female-dominated shops; 22 percent in culture, health and care; only 5 percent in industrial companies; 4 percent in energy; and 1 percent in building and construction (Skalpe, 2006).

A private organization, Lederne (The Norwegian Organization for Managers and Executives) which has over 15,000 members, recently did a survey and found that in their sample female managers and leaders earned 26 percent less than their male counterparts[2] (Nordrik and Stugu, 2009). To understand the differences they examined salary disparities within industries (see Table 8.1). They found that across all industries (except IT where the sample was very small), and at the same managerial level, men earned more than women, even in female-dominated sectors such as pre-schools (Nordrik and Stugu, 2009). Research done on foreign women in Norway showed they earned less than Norwegian women and did not achieve as high subjective career success (Traavik and Richardsen, 2009). From the data available, it appears that in management the salary gap is wide.

Table 8.1   Management salaries for men and women

	Women's salary (NOK)	Men's salary (NOK)	Women's salary as a percentage of men's salary
Pre-schools	442,671	498,414	88.8
Building and construction	416,875	494,682	84.3
Trade	385,174	485,487	79.3
Hotel and restaurants	376,707	416,000	90.6
Information technology	529,500	523,357	101.2
Industry	414,514	482,290	85.9
Aviation	542,714	567,667	95.6
Public sector	383,798	467,750	82.1
Oil and gas	587,704	735,545	79.9
Shipping	384,731	633,368	60.7
Travel	372,222	532,225	69.9
Service	381,846	492,871	77.5
Transport	384,545	452,250	89.3

Source: Research report *Lederne* (Nordrik and Stugo, 2009)

---

2   The study controlled for part-time work.

Women Entrepreneurs

The literature in the area of women in management indicates that the trend for women to start their own businesses is increasing worldwide, and is quickly emerging as an area of growing research interest. However, research on women entrepreneurs in Norway is scarce and studies often have serious methodological limitations (Richardsen and Burke, 2000).

The latest research from The Global Entrepreneurship Monitor (Bullvåg et al., 2008) calculated the total early-phase entrepreneurial activity (percentage of the population that attempts to start their own company) (TEA) for women in Norway to be 4 percent in 2003, 6 percent in 2006, 4 percent in 2007 and 5 percent in 2008. Female involvement in early phase entrepreneurship fell evenly between 2000–2004 to under 4 percent, however, the percentage of women actually establishing their own business increased from 25 percent in 2004 to 33 percent in 2007 (Kolvereid, Bullvåg and Aamo, 2007). The most recent Norwegian report shows that men continue to be twice as active as women in early-stage entrepreneurship and that women represent only one-third of entrepreneurial activity (Bullvåg et al., 2008). Female businesses tend to be smaller than men's (Foss and Ljunggren, 2006) and men are often involved in high-growth start-ups (Bullvåg et al., 2008). Isaksen and Kolvereid (2005) found that although both men and women expected their new start-ups to provide full-time employment, significantly more men (27 percent) than women (18 percent) aspired to having employees. Furthermore, Skalpe (2006) reported in his study that only 7 percent of companies in his sample had women as majority owners. There have been large discrepancies between men and women in terms of the type of industry in which registrations are made (Spilling, 2001). While 54 percent of male start-ups were in construction, primary industries and agriculture, producer services and transport; 64 percent of female start-ups were in wholesale and retail trade, and community and social services (Spilling, 2001).

In summary, data indicate that women's enterprises in Norway tend to be small with one or two employees, and tend to be concentrated in two commercial sectors. As a rule, therefore, women-led enterprises are often operating in a local market economy and have only local competition. Women-led businesses are also more often sole proprietorships than businesses led by men, which more often tend to be limited companies.

Country Legislation

Norway prides itself on a strong social democratic tradition, which is based on the assumption that men and women should be treated equally and fairly. The Gender Equality Act was first passed in Norway in 1978 and put in practice in 1979 and has undergone many reformulations over the years, with the most recent taking place in 2005 (Ministry of Children and Equality, 2009). This act provides the framework for ensuring that women have the same rights, obligations and opportunities as men and vice versa. The recent amendments (2002, 2005) to the law require a much more proactive approach from companies and organizations. The law states that public authorities, employers, and enterprises must "make active, targeted and systematic efforts to promote gender equality" (Ministry of Children and Equality, 2009). Companies that are required to prepare annual reports must include information on the current gender equality in the organization, as well as plans for promoting gender equality. The law also allows for affirmative action and prevents job advertisements restricting applicants based on their sex. Norway has also set up institutions, such as the The Equality and Anti-discrimination Ombud, to provide guidelines, information and to assist people in making discrimination complaints.

The other pioneering legislation that we have mentioned previously, were the laws requiring equal representation of women in important boards and committees in both public organizations and private companies. In 1981 the law requiring gender balance on all boards and committees in public sector organizations was enacted. The law that there must be 40 percent female representation on the boards of all publicly owned and privately owned publicly listed enterprises was passed in 2003 and came into effect from 1 January 2004 for publically owned enterprises. Privately owned publicly listed companies were given until 2007 to comply with the new law. The new laws were incorporated into The Norwegian Companies Act which meant non-compliance to the regulation would lead to dissolution of the companies (Hoel 2008: Lovdata, 2009). These laws have undoubtedly had a positive impact. The facts and figures in our earlier section on women in management show this legislation has led to the reality of gender balance in committees, councils and now boardrooms.

The legislation directed at giving women equal status and rights has not been able to redress all the imbalances between men and women in the workplace. For example, Hovde (2008) found that only 24 percent of 50 companies surveyed in central Norway were complying with the new proactive section of the Gender Equality Act, and 22 percent did not deem it necessary to have any measures or policies to promote gender equality. Possible explanations for this situation are that sections of the Gender Equality Act do not have the legal clout or ability to impose sanctions easily or in such a way to act as a powerful deterrent. When there is a powerful deterrent, such as dissolving or fining companies not complying with the law, the legislation works (Hoel, 2008). Hovde (2008) also found that larger companies had the most proactive integrated policies and plans.

There are also examples of legislation which might have adverse effects on female advancement and equality. In 1999, the Christian Democratic Government passed a bill to give families with children added financial support in order to provide parents opportunities to spend more time at home with their children. A recent study demonstrated short-term negative effects on women's employment as more women chose to remove themselves from the labour market and receive the Government benefits (Schøne, 2004).

Initiatives Supporting Women in the Workforce

To address the paucity of women in higher management and the continued salary disparity, many initiatives have been launched over the years. In this section we highlight projects assisting women in management and entrepreneurship, and comment on the roles of networks.

In Norway a very influential actor is The NHO, The Confederation of Norwegian Enterprises. This organization is the most important representative body for Norwegian companies with a current membership of over 18,500 enterprises. In 1995 The NHO began a mentoring programme with the goal of helping women obtain leadership positions and corporate board positions. At the end of the year 2008, they had had 900 participants (Anderson, 2008). The Confederation of Norwegian Enterprises also started the Female Future project in 2003 to mobilize and develop talent, and create a meeting place for women in order to move into leadership positions. Since its inception Female Futures has had over 1,000 participants, and reported results from the last two years show that 33 percent of participants had received advancement into leadership positions and board work (NHO, 2009). A unique approach is that it is the business leaders themselves who are the driving force behind the programme since they are responsible for recruiting the women.

Innovation Norway is a State-owned company which promotes nationwide industrial development, Norwegian products and services internationally, and entrepreneurship. Women are a priority target group in the organization, and with the programme "Women in Focus" they seek to strengthen the role of women in the private sector, leadership and as entrepreneurs. The programme finances entrepreneurs, offers consultancy services and sponsors women-focused projects. In 2008, Innovation Norway contributed 1.4 billion Norwegian crowns to female projects and companies (Innovation Norway, 2009).

In order to counteract the "old boys network" and its effects on important management decisions, a number of women in business have realized the need for women to create their own networks. New women's networks are growing fast, and many of these work actively to break the glass ceiling and help promote women in management. Women's networks have been established within politics, business, among students as well as in cultural areas, and they arrange a variety of activities, training and opportunities for sharing information. Examples are "Women Innovation" (http://kvinnovasjon.no/) for female entrepreneurs and "Association of International Professional and Business Women" (www.aipbw.no), a network for business women in Norway of international background. Common to all the fast-growing networks is a belief that not much will change unless women themselves take action and build networks and contacts the way men do.

The Future

Although Norway has enjoyed an excellent reputation for equality, the reputation hides the statistical truth that women still work in stereotypically female jobs, face discrimination and are paid less than men. Considering the most recent statistics, one has to conclude that despite a number of political initiatives and social welfare policies that promote equality, Norway has failed to completely close the gender gap. However, Norway has shown that gender balance can be achieved through quotas, legislation and political pressure.

The Equal Pay Commission submitted a report to the Government recommending several actions to increase the equality between men and women in Norway (NOU, 2008:6). Some of their suggestions were to increase the percentage of parental leave that must be taken by the father (which as of 1 July, 2009 has been increased to ten weeks (NAV, 2009), increases in the funding to the Equality and Anti-discrimination Ombud, and a salary raise to chosen female-dominated professions within the public sector.

Authorities are also doing more to encourage non-traditional choices in education (for example, offering extra points needed to get into studies that are currently under represented by women, such as engineering), and putting more muscle behind their policies. The changes in the Gender Equality Act have also shifted the pressure to companies who are now required to be proactive, rather than non-discriminatory, and to deliver policies and plans. There has been a clear shift in the last five years in Norway with the Government playing a larger role to redress the gender inequalities that exist today. The legislation has pushed Norwegian organizations to take responsibility.

Gender inequality cannot be eliminated over night nor can it be easily understood. The research in this area points to a number of obstacles to women's advancement to senior levels (Morrison, White and Van Velsor, 1992; Burke and McKeen, 1995). The most common obstacles mentioned are lack of mentors, role models, visible jobs and flexible work arrangements, and being excluded from so-called "old boys' networks". There has been relatively little research conducted in Norway concerning the barriers to women's equal participation in the labour market, but a few studies indicate that such barriers are related to career and job satisfaction, career advancement opportunities and health (Richardsen, Mikkelsen and Burke, 1997; Richardsen, Burke and Mikkelsen, 1999). Despite the increased knowledge of obstacles, the keys to success for women are largely unknown. Through interviews with successful women, some areas of importance are emerging, but the studies also suggest that there are individual differences among the women, for example, background, ethnicity, religion, education, work experience and values (White, 2000). It is important to expose the range of these individual differences, which women can use in their career planning. Some authors have argued that there is much more to be learned from studies of successful women than comparing women's career success with that of men's (Morrison, White and Van Velsor, 1992; White, 2000). Career development issues would be an important area of research in order to promote gender equality in Norway.

A clear message from the Norwegian experience is that affirmative action, quotas and clear goals lead to increases in the number of women in boardrooms and in politics. Recent research assessing diversity management policies in the USA concluded that it is the structural variables that are most important (Kalev, Dobbin and Kelley, 2006). Organizations which establish practices that assign responsibility for achieving change, achieve the change they seek (Kalev, Dobbin and Kelley, 2006). In a land of equality, the values of same worth are in place, and the recent focus on goals and organizational accountability is promising. However, Norway still must address the gender-segregated education system and the paucity of women in top leadership in the private sector. As the Minister of Children and Equality warned at a recent United Nations Commission on the Status of Women (UN CSW) meeting in March 2009, Norwegians must not become too self-righteous as there are still hurdles to overcome before equality is reached.

References

Anderson, H. A. (2008) *Ledere som Utvikler seg Sammen med Ledere [Leaders who Develop Together with Leaders]* AFF, http://www.aff.no/AFF/lnnyhet.nsf/wP rId/8A387C80BC9ECDFCC1257443003B7C0B!OpenDocument, accessed 29 April, 2009.

Bullvåg, E., Jenssen, S. A., Kolvereid, L. and Aamo, B. W. (2008) *Global Entrepreneurship Monitor: Entrepreneurship i Norge 2008*, http://www. gemconsortium.org/document.aspx?id=891, accessed: 4 May, 2009.

Burke, R. J. and McKeen, C.A. (1995) Work experiences, career development, and career success of managerial and professional women, *Journal of Social Behavior and Personality*, 10(6), 81–96.

Den norske legeforening (2009) http://www.legeforeningen.no.

The Equality and Anti-discrimination Ombud (2008) http://ldo.no/no/.

Eurostat (2007) *Labour Market Statistics*, http://epp.eurostat.ec.europa.eu/portal/ page/portal/eurostat/home.

Foss, L. and Ljunggren, E. (2006) Women's entrepreneurship in Norway. Recent trends and future challenges. In C. G. Brush (ed.) *Growth-Oriented Women Entrepreneurs and Their Businesses* (Cheltenham: Edward Elgar Publishing Ltd).

Hausmann, R., Tyson, L. and Zahidi, S. (2008) *The Global Gender Gap 2008* (Geneva: World Economic Forum).

Hoel, M. (2008) The quota story: five years of change in Norway. in S. Vinnicombe, V. Singh, R. J. Burke, D. Bilimoria and M. Huse (eds) *Women on Corporate Boards of Directors: International Research and Practice* (Cheltenham: Edward Elgar Publishing Ltd, pp. 79–87).

Hovde, K. (2008) *Bedrifters Redegjørelse for Likestilling – Undersøkelse av 50 Bedrifter sin årsberetning for 2006 [Companies Description of their Equality*

Policies – A Study of 50 Companies Annual Reports], http://www.kun.nl.no/no/ publikasjoner_fra_kun/rapporter/, accessed 30 April, 2009.

IMDi (Directorate of Integration and Diversity Norway) (2009) *I Fakta: Faktahefte om Invvandrere og Integrering, Integrerings-og Mangfoldsdirektoratet [Focusing on Women]*.

Innovation Norway (2009) *Satser på Kvinner*, http://www.innovasjonnorge.no/ Satsinger/Kvinner-i-fokus/, accessed 30 April, 2009.

Isaksen, E. and Kolvereid, L. (2005) Growth objectives in Norwegian start-up businesses, *International Journal of Entrepreneurship and Small Business*, 2(1), 17–26.

Kalev, A., Dobbin, F. and Kelly, E. (2006) Best practices or best guesses? Assessing the efficacy of corporate affirmative action and diversity policies, *American Sociological Review*, 71, 587–617.

Kolvereid, L., Bullvåg, E. and Aamo, B. W. (2007) *Global Entrepreneurship Monitor: Entrepreneurship i Norge 2007*, http://www.gemconsortium.org/ document.aspx?id=701, accessed 27 April, 2009.

Liebig, T. (2009) *Jobs for Immigration Labour Market Integrtion in Norway*, OECD Working Papers No. 94, http://www.olis.oecd.org/olis/2009doc.nsf/ LinkTo/NT00004EA6/$FILE/JT03269718.PDF, accessed and downloaded 25 September, 2009.

Lovdata (2009) http://www.lovdata.no/.

Ministry of Children and Equality (2009) http://www.regjeringen.no/nb.html?id=4.

Morrison, A. M., White, R. P. and van Velsor, E. (1992) *Breaking the Glass Ceiling* (Reading, MA: Addison-Wesley).

NAV (The Norwegian Labour and Welfare Administration) (2009) http://www. nav.no, accessed 25 September, 2009.

NHO (The Confederation of Norwegian Enterprise) (2009) *Female Future – en Suksesshistorie*, http://www.nho.no/female-future/female-future-en- suksesshistorie-article20406-63.html, accessed 30 April, 2009.

Nordrik, B. and Stugu, S. (2009) *Norsk Ledelsesbarometer: Noen Vudering av Lønn [Norwegian Leadership Barometer: Some Salary Evaluations]*, Lederne rapport, www.lederne.no.

Norwegian Ministry of Children and Equality (2009) *Women in Norwegian Politics*, http://www.norway.org/policy/gender/politics/politics.html, accessed 14 April, 2009.

Norwegian Research Council (2009) *Annual Report 2008*, http://www. forskningsradet.no/no/Forsiden/1173185591033.

Norwegian Social Science Data Service (2009) http://www.nsd.uib.no.

NOU (Official Norwegian Reports) (2008:3) *Ny Struktur i høyre Utdanning [New Structures in Higher Education]*, http://www.regjeringen.no/pages/2044137/ PDFS/NOU200820080003000DDDPDFS.pdf, accessed 14 April, 2009.

NOU (Official Norwegian Reports) (2008:6). *Kjønn og Lønn [Gender and Salary]*, http:// www.regjeringen.no/pages/2052468/PDFS/NOU200820080006000DDDPDFS. pdf, accessed 14 April, 2009.

OECD (Organisation for Economic Cooperation & Development) (2007) *OECD Employment Outlook 2007*, Vol. 2007 (1) (Organisation for Economic Cooperation & Development).

Richardsen, A. and Burke, R. J. (2000) Women entrepreneurs and small business owners in Norway and Canada'. In M. Davidson and R.J. Burke (eds) *Women in Management: Current Research Issues, Vol. II* (London: Sage Publications).

Richardsen, A. M., Burke, R. J. and Mikkelsen, A. (1999) Job pressures, organizational support and health among Norwegian women managers, *International Journal of Stress Management*, 6(3), 167–178.

Richardsen, A. M., Mikkelsen, A. and Burke, R. J. (1997) Work experiences and career and job satisfaction among professional and managerial women in Norway, *Scandinavian Journal of Management*, 13(3), 209–218.

SALDO (2008) *Et Samfunnsregnskap for Likestilling og Diskriminering [Social Accounting of Equality and Discrimination]* (Oslo: The Norwegian Equality and Anti-discrimination Ombud).

Schøne, P. (2004) Kontantstøtten og mødres arbeidstilbud; Varig effekt eller retur til arbeid [Cash benefits and mother's employment; Long term effects or return to work], *Norsk Økonomisk Tidsskrift*, 118, 1–21.

Skalpe, O. (2006) Kvinner leder små bedrifter i lite lønnsomme brasnjer [Women lead small companies in not very profitable sectors], *Magma*, 9(2), 51–59.

Spilling, O. R. (1998) Kjønn og ledelse i SMB [Gender and leadership in SMB]. In O.R. Spilling (ed.) *SMB 98 – Fakta om Små og Mellomstore Bedrifter i Norge [SMB 98- Facts about small medium sized companies in Norway]* (Bergen: Fagbokforlaget).

Spilling, O. R. (2001) *Women Entrepreneurship and Management in Norway: A Statistical Overview*, Discussion Paper, Norwegian School of Management BI.

Spilling, O. R. and Berg, N. G.(2000) Gender and small business management: The case of Norway in the 1990's, *International Small Business Journal*, 18(2), 38–59.

Statistics Norway (2001) *Labour Market Statistics 2000*, Report on official statistics of Norway.

Statistics Norway (2006) *Dette er Kari og Ola Oppdatert [This is Kari and Ola Updated]*, 2006, Report on official statistics of Norway, http://www.ssb.no/ emner/00/02/10/ola_kari/main_2006.html, accessed 14 April, 2009.

Statistics Norway Horge, E. H. and Rønning, E. (2008) *Norsk Sysselsetting på 'Europa-toppen' [Norwegian employment at 'European Top']* Samfunnsspeilet, 5–6, http://www.ssb.no/samfunnsspeilet/utg/, accessed 14 April, 2009.

Statistics Norway (2009) http://www.ssb.no.

Traavik, L. E. M. and Richarsdsen, A. M. (2010) Career success for international professional women in the land of the equal. Evidence from Norway, *International Journal of Human Resource Management*, 21(15), 2798–2812.

UNHD (United Nations Human Development) (2008) *United Nations Human Development Report*, http://hdrstats.undp.org/2008/countries/country_fact_sheets/cty_fs_NOR.html, accessed 6 April, 2009.

White, B. (2000) Lessons from the careers of successful women. In M. Davidson and R. J. Burke (eds) *Women in Management: Current Research Issues, Vol. II* (London: Sage Publications, pp. 166–176).

9

Women in Management in Russia

Carianne M. Hunt and Sarah E. Crozier

Introduction

This chapter aims to discuss a number of factors relevant to women in management in Russia. The characteristics of women in the labour market are uncovered, and issues such as wage discrimination, education statistics and the specific role of women managers in Russia are explored. Further, details on women entrepreneurs are discussed alongside legislative initiatives and trends for the future.

In introducing the topic and its political and historical background, the Soviet State pre-1989 appeared to be based on an egalitarian system, whereby men and women were seen as equal. However, this supposed egalitarian state was based on Marxist principles of class and therefore a woman's role was viewed as supporting her husband and family in the war against class. Organizations had numerous "family-friendly" policies in the sense that they offered flexible working and reduced hours for women. These policies were implemented so that women were able to work and also look after their family. One may suggest that such policies simply re-emphasized the view that childcare and looking after the family was women's work and therefore the father was not involved to the same degree. The fact that men were not allowed to take advantage of flexible working patterns emphasizes this point.

Post-1989 and during the development of Russia as an independent state, the country needed to restructure and organizations were required to become more profitable to survive the economic conditions. To become more competitive many organizations began to restructure and downsize their workforce and the first workers to go were women as they were seen as being more important to the home than to work – as one State official stated:

> *Why should we employ women when men are unemployed? It is better that men work and women take care of the children and do the housework. I don't want women to be offended but I don't think women should work while men are doing nothing.*
>
> (Kay, 2001:57)

The extent of female labour force participation has often been linked to economic need. Many held the view that if the right conditions prevailed, that is, that men's wages could support the family, many women would in fact no longer need to work outside the home. Furthermore, in the past, the high level of female labour force participation was often condemned by many, in terms of the negative impact this could have on the birth rate and the family (Kiseleva, 1982).

Labour force participation rates for men in 1992 were extremely high with rates above 90 percent in the prime working ages (25 to 50). This employment rate equalled levels which had been observed in the US and western Europe. In 1992, female participation in the labour force was nearly as high as that for males with rates also surpassing 90 percent for women who were aged between 30 and 40. In contrast, the labour force participation rates in the US for the same age ranges was around 70 to 75 percent throughout the 1990s (US Census Bureau, 2002). These figures suggest that there was equality between men and women in Russia, at least in terms of labour force participation.

Labour Force Characteristics

The overall level of women's economic activity remains high in Russia. This is largely due to their necessity in the labour force in relation to contributing to the family budget. In Russia, in the majority of households one worker is not able to ensure that the necessary level of consumption and prosperity is achieved; therefore households require incomes from two individuals. The United Nations (2005) report found that analysis of factors affecting the rate of labour activity revealed a number of gender differences. In contrast to men, the number of children negatively affects women's economic activity. However, educational attainment has a positive impact on women's participation in the labour market when compared to men, that is, women receive more returns from their education in terms of improving their position and status in the labour market.

The position of employed women declined steadily for all sectors of the Russian economy (from 51 percent in 1990 to 48 percent in 1998) (Rzhanitsyna, 2000). Furthermore, the traditionally "female" sectors where the number of women has always been larger, such as finance, communications and housing, have also witnessed a process whereby women were being displaced by men. Rzhanitsyna (2000) states that there have been unfavourable shifts in women's employment patterns. Moreover, this can be seen when examining the share of industrial labour which has dropped steadily in the 1990s: 37 percent of those working in industry, transport, construction and other sectors of production were women in 1998, as opposed to 50 percent in 1990. When examining employment in the social sectors – health care, education and culture, there has been a general increase in relative terms, however the number of women in these roles has remained constant. One area where women have gained advantage is in the development of the information and market infrastructure. As well, the army has also become a place where women are witnessing an increase in employment, although only 3 percent of women serving in the armed forces hold officers' ranks. In terms of educational attainment, employed women have higher education, particularly secondary and professional qualifications, when compared with men. However, they also make up the majority of individuals registered as unemployed with secondary and higher professional education (73 percent) (Rzhanitsyna, 2000) thus illustrating how educational attainment does not always transfer to employment, particularly for women. Moreover, statistics reported by the Russian Statistical Agency (1999) showed that the number of women who wanted to work had increased dramatically from October 1997 to August 1999, from 2,384,000 to 3,417,000 (see Table 9.1).

Table 9.1   Women in the household (000s)

	Do not want to work	Want to work	Including those who have stopped looking for work
October 1997	2853	2384	456
August 1999	1850	3417	649

Source: Rzhanitsyna (2000), Population Study of Employment Problems, August 1999, Moscow, Russian Statistical Agency, 1999, 82

Despite respondents stating that they "wanted to work", Table 9.2 shows that more women than men appear to believe that they have fewer qualities which may be of value in the current economic situation. These perceptions may result in women being less likely to apply for certain jobs as they do not feel that they have the appropriate qualities and skills for the position. In addition, the fewer women in those positions is likely to have a further negative impact on women's perceptions of gaining employment (Rzhanitsyna, 2000).

Table 9.2   Qualities of value in economic situation

To the question "I seem to have few qualities of value in the current economic situation" the following responses were shown:

	Exactly		Very likely		Rather unlikely		Unlikely	
	1998	2000	1998	2000	1998	2000	1998	2000
Men	20.35	17.74	28.42	27.42	27.29	31.7	12.34	11.39
Women	26.18	24.66	32.02	29.88	23.29	26	7.40	9.00

Source: United Nations (2005)

The centralized pay scale policies in Russia which were set to uniform rates of pay, particularly in relation to gender, have in fact given preference to traditionally "male" sectors such as the heavy and extraction industries, construction and transport. On the other hand, the sectors which hold less national economic significance such as the light and food industries, and health care (where female employment has predominated), have experienced lower pay rates (United Nations, 2005).

Differences in wages experienced by men and women are typically explained by unequal gender discrimination across different professions and industries (horizontal segregation), unequal wages within professions and types of activity (vertical segregation), and low recognition of women's labour (United Nations, 2005). In 1998, female average wages in the Russian economy made up 70 percent of male average wages, in 2000 this fell to 63.2 percent, in 2001 63 percent and in 2003 experienced a slight increase to 64 percent

(RF Goskomstat data) (United Nations, 2005). Alongside these figures one must also consider two key factors, firstly in the 1990s, non-payments and wage arrears were an acute problem in the Russian economy and affected more men than women and, secondly, wage rates were typically based on primary workplaces, however, many individuals had secondary employment. This secondary employment is, on the whole, conducted by men and they tend to command higher wages than women. Therefore, the differences in male and female wages reported above may be underestimated.

Russian Longitudinal Monitoring Survey (RLMS) data for 2001 revealed that the largest gender gaps in wages were in professional occupations, for example, in professionals who require specialist secondary and university education, women make less than men by 47percent and 45 percent respectively on average. Employees with complete or incomplete postgraduate education were highest earners; however women with postgraduate education on average earned less than men with secondary education. Women who had university education earned more than only one category of men, that being those with incomplete university education (United Nations, 2005).

Table 9.3 shows the trends of the percentages of women across different industries and the changes in the level of income in those sectors between 1996 and 2002. It is evident from these figures that the occupations which show a large percentage of women, health care and education, are the occupations which have some of the lowest ratios of pay.

Table 9.3   Percentages of women among employees and level of wages
by industries, 1996–2002

	Share of women among the employed (%)				Ratio of monthly wages in branch to average wages in economy			
Year	1996	1998	2000	2002	1996	1998	2000	2002
Total economy	47	48	48	48	100	100	100	100
Industry	41	38	38	38	110	115	123	118
Agriculture	34	32	35	40	48	45	40	40
Construction	24	24	24	24	122	127	126	120
Transport	26	26	26	23	144	144	150	136
Communication	62	60	61	60	130	140	130	130
Trade, public catering, mobile telesystems	62	62	64	63	77	82	71	70
Communal and public services	46	46	47	47	106	105	88	85
Health care, sport, social security	82	81	81	80	77	69	62	74
Education	82	80	80	79	70	63	56	67
Art and culture	69	68	69	72	65	62	55	66
Science	51	50	50	49	83	99	121	126
Finance and credits	74	71	71	69	193	199	243	285
Public administration	50	48	45	38	120	129	120	118

Source: United Nations (2005)

Wage differentials were also apparent across different regions in Russia as
Table 9.4 illustrates. Interestingly, the regions which are least developed show
gender equality in favour of women, whereas the most developed regions, for
example, Moscow, has the highest educational level but show some disparities.
However, the strongest disparities tend to be in the north-eastern regions where
the industries rely on export-oriented mining.

Table 9.4   Types of regional gender disparities in wages

Ratio of female wages to male wages (%)	Regional types as per combination of gender disparity factors	Regions
Strongest disparities (56–64)	a) Northern and eastern regions, prevalence of export-oriented mining industry and relatively young population	Nenetsky, Yamalo-Nenetsky, Khanty-Mansiisky Autonomous Districts, Kemerovskaya, Murmanskaya, Tomskaya, Tyumenskaya Oblasts, Krresnoyarsky Kray, Komi Republic, Khakassia
	b) European Russia, prevalence of export-oriented industries, higher income level and average educational level	Astrakanskaya, Belgorodskaya, Vologodskaya, Lipetskaya, Samarskaya, Sverdlovskaya and Orenburgskaya Oblasts, Tatarstan, Baskortostan
Close to average across Russia (64–69)	Predominately average with regard to level of development, different educational levels and age structure	Over 30 regions
Less stronger disparities (69–80)	a) Most developed, with highest educational level	Moscow
	b) Below average by level of income, older age structure and low educational level	Bryanskaya, Vladimirskaya, Voronezhskaya, Ivanovskaya, Kaluzhhskaya, Kostromomskyay, Kirovskaya, Penzenskaya, Novgorodskyay, Orlovskaya, Pskovskaya, Tambovskaya, Tverskaya Oblasts
	c) Semi-agrarian with lower educational levels and the level of incomes	Krasnodrasky, Stavropolsky, AltayskyKrays, Kurganskaya Oblasts
	d) Eastern regions with income below average and younger age structure	Taimyrsky, Evenkiysky Autonomous District, Chitinskaya Oblast, Buryaita Republic and most Far East regions
	e) Undeveloped semi-agrarian republics with younger age structure	Adygeya, Imgushetia, Kabardino-Balkaria, Karacheavo-Chekessia, Northern Ossetia, Kalmykia, Mari El, Mordovia, Chuvashia
Gender equality or gender disparity in favour of women (82–113)	Least developed	Altay Republic, Tuva, Komi-Permyatsky, Agynsky Buryatsky, Ust-Ordynsky Autonomous Districts

Source: United Nations (2005)

Women Pursuing Education

Table 9.5 highlights that the number of women and men completing a university education were similar in 2002, however slightly more women achieved this level of education. Women were more likely to have a secondary professional qualification in 2002 compared to men, whereas men were more likely to have secondary education in 2002. Despite some differences, these figures illustrate that educational attainment of men and women appears to be relatively equal across educational levels. However, as previously stated, this attainment does not appear to transfer to the labour market.

Table 9.5   Level of education of men and women above 15 years old per 1,000 people

Years	University education		Secondary professional education		Secondary education		Universal primary education	
	Men	Women	Men	Women	Men	Women	Men	Women
1970	57	44	78	88	126	121	325	253
1989	117	110	166	214	323	233	231	192
1994	138	130	190	242	327	250	216	190
2002	142	144	213	262	349	272	175	156

Source: United Nations (2005)

The United Nations (2005) report stated that currently among young and able-bodied age groups, women's educational attainment is slightly higher than men's. However, it is evident that women and men apply different strategies to their education and preparing for work. Women were more inclined to obtain secondary education in general schools and were oriented at receiving top-level professional training, whereas men were more likely to receive incomplete general secondary education in schools and continued studies in vocational training situations. These differences in educational strategies may be due to the professional segregation and different returns on investment of men and women. For women, only university education can ensure higher wages, whereas for men even unskilled occupations, which require vocational training, can provide sufficient returns on education.

The *St Petersburg Times* reported in September 2008 that women were applying to MBA programmes in greater numbers than ever before. The Graduate Management Admission Council (GMAC) maintained that in September 2008, 44 percent of those who were taking the Graduate Management Admission Test were women (Coutat, 2008). This trend was also confirmed by the Forte Foundation, an organization developed to promote women in management. The Forte Foundation found that for the first time in 15 years the number of women in business schools had raised significantly and it appears that Russian women seem to be more active than the world average. Women accounted for 54 percent of all the Graduate Management Admission Test takers holding Russian citizenship (Coutat, 2008).

Women in Management

Table 9.6 shows the trend in the changing number of women employed in some sectors of the Russian economy from 1994 to 2001. In 2001, the most popular occupations for women were office clerks and client services and occupations in the public services. Whilst there were a high number of women employed in public services, this does not appear to imply that they were in positions of decision making. For example, in senior government levels, there were no women and only one woman among the heads of Russian Federation subjects – governors or heads of national autonomies (in St. Petersburg). Among deputies of the State Duma of the first convocation (1993–1995), 13.6 percent were women, of the second convocation (1995–1999) 10 percent were women. Moreover, of the third convocation elected in December 1999, only 7.7 percent were women, and in 2003 this rose to 10 percent. In the upper chamber, Council of the Federation, which has 178 members, there were only seven women in 2002. While women make up a large percentage of the public sector they do not appear to be gaining access to the higher echelons of power.

Table 9.6   **Share of women across occupational groups, 1994–2001 (RLMS data)**

Occupational groups	1994	1995	1996	1998	2000	2001
Armed forces	6.1	16.9	11.9	10.6	11.6	11.1
Heads of government bodies, enterprise and organizations	25.3	32	32.7	41.8	40.9	46.5
Professional with university education	64.2	69.4	69.2	71.8	73.3	74
Professionals with secondary education	81	77.1	76.8	74.3	76.4	74.1
Office clerks and client services	92.3	89.2	91.2	89.7	91.1	88.5
Public services workers	68.7	66.8	70.2	76.1	78.8	77.9
Skilled agricultural and fishery workers	10.3	0	16.7	10.5	9.4	7.4
Plant and machine operators and assemblers	19.1	16	17.4	16.7	16.7	15.2
Industrial workers	17.4	18.3	19.6	19.8	18.4	22.1
Unskilled workers	64	66	59.7	56.2	55.6	53.1

Source: United Nations (2005)

Unsurprisingly, the RMLS (United Nations, 2005) showed that more men than women felt that there were equal opportunities for men and women in the labour market (see Table 9.7). More women than men felt that men had better opportunities, and only a small proportion of both men and women felt that women had better opportunities in the labour market.

Table 9.7   **Opportunities for employment**

	Men and women have equal opportunities for well-paid job placement	Men have better opportunities	Women have better opportunities
Men	39.6	51.27	4.21
Women	32.32	61.9	2.27

Source: United Nations (2005)

More recent publications highlight the comparisons between women and men in different employment sectors. The Federal State Statistic Service (2009) showed that in the year of 2008, as exemplified in Table 9.8 below, there were still marginally more men than women in the most senior roles available. However, more women than men were specialists of high and medium qualifications. Similarly, more women were shown to hold medium-level personnel positions. Higher proportions of men were found in manual jobs of different descriptions, and there were an approximate equal number of men and women in unskilled labour positions.

Table 9.8   **Employment by sex and occupation in 2008, as a percentage of the total employed population**

Occupation Type	Total (%)	Men (%)	Women (%)
Heads of public authorities and administration	7.0	8.7	5.3
Specialists of high qualifications	19.0	14.7	23.8
Specialists of medium qualifications	8.7	4.8	12.0
Medium-level personnel	6.4	4.0	8.9
Employees in administrative roles and services	3.1	0.6	5.6
Workers of other services, housing and public utilities	6.5	5.1	7.9
Skilled workers in agriculture, forestry, hunting and fisheries	3.4	3.3	3.5
Mining, construction and repair work employees	4.5	7.8	1.1
Workers in machine building and metal industry	5.8	10.3	1.2
Transport and communication employees	1.7	2.5	0.8
Other skilled professions in industry	2.6	1.0	3.2
Operators and drivers	12.5	21.7	3.0
Unskilled workers in all types of industries	9.5	9.2	9.9

Source: Adapted From Federal State Statistics Service, 2009

A study by Metcalfe and Afanassieva (2005 a;b) based on a total of 30 semi-structured interviews, examined the social and economic changes that have shaped Russian women's work identity. Interviews were conducted with professional women in a range of industries including education, manufacturing, public management, marketing and law. The interviews were based on a life history research methodology and asked women to describe their management roles, career histories and explore significant work-life events. The study found that when women were asked to describe effective management characteristics they tended to highlight stereotypical characteristics, such as assertiveness, toughness and resilience and women reported that men were "naturally" suited to authoritative roles. The study also found that:

> women supported the double burden and the essentialist gender order and did not expect or receive help from their partners or husbands with childcare or household tasks. Inequalities in family and work responsibilities were perceived as public administration issues associated with the dismantling of state child services, rather than about gender relations within the family sphere.
>
> (Metcalfe and Afanassieva, 2005b: 442)

Women in the study referred to how the transition had enabled them to "transform" themselves and to become "real women". The expansion of business services, particularly in fashion, food, retailing and cosmetics had changed the lifestyles of Russian women. Earlier research suggested that the increased consumer choice experienced by women had assisted in reconstructing the traditional gender identity of a female masculinized Russian (Rubchak, 2001). Moreover, the construction of a feminine identity was considered an important part of a Russian woman creating a professional work identity. Rubchak (2001) maintained that displaying and performing a feminine work identity provided Russian women with confidence and the assurance that they could be successful in business. This value was also supported by the training services of the International Federation of Businesswomen in St Petersburg which focused on colour analysis, grooming and dress decisions. Women were seen as needing to portray an image of "feminism". The interviews with women managers in the study by Metcalfe and Afanassieva (2005b) showed that women themselves viewed their role as managers second place to their husbands' position and also how it was important for them to ensure that they looked and acted feminine in the workplace and how this could result in a successful career.

Dakin (1994) found that in the private sector, numerous newspapers (for example, *Rabota dlia leas [Work for You]*, and *Priglashaem na rabotu [Invitation to Work]*) showed job listings and advertisements which listed one or the other sex as a requisite for the position, that is, positions that specify "men" are usually management positions, whereas those that request "girls" were typically for secretarial or assistant-type positions. In line with the more recent findings by Metcalfe and Afanassieva (2005b) appearance was often mentioned, and adverts also commonly specified age. Most positions sought a woman under 30 or 25, attractive, "without complexes", with a range of job qualifications (degree, foreign languages, and so on); also the suggestions that applicants wore a short skirt or that there would be a beauty competition involved in the application process have even appeared! Recruitment and selection advertisements in St Petersburg stated that women needed to have "long hair", wear "short skirts" and "wear makeup". In addition to specifying only "young pretty candidates preferably under 25 years of age", there was also a reluctance to employ women who were married (Metcalfe and Afanassieva, 2005b).

Despite the need for organizations to develop policies to show commitment to gender equality, a survey in 2004 revealed that Russian companies now seem the most likely in the world to have female managers. A report by the Grant Thornton consultancy stated that 89 percent of the Russian enterprises it interviewed in a survey of 6,900 businesses in 26 countries, had women in management. The Philippines were second with 85 percent and the US third with 75 percent. Despite these findings, only 42 percent of senior management posts in Russia were held by women. The figures probably reflect the resurgent economy and the high divorce rate, which has forced many women to provide for their families (Paton Walsh, 2004).

According to a study in 1997 by the Institute of Sociology in the Russian Academy of Science, women managers head or belong to the directorship of about 20 percent of businesses (Gvozdeva and Gerchikov 2002:56; see also Chirikova and Krichevaskai, 2002). Similar to western businesses, there was also found to be segregation in managerial roles. The study revealed that women accounted for about 54 percent of managers in the housing and social services sector, 5 percent in transport, 7 percent in construction and 11 percent in science.

Women Entrepreneurs

Gale and Polnareva (2004) described an increasingly positive picture with respect to female entrepreneurial activity in Russia, and more recent statistics would also support this view. Research sources suggest a sharp rise in women's self-employed statistics, thought to be intrinsically linked to the increase of unemployment and discrimination towards women, as a function of traditional gender roles. Research addressing entrepreneurship globally hypothesises that female entrepreneurship is more common in low/middle-income countries than in higher-income countries where male entrepreneurship is more common (GEM, 2006), and this is typically prevalent in Russia, where the rate of female entrepreneurs is believed to be one of the highest of low/middle-income countries.

There are important complexities in assessing female entrepreneurial activity in Russia. The high proportions of entrepreneurial activity in females are clustered in "early-stage entrepreneurship" as opposed to established successful businesses (GEM, 2006). It is believed that the prevalence rate of early career female entrepreneurship in Russia has a prevalence rate of 39.3 percent, compared to higher income countries such as Sweden, where the rate is much less at 2.3 percent. These recent statistics suggest a further rise in women's entrepreneurship, where earlier research specified that women as employers in Russia occupied 21 percent of the workforce in 1997 and rose to 30 percent in 1999 (Gale and Polnareva, 2004; Goskomat, 2000).

The Russian Federation (2002) publish case studies on their successful female entrepreneurs, where such women present an overview of their entrepreneurial activity and success, citing the types of industries they work in and their motivations and previous experiences. Core themes evident from these case studies include a high prevalence of higher education qualifications and experience in senior roles before leaving to set up independent enterprises. Common industries encompassed both small, medium and large enterprises in areas such as light manufacturing, food production and distribution, clothing and fashion, construction, music and entertainment, business support services for other women, and business consultancy (The Russian Federation, 2002).

Country Legislation and Initiatives Supporting Women in the Workforce

Women's labour market participation in the USSR has been amongst the highest in the world (Ashwin, 2002; Rzhanitsyna, 2000; Standing, 1994). Women's share in industrial and service employment was 24 percent in 1928, and 51 percent by the beginning of the 1990s. For agricultural employment women's share was 52 percent in 1939 and 45 percent by the end of the 1990s (Goskomstat, 1990). Women also had an increased role in the public sector, unlike in western countries (Metcalfe and Afanassieva, 2005b).

Whilst there is evidence of gender segregation in employment, with women primarily in the public sector fields such as health and education, women's representation in political administration and scientific disciplines was significant when compared with the West (Kay, 2001; Standing, 1994). However, a lack of attention to women's issues is seen in international employment constitutions. The Russian Federation, although signed up to the United National Confederation for the Elimination of Discrimination against Women (CEDAW) has not made any progress in advancing women and addressing employment issues. While a commitment to social policy reform is to be encouraged, employment advancements and real wages equivalent to men would help alleviate inequalities. The concept of gender mainstreaming is not commonly used within political discourse and the UN report (UN, 2000) made no mention or acknowledgement of it (Metcalfe and Afanassieva, 2005b). A study of public sector employees in the Moscow and Saratov region of Russia found that organizations needed to actively show commitment to gender equity within the workplace and direct and visible support for the advancement of women into executive position particularly in the public services (Antonova, 2002).

Some protective legislation has been in the past introduced, for example banning women from night work, overtime and from occupations which were deemed as detrimental to their health (Ilic, 1995). This protection of female workers often fluctuated, particularly in times of greater demand and in such circumstances the legislation was often relaxed. During the New Economic Policy (NEP), for instance, employment restrictions in relation to overtime and underground work were enforced, however these restrictions were abandoned in 1940 when the need for female labour was greater (Dewar, 1956). Therefore, legislation which was initially introduced to protect mothers was often transitory and would be changed in light of the current situation. In addition, the redistribution of women to certain industry sectors was in fact introduced to adapt to changing economic circumstances. For example, women's movement from industrial work to the service sector was seen as *"economically and socially justifiable"* (Boginya and Bon, 1988:19). However, the transfer of women from industry was not necessarily based on protecting women from heavy work, rather it suited the plan to reduce the labour force in the industrial sector. This is particularly evident when considering the work within the service sector which is often just as heavy as work within the industrial, sector, for example sales women are often required to lift heavy boxes and so on (Boldyreva, 1989).

Protective legislation also had a severe negative impact for some women. Legislation often resulted in women being excluded from skilled jobs, in particular when legislation was attempting to "protect" women from the dangers of mechanization (Filtzer, 1992). Protective legislation forced managers to provide childcare facilities, paid maternity leave, time off when children were sick and so on. However, it was believed that instead of providing women with benefits and privileges as the State claimed, they were instead categorizing women as weaker and a second class group of workers who needed this protection (Harden, 2002).

Human Rights Watch has concluded that gender-specific protective legislation were in fact discriminatory and could make it impossible for Russian women to compete for work on an equal basis. Therefore such legislation can be seen to be violating women's right to freedom from discrimination. Human Rights Watch also concluded that despite rhetoric regarding women and equality, the Russian Government had failed to enforce any of the existing sex discrimination laws (Dakin, 1994).

Metcalfe and Afanassieva (2005 a;b) provide some practical proposals to assist in the development of gender-sensitive employment and organizational policy. The following are a list of equal opportunity initiatives that these authors propose could be promoted by government administration and employee organizations:

- CEE could further encourage entrepreneurial training and development for women (see Wirth, 2001; Dickens, 1998).

- Training and education opportunities could be encouraged especially in relation to computing and ICT development (Jalusic and Antic, 2000).

- Employer and employee organizations and professional bodies could devise partnerships with UN agencies to help devise managerial strategy and development programmes.

- Evaluation of Central and Eastern European (CEE) human resources policies in organizations needs to incorporate diversity and equal opportunity priorities.

- The significance of gender audits has been strongly promoted by EU administration and can be encouraged by CEE and new member states. In the UK, the former Equal Opportunities Commission (now part of EHRC) supported gender and equal opportunity audits and frameworks and this policy framework could be benchmark within CEE Government administration (See Ely and Meyerson, 2000; Walby 1999).

The Future

It is evident that post-1989 female and male unemployment was low and the difference between the two rates was not significant. However, when examining the employment practices of men and women in Russia, it is clear that there are differences, for example, women tend to be concentrated in certain occupations, for example office clerks and public sector services. These occupations tend to demand lower wages in comparison to the more technical roles which tend to be dominated by men. The picture for female entrepreneurs, however, is positive and suggests an empowerment of women in self-employment. Today, Russian women are more likely to want to work, however they often feel that they do not have the appropriate skills or qualities to find work in the current climate. This is a surprising finding considering that women tend to be educated to the same level as men, and in some areas, their education attainment surpasses their male counterparts (for example: secondary, vocational qualifications). It appears this educational achievement does not have a positive impact on women's careers.

The protective legislation which superficially was implemented to protect women from discriminatory practices has often been shown to do the opposite of what it is trying to achieve. Protective legislation often limits women's careers and appears to be based on current situations with legislation changes occurring when it is felt needed, therefore not providing legislation which portrays a clear and consistent message to individuals, organizations and society. In addition, it is often felt that the legislation which is supposedly implemented to protect women, has simply been adopted because of the change in the economic situation.

Women managers in Russia appear to be making the transformation in the new Soviet State, however the concentration appears to be on emphasizing their differences in terms of showing their femininity and performing a feminine work identity which appears to provide women with confidence and assurance that they can be successful. Afanassieva (2005b) showed that women themselves viewed their role as managers as being second place to their husbands' position and specified how it was important for them to ensure that they looked and acted feminine in the workplace in order to ensure a successful career. Moreover, women managers do not appear to have the social capital and networks which men have access to. This will continue if women do not feel that they have the necessary skills to enter employment and if women, particularly those with high educational attainment, are not reaching top positions, this will result in reduced opportunities for networking for women who do break through the glass ceiling.

References

Antonova, V. K. (2002) Women in public service in the Russian Federation: equal capability and unequal opportunity, *Review of Public and Personnel Administration*, 22(3), 216.

Ashwin, S. (2002) The influence of the Soviet gender order on employment behaviour in contemporary Russia, *Sociological Research*, 41(1), 27–37.

Boginya, D. P. and Bon, A. V. (1988) Sovershenstvovanie strukturi zhenskoi zanyatosti – vazhnii faktor rosta effektivnosti truda. In Harden, J. (2002) Beyond the dual burden: Theorizing gender inequality in Soviet Russia, *Critique*, 30(1), 43–68.

Boldyreva, T. (1989) You won't stop the revolutionary horse in its tracks, *Soviet Sociology*, 2, 102–118 .

Chirikova, A. E. and Krichevaskai, O. N. (2002) The woman manager, *Sociological Research*, 41(1), 38–54.

Coutat, C. (2008) Russian women take the lead in MBA studies, *Education, The St Petersburg Times*, 1410(74), 23 September.

Dakin, M, I. (1994) *Women and Employment Policy in Contemporary Russia,* Paper presented at the 1994 Annual Convention of the American Association for the Advancement of Slavic Studies.

Dewar, M. (1956) *Labour Policy in the USSR* (Oxford: Oxford University Press).

Dickens, L. (1998) What HRM means for gender equality, *Human Resource Management,* 8(1), 23–40.

Ely, R. and Meyerson, D. E. (2000) Theories of gender in organizations: a new approach to organizational analysis and change. In B. Staw and R. Sutton (eds) *Research in Organizational Behaviour* (New York, NY: JAI Press).

Federal State Statistics Service (2009) *Russia in Figures, Statistical Handbook: Official Publication* (Moscow, Russia: Federal State Statistics Service).

Filtzer, D. (1992) *Soviet Workers and De-Stalinisation: The Consolidation of the Modern System of Soviet Production Relations 1953–1964* (Cambridge: Cambridge University Press).

Gale, A. and Polnareva, L. (2004) Women in management in Russia. In M. J. Davidson and R. J. Burke (eds) *Women in Management Worldwide: Facts, Figures and Analysis* (Aldershot: Gower Publishing).

GEM (Global Entrepreuneurship Monitor) (2006). *Report on Women and Entrepreneurship.*

Goskomstat: Sate Statistical Committee, (2000) *Men and Women of Russia in 2000.*

Gvozdeva, E. S. and Gerchikov, V. L. (2002) Sketches for a portrait of women managers, *Sociological Research,* 41(1), 55–68.

Harden, J. (2002) Beyond the dual burden: Theorizing gender inequality in Soviet Russia, *Critique,* 30(1), 43–68.

Illic, M. (1995) Equal rights with restrictions: women, work and protective legislation in Russia. In S. Bridger (ed.) *Women in Post Communist Russia* (Interface 1) (Bradford: University of Bradford Press).

Jalusic, V. and Antic, M. (2000) *Prospects for Gender Equality Policies in central and eastern Europe, Social Consequences of Economic Transformation in East-Central Europe.* (Vienna: Institute for Human Sciences).

Kay, R. (2001) Liberation from emancipation? Changing discourses of women's employment in soviet and post-Soviet Russia, *Journal of Communist Studies and Transition Politics,* 18(1), 51–71.

Kiseleva, G. (1982) The position of women and demographic policy. In G. Lapidus (ed.) *Women, Work and the Family in the Soviet Union* (New York, NY: M. E. Sharpe).

Metcalfe, B. D. and Afanassieva, M. (2005a) The woman question? Gender and management in the Russian Federation, *Women in Management Review,* 20(6), 429–445.

Metcalfe, B. D. and Afanassieva, M. (2005b) Gender, work, and equal opportunities in central and eastern Europe, *Women in Management Review*, 20(6), 397–411.

Paton Walsh, N. (2004) Russia tops the table for women managers, *Guardian*, 23 February.

Rubchak, M. J. (2001) In search of a model: evolution of feminist consciousness in Ukraine and Russia, *European Journal of Women's Studies*, 8(2),149–160.

Rzhanitsyna, L. (2000) Working women in Russia at the end of the 90s, *Problems of Economic Transition*, 43(7), 68–86.

Standing, G. (1994) The changing patterns of women in Russian industry, *World Development*, 22(2), 271–84.

The Russian Federation (2002) *Female Entrepreneurs in Russia: Case Studies*, http://www.unece.org/operact/gallery/ru/ru-gal.htm.

United Nations (2000) *Convention on the Elimination of Discrimination Against Women*, Russian Federation, Fifth Periodic Report. (Washington, DC: UN).

United Nations (2005) *Gender Equality and Extension of Women Rights in Russia in the Context of UN the Millennium Development Goals*, http://www.undp.ru/Gender_MDG_eng.pdf.

US Census Bureau (2002) *Statistical Abstract of the United States: 2001* (Washington DC: US Government Printing Office).

Walby, S. (1999) The European union and equal opportunity policies, *European Societies*, 1(1), 59–80.

Wirth, L. (2001) *Shattering the Glass Ceiling* (Geneva: ILO).

PART III

Women in Management – North and Central America

10

Women in Management in Canada

Golchehreh Sohrab, Rekha Karambayya and Ronald J. Burke

Introduction

In this chapter we revisit the status of women in management in Canada to take stock of changes in women's participation in the workplace and recent initiatives on the part of employers to improve the roles and retention of women in managerial ranks. Although our primary interest is in the experience of women in management, we offer some national data on employment, education and income differences among men and women in Canada.

While labour force participation in Canada has remained relatively stable at 67.5 percent since 2004, the rate for men has dropped marginally to 72.7 percent and that for women has risen marginally to 62.8 percent (Statistics Canada, 2008a). Women made significant inroads into employment in the 1970s and 1980s, experienced some declines during the recession of the early 1990s and then achieved some marginal increases again after the turn of the century. Yet some occupational patterns seem to persist, such as the concentration of women in occupations such as teaching, health care and service sectors while some gains have been made in business, medicine and law (Statistics Canada, 2008f).

While women have made significant gains in terms of labour force participation, those gains have not always translated into inroads at the most senior levels of management. Among managers, women appear to be better represented at lower levels, accounting for only 26 percent of senior managers compared to 37 percent of managers at other levels (Statistics Canada, 2006).

We begin with a reflection on the status of women in the Canadian labour force, their representation in educational institutions and in managerial ranks. We then outline changes in the context of women's employment including a discussion of organizational and research initiatives directed at women in the workplace. Finally we conclude with some speculations on what the future might hold for women in management in Canada through an exploration of the challenges that remain and the initiatives that might hold the most promise for the advancement and retention of women.

Labour Force Characteristics

Table 10.1 summarizes Canadian labour force statistics during the last decade. Between 1998 and 2008, women's participation rate increased from 58.4 percent to 62.8 percent and their employment rate increased from 53.7 percent to 59.3 percent. In 2008, women formed 47.1 percent of the labour force, compared to 45.6 percent in 1998 (Statistics Canada, 2008a). Despite these positive trends, women still lag behind men both in participation rate and employment rate roughly by 10 percentage points. In addition, women still demonstrate somewhat traditional patterns in employment including their involvement in part-time work and concentration in lower-paying occupational sectors.

Compared to men, women are disproportionately represented in the part-time workforce, including part-time, contract and non-standard work arrangements. Overall, about 40 percent of working women are involved in part-time or non-standard work compared to less than 30 percent of men. That said, the gap between women's and men's rate of part-time employment has narrowed during the past few decades. Women's part-time employment rate declined from 28.6 percent in 1998 to 26.4 percent in 2008, while the rate for men increased from 10.5 percent to 11.2 percent in the same period (see Table 10.1).

Table 10.1   Labour force statistics (%), 1998–2008

	1998	1999	2000	2001	2002	2003	2004	2005	2006	2007	2008
Participation rate (%)											
Women	58.4	58.9	59.4	59.7	60.9	61.9	62	61.8	62.1	62.7	62.8
Men	72.1	72.4	72.4	72.3	73	73.4	73.2	72.8	72.5	72.7	72.9
Employment rate (%)											
Women	53.7	54.6	55.4	55.6	56.6	57.4	57.8	57.8	58.3	59.1	59.3
Men	65.9	66.7	67.3	66.8	67.1	67.6	67.8	67.7	67.7	68	68.1
Unemployment rate (%)											
Women	8	7.3	6.7	6.9	7.1	7.2	6.9	6.5	6.1	5.6	5.7
Men	8.5	7.8	6.9	7.5	8.1	7.9	7.5	7	6.5	6.4	6.6
Part time to total (%)											
Women	28.6	27.9	27.2	27	27.7	27.9	27.2	26.8	26.1	26.1	26.4
Men	10.5	10.3	10.3	10.5	11	11.1	10.9	10.8	10.8	11	11.2
Women in the labour force (%)											
	45.6	45.7	45.9	46	46.3	46.5	46.6	46.7	46.9	47.1	47.1

Source: Statistics Canada, 2008a

When examining the gender gaps in terms of pay, in 2006, Canadian women earned, on average, 64.7 cents for every dollar that men earned. Figure 10.1 shows the female to male earning ratio during the past 40 years, demonstrating that although the earning gap has narrowed, the rate of change has significantly decreased (Statistics Canada, 2008b). The earning ratios demonstrate that the earning gap for those working full time and full year is much narrower. In 2006, the female to male earning ratio for those working full time and full year was 71.9 percent, somewhat higher than that for all employees. Comparison of hourly wage rates suggests an even more positive picture. In 2008, the hourly wage rate for women who were working temporarily was .92 of men's hourly wage rate. In the same year, the female to male hourly wage rate ratio for those who were working permanently was .83 (Statistics Canada, 2008b).

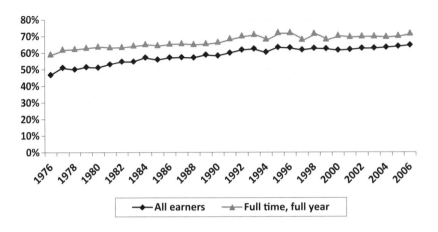

Figure 10.1   Female to male earning ratio, 1976–2006
Source: Statistics Canada, 2008b

One factor that may explain part of the discrepancy between average earning ratio and hourly wage ratio is the hours an individual works during the week. Statistics Canada (2008c) reports show that in 2008, men on average, worked 35.9 hours per week while women worked 29 hours per week. Similar differences exist between self-employed men and women. While self-employed men on average worked 39.5 hours per week, self-employed women worked 29.5 hours per week (Statistics Canada, 2008c).

Women Pursuing Education

In the academic year 2006/2007, 57.8 percent of university students were women, a proportion that has remained almost steady since 2001 (Statistics Canada, 2009). Although women account for large numbers of university graduates, their representation among those with a degree declines at postgraduate levels. In 2006, women formed 58.49 percent of registered undergraduate students. This ratio decreases to 54.44 percent at master's level and 46.32 percent at doctorate level (Statistics Canada, 2008d).

It is of interest to note that women's participation in business studies shows an unusual pattern. The percentage of female students at undergraduate level shows a gradual growth from 1992 (54.35 percent) until 2001 (57.76 percent. However, after 2001, women's presence at undergraduate level shows a gradual decline, with 53.58 percent in 2006. At the graduate level, however, women's enrolment in business studies has gradually increased during the past 15 years. In 2006, 45.14 percent (compared to 40.77 percent in 1992) of master's students were women and 46.25 percent (compared to 32.88 percent in 1992) of doctorate degrees were earned by women (Statistics Canada, 2008d).

While the number of women in professional programmes such as law and medicine has risen gradually over the past two decades, the percentage of women in MBA programs appears to be stalled at about 30 percent on average. Women earned 35.3 percent of all MBAs (Catalyst, 2009a) in 2007–2008 and they made up 30.8 percent of MBA classes in the top five Canadian business schools in 2008 (Financial Times, 2009a), up from 29.8 percent in 2007 (Financial Times, 2008).

Women in Management

This section is organized based on the Catalyst[1] pyramid illustrated in Figure 10.2 (Catalyst, 2009c). We first discuss women in managerial occupations, followed by women corporate officers and board directors. Then, we briefly mention women's standing among top earners and organization heads.

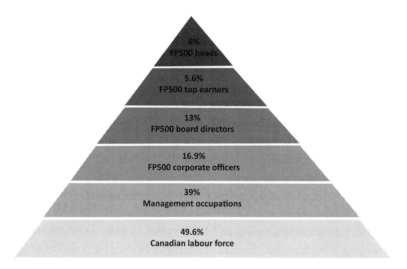

Figure 10.2   The Catalyst pyramid
Source: Catalyst, 2009c

---

1   Founded in 1962, Catalyst is the leading non-profit membership organization working globally with businesses and the professions to build inclusive workplaces and expand opportunities for women and business. With offices in the United States, Canada and Europe, Catalyst is the trusted resource for research, information and advice about women at work.

Representation of women in managerial positions has grown very slowly during the past two decades. In 1987 women held 30.62 percent of total managerial positions. Women's share of managerial positions steadily grew up to 38.43 percent in 1998, and then dropped to 35.09 percent in 1999. Since then, women's representation in managerial occupations has grown very slowly to 36.04 percent in 2008 (Statistics Canada, 2008f). While the popular press has pointed to a tendency among managerial women to "opt out" of promising careers, it is not clear that we have begun to truly understand the complexities of the phenomenon.

In general, visible minorities make up 15.4 percent of the labour force and 11.2 percent of the management occupations. Visible minority women make up 47.9 percent of the visible minority labour force and 35.3 percent of visible minorities in management occupations (Catalyst, 2008).

Corporate officers are those with day-to-day responsibility for corporate operations and the power to legally bind their companies. Since 1999, Catalyst has tracked the representation of women corporate officers among FP500 (Financial Posts ranking of top 500 largest Canadian businesses) companies in Canada. In 2008, 16.9 percent of corporate officers in FP500 companies were women. This represents an increase of 1.8 percent since 2006 and 2.9 percent since 2002 (Jenner and Ferguson, 2009). The percentage of FP500 companies with multiple women corporate officers increased from 39.4 percent in 2006 to 44.9 percent in 2008, while the percentage of companies with no woman corporate officer decreased from 34.0 percent in 2006 to 32.0 percent. Yet, one-third of Canada's largest companies still have no woman corporate officer (Jenner and Ferguson, 2009). Although the proportion of women among FP500 corporate officers shows a relatively large growth during the past two years, the representation of women in corporate officer positions (16.9 percent) is still much lower than their participation in the labour force (47.1 percent) and their representation in managerial positions (36.4 percent) (Statistics Canada, 2008e).

WOMEN ON BOARDS OF DIRECTORS

Catalyst's (Jenner, Dyer and Whitham, 2008) most recent report on women on boards of directors of FP500 companies shows that women hold only 13 percent of all FP500 board seats in Canada (see Figure 10.3). This report shows that, in 2007, 43.2 percent of the FP500 companies had no women board directors and 28.2 percent had only one woman on their board of directors (Jenner, Dyer and Whitham, 2008).

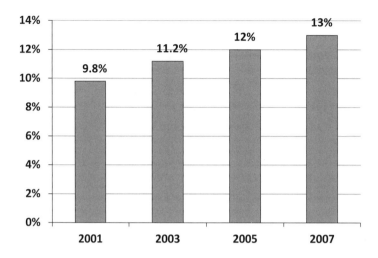

Figure 10.3   Percentage of women on FP500 boards of directors
Source: Jenner, Dyer and Whitham, 2008

We summarize the data on women on corporate boards in terms of some bad news and some good news. First the bad news:

* slow progress of women to executive ranks;

* slow increase in women on corporate boards;

* no government monitoring and intervention.

Now the good news:

* heightened interest and glaring failures in governance;

* some educational offerings for directors, with lots of women graduates;

* an increasing pool of "board-ready" women.

In 2008, 6.0 percent (N=30) of FP500 companies were headed by a female CEO or president, up from 4.2 percent in 2006 and 2.8 percent in 2002 (see Figure 10.4). In this year, only 5.6 percent (58 out of 1,044) of top earners in FP500 companies were women, up from 3.9 percent in 2002 (44 out of 1,128) (Jenner and Ferguson, 2009).

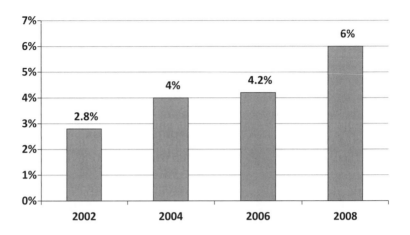

Figure 10.4   Percentage of women heading FP500 companies
Source: Jenner and Ferguson, 2009

Women Entrepreneurs

In 2009, over one in ten employed women were self-employed (11.51 percent), representing 34.66 percent of all self-employed individuals in Canada. While historically, there have always been more self-employed men, over the past three decades, the *number* of self-employed women has increased at a faster rate than men; showing 212 percent increase (versus 109 percent for men) between 1976 and 2009 (Statistics Canada, 2008g). The roots of this pattern may reflect the fact that the number of women in the labour force has grown almost 118 percent, while the number of men in the labour force has only grown 47.4 percent.

Figure 10.5 highlights that the general trend in self-employment during the past three decades has been very similar among men and women (Statistics Canada, 2008h). However, after the IT crash in 2000, the percentage of self-employed women has stayed stagnant (only 0.51 percent growth) compared to 5.3 percent growth in the percentage of self-employed men to all employed men (Statistics Canada, 2008h). This could reflect either a movement of women into more stable employment or a general reluctance among investors and institutions to support women entrepreneurs.

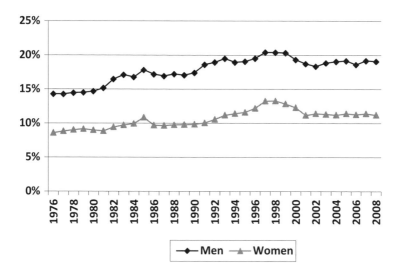

Figure 10.5   Percentage of self-employed to total employed, 1976–2008
Source: Statistics Canada, 2008h

Country Legislation

Canadian legislation to support women in the workplace is enshrined at the constitutional, federal and provincial levels. Federal employment and labour laws, such as the Canada Labour Code (1965) and the Canadian Human Rights Act (1977) cover less than 10 percent of the Canadian workforce. Provincial laws, which cover the majority of the Canadian workforce, include employment standards legislation, labour relations legislation, health and safety legislation, workers' compensation and human rights legislation.

Although there has been no new legislation enacted in the last five years, there is some emerging evidence that provincial and federal governments have cut funding to initiatives intended to enforce legislation and made it more difficult to qualify for benefits such as unemployment insurance or file pay equity claims (Klie, 2009).

Initiatives Supporting Women in the Workforce

In this section, we provide an overview of organizational initiatives intended to support women's career advancement based on three pillars: empowering women, developing unbiased procedures, and building inclusive environments.

Many organizations have introduced initiatives focusing on empowering women and helping them develop the skills and resources necessary for career advancement. Mentoring and networking opportunities for women are two of the most popular strategies in this category. Providing women with access to relevant training and development is another strategy Canadian organizations use to empower women. For example, Blake, Cassels and Graydon LLP, a law firm in Toronto, partners with the Rotman School of Management to develop career development programmes for its senior women employees (Canada's Best Diversity Employers, 2009).

The second group of initiatives targets top managers to ensure that the recruitment, selection and performance evaluation systems and procedures are unbiased. For example, senior employees in HSBC Bank Canada receive training on how to develop talented employees from diverse groups. BMO, taking the initiatives one step further, holds executives accountable for the progress of diversity goals by including a diversity scorecard in the bank's performance assessments (Canada's Best Diversity Employers, 2009).

Canadian businesses have initiated various programmes and policies in order to create inclusive workplaces that are attractive to and supportive of women. While some organizations develop flexible work arrangements or on-site childcare programmes to help women address the conflicting demands of their life and work, others try to educate all employees on the importance of diversity and inclusiveness. In 2007, Ernst and Young launched a campaign to communicate their inclusiveness philosophy and goals to all employees. Their brochure entitled "Inclusiveness Matters", described the firm's commitment to inclusiveness in the workplace and its importance to their overall company goals (Canada's Best Diversity Employers, 2009).

There are a number of initiatives currently being undertaken in Canada that give recognition to managerial women, and keep the issues of women's progress front and centre. These include:

- The Women of Influence luncheon series held in several large Canadian cities which features successful women as speakers and permits networking.

- An annual listing and profile of Canada's Most Powerful Women.

- The Ivey School of Business at the University of Western Ontario has developed a seven-day intensive programme to help women with five to ten years of management experience who have been out of the workforce for at least two years plan for their re-entry into the work world.

- The Rotman School of Business at the University of Toronto, through their Judy Programme, offers short courses to assist managerial and professional women with their careers.

RESEARCH INITIATIVES

Although our search of the academic literature suggests that the pace of Canadian research on women in management has slowed somewhat, there are some interesting research initiatives that deserve attention. Although attitudes and behaviours around gender roles at work and in the family are changing in Canadian society, family roles are still placing an unfair burden on women. Some research shows that gender differences still exist such that women disproportionately experience work–family conflict (McElwain, Korabik and Rosin, 2005). Further, co-workers' support and resentment play a major role in the experience of and reactions to work–family conflict (Korabik et al., 2007).

Within organizations, attempts to integrate work and family through reduced workload arrangements do not seem to have the stigma or the career limiting consequences they once did (Friede et al., 2008). However, an overwhelming majority of those taking advantage of such arrangements are married women who report choosing a reduced workload primarily because of their commitment to family (Dean Lee and Kossek, 2005).

Nonetheless, other challenges exist in the workplace. For example, Berdahl (2007) found that women in male-dominated environments were sexually harassed more than those in female-dominated environments and that women who were assertive, dominant and independent were harassed most of all.

Other research is suggesting that gender differences may not provide as much explanatory power as we might think. Zikic, Burke and Fiksenbaum (2008) found that men and women experienced the job loss and re-employment process in very similar ways, although men were more likely to use networking in their job search process, perhaps reflecting their more extensive networks. In addition, Burke and Fiksenbaum (2009) found that women were only slightly less likely to be employed in "extreme jobs" requiring long working hours, but those that did were more likely to be younger, and less likely to be married or have children than men in extreme jobs.

Summing up, there appear to be two research directions; the first reflects somewhat traditional research that assumes gendered roles and focuses on adaptations to them, while the second examines explanations that go beyond gender differences to explore the dynamics of women's engagement in work and its consequences for their professional and personal lives.

The Future

Looking at women in the workplace across comparable nations, it appears that while Australia, Canada and the US show very similar population gender splits at around 50 percent, Canada has higher female labour force participation at 46.9 percent compared to 45.3 percent for Australia, and 46.4 percent for the US (Catalyst, 2009b). However, the composition of women in managerial ranks and professional specialty positions shows a reversal of those rankings, with the US at 50.6 percent, Australia at 45.5 percent and Canada at 39 percent. Canada with 16.9 percent of female corporate officers and professional positions is squarely in the middle between the US at 25.3 percent, and Australia at 10.7 percent (Catalyst, 2009b).

In the workplace, women still earn, at best, 72 percent of the income earned by men. According to the Global Gender Gap Report (2007), Canada is ranked thirty-eighth among nations on wage equality between the sexes. Almost two-thirds of employed women are still concentrated in relatively low-paying sectors, such as nursing, teaching, administrative and retail sales (ACTEW, 2007). Clearly there is much work to be done here on income parity. Women are never going to make significant progress in the workplace or the family if we cannot explain or close that gender wage gap.

In terms of family roles, although there is evidence of some change, women still seem to bear the greater responsibility for child and elder care (ACTEW, 2007). Women's decisions about employment are often driven by family or marital pressures (ACTEW, 2007). One-third of working women return to work when their child is between six and 12 months old compared to 67 percent of men who return to work by the time their child is a month old (ACTEW, 2007). Also, women work an average of 4.3 hours a day of unpaid work while the comparative figure for men is a mere 2.5 hours (ACTEW, 2007). Some research (Beagan et al., 2008) suggests that women and their families often rationalize this gendered division of family roles in terms of women's availability, schedules, standards for family care and desire to reduce conflict. These unspoken, implicit assumptions about gender roles in the family might prove more challenging to address and change than more explicit social norms.

Employers have made concerted efforts to promote and support the advancement of women in the workplace, and we have now accomplished better access for women into workplaces and more opportunities for advancement. However, gendered perceptions about what it takes to succeed in management may have been rendered silent and relatively impervious to change much like those around family roles (Pletsch, 2008).

The role of government in promoting the interests of women in the workplace has not been exemplary in the last decade. While Canada's implementation of Employment Equity legislation and support of parental leaves had a significant impact on women's employment in the 1980s and 1990s, some recent changes have created a reversal of that impact. Despite differences across provinces in this regard, it is now generally much more difficult to qualify for unemployment benefits (Klie, 2009). Given women's precarious employment and career interruptions they tend to be disproportionately paying the price.

The Ontario Pay Equity had a remarkable impact during the first ten years of its existence; however lax enforcement seems to be contributing to the persistent gender wage gap. The Government has also stopped paying equity settlements to close pay gaps to women in public sector workplaces and by their own accounts will end up owing women $1.32 billion from 2008 to 2011 (Cornish, 2008).

It is possible that women will not suffer significant job losses during this recession (Klie, 2009) because the sectors that are experiencing the worst consequences, such as manufacturing and construction, tend to employ more men. However, women are also less likely to benefit from the federal government programmes that will pump about $8 billion into the economy over the next two years because most of that money is directed at infrastructure projects in construction and transportation (Klie, 2009).

We appear to be at a critical juncture on the road to women's equality in the workplace. We have managed to improve access to fair treatment in workplaces over the last 30 years. However, we have not managed to change perceptions about work and family roles or encourage women to enter sectors that were traditionally occupied by men. We are now faced with a set of paradoxes that hold women captive in a series of double binds. If roles in the home and family continue to be allocated based on the assumption that women will bear primary responsibility for the home and children, their work roles and advancement are likely to suffer. On the other hand, as long as women continue to earn less than men they cannot be considered the primary breadwinners in the family, and will continue to respond to family needs with adaptations in their work lives.

Future research and policy initiatives need to proceed in a couple of different directions. First, we need to begin to explore the causes and consequences of the enduring wage gap between men and women. Blau and Kahn (2007) in the US suggest that over 40 percent of this gap is explained by occupational and industry concentrations and about 10 percent by experience, leaving about 40 percent of the wage gap unexplained by labour market factors. That kind of research is important to begin to unpack the roots of the gender wage gap, and could encourage women to enter fields, such as information technology, that may be free from the traditional gender biases.

Second, if we acknowledge that women face a labyrinth (Eagly and Carli, 2007), rather than a glass ceiling, on their path to the top of organizations, we could begin to explore the nature and shape of the barriers that make up the labyrinth. Some of those barriers may exist in the workplace, such as restricted access to mentoring, and stereotypes about women's skills and abilities (Eagly and Carli, 2007; Jenner, Dyer and Whitman, 2008). Others may exist outside the workplace, in the family and the community, and have serious implications for women's involvement in work and motivation to invest in it.

Finally, there are a number of research questions that are particularly relevant in the current business and social context. In light of the large cohort of women managers who belong to the baby boom generation, it might be useful to focus some attention on how and why older managers make decisions about withdrawal from work. Emerging research from Australia (Shacklock, Brunetto and Nelson, 2009) suggests that gender differences may be at play here too. There are also unresolved questions about the impact of the current financial crisis on women in management. The popular press is suggesting that women managers, being more risk-averse and more focused on the long term, may be in a better position to weather the unpredictability of the financial markets (Financial Times, 2009b), but the research is not in evidence yet.

In conclusion, improving the lot of women in management may require concerted effort on three fronts: government, employers and the general population. Government will need to invest in education and make serious attempts to understand and close the wage gap. Employers seem to be doing their part by making some progress in addressing issues of access and treatment in the workplace. Individuals of both sexes need to understand and reflect on the dynamics of gendered roles and their impact on the work and family lives of women and men.

References

ACTEW (A Commitment to Training and Employment for Women) (2007) *Women in the Canadian Labour Market: Employment Facts*, http://www.actew. org/projects/pwpsite/snapshots/Cdn_women_labourmarket.pdf, accessed 30 March, 2009.

Beagan, B., Chapman, G. E., D'Sylva, A. and Bassett, B. R. (2008) 'It's just easier for me to do it': rationalizing the family division of foodwork, *Sociology*, 42(4), 653–671.

Berdahl, J. L. (2007) The sexual harrassment of uppity women, *Journal of Applied Psychology*, 92(2), 425–437.

Blau, F. D. and Kahn, L. M. (2007) The gender pay gap: have women gone as far as they can? *Academy of Management Perspectives*, 21(1), 7–23.

Burke, R. J. and Fiksenbaum, L. (2009) Are managerial women in "extreme jobs" disadvantaged? *Gender in Management: An International Journal*, 24(1), 5–13.

Canada's Best Diversity Employers (2009) *2009 Winners*, http://www. canadastop100.com/diversity/, accessed 29 April, 2009.

Catalyst (2008) *Visible Minorities*, http://www.catalyst.org/publication/243/ visible-minorities, accessed 2 April, 2009.

Catalyst (2009a) *Women MBAs*, http://www.catalyst.org/publication/250/ women-mbas, accessed 8 March, 2011.

Catalyst (2009b) *Australia, Canada, South Africa, & United States*, http://www. catalyst.org/publication/239/australia-canada-south-africa-united-states, accessed 23 April, 2009.

Catalyst (2009c) *Canadian Women in Business*, http://www.catalyst.org/ publication/198/canadian-women-in-business, accessed 23 April, 2009.

Cornish, M. (2008). Much work to be done on pay equity, *Canadian HR Reporter*, 21(4), February 25, p. 22.

Dean Lee, M. and Kossek, E. E. (2005) *Crafting Lives That Work: A Six-year Retrospective on Reduced-load Work in the Careers & Lives of Professionals & Managers*, http://www.polisci.msu.edu/kossek/final.pdf, accessed 11 March, 2011.

Eagly, A. H. and Carli, L. L. (2007) Women and the labyrinth of leadership, *Harvard Business Review*, 85(9), 63–71.

Financial Times (2008) *Global MBA Rankings 2008*, http://rankings.ft.com/businessschoolrankings/global-mba-rankings-2008, accessed 24 April, 2009.

Financial Times (2009a) *Global MBA Rankings 2009*, http://rankings.ft.com/businessschoolrankings/global-mba-rankings, accessed 24 April, 2009.

Financial Times (2009b) Why women managers shine in a downturn, 2 March, p. 15.

Friede, A., Kossek, E. E., Dean Lee, M. and Macdermid, S. (2008) Human resouce manager insights on creating and sustaining successful reduced-load work arrangements, *Human Resource Management*, 47(4), 702–727.

Jenner, L., Dyer, M. and Whitham, L. (2008) *2007 Catalyst Census of Women Board Directors of the FP500: Voices From the Boardroom*, http://www.catalyst.org/publication/261/2007-catalyst-census-of-women-board-directors-of-the-fp500-voices-from-the-boardroom, accessed 11 March, 2011.

Jenner, L. and Ferguson, R. (2009) *2008 Catalyst Census of Women Corporate Officers and Top Earners of the FP500 Catalyst*, http://www.catalyst.org/publication/295/2008-catalyst-census-of-women-corporate-officers-and-top-earners-of-the-fp500, accessed 11 March, 2011.

Klie, S. (2009) Federal budget leaves women behind: Advocates, *Canadian HR Reporter*, 22(4), 23 February, p. 1.

Korabik, K., McElwain, A. K., Warner, M. and Lero, D. (2007) *The Impact of Coworker Support and Resentment on Work–family Conflict*, paper presented at the 2nd IESE Conference on Work and Family, Barcelona, Spain.

McElwain, A. K., Korabik, K. and Rosin, H. M. (2005) An examination of gender differences in work–family conflict, *Canadian Journal of Behavioral Science*, 34(7), 269–284.

Pletsch, A. (2008) The paternal cycle, *Canadian Business*, 81(10), 16 June, pp. 27–28.

Shacklock, K., Brunetto, Y. and Nelson, S. (2009) The difference variables that affect older males' and females' intentions to continue working, *Asia Pacific Journal of Human Resources*, 47(1), 79–101.

Statistics Canada (2006) *Women in Canada: Work Chapter Updates*, Statistics Canada Catalogue No. 89F0133XIE, accessed 24 April, 2009.

Statistics Canada (2008a) CANSIM Table 2820002 – Labour force survey estimates (LFS), by sex and detailed age group.

Statistics Canada (2008b) CANSIM Table 2020102 – Average female and male earnings, and female-to-male earnings ratio, by work activity, 2006 constant dollars, annually.

Statistics Canada (2008c) CANSIM Table 2820022 – Labour force survey estimates (LFS), by actual hours worked, class of worker, North American Industry Classification System (NAICS) and sex, annually.

Statistics Canada (2008d) CANSIM Table 4770013 – University enrolments, by registration status, program level, Classification of Instructional Programs, Primary Grouping (CIP_PG) and sex, annually.

Statistics Canada (2008e) CANSIM Table 2820008 – Labour force survey estimates (LFS), by North American Industry Classification System (NAICS), sex and age group, annually.

Statistics Canada (2008f) CANSIM Table 2820010: Labour force survey estimates (LFS), by National Occupational Classification for Statistics (NOC-S) and sex, annually.

Statistics Canada (2008g) CANSIM Table 2820011 – Labour force survey estimates (LFS), employment by class of worker, North American Industry Classification System (NAICS) and sex, monthly.

Statistics Canada (2008h) CANSIM Table 2820012 – Labour force survey estimates (LFS), employment by class of worker, North American Industry Classification System (NAICS) and sex, annually.

Statistics Canada (2009) University Enrolment, *The Daily*, 11 March, http://www.statcan.gc.ca/daily-quotidien/090311/dq090311a-eng.htm, accessed 24 April, 2009.

Zikic, J., Burke, R. J. and Fiksenbaum, L. (2008) Gender differences in involuntary job loss and the reemployment experience, *Gender in Management: An International Journal*, 23(4), 247–261.

11

Women in Management in Mexico

Gina Zabludovsky[1]

Introduction

The dramatic increase in the number of women working outside the home constitutes an unprecedented social change, one that has radically transformed societies over the past 30 years. The growing insertion of women is reflected in different areas of the economy, particularly in higher education, and in many professions. The following chapter analyzes women's participation in the Mexican labour force and the proportion of women holding leadership positions as managers, officers, members of boards of directors and entrepreneurs. Thus, as we shall observe, the active presence of women has become evident in every environment.

Labour Force Characteristics

The increased participation of Mexican women in the nation's labour force has been one of the fastest-paced changes taking place in Latin America, increasing from 20.6 percent in 1970 to 37.5 percent in 2008 in an economically active population of 39,633,842 in the latter year (16,465,017 women and 27,401,679 men). The aforementioned percentage is even higher in the urban areas of the country, where women comprise 40.8 percent (2008) of the total economically active population of 23,332,692. (INEGI, 2009b) As shown in Table 11.1, over the last 17 years, this percentage has been steadily increasing.

---

1 The author appreciates the work of Rosa Elvira/Cedillo as a research assistant for this article.

Table 11.1   Male and female labour force (urban areas), 1991–2008

Year	Men	Women	Total
1991	65.5%	34.5%	100.0%
1997	63.4%	36.6%	100.0%
2003	63.3%	36.7%	100.0%
2008	59.2%	40.8%	100.0%

Source: Developed by Gina Zabludovsky, data from INEGI, National Employment Survey, urban areas, National Employment Survey (1991–2000) and 2008 National Survey of Occupations and Employment

The majority of women (that is, 82.6 percent) work in the service sector compared to 65.8 percent of men (see Figures 11.1 and 11.2).

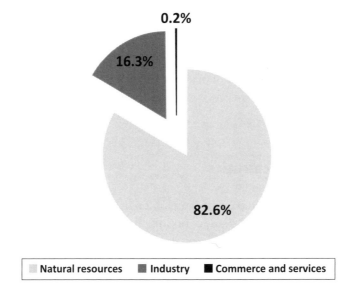

Figure 11.1   Women in the workforce, Mexico, 2008
Source: INEGI, National Employment Survey, Urban Areas, National Employment Survey (1991–2000) and 2008 National Survey of Occupations and Employment

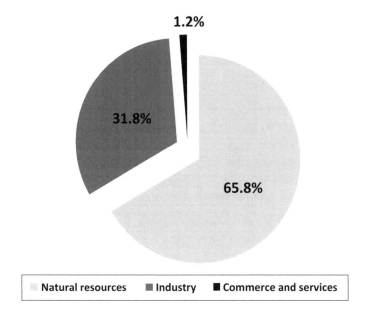

1.2%

31.8%

65.8%

Natural resources   ■ Industry   ■ Commerce and services

Figure 11.2   Men in the workforce, Mexico, 2008

Source: INEGI, National Employment Survey, Urban Areas, National Employment Survey (1991–2000) and 2008 National Survey of Occupations and Employment

Women have an especially important presence and outnumber men in such areas of business as social services (63.9 percent), hotels and restaurants (53.2 percent) and other services (51 percent). They also have a significant presence in commerce (47.8 percent). In contrast, females have an extremely low presence in traditionally masculine sectors, such as construction (5.4 percent) and agriculture and livestock (12.1 percent), as well as in mining (12.1 percent). (INEGI, 2009a) However, the percentage of females in the latter sectors has increased significantly in recent years (in 2000 women comprised only 5.9 percent of mine workers). The same holds true in the transportation and related services sector, where although women now comprise only 14.6 percent, this figure is significantly higher than in 2000, when women made up only 8.2 percent of the labour force in transportation and 12.6 percent in agriculture and livestock (see Figure 11.3) (INEGI, 2000).

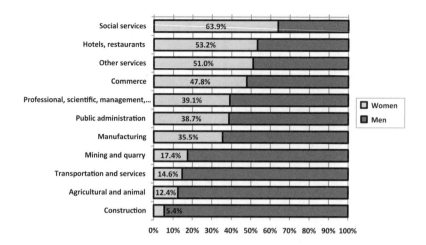

Figure 11.3   Male and female labour force by industry categories, Mexico, 2008
Source: Developed by Gina Zabludovsky, from INEGI 2008 National Survey of Occupations
and Employment, Strategic Indicators for Occupations and Employment, as of February 26,
2009,   at:http://www.inegi.org.mx/est/contenidos/espanol/sistemas/enoe/infoenoe/default.
aspx?c=8433

Despite women's growing presence in the labour force, it is interesting to note
the inequalities that appear when comparing the women's and men's earnings
(Zabludovsky, 2004). Figure 11.4 shows that regarding the total workforce earning
less than one minimum wage, the percentage of women reaches 65.1 percent,

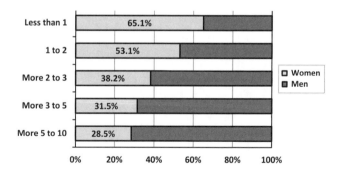

Figure 11.4   Male and female labour force in relation to salary, Mexico, 2008
Source: INEGI 2008 National Survey of Occupations and Employment, strategic
indicators of occupations and employment as of February 26, 2009, at http:www.inegi.
org.mx/est/contenidos/espano/sistemas/enoe/infoenoe/default.aspx?c=8433

while, in contrast, the percentage of women in the areas of the labour force earning over five times the minimum salary drops to 28.5 percent (INEGI, 2009a).

This difference between men's and women's income appears in all the 36 states comprising the Republic of Mexico, both in the nation's richest states, located in the north and thus closest to the United States, such as Baja California and Nuevo León, as well as in the poorer southern states, namely Oaxaca, Tlaxcala and Guerrero. (The exception is Chiapas, the poorest state in Mexico, where men and women earn the same and their income falls within the lowest wage category) (STPS, 2009a).

Women Pursuing Education

In the 1990s, the percentage of women enrolled in higher education in many countries began to exceed that of men (Avelar and Zabludovsky, 1996). In line with these international trends, the number of women enrolled in higher education in Mexico has grown significantly and at an accelerated pace (Zabludovsky, 2004; 2007).

According to national statistics, in 2007, the proportion of males and females among college graduates in major cities was 51 percent men and 49 percent women (ANUIES, 2009). If we view the percentage distribution in higher education by sex from 1970, significant changes can be observed. The student population in that year was 19 percent female, increasing to 30 percent in 1980, 40 percent in 1990, 46 percent in 1998 and 49 percent in 2007 (see Figure 11.5) (ANUIES, 2009).

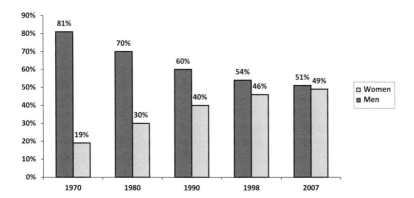

Figure 11.5   Men and women enrolled in higher education, 1970–2007
Source: Developed by Gina Zabludovsky, based on data from ANUIES Statistical Yearbooks, 1970–2007

Figure 11.6 illustrates that women's presence in universities tends to be higher in the fields of education and the liberal arts (67.8 percent women), health sciences (64.1 percent) and the social sciences and business administration (58.4 percent); in contrast to engineering and the technological sciences, where the percentage of female students is only 30.2 percent (ANUIES, 2009). In fact, the index of masculinization in engineering and technology is 230.9 percent, while the index of feminization in the liberal arts and education is 210.5 percent (ANUIES, 2009).

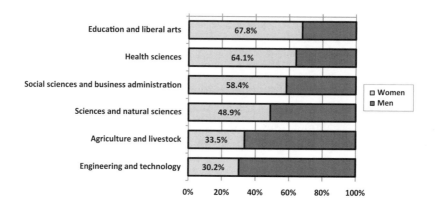

Figure 11.6   Percentage of women in universities, 2006–2007

Source: ANUIES 2006–2007 Statistical Yearbooks, May 2009, at : http://www.anuies.mx/servicios/e_education/index2.php'

When examining degree programmes which constitute the largest number of students in the country, based on data from 2004, women show a greater propensity for studying business administration, accounting and psychology, but continue to have low participation rates in the various fields of engineering (ANUIES, 2009).

If we look beyond strictly university degree programmes and consider the entirety of jobs in the country and the training programmes available at other types of facilities (such as hospitals, seminars, teacher training centres and other centers and institutions), it can be seen that the occupations where women predominate are nursing, training in special education, nutrition, psychology and education. In contrast, the fields with the fewest women are physics, veterinary and animal sciences and the various fields of engineering (ANUIES, 2009). This situation indicates that despite women's major advances in the professional spheres, most are involved in fields considered "appropiate" for women, where they are dedicated to educating and taking care of others.

Women in Management

As stated previously, females comprise an estimated 40.8 percent of the economically active population in the urban areas of Mexico as a whole. However, in the specific ranks of employment that the Census Bureau ranks as officers and directors in the public and private sectors, women's presence drops to 31.1 percent. The highest percentage of women officers is in the service industry (67.5 percent), followed by commerce (20 percent). In contrast, only 8.5 percent of women (as opposed to 14.5 percent of men) are in manufacturing and 2.3 percent in construction (STPS, 2009b).

Nevertheless, the 31.2 percent figure for female managers should not be taken at face value, since the pay levels for these echelons are not generally on a par with the salaries usually paid to executives. If we include only those officers paid over five times the minimum salary (the others could hardly be considered officers with any decision-making responsibility), the inequity becomes even more marked, since women's presence falls to 28 percent. This disparity becomes more evident the higher the position. Based on the authors own interpretation of a micro data sample from the National Employment Survey (INEGI, 2009b), it became apparent that the percentage of women officers and directors comprises only 15.5 percent of the top salary levels.

Furthermore, if one analyzes the data related to the top positions in the 500 largest companies in Mexico, among the eight highest positions comprising the general directorships of areas (general director or CEO, general directors of administration and finance, operations, marketing, commercial, computer systems, human resources and public relations), in 2005 women held only 13.4 percent of these posts (Expansion, 2005). There were only four women CEOs, which means that women did not even figure among the top one percent of positions.[2] However, women's presence in certain specific areas, such as directors of public relations, marketing and human resources has increased significantly as shown in Figure 11.7.

---

2   The major corporations in Mexico headed by women in 2006 were: Sam's Club (self-service and commerce sector, ranking 31 out of 500) headed by Simona Viztova; Federal District Subway System (ground transportation sector, rank: 269) headed by Florencia Serranía Soto; Softek (computer and services sector, rank: 332) headed by Blanca Treviño; and Zimag Logistics (logistics and transportation sector, rank: 472) headed by Ileanea Gómez.

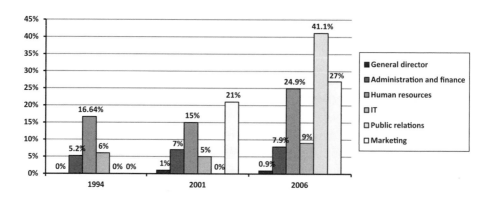

Figure 11.7   Percentage of executive positions where women's presence has increased, 1994–2006

Source: Developed by Gina Zabludovsky, data from *Expansion* magazine

These data indicate that, apart from the vertical segregation demonstrated by the larger number of women in the lower levels of the hierarchy, there is a high degree of horizontal segregation as well, related to women's presence as managers and directors, since women are concentrated in a restricted number of areas. Figure 11.7 shows that the largest incidence of women as general directors is in the public relations area. In fact, this directorship, which did not previously appear in companies' organization charts, now contains the largest percentage of women top executives, since women hold 41 percent of these positions. The second most important ranking of women in general director positions is in marketing (which has also been created recently) where the figure is 27 percent, followed by human resources with 24.9 percent. Outside these areas, the percentage of women directors falls drastically, as shown by the figures for computers and systems (8.6 percent), administration (7.9 percent), the commercial area (7.2 percent) and operations (5.1 percent). (Expansion, 2005)

Mexico is not unique as regards its profile of women directors. For example, based on figures for the directorships of the Fortune 500 list, comprised of the 500 largest companies in the US, the magazine has noted that there are ten times more women directors in human resources than in production. (Catalyst, 2008) Likewise, in Latin American countries the presence of women as CEOs and in production is almost non-existent, while, in contrast, they hold an important share in the commerce, sales, marketing, human resources, administration and finance areas (Maxfield et. al., 2008).

The exclusion of women executives from certain areas is much more significant from a strategic standpoint than what is evident by mere numbers, since it often means that women are barred from the positions that confer functional responsibilities and offer more opportunities for ascending the administrative hierarchy (Hola and Todaro, 1992; Kanter, 1993).

Women's segregation into certain occupations may be partially explained by differentiated socialization in early life that has a significant influence on the choice and practice of a profession and leads women to be inclined towards certain occupational areas, while rejecting others (Bauman, 1994; Elias and Scottson, 1965; Kanter, 1993; Simmel, 1998; Zabludovsky, 2005). Expectations for academic and non-academic education related to the different patterns of success for men and women in traditional contexts have influenced the fact that certain positions of authority and leadership are considered as prototypically masculine. Consequently, it is not at all far-fetched to assume that women themselves consider that some positions are not an option for them and therefore pursue job opportunities considered "more feminine" and limit their aspirations to holding less strategic positions.

However, apart from these general cultural patterns comprising a large portion of the differentiating axes of men's and women's "roles" in our society, there are also other factors in "corporate culture" where the distinct characteristics of "feminine" and masculine" are reproduced exponentially (Albrow, 1997; Burell and Hearn, 1989; Mills, 1989; Sheppard, 1989; Zabludovsky, 2003). Organizations tend to replicate aspects of their social context, while considering that their own corporate culture is neutral and objective, although in practice, it in fact corresponds to a masculine organization of power.[3]

As a result of assigning occupations based on gender, bureaucracies in the public and private sectors determine the distinct behaviours for men and women. Organizational life significantly contributes to the construct of what is "feminine" and what is "masculine" since the descriptions of job profiles for the different positions and ranks are based on presuppositions related to employees' general characteristics as determined by gender. These formal and informal practices are often not recognized but rather perceived as "natural" and consequently limit women's opportunities (Williams, 1995:8).

---

3   Because males are the sex that created art, industry, science, commerce, the State and religion, for centuries, women have been considered as "foreigners" or outsiders, as intruders with no right to belong to the various environments of economic, scientific, political and culture leadership. Concerning the social construct of "foreigners" the following sources may be consulted Elias and Scottson, 1965; Bauman, 1994; Kanter, 1993; Simmel, 1911/1998; Zabludovsky, 2005.

The absence of women in leading companies' most important directorship positions and their major presence in a limited number of areas can thus be explained by an organizational culture that exponentially reproduces the assignment of occupations in relation to social gender roles. This exclusion becomes more acute due to other features of corporate life, among which is the fact that the expected stance of unconditional loyalty to a company often means that officers can not set a limit to working hours and that, on the contrary, they must be available and totally dedicated around the clock. These values can hardly be accommodated to women's social responsibilities. In practice, women face enormous obstacles to fulfilling their different roles and striving to carry out their family and professional duties (Serna, 2001; Zabludovsky, 2001a; 2001b; 2007).

While the number of married male officers and directors in Mexico was 73 percent, the number of married women managers was only 48.7 percent and more women (that is, 7.7 percent) were divorced compared to 1.6 percent of men (INEGI, 2009b). As far as women on "corporate boards" are concerned, a review of the boards of directors of companies quoted on the Mexican Stock Exchange (Bolsa Mexicana de Valores, 2008) showed that females have a significantly lower presence on boards than in other leadership positions, with women representing only 6.6 percent of the total positions on boards of directors. Moreover, only one woman held the position of chairman of the board[4] and only four women were vice presidents (three of these women are active in the communications and transportation sectors). Despite women's extremely small presence at these levels, it does appear that their presence is gradually increasing as, in 2000, no woman was chairman of a board of directors, only one was a vice president and women held a total of only three other positions at this level (Bolsa Mexicana de Valores, 2008).

Another interesting fact to consider is that several members of the board were found to have the same last name. The companies with the largest percentage of women sitting on the board are family-owned companies. In this regard, it is interesting to note that, as the author has indicated in previous articles, the importance of women in family business in Mexico is not limited to the companies quoted on the stock exchange but includes all sizes of women-owned businesses (Grabinsky and Zabludovsky, 2001).

---

4   The person in question is Cynthia Grossman of Grupo Continental, one of the largest Coca-Cola bottling companies in the world.

Women Entrepreneurs

In addition to participating in the workforce as salaried employees, women in Mexico are also entering the ranks of remunerated work as independent owners of small businesses. Women of all ages and economic levels are running companies on their own, with their husbands or other relatives (Grabinsky, 1996; Grabinsky and Zabludovsky, 2001).

Concerning entrepreneurship, women represent 36.5 percent of the country's business owners (including own-account workers and employers) (INEGI 2000). This figure has increased in recent years, so that while in 1991, the percentage of women entrepreneurs was 25.3 percent, in 1995 it had reached 28.4 percent and rose to 36.5 percent in 2008 (see Table 11.2).

Table 11.2   Women employers and entrepreneurs, 2008

Percentage of employers	22.4%
Percentage of own-account workers	77.6%
Percentage of female entrepreneurs	36.5%

Source: Developed by Gina Zabludovsky based on INEGI, National Survey of Occupations and Employment 2008

However, due to the major differences between employers and own-account workers, for purposes of the different surveys we have conducted in the country, we considered women entrepreneurs to be comprised solely of those women business owners who are employers, meaning that they hire at least one employee apart from themselves. This definition coincides with that adopted in Mexico's statistical instruments and allows us to make adequate comparisons. Under this definition, women now comprise 19.7 percent of the total number of business owners, a percentage that has gradually increased in recent years, rising from 13.6 percent in 1991, to 15 percent in 1997, to 17 percent in 2000 and to 19.7 percent in 2008.

Women entrepreneurs in Mexico are particularly important as the owners and directors of micro-businesses, the size that accounts for the largest number of businesses operating in Mexico. According to national statistics, women comprise 20.9 percent of employers with two to five employees and only 5.4 percent of those with over 51 employees (see Table 11.3).

Table 11.3   Percentage of employers by number of employees and gender, ENOE 2008

Employees	Women	Men	Total
From 2 to 5	20.9%	79.1%	100.0%
From 6 to 10	16.3%	83.7%	100.0%
From 11 to 50	15.2%	84.8%	100.0%
51 and over	5.4%	94.6%	100.0%
Total	19.7%	80.3%	100.0%

Source: Developed by Gina Zabludovsky based on INEGI National Survey of Occupations and Employment, 2008

In this respect, it is important to stress that the small number of employees is not due to the fact that companies are highly sophisticated enterprises where technology has replaced the number of employees. On the contrary, these establishments tend to be very simple operations, as shown by the number of minimum salaries comprising the women's pay. Table 11.4 shows how the percentage of women employers decreases as salaries increase.

Table 11.4   Percentage of employers by income level and gender, ENOE 2008

No. of Minimum Salaries	Women	Men	Total
Up to 1	36.3%	63.7%	100.0%
Over 1 up to 2	35.6%	64.4%	100.0%
Over 2 up to 3	27.0%	73.0%	100.0%
Over 3 and Up	16.5%	83.5%	100.0%
No Income Paid	100.0%	0.0%	100.0%
Total	19.7%	80.3%	100.0%

Source: Developed by Gina Zabludovsky based on INEGI, National Survey of Occupations and Employment 2008

Concerning the different sectors of activity, the percentage of women entrepreneurs shows sharp variations depending on the type of business. Most women entrepreneurs are involved in commerce and services (41.5 percent and 44.5 percent of the total, respectively). These percentages coincide with the data from la *Red de Mujeres Empresarias* (Women Business Owners' Network), indicating that most are involved in services.[5]

However, recent data also show that women-owned businesses are becoming increasingly diversified, so that women's presence is no longer restricted to traditional sectors. There are many activities in which the percentage of women approaches 19.7 percent, which is their representation in the total number of businesses in the metropolitan areas (Zabludovsky, 2002). Currently, more women are involved in a wider variety of sectors, including such industrial activities as durable manufacturing, a field where very few women were active up to just a few years ago. If we consider the presence of women among the total number of employers in the country, we note that their presence in manufacturing has more than doubled, rising from 7.6 percent in 1995 to 18.4 percent in 2008 (INEGI, 2009b).

Country Legislation

With respect to the actions taken by the legislative branch, the Chamber of Deputies and the Senate have had their own Equality and Gender Commission in place since 1997. They also organized the "Women's Parliament" to give impetus to a national legislative agenda intended to contribute to eliminating all forms of discrimination against the female sex, promoting Government policies that fully ensure women's rights and the implementation of programmes to benefit them. Among the legislative results of these actions, various laws have been enacted and decrees implemented in line with the Beijing Action Plan and are centered especially on ways to prevent and prosecute acts of violence against women (PRONAM, 1999).

For several decades, no changes have been made to the chapter on women in the Federal Labor Law, so that the law now in effect continues to relate solely to matters of pregnancy, maternity and breastfeeding. These laws forbid companies to oblige women to carry out activities that could endanger their

---

5   The network of the Women Entrepreneurs Organization, founded in 2004, operates via the Internet (Empresarias Mexicanas network, http://200.94.94.228/empresarias/DefaultNoAuth. aspx).

health during pregnancy and require them to grant pregnant females a six-week leave prior to and another six-week leave after childbirth, as well as two extraordinary rest periods during the workday, while they are breastfeeding. In practice, to avoid granting these benefits, some companies have resorted to pregnancy tests as a requirement for hiring women, which has led to a growing number of protests and campaigns in the press by feminist associations and by the Government itself, stating that this procedure is a violation of women's human and labour rights.

Concerning women's presence in positions of authority and political power, in 2002 important changes were made to the Federal Electoral Code concerning gender, which now requires political parties to register a certain quota of women as candidates. This decree forbids registering over 70 percent of candidates from the same gender, which in practice means that a 30 percent minimum of women candidates is the now the norm (Cámara de Diputados, 2009b). This decision had a direct impact on the number of women in the nation's legislative chambers. While women comprised 16 percent of the members of the Chambers of Deputies and the Senate in the 2000–2003 period, by the 2003–2006 period, they comprised 23 percent of legislators.[6]

One of the most relevant recent laws is the General Law for the Equality of Men and Women (*Ley General para la Igualdad entre Mujeres y Hombres*, LGIMH) enacted in August 2006, intended to ensure fairness and non-discrimination based on gender and to propose institutional guidelines and procedures that ensure equality and promote the "empowering" of women. (Cámara de Diputados, 2009b). To achieve these objectives, the law proposes ensuring that budget planning should include a gender perspective, so as to encourage women's participation, achieve balanced political representation, promote equal access and women's full enjoyment of their social rights and strive towards the elimination of gender stereotypes. The National Women's Institute[7] is in charge of coordinating the programme derived from this law,

---

6 These percentages are similar to those in other Latin American countries and lower than those for Nordic countries, where women comprise up to 41 percent of the members of parliament. In contrast, the lowest percentages for women are in the Arab countries where women only comprise 9 percent of parliaments. WLCA, "Women's Leadership Conference of the Americas", *Women and Power in the Americas, A Report Card, Inter-American Dialogue*, Washington, 2001; United Nations Organization, Inter-Parliamentary Union of Women in Public Life, Geneva, Switzerland, 1999, pp. 24–25.

7 In 2001, the State programmes specifically addressed to women's issues achieved a new visibility in the Government agenda, when the National Institute of Women (INMUJERES) was created as an autonomous, decentralized public sector agency, with its own legal status and funding (INMUJERES 2002; PRONAM, 1999). The Institute has gained strength in recent years, because of the important role it was assigned by the Law for the Equality

while the National Commission of Human Rights is responsible for evaluating and monitoring the results.

The law stresses the importance for federal budgets to allocate specific funding to achieve its objectives and also promote cooperation initiatives and policies in the economic sphere and in decision-making processes, including some compensation measures, such as affirmative action in social, cultural and civic life. The law also prescribes that various authorities must take action to support parliamentary work from the gender viewpoint, create an awareness of the need to eliminate all forms of discrimination and ensure that every level of education operates within a framework of equality for men and women (Cámara de Diputados, 2009a).

Initiatives Supporting Women in the Workforce

Concerning the work to strengthen equity in economic matters, the law calls for the inclusion of a gender perspective in public policies intended to reduce poverty. To achieve these objectives, funds should be allocated to raise awareness and promote equality at work and in production processes to avoid segregation, promote equality in leadership and encourage access to work for people who are relegated to certain areas and levels based on their gender, especially with respect to directorship positions. Special programmes should be implemented, such as the incentives and certificates of equality to be granted yearly to those companies that have gender policies and practices in place (INMUJERES, 2007).

Concerning the pursuit of equal opportunities in the corporate world, in 2003, INMUJERES established a gender equity model *(Modelo de equidad de género MEG)*, as a means of acknowledging the implementation of equity policies in public and private sector organizations and of enforcing top management's

of Men and Women to act as the coordinator of the actions and programmes derived from that law.

commitment to eliminating discrimination against women and the unequal treatment given to them (INMUJERES, 2007). To promote these policies and attitudes, INMUJERES grants gender equity certification to those organizations that voluntarily elect to participate in and be evaluated on practices for promoting gender equity in the workplace. The award consists of a seal that may be affixed to the organization's products and used in its services and institutional image. By 2009, 132 organizations had been granted the gender equity seal, 93 of which were in the private sector and 39 in the public sector.[8]

As to the public sector programmes aimed at women business owners, the few existing Government programmes are specifically aimed at extremely small-sized businesses and are intended to reduce poverty levels. Within the Ministry of the Economy's sphere of influence, the two projects of this type are the Trust to Fund Micro-Financing to Rural Women (*Fideicomiso del Fondo de Microfinanciamiento de Mujeres Rurales*, FOMMUR) and the National Fund for Solidarity Enterprises (*Fondo Nacional de Empresas de Solidaridad*, FONAES). FOMMUR supports impoverished women by providing micro-funding for their production projects. FONAES, in turn, spurs job creation by encouraging the generation, implementation and consolidation of production projects related to commerce or services created by individuals, social organizations or groups in rural areas, among the indigenous population or low-income groups (*Directorio de Apoyos Institucionales* INMUJERES).

Meanwhile, women involved in small, medium and large enterprises have organized themselves on their own to create networks, form relationships and fight for their rights. Some of the most important associations of this type are the Mexican Association of Executive Women (*Asociación de Mujeres Ejecutivas*, AMME) and the Association of Women Business Owners (*Asociación de Mujeres Jefas de Empresa*, AMMJE). AMME groups women executives from all types of public or private companies, partnerships, institutions or associations to create and project the image of women managers in the professional, intellectual, cultural and social spheres. Its mission is to promote professional development and further the advancement of women executives to attain top management

---

8   In 2008, the Gender Equity Model seal was awarded to various public and private sector organizations, including: Addition Human Resources; American Express; State of Guerrero General Auditing Department; Best Day Travel; Chihuahua National Chamber of Commerce and Services; Campbell's de México; National Chamber of the Electronics, Telecommunications and Information Technology Industries; Casa Rufino; Chivagente; Chivas de Corazón; Combustibles de Oriente: Storage and Distribution Terminal, Corporate, Transportation; Federal Electricity Commission; Transmision Oriente Management; Puebla State Congress; State of Jalisco Controllership.

positions, while achieving a balance between their enjoying a high quality of life and fully achieving their professional objectives. AMME's objective is to bring women executives together and facilitate their access to directorship positions, create a fund for granting training scholarships, organize conferences and congresses and convey its viewpoint on women-related matters to all public and private institutions (AMME, 2009). Insofar as The Association of Women Business Owners or AMMJE is concerned, the Mexican chapter is part of a world association, *Femmes Chefs D'Entreprises Mondiales*, founded in France in 1946, which from the very beginning has encouraged and supported women's entrepreneurial activities in 42 countries.

Some of the association's objectives are: to promote the exchange of information and the sharing of experience and knowledge; contribute to the development of professional skills through conferences, seminars and workshops; expand communications and support networks; offer assessment on legal matters and promotional areas; create financial instruments and foster the development of its women business owner members. AMMJE has grown significantly in recent years, increasing from eight city chapters in 1998 to 36 at present, while the membership base of 400 in 1998 has risen to 4,000 in 2009 (AMMJE, 2009).

Also, since 1997, women's associations have been founded within important business chambers, such as the women's business chapters in the Employers Federation of Chambers of the Mexican Republic (*Confederación de Patronal de la República Mexicana*, COPARMEX) and the Women Industrialists of the National Chamber of the Transformation Industry (*Camara Nacional de la Industria de Transformación*, CANACINTRA). These entrepreneurial women's associations have held several national conferences in different Mexican cities. Moreover, by making use of new technologies, some women business organizations, supported by INMUJERES, created the National Network of Women Business Owners (*Red de Mujeres Empresarias*).

The Future

Over the past few years, women business owners and executives in Mexico have achieved an increasing visibility. The programmes implemented by INMUJERES and the organizations of women entrepreneurs and executives have helped create a greater awareness of the importance of providing equal opportunities for advancement to both men and women.

In addition, women have achieved extraordinary advances in higher education and are entering a wide range of working environments, including business administration. However, despite these major changes, women business owners have tended to be concentrated in smaller businesses, while in corporations, women directors solely hold positions linked to certain types of activities considered "feminine" which generally provide fewer opportunities for advancement. Moreover, the assumption still holds that the responsibility of running a home is considered to be primarily women's work, so that females must take on the burden of working the equivalent of double and triple shifts every day.

Therefore, it is important to give impetus to revamping the assignment of responsibilities at home and in marriage. Efforts should also be made to convince companies to support employees with paternity and maternity leave and an additional series of measures to generate greater awareness in corporations of the wealth that they can have at their disposal, by having a diversified workforce at every level, specifically in director positions in charge of certain areas. To change the still prevalent stereotypes in the workplace, it is important to question the traditional separation of "feminine" and "masculine" positions, furthering the placement of men in more positions in the "public relations" and "human resources" areas and offering women more opportunities for entering the directorships of production and other strategic positions.

References

Albrow, M. (1997) *Do Organizations Have Feelings?* (London: Blackwell).

ANUIES (2009) Anuarios Estadísticos 2004–2007. In: *Estadísticas de la Educación Superior [Higher Education Statistics]*, http://www.anuies.mx/servicios/e_educacion/index2.php, accessed 6 May, 2009.

AMME (Asociación de Mujeres Ejecutivas) (2009), http://www.amme.org.mx/tiendavirtual.cfm?ma68mtno=4012, accessed 9 June, 2009.

AMMJE (Asociación de Mujeres Jefas de Empresa) (2009) *Asociación Mexicana de Mujeres Empresarias, Asociación Civil [Mexican Association of Women Business Owners]*, http://www.ammjenacional.org/, accessed 9 June, 2009.

Avelar de, S. and Zabludovsky, G. (1996) Women's leadership and glass ceiling barriers in Brazil and Mexico. In A. M. Brasileiro (ed.) *Women's Leadership in a Changing World* (New York, NY: UNIFEM, pp. 31–41).

Bauman, Z. (1994) *Pensando Sociológicamente [Thinking Sociologically]* (Argentina: Nueva Visión).

Bolsa Mexicana de Valores (2008) *Annual Financial Facts and Figures* (Mexico: Bolsa Mexicana de Valores).

Burrell, G. Y. and Hean, J. (1989) The sexuality of organizations, In J. Hearn, D. L. Sheppard, Tancred, P. and Burrell. G. (eds) *The Sexuality of Organizations* (London: Sage Publications).

Cámara de Diputados (2009a) *Ley Federal del Trabajo [Federal Labour Law]*, http://www.ordenjuridico.gob.mx/Federal/Combo/L-130.pdf, accessed 9 June, 2009.

Cámara de Diputados (2009b) *Ley General para la Igualdad entre Mujeres y Hombres [General Equity Law for Women and Men]*, ,http://www.cddhcu.gob.mx/LeyesBiblio/pdf/LGIMH.pdf, accessed 9 June, 2009.

Catalyst (2008) *Catalyst Member Benchmarking Report*, http://www.catalyst.org/publication/279/2008-catalyst-member-benchmarking-report, accessed 1 March, 2009.

Elias, N. and Scottson, J. (1965) *The Established and the Outsiders* (London: Frank Cass).

EXPANSION (2005) *Las 500 de Expansión [The 500 Biggest Companies]*, http://www.cnnexpansion.com/especiales/las-500-de-expansion-2008/a-rio-revuelto, accessed 2 March, 2009.

Fielden, S., Davidson M., Gale, A. and Davey, C. (2001)Women, equality and construction. In R. Burke and D. Nelson (eds) *The Journal of Management Development, Developing Women as Managers* (Cambridge, MA: Emerald Library).

Grabinsky, S. (1996) Crisis in Mexico:Mexico in Crisis Its effects on the family-owned business, *Journal of Entrepreneurship Culture*, 4 (September), http://www.worldscinet.com/jec/jec.shtml, accessed 14 March, 2009.

Grabinsky S. and Zabludovsky G. (2001) *Mujeres, Empresas y Familias [Women: Business and Families]* (México: Del Verbo Emprender).

Hola, E. and Todaro R. (1992) *Los Mecanismos de Poder: Hombres y Mujeres en la Empresa Moderna [Power mechanisms between Men and Women in The Modern Enterprese]* (Santiago, Chile: Grupo Editor Latinoamericano).

INEGI (2000) *Encuesta Nacioal de Empleo [National Employment Survey]*.

INEGI (2008) *Consulta de Indicadores ENOE 2008 [Indicators Report]*, p. 1, México, DF, http://www.inegi.org.mx/est/contenidos/espanol/sistemas/enoe/infoenoe/default.aspx?c=8433, accessed 1 November, 2009.

INEGI (2009a) *Consulta de Microdatos de la ENOE 2005 — 2008 [ENOE'S Microdata]*, http://www.inegi.org.mx/est/contenidos/espanol/soc/sis/microdatos/enoe/default.aspx?s=est&c=14439, accessed 2 March, 2009.

INEGI (2009b) *Encuesta Nacional de Ocupación y Empleo 2008 [National Employment Survey]* (Mexico: Instituto Nacional de Estadística e Informática).

INMUJERES (2002) *Propuesta del Instituto Nacional de las mujers para incorporar la Perspectva de* Género en la Modernizacion de la Ley Laboral *[National Institute of Women's Propositions to incorporate a gender perspective for the modernization of Mexican Labor Laws]*, México, DF.

INMUJERES (2007) *Modelo de Equidad de Género MEG: 2003 [Gender Equity Model]* (Mexico: Instituto Nacional de las Mujeres).

Kanter, R. M. (1993) *Men and Women of the Corporations* (New York, NY: Basic Books).

Maxfield, S. Cárdenas, M. C. and Heller, L (2008) *Mujeres y Vida Corporativa en Latinoamérica, Retos y Dilemas [Women and Corporate Life in Latin America]* (Colombia: Universidad de los Andes-Facultad de Administración).

Mills, A.(1990), Gender, sexuality and organizations theory. In J. Hearn, D. L. Sheppard, Tancred, P. and Burrell. G. (eds) *The Sexuality of Organizations* (London: Sage Publications).

Parlamento de Mujeres (1998) *Parlamento de Mujeres de México [Mexican Women's Parliament]* (Mexico, 2000).

PRONAM (1999) *Alianza para la Igualdad, Informe de Avances de Ejecución [Equality Agreement, Advancement Report]* (Mexico: PRONAM).

Serna María Guadalupe. (2001) Empresarias y relaciones de género en dos ciudades de provincial. In Barrera Bassols, D. (comp.) *Empresarias y Ejecutivas, Mujeres con Poder [Women of Power: Entrepreneurs and Managers]* (Mexico: Colegio de Mexico).

Sheppard, D. (1990) Organizations, power and sexuality: the image and self-image of Women Managers. In J. Hearn, D. L. Sheppard, Tancred, P. and Burrell. G. (eds) *The Sexuality of Organizations* (London: Sage Publications).

Simmel, G. (1998) *Sobre la Aventura, Ensayos Filosóficos [On Adventure. Philosophical Essays]* (Barcelona: Península).

STPS (2009a) *Secretaría del Trabajo y Previsión Social, Subsecretaria de Empleo y Productividad Laboral, Información Laboral [Mexico's Labour Information]*, http://www.empleo.gob.mx/pdf/perfiles/perfil%20distrito%20federal.pdf, accessed 6 May, 2009.

STPS (2009b) *Secretaría del Trabajo y Previsión Social, Portal del Empleo, Información sobre empleo en México [Information about Employment in Mexico]*, www.empleo. gob.mx/wb/BANEM/BANE_que_carreras_ocupan_mas_profesionistas_/_ rid/1725/_mod/edit, accessed 6 May, 2009.

Williams, C. (1995) *Still a Man's World.* (Berkeley and Los Angeles, CA: University of California).

Zabludovsky, G. (1994) *Presencia de la Mujer Empresaria en México [Women Business Owners in Mexico]* (Mexico: Documento de Trabajo, CIDE).

Zabludovsky, G. in collaboration with NFWBO (1998) *Women Business Owners in Mexico, an Emerging Economic Force* (Mexico, DF: UNAM–IBM).

Zabludovsky, G. (2001) Women managers and diversity programs in Mexico. In R. J. Burke and D. L. Nelson (eds) *The Journal of Management Development, Developing Women in Management*, 20(4), (UK: MDC University Press).

Zabludovsky, G. (2001) Ejecutivas en México [Women Executives in Mexico] In G. Zabludovsky and Avelar (eds) *Empresarias y Ejecutivas en México y Brasil* (Mexico, DF: Miguel Ángel Porrúa/UNAM).

Zabludovsky, G. (2002) Trends in women's participation in Mexican Business, *Journal of Entrepreneurship and Innovation*.

Zabludovsky, G, (2003) Burocracia y comportamiento organizacional, de la jerarquía moderna a la sociedad-red *[Bureaucracy and Organitational Behavior. From Modern Hyerarchies to Net-Society]*. In M. Guitián and G. Zabludovsky (eds) *Sociología y Modernidad Tardía: Entre la Tradición y los Nuevos Retos [Sociology and Late Modernity: Between Tradition and the New Challenges]* (México: Juan Pablos/UNAM).

Zabludovsky, G. (2004) Women in management in Mexico. In M. J. Davidson and R. J. Burke (eds) *Women in Management Worldwide: Facts, Figure and Analysis* (Aldershot: Gower, pp. 179–194).

Zabludovsky, G. (2005) Zigmunt Barman and Norbert Elias. In *Zygmunt Bauman, Teoria Social y Ambivalencia [Ambiguity and Social Theory] in Revista Anthropos, Vol. 206*, (Barcelona, pp. 196–209.)

Zabludovsky, G. (2007) México: mujeres en cargos de dirección del sector privado [Women in decision–making positions in the private sector. In *Revista Latinoamericana de Administración, No. 38, Primer Semestre* (Bogotá, pp. 9–26).

12

Women in Management in the USA

Kimberly Mathe, Susan Michie and Debra L. Nelson

Introduction

The purpose of this chapter is to present the current state of women in business in the United States. Although the advancement of women shows strong progress, there are still many challenges to overcome in addition to great accomplishments. The chapter begins by introducing a current profile of women in the workforce and trends over the past ten years. Next, we explore the progress of women in education, management and entrepreneurship. We then examine legislation supporting women in management and current initiatives supporting employed women. We conclude the chapter by exploring future avenues for progress of women in the workforce.

Labour Force Characteristics

The portrait of women in the workforce has changed very little in the last seven years. In 2008, 46.5 percent of women were employed in the US labour force, a slight increase from 46.4 percent in 2007 and 46.3 percent in 2006 (see Figure 12.1). Women's participation in the labour force has remained fairly constant, with the highest participation rate in the last ten years occurring between the years 2002–2003 at which time 46.6 percent of women were employed (US Department of Labor, 2008).

Many factors may be contributing to the slight fluctuations in labour force participation rates, including increases in education, the return of working mothers to the workforce and women who are continuing to work later in their working years (US Department of Labor, 2008).

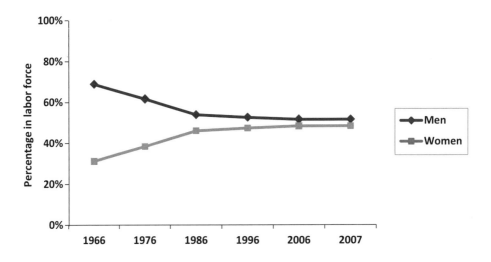

Figure 12.1   Private sector employment of women versus men, 1966–2007
Source: Equal Employment Opportunity Commission, Employer Information Reports
(EEO-1 Single and Consolidated Reports), 2007

The rate of mothers employed in the labour force has steadily risen since 1975. Collectively, mothers with children under the age of 18 totaled just less than 27 million in 2007. Forty percent of these mothers have children under the age of six. For the remaining 60 percent of working women, their children's ages range from six to 17. From 1975 to 2007, the percentage of women with children under the age of 18 increased 24 percent for total participation rate of 71 percent. The all-time high participation rate for working women with children in the labour force was 73 percent in 2004; however, the rate has dropped slightly and has remained relatively constant since then (US Department of Labor, 2008).

Married women currently comprise 52.9 percent of all employed women in the labour force and 32.8 percent of those women who are currently unemployed. The contribution of women's salaries to the total family income has been increasing since 1970 with minor fluctuations throughout (see Figure 12.2). In 2006, women's contributions to total family income were 35.6 percent. Further, the percentage of marriages in which women's earnings exceed that of their husbands has also been on the rise. In 2006, 25.7 percent earned more than their husbands, compared to 19.2 percent in 1990 and 22 percent in 1995. The occupations that make up the top five highest average weekly earnings for women are pharmacist, CEO, attorney, information system manager and software engineer (US Department of Labor, 2008).

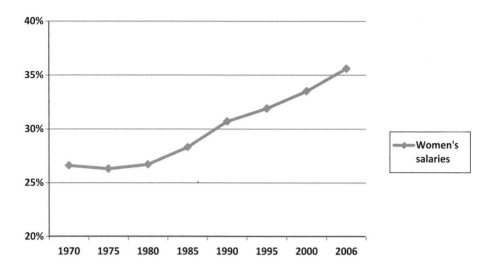

Figure 12.2   Percentage of wife's contribution to total family income, 1970–2006

Source: US Department of Labor, US Bureau of Labor Statistics, *Women in the Labor Force: A Databook*, December, 2008

Women of various racial backgrounds (Caucasian, African–American, Asian and Hispanic) populate different occupations. Women of Hispanic background are most often employed jobs in sales and office occupations. Women of Asian descent on the other hand, were mostly employed in management or professional occupations, as were Caucasian women. African–American women occupied sales and office positions most frequently and were also highly employed in the service occupations (US Department of Labor, 2008).

The average weekly earnings of women of all races has been increasing over the last seven years with the exception of African–American women experiencing a slight decline in 2005 (see Figure 12.3). Asian women were earning the highest salaries of the races examined, topping the weekly earnings average at $731 per week in 2007. Conversely, Hispanic women were taking home the lowest average weekly earnings at $473 per week in 2007 (US Department of Labor, 2008).

The aging women's workforce is also of particular interest. Currently, two-thirds of women, aged 65 or older, are using social security as the majority of their monthly income. Without the aid of social security, more than one-half of these women over the age of 65 would be living in poverty. In light of this evidence, the Government has introduced the American Recovery and Reinvestment Act to help in addressing aging women's needs. The $80 million initiative bans discrimination on the basis of gender and also provides increased funding programmes for health care, education and childcare. This will serve to preserve jobs and create jobs in these fields that are currently composed of mostly women (National Women's Law Center, 2009).

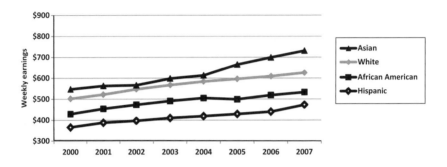

Figure 12.3   Average weekly earnings by ethnicity, 2000–2007
Source: US Department of Labor, US Bureau of Labor Statistics, *Women in the Labor Force: A Databook*, December, 2008

Women Pursuing Education

For women and men, the higher a person's educational achievements, the more likely they will be employed (US Department of Labor, 2007). The unemployment of women with at least a bachelor's degree has been decreasing since 2003. Specifically, in 2003 the unemployment rate of women with a bachelor's degree was 2.9 percent. In 2004 this number fell to 2.4 percent and in 2007 fell to 2.1 percent (US Department of Labor, 2008).

Women are currently earning more bachelor's and master's degrees than their male counterparts. Specifically, from 2005–2006 women were obtaining 57.5 percent of bachelor's degrees and 60 percent of master's degrees but were slightly edged out in doctoral degrees at 48.9 percent. In 2007 women earned more than three times the number of bachelor's degrees than in 1970 at 34.9 percent and only experienced one year of decline of bachelor's degree attainment in 1992, dropping from 25.2 percent to 25 percent (US Department of Labor, 2008). In 2006, African–American women made up 6.4 percent of all graduates receiving bachelor's degrees and 7.1 percent of all those earning master's degrees, both of which doubled their male counterparts' educational attainments. African–American women obtained 3.6 percent of all PhDs granted in 2005 (Catalyst, 2008) down slightly from 3.9 percent in 2004 (National Center for Education Statistics, 2007).

In 2007, women college graduates composed 34.9 percent of the civilian labour force, up from 31.3 percent in 2002 and 28.4 percent in 1997. Comparatively male college graduates composed 32.9 percent of the civilian labour force in 2007 (see Figure 12.4).

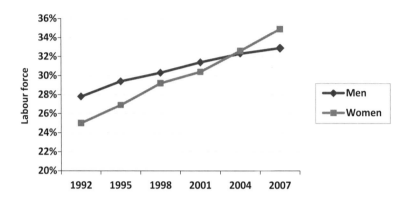

Figure 12.4   Percentage of men and women college graduates in labour force, 1992–2007

Source: US Department of Labor, US Bureau of Labor Statistics, *Women in the Labor Force: A Databook*, December, 2008

Although women are graduating with more bachelor's and master's degrees than men, one contributing factor to their overall lower pay than men may be their occupations of choice. More women at colleges and universities are majoring in such areas as education, health and psychology whereas men compose the majority of engineering, physical science and mathematics students, who typically earn higher pay (Mantey, 2007).

Women in Management

Women in the workplace are making significant progress in obtaining managerial and professional positions. In fact, of the 46.5 percent of women in the labour force, 50.8 percent held positions in a managerial or professional occupation, the highest share to date (US Department of Labor, 2008). In 1950, only 13.8 percent of women held managerial positions and this rate has continuously been increasing. In 2001 more than half of the women employed were working in a managerial or professional position for the first time (US Department of Labor, 2008). Of the managerial and professional occupations, women were most often employed as human resource managers, social and community service managers, medical and health services managers and education administrators and insurance underwriters (US Department of Labor, 2008). Women of minority backgrounds in management compared to total population can be seen in Figure 12.5. Although women of Asian backgrounds are earning the highest weekly incomes, they are the least represented in managerial positions at only 2.8 percent, likely due to the fact that they have the least amount of participation in the labour force (Catalyst, 2009a).

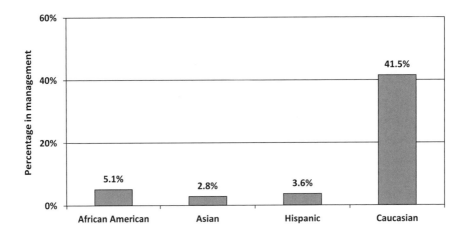

Figure 12.5   Total percentage of women by ethnicity employed in management

Source: US Department of Labor, US Bureau of Labor Statistics, *Women in the Labor Force: A Databook*, December, 2008

Despite the fact that more than half of the employed women obtain managerial positions, women CEOs are still very rare. Among the Fortune 500, only 3 percent of women hold the title CEO and 7.8 percent hold the title of CFO (Catalyst 2009b, Catalyst 2009c). A significant achievement for women of colour occurred in 2009 as Ursula Burns was named the first African–American CEO of a Fortune 500 company at Xerox Corporation (Evans, 2009). Although the top spot is held by less than 3 percent of women, in 2008 15.7 percent of women held corporate officer positions in the Fortune 500. The percentage of women holding these corporate officer spots has been holding relatively steady since 2002 with a peak at 16.4 percent in 2005. Similar trends are occurring with women on boards of Fortune 500 companies as well. Less than 10 percent of women held corporate board positions in 1995, but in 2008 15.2 percent of women held these positions, an all time high (Catalyst 2009b). Of these corporate board positions, the number of Hispanic women has increased from 16 positions in 2001 to 24 positions in 2009 (Kuznia, 2009). Also noteworthy is the fact that there has not been a decline in the number of women holding board positions in the past 13 years (Catalyst, 2009b). In 2008, only 1.84 percent of African–American women held the title of partner in US law firms (Catalyst, 2009d).

Women holding positions in elected offices have been increasing since 1979. In 2009 women held 16.8 percent of US Congress positions, up from 12.1 percent in 1999, and just 3 percent in 1979. Women holding the highest state-level position of governor totaled 16 percent. Similarly, the position of lieutenant governor was also made up of 16 percent women. Individual states with the highest percentage of women legislators in State government are Colorado (39 percent), Vermont (37.2 percent), New Hampshire (37 percent), Minnesota (34.8 percent), and Hawaii (32.9 percent) (Center for American Women and Politics, 2009).

In 2009, when the first African–American President, Barack Obama, was elected, women of colour in Congress constituted 3.9 percent. These included 12 African American, 6 Latina and 2 Asian Pacific Islander congresswomen. Also at the beginning of the Obama Administration, 15 women were named to the Cabinet, Cabinet Level or other top positions within the administration. These top positions included Hillary Rodham Clinton (Secretary of State), Karen Gordon Mills (Administrator, Small Business Administration) and Hilda L. Solis (Secretary of Labor). American politics in the election year 2008 experienced many firsts for women including the first woman on a national Republican ticket, Sarah Palin; and the first woman to be a presidential candidate in every primary and caucus elections, Hillary Rodham Clinton (Center for American Women and Politics, 2009).

With the increasing proportions of women in management, women business owners and women holding political office, the types of leadership styles that women exhibit is of great interest to organizations and society alike. A meta-analysis by Eagly, Johannesen-Schmidt and van Eagen (2003) revealed that female leaders were more transformational; that is, they work to gain the trust and confidence of followers to a greater degree than do their than male peers. In contrast, male leaders were more likely to engage in transactional leadership, a more typical exchange relationship involving rewards for meeting objectives and corrections for failing to meet objectives. Another study by Koneck (2006) involving women in management positions confirmed the finding that women were more transformational in leadership style. The same study also revealed that a growing number of women do not perceive the glass ceiling as a barrier to advancing to higher ranks within the organization (Koneck, 2006). Other research has shown that women, particularly women of colour, are still experiencing difficulties in making the climb to the top of the corporate ladder. In a study of women in the law profession, US-born women of colour reported a variety of hardships and disadvantages including lower organizational commitment and dissatisfaction with client assignments. They also perceived diversity initiatives as ineffective and did not believe other employees made an effort to be inclusive to all individuals (Catalyst, 2009d). Despite these perceived inequities, some women may not aspire to achieve the highest ranks within the organization. In a study of women senior managers in the accounting industry, only 41 percent aspired to be a partner within the firm, as opposed to 65 percent of men. Similarly, 25 percent of women staff accountants aspired to partnership within the firm, compared to 62 percent of men (Catalyst, 2009c).

Women Entrepreneurs

Female entrepreneurs are creating a large economic impact, totaling $1.9 trillion in revenues for 2008. This is up from $1.15 trillion in 2001. The 10.1 million woman-owned businesses in the US create this economic effect. Of these 10 million businesses, three-quarters are majority-owned by women. Women of colour owned 1.9 million of these firms and between 2002 and 2008 these firms grew faster than all privately owned firms. Women-owned businesses employed more than 13 million workers, which is nearly 4 million more than in 2002, and double the number employed in 1997 (Center for Women's Business Research, 2008). Women as new business owners or established business owners are still lagging behind men in overall business ownership, 18.45 percent to 10.73 percent in 2007 (Allen et al., 2008). Service firms made up 53 percent of all women-owned businesses and retail composed 16 percent of all women-owned businesses followed by finance, insurance and sales at 9 percent (Women's Business Center, 2009). Venus and Serena Williams, professional tennis players, made a first for women business owners in 2009. The sisters became the first African American females to own a share in a National Football League franchise with their buy-in to the Miami Dolphins (ESPN, 2009).

What motivates American women to start their own business? The Global Entrepreneurship Monitor distinguished between two types of motivation: opportunity motivation and necessity motivation. Opportunity motivation exploits a perceived opportunity, whereas necessity motivation is created when all other options for work are exhausted or unsatisfactory. More than 60 percent of American women declared they pursued owning their own business for opportunity, around 20 percent for necessity and more than 10 percent a combination of both motivations. The female opportunity to necessity ratio was 3.01 while this ratio for men was higher at 4.82. In other words, women start their own businesses three times more often for opportunity than because there are no other viable options to explore (Allen et al., 2008).

Because of women's strong impact in small and entrepreneurial businesses, an initiative was created to examine the discrepancies between funding opportunities and resources for rapidly growing women-owned businesses. The Diana project, founded at Babson University, has two primary purposes. (Arthur M. Blank Center for Entrepreneurship, 2009) First is to "to raise awareness and expectations of women business owners for the growth of their firms, to educate women business owners about the characteristics of equity-funded businesses, and to provide detailed information about how the equity funding process works". The second goal is "to educate equity capital providers about opportunities for enhanced portfolio diversification and new investment possibilities through investment in women-owned businesses" (Arthur M. Blank Center for Entrepreneurship, 2009). Programmes like this are helping to increase the motivation and success of women entrepreneurs in taking the first step of starting a business or taking the next leap in making the business more successful.

Country Legislation

Women in the US were granted the right to vote in 1920. This single act of legislation provided the precedent for other laws aimed at improving the conditions for women overall. Substantial improvements for women in the workplace, however, did not happen until after the Civil Rights Movement of the 1960s. Since then several laws have passed to prevent workplace discrimination against women in three major areas – equal employment opportunity, pay equality and work/family issues.

Perhaps the most important act of legislation for women that came out of the US civil rights movement was the Civil Rights Act of 1964. This act included a chapter sub-division called Title VII that prohibited employment discrimination based on race, creed, religion, national origin or sex. Title VII provided several forms of judicial relief, including hiring, reinstatement and back pay with interest. In 1991, an amendment to Title VII added compensatory and punitive damages as well, which gave women a very powerful tool for challenging employment inequalities.

Another critical piece of legislation, following the 1960s, was the Education Amendments of 1972 (Title IX). This act prohibited sex discrimination in the public education system and created opportunities for women to obtain degrees required for a number of occupations and professions from which they had previously been barred. Following the passage of Title VII and Title XI, the proportion of women working in non-traditional (male-dominated) occupations increased, but progress was slow in many areas. Women in certain skilled professions, including accounting, medicine and law, represented most of the gain (Maclean, 1999). Professions involving technology or engineering skills and blue-collar jobs requiring manual labour continued to be segregated by sex (Maclean, 1999).

Beginning in the late 1960s, the Federal Government implemented several affirmative action programmes designed to advance women and minorities in jobs from which they had traditionally been excluded (Maclean, 1999). For example, Executive Order 11375 banned sex discrimination, and required affirmative action by federal contractors and sub-contractors in 1967. However, the outcomes for women affected by these programmes were not always positive. Due to past employment practices, there was a shortage of qualified female applicants to fulfil the hiring mandates. Thus, the required quotas were difficult to meet at times and led to hiring women who were inexperienced or lacked the resources to perform well (Eberhardt and Fiske, 1994). The overall impact of affirmative action programmes on the advancement of women in the US workforce is still a very controversial topic (West-Faulcon, 2009).

In 1960, women in the US earned approximately 60 cents for every dollar earned by men. Passage of the Equal Pay Act in 1963 required that men and women be paid equal wages for equal work. But the law applied only to situations where women and men were employed in the same, or very similar, jobs. It did not address the issue of occupational segregation by sex that resulted in low pay for women in "female occupations" that rarely employ men. Furthermore, the law did not take into account male and female jobs that were viewed as "different" but still required similar levels of skill, effort and responsibility. The gender pay gap has been narrowing steadily, but slowly, since 1973. Women today earn 80 cents for every dollar earned by men in the US, which amounts to an increase of about 3 cents over the last decade (US Department of Labor Women's Bureau, 2007). The recent passage of a new bill, the Lilly Ledbetter Act, in January 2009 may help to speed this process. The bill amends the Civil Rights Act of 1964 by stating that the 180-day statute of limitations for filing an equal-pay lawsuit resets with each new discriminatory paycheck as opposed to commencing on the date the pay was originally agreed upon. This new law will enable women and other victims of pay discrimination to challenge unequal pay more effectively (Wall Street Journal, 2009).

Although households with dual career partners have increased dramatically in the US since the 1960s, sharing the burden of family care has not kept pace with the increasing number of double income families. Women still bear the responsibility of primary caregiver in most US households and, as a result, are subject to biases against their commitment to work (Vogel, 1993). As the number of women in the workforce increased, for example, so did the incidents of pregnancy discrimination. By the late 1970s, women made up more than 45 percent of the labour force, but only one-quarter had insurance plans that allowed sick leave for pregnancy-related illness (Vogel, 1993). In 1976, a Supreme Court decision *(General Electric v. Gilbert)* held that denial of benefits for pregnancy-related disability was not discrimination based on sex. This holding reflected common management decisions by which married women faced job discrimination and pregnant women were routinely fired. Reaction to the *Gilbert* decision was swift; however, and in 1978 an amendment to Title VII was passed that prohibited workplace discrimination on the basis of pregnancy. The Pregnancy Discrimination Act prohibits employers with 15 or more employees, including state and local governments, from discriminating against women because of pregnancy, childbirth or related medical conditions.

In 1993, the US Congress passed the Family and Medical Leave Act (FMLA), which guaranteed *both* female and male employees up to 12 weeks of unpaid job-protected family or medical leave per year. The law applies to companies with more than 50 workers, and requires continuation of group health benefits during the unpaid leave. By recognizing the family care obligations of both mothers and fathers, this act implied that employers should not see child or elder care as solely a woman's responsibility (Cushman, 2001).

Initiatives Supporting Women in the Workforce

Increasing legal actions against sex discrimination have prompted many companies to develop initiatives for recruiting, retaining and advancing women in management. Important areas of focus include women's leadership development, women of colour, work–life balance, globalization and women on boards.

Catalyst, a well-known and respected non-profit organization working to expand opportunities for women in business, honours organizations that have exemplary initiatives for the advancement of women (Catalyst, 2009a). The annual Catalyst Awards recognize innovative organizational approaches with proven, measurable results that promote the recruitment, development and progress of all women, including women of colour. In 2009, Baxter International received a Catalyst Award for its pan-Asian Pacific management initiative that strives to develop a 50/50 gender balance across management and other critical positions throughout 14 countries. Baxter aimed to reach the 50/50 target by 2010, but achieved its goal two years ahead of schedule through aggressive recruitment and development strategies based on accountability and strong communication. Women in management and executive positions increased from 31 percent in 2004 to 50 percent in 2008, and four out of 16 general management positions at Baxter are currently held by women (Catalyst, 2009e).

In the traditionally male-dominated industry of engineering and construction, CH2M Hill provides a model for advancing women and achieving business success. The company launched an "inclusive workplace" initiative in 2003 that increased women's representation in senior leadership positions from 2.9 percent to 18.0 percent. Women of colour lead two of the company's 13 geographic regions and the percentage of women project managers has increased from 20.5 percent in 2005 to 30.3 percent in 2008 (Catalyst, 2009e).

Gibbons P. C. is a top law firm in the New York, New Jersey, Philadelphia and Delaware metropolitan regions of the US. The firm employed 230 attorneys and was recently ranked as one of the best firms for working women by *Working Mother* magazine (Catalyst, 2009e). A workplace culture that is flexible, innovative, engaging and inclusive is embedded in the firm's business development strategy. In 2007, the firm's initiatives for women generated more than 6 percent of its annual revenue. Women held 21.1 percent of equity director positions, and the number of women directors overall increased from 13 percent in 1997 to 19 percent in 2008. Also during that time, women of colour directors increased from zero to 4.1 percent, and women now chair three of the firm's nine practice groups (Catalyst, 2009e). By recognizing, sharing and celebrating successful initiatives, these companies and Catalyst provide replicable models to help other organizations create initiatives that are good for women and good for business (Catalyst, 2009e).

Catalyst is just one of many organizations dedicated to the advancement of women in the US. The InterOrganization Network (ION) has regional organizations located across the US working to advance women to executive suites, boards of directors and other positions of power in the business world. Furthermore, The National Association of Women MBAs (NAWMBA) is a non-profit organization dedicated to empowering and promoting more women into leadership positions in corporate America, and The Women's Museum™ is a Smithsonian affiliate that uses the latest technology and interactive media to publicize diverse, unique and revealing stories of US women in exhibits and programmes that increase knowledge of how women participated in shaping the nation's history (Catalyst, 2011). The Alfred P. Sloan Work and Family Research Network is a global online resource for information about work and family research. The National Women's Law Center (NWLC) uses the law in all of its forms to improve public policy for women and their families.

Women and their families are also receiving support from the Government. A recent Executive Order signed by President Barack Obama created the White House Council on Women and Girls. President Obama founded the council "to ensure that American women and girls are treated fairly in all matters of public policy" (The White House, 2009). The Council will work to enhance current programmes for women and girls. In particular, during the first year the council seeks four objectives including: improve women's economic security, establish a balance between family and work, prevent violence against women and build healthy families (The White House, 2009). These examples represent only a handful of the numerous and ongoing efforts aimed at advancing women in the US.

The Future

Although the initiatives above provide reasons to be optimistic about US women in management, progress in some areas continues to be extremely slow. One avenue that needs improvement is the retention of women in certain professional and non-traditional career fields. Since 1985, for example, over 40 percent of annual law school graduates in the US have been women. Consistently over the years, 70 percent of all newly minted female and male lawyers enter firms upon graduating. By 1995, 14.2 percent of law firm partners were women; but a decade later in 2005, only 17.2 percent of partners were women. Based on these current rates, it will take until 2115 to reach parity (50 percent women partners). (Women's Bar Association of DC, 2006). Another area of concern is the limited number of women holding positions in the upper echelons of major corporations. Women held 15.2 percent of board director positions in 2008 compared to 12.4 percent in 2001, an increase of less than 3 percent (Catalyst 2009b). Furthermore, between 2007 and 2008 a slight increase in companies with three or more women directors was offset by a slight increase in companies with no women on the board. Representation of women corporate officers and top earners in the Fortune 500 appears to be slowing, perhaps due in part to the current global economic recession (Catalyst, 2009f). Women held 12.5 percent of corporate officer positions in 2000 compared to 15.4 percent in 2007, and 15.7 percent in 2008 (Catalyst, 2009b). Although top earner positions held by women increased from 4.1 percent in 2000 to 6.7 percent in 2007, they decreased to 6.2 percent in 2008 (Catalyst, 2009f). Thus, in critical areas of management and influence, women remain grossly under-represented.

Perhaps what is needed is a greater understanding of women's career trajectories and the barriers they face. One perspective was put forth by Eagly and Carli (2007) who proposed that the glass ceiling is outdated as far as depicting women's careers. Instead, they argued that women's careers be depicted as labyrinths, which better capture the twists and turns and the need to face challenges immediately as they arise. Lack of access to professional networks, increased hours demanded by work, increased parenting demands, and the remains of prejudice and discrimination against women managers can all stall a woman's progress up the career ladder. Inventive solutions will be required in order to advance women in management in the US.

References

Allen I. E., Elam, A., Langowitz, N. and Dean, M. (2008) *2007 Global Entrepreneurship Monitor Report on Women and Entrepreneurship*, Babson College, The Center for Women's Leadership.

Arthur M. Blank Center for Entrepreneurship (2009) Diana Project, http://www3.babson.edu/ESHIP/research-publications/dianaproject.cfm, accessed 25 March, 2009.

Catalyst (2008) *Quick Takes: African American Women*,http://www.catalyst.org/file/204/qt_african_american_women.pdf, accessed 26 August, 2009.

Catalyst (2009a) *Statistical Overview of Women in the Workplace*, http://www.catalyst.org/publication/219/statistical-overview-of-women-in-the-workplace, accessed 26 August, 2009.

Catalyst (2009b) *Women in U.S. Management*, http://www.catalyst.org/publication/206/women-in-us-management, accessed 26 August, 2009.

Catalyst (2009c) *Women in Accounting*, http://www.catalyst.org/publication/204/women-in-accounting, accessed 27 August, 2009.

Catalyst (2009d) *Women of Color in US Law Firms*, http://www.catalyst.org/publication/344/women-of-color-in-us-law-firmswomen-of-color-in-professional-services-series, accessed 27 August, 2009.

Catalyst (2009e) *Catalyst Honors Initiatives at Baxter, CH2M HILL, Gibbons, and KPMG With the 2009 Catalyst Award*, http://www.catalyst.org/press-release/142/baxter-ch2m-hill-gibbons-and-kpmg-initiatives-honored-with-the-2009-catalyst-award, accessed 26 August, 2009.

Catalyst (2009f) *Catalyst 2008 Census of the Fortune 500 Reveals Women Gained Little Ground Advancing to Business Leadership Positions*, http://www.catalyst.org/press-release/141/catalyst-2008, accessed 26 August, 2009.

Catalyst (2011). *Partners and Friends*. http://www.catalyst.org/page/113/partners-and-friends, accessed 12 March, 2011.

Center for American Women and Politics (2009) *Fast Facts on Women Officeholders, Candidates and Voters*, http://www.cawp.rutgers.edu/fast_facts/, accessed 7 April, 2009.

Center for Women's Business Research (2008) *Key Facts about Women-owned Businesses*, http://www.nfwbo.org/facts/index.php, accessed 23 April, 2009.

Cushman, C. (2001) *Supreme Court Decisions and Women's Rights*, Congressional Quarterly Press, Washington DC.

Eagly, A. H. and Carli, L. L. (2007) *Through the Labyrinth: The Truth about How Women Become Leaders* (Boston, MA: Harvard Business School Press).

Eagly, A. H., Johannesen-Schmidet, M. C. and van Eagen, M. L. (2003) Transformational, transactional, and lassiez-faire leadership styles: a meta-analysis comparing women and men, *Psychological Bulletin*, 129(4), 569–591.

Eberhardt, J. and Fiske, S. (1994). Affirmative action in theory and practice: issues of power, ambiguity, and gender versus race, *Basic & Applied Social Psychology*, 15(1/2), 201–220.

Equal Employment Opportunity Commission (2007) *Employer Information Reports* (EEO-1 Single and Consolidated Reports).

ESPN (2009) *Williams Sisters Buy into Dolphins Group*, http://sports.espn.go.com/nfl/news/story?id=4422313, accessed 13 March, 2011.

Evans, H. (2009). Ursula Burns to head Xerox, will be first black woman to be CEO of Fortune 500 Company, *NYDailyNews.com*, 23 May, http://www.nydailynews.com/money/2009/05/23/2009-05-23_1st_black_woman_xerox_ceo.html.

Koneck, C. M. (2006) A study of women leadership styles and the glass ceiling. *Dissertation Abstracts International: Section B: The Sciences and Engineering*, 67(10-B), 6103.

Kuznia, R. (2009) Hispanic women soar to leadership positions, *New America Media*, 7 April, http://news.newamericamedia.org/news/view_article.html?article_id=576734b25b0b01e09904b8f61d7f34cc, accessed 12 March, 2011.

Maclean, N. (1999) The hidden history of affirmative action: working women's struggles in the 1970s and the gender of class, *Feminist Studies*, 25(1), 42.

Mantey, J. (2007) College majors could cause women to earn less, *US News*, 21 June, http://www.usnews.com/usnews/news/articles/070621/21wagegap.htm, accessed 12 March, 2011.

National Center for Education Statistics (2007) *Status and Trends in the Education of Racial and Ethnic Minorities*, http://nces.ed.gov/pubs2007/minoritytrends/tables/table_25_1.asp?referrer=report, accessed 12 March, 2011.

National Women's Law Center (2009) *How the American Recovery and Reinvestment Act Addresses Women's Needs: Job Opportunities for Women*, http://www.nwlc.org/resource/how-american-recovery-and-reinvestment-act-addresses-womens-needs-job-opportunities-women, accessed 13 March, 2011.

The White House, Office of the Press Secretary (2009) *President Obama Announces White House Council on Women and Girls*, http://www.whitehouse.gov/the_press_office/President-Obama-Announces-White-House-Council-on-Women-and-Girls/, March 11, Washington, DC, accessed 6 April, 2009.

United States Department of Labor, Department of Labor, U.S. Department of Labor Statistics (2008) *Women in the Labor Force: A Databook*, Washington, DC: Report 1101.

United States Department of Labor, Women's Bureau (2007) *20 Facts on Women Workers: March 2007*, Washington, DC: U.S. DOL/00-02.

Vogel, L. (1993) *Mothers on the Job: Maternity Policy in the U.S. Workplace* (New Brunswick, NJ: Rutgers University Press).

Wall Street Journal (2009) U.S. News: Pay-discrimination Bill Signals Pro-labor Shift in Washington (Eastern edition), New York, NY: January 24, p. A.3

West-Faulcon, K. (2009) The river runs dry: When Title VI trumps state anti-affirmative action laws, *University of Pennsylvania Law Review*, 157(4), 1075–1160.

Women's Bar Association of the District of Columbia (2006) *Creating Pathways to Success: Advancing and Retaining Women in Today's Law Firms*, Washington, DC.

Women's Business Center (2009) *US Women's Business Ownership Statistics*, http://www.womenbiz.org/index.php?content=resources/usstats&section=resources, accessed 7 April, 2009).

PART IV

Women in Management – Australasia

13

Women in Management in Australia

Glenice J. Wood

Introduction

This chapter aims to present a current picture of women in Australia in relation to their participation in the labour force, the roles they typically fill, their educational achievements and their entrepreneurial activities. Where possible a picture is presented which is inclusive of Indigenous Australian women, however, the majority of the statistics that are readily available skew the picture to reflect what is the reality for non-Indigenous women in Australia, as the Indigenous population are a minority in their own country. Hence, statistics combining "all Australian women" make any differentiation between Indigenous women and non-Indigenous women difficult. The following report illustrates this phenomenon well.

The Global Gender Gap report (2008), which measures the size of the gender gap between women and men in four critical areas of inequality, ranks Australia as twenty-first in the world, down four points from the ranking achieved in 2007 (Hausmann, Tyson and Zahidi, 2008). This ranking places Australia just out of the top 20 countries, and as such, it does provide a sobering reminder of how far we have to go to close the gender gap on all areas measured. Although there are obvious difficulties in the collection of data between the ranges of countries covered, this measure is indicative of where Australia sits in areas which include economic participation and opportunity, education attainment, political empowerment and health and survival (Hausmann, Tyson and Zahidi, 2008).

Specifically, Australia is reported as not achieving equality in economic participation and opportunity in the areas of labour force participation, wage equality for similar work, estimated earned income, and numbers of legislators, senior officials and managers. In educational attainment, we have only achieved equality on the measure of enrolment in tertiary education. In terms of health and survival, we have achieved equality in health life expectancy (78.5 for males, and 81.7 for females), although this is markedly different for the Australian indigenous population (67 for males and 72 for females) (ABS, 2009c). In political empowerment, despite having a female Prime Minister, we have a long way to go to achieve equality in terms of the numbers of women in parliament, women in ministerial positions and heading up states (Hausmann, Tyson and Zahidi, 2008).

These statistics are particularly sobering when we consider the proportion of women who are now engaged in the workforce. The following section will explore the current position of women in various work-related areas in Australia.

Labour Force Characteristics

In March, 2009, 4,945.600 males were employed full time in the Australian labour force (64.6 percent), compared with 2,703.000 females (35.3 percent). The number of indigenous people in the labour force has been estimated at 183,800, with participation rate being higher for Indigenous males (65 percent), cf. 48 percent for Indigenous females) (ABS, 2008e).

In the amalgamated data (non-Indigenous and Indigenous population), fewer males were employed on a part-time basis (918,900; 29 percent), with 2,224.700 (70.7 percent) of females in the same category (ABS, 2009a). Therefore, while there are greater numbers of women in the workforce, the majority of these are employed in casual or part-time jobs where there are typically less avenues for progressing in careers (Fastenau, 2006). In the 30 Organisation for Economic Co-operation and Development (OECD) countries, Australia is ranked thirteenth in relation to its female participation in the labour force (Women in Australia, 2009). Women made up 50 percent of the population in Australia in March, 2009 with 58 percent of all women over 15 years of age in the workforce (Women in Australia, 2009). In terms of the Australian workplace, 46 percent of the total labour force is made up of women (ABS, 2009a).

Women in Australia who are aged between 25–54 tend to have a lower labour force participation (that is, employed or looking for employment) than women in countries such as Canada, New Zealand, Sweden, UK and the US (ABS, 2007), with 58 percent of the Australian female population participating in the labour force (Women in Australia, 2009). However, in Australia, indigenous women have a lower rate of participation, with 48 percent estimated to be participating in the labour force in 2007 (ABS, 2008e). One key reason for the lower labour force participation is the lack of government childcare availability, and in countries where childcare is seen as a responsibility of the country, such as Sweden, participation rates of women actually increase, rather than dip, during this period (ABS, 2007).

Analyses of workforce participation have indicated that people between 55–64 years of age reduce their participation in the labour force in all countries. However, there have been recent increases in the participation rate of Australians in this age category, with a rise of 8 percentage points between 2000–2005, which exceeds the rise in the OECD average. Despite this, Australians over the age of 55 have a lower participation in the workforce than that of similar countries (ABS, 2007).

In Australia, there is a clear segmentation of the workforce according to gender, with the majority of women being employed in the areas of health and community services and education. Men make up the majority of workers in the areas of wholesale trade industries, transport and storage, mining, manufacturing and construction (Women in Australia, 2009). Women tend to dominate in clerical, sales and service areas at the elementary, intermediate and advanced levels as well as in the category of "professional" occupations. For males, the dominant occupations are in labouring, transport, and in the areas of trades, associate professionals and managers and administrators (Women in Australia, 2009).

However, in no industry do women fill more senior roles than their male counterparts. For example, within the Australian Public Service, women make up the majority of employees (57 percent of the workforce). Despite this, women are under-represented at all three senior executive levels, ranging from 37.6 percent of the cohort, to 27.5 percent at the highest Senior Executive Service (SES) level (Women in Australia, 2009). In terms of women and the law, in 2007/8 in the Federal Court of Australia, women made up 13 percent of the bench (AHRC, 2009). Further elaboration of this phenomenon is presented in the Women in Management section of this chapter.

In addition to the under-representation of women at senior levels, there are significant pay differences in the earnings of men and women in Australia. For example, in 2008, the average weekly earnings for women was $702.30 AUD, compared with $1,075.10 AUD for male employees (ABS, 2008b), indicating a ratio of female to male earnings of 65.3 percent – effectively a gender pay gap of almost 35 percent (Women in Australia, 2009). When full-time employees are considered, the ratio is even higher (80.5 percent). Despite the fact that it is now approaching 40 years since legislation was passed in Australia to ensure equal pay for equal work, "women working full-time still earn an average of 16 percent less than men" (Burrows, 2008: 11).

Pay inequities are also reported at the graduate starting salary level, with males earning $47,000 and female graduates $45,000 (up from $42,000 in 2007) for first time employment. In addition, women earn less than men in areas such as medicine, dentistry, architecture, optometry and art and design, but do achieve an equal starting salary in the field of accounting (Women in Australia, 2009). In fact, according to the Equal Opportunity for Women in the Workplace Agency (EOWA), in nine out of ten industry sectors, the median female top salary is less than that of their male colleagues. Only 7 percent of the top earner positions (80 out of 1,136) are held by women, with female CEOs earning two-thirds of the male CEO salary. Even in the human resources (HR) sector, typically seen as an area where women predominate, the median remuneration for women is only 57 percent of that received by their male counterparts (EOWA, 2008b).

Such disparities in pay across such a broad spectrum are difficult to understand, given the legally sanctioned legislation for equal pay to be received for equal work as mentioned previously, and the increasing numbers of women pursuing education in Australia.

Women Pursuing Education

According to statistics from the Department of Education, Science and Training (DEST), females have been enrolling in courses in greater numbers than males since 1987 in Australia (Bagwell, 1993), and this trend is continuing (ABS, 2008a), with more than half (56 percent) of all student enrolments being female in the first half of 2008 (DEST, 2008).

Some patterns of enrolment are particularly interesting. In 1993, 55 percent of all students enrolled in undergraduate courses were women, and in disciplines such as law, women have been successfully graduating in numbers equal to their male colleagues since the late 1980s (Bagwell, 1993). In 2007, 56 percent of all award course completions were female (Women in Australia, 2009). The three most common fields of study for women are now management and commerce (30 percent), followed by society and culture (17 percent) and health (16 percent) (Women in Australia, 2009).

In recent figures released by ABS (2008a), 52 percent of students enrolled in a postgraduate degree are males, compared to 48 percent who are females. The trend continues for undergraduate bachelor degree enrolments; the dominant group of enrollees is women (56 percent) compared to 44 percent being male (ABS, 2008a).

Women have been reported to be graduating in higher numbers in business-related areas since the mid 1900s, when women made up more than 44 percent of commencing business students in Australian universities. Recent ABS data report a similar trend with 53 percent of students being female in management and commerce courses (ABS, 2008a). Despite the increasing numbers of female graduates in business-related areas generally, and in management courses in particular, these numbers do not translate into women filling equal numbers of management roles as their male counterparts.

In relation to Aboriginal and Torres Strait Islander Australians, for more than 55,000 Indigenous Australians over 15 years of age, Year 12 was the highest level of schooling achieved. A greater number (79,000) in the same age group reported that Year 10 was the highest level of schooling completed (ABS, 2006a). In the Census of 2006, only 7 percent of the Indigenous population in the same age bracket, were attending a university or a technical or further educational institution, with the latter educational settings being the most common form of education.

Of interest in this Census is the finding that a greater proportion of Indigenous females (59 percent) were involved in technical or further education than non-Indigenous Australian females (51 percent). The figures for involvement in university or other tertiary institution education were even more striking. Two-thirds of the Indigenous enrolments in full-time and part-time study were females (67 percent), and again this is a higher proportion than for non-Indigenous Australian females (56 percent) (ABS, 2006b).

Women in Management

There have been dramatic changes in the employment of full-time managers in Australia over the past decade. In 1996, there were 681,500 male managers in full-time employment (76 percent), compared to 217,000 female managers (24 percent) (ABS, 2009b). In February 2009, there has been an increase in the numbers of both male and female managers in full-time employment: 847,400 (70 percent) male, compared to 360,500 (30 percent) female managers (ABS, 2009b). These data indicate a steady growth in the numbers of managers employed in a full-time capacity over more than a decade, with female managers now approaching one-third of managers overall.

However, it appears that the higher the level of management, the lower the proportion of females in this occupation. In a recent report focusing on the current status of equal opportunity in Australia (EOWA, 2008a), data was presented for the top 200 companies listed on the Australian Stock Exchange, referred to as the ASX 200. (Equal Opportunity implies that employees will have similar access to the available opportunities; are treated with fairness and respect, and do not experience any discrimination or harassment while engaged in their work) (EOWA, 2009). The EOWA report compared the current results obtained with similar measures of Australian women in leadership in 2006, indicating a disturbing slowing down of the progress of women leaders in this country. In addition, it highlights that women in Australia remain under-represented in the most senior corporate positions of the ASX 200. The Director of EOWA, Anna McPhee, summed up the situation as follows: "At the 2006 Census we described the pace of change as glacial, in 2008, the results show that women's progress is melting away" (EOWA, 2008b:2).

In terms of company data relating to women in executive management positions in Australia's top companies, there are now 10.7 percent of executive manager roles filled by women, a decline from 12.0 percent in 2006. Australia has the least amount of women executive managers in the top 200 companies when compared to the UK (12.2 percent), Canada, (15.1 percent), US (15.4 percent) and South Africa (25.3 percent) (EOWA, 2008b). The reasons for this low number, and for the decline from that recorded in 2006, are a cause of consternation. There has also been a slight decline in the proportion of board directors who are women; in 2006 there were 8.7 percent, and in 2008, 8.3 percent. It is illuminating to ponder this statistic, and to comprehend that in 2008, 22 years after the Affirmative Action (Equal Employment Opportunity for Women) Act was passed as legislation in this country, that 91.7 percent of board directors are men. In fact, over half of the ASX 200 companies have no women directors on their boards (51 percent), with only 11.5 percent of companies having two or more women directors.

In relation to the role of CEOs, in 2006, 3.0 percent of CEOs were women, whereas in 2008 this figure had dropped to 2.0 percent. Finally, in 2006, 2 percent of chairs were held by women, and this figure is the same in 2008 (EOWA, 2008a).

The proportion of women who fill the role of board directors is currently lower in Australia than in all of the comparison countries included in Table 13.1.

Table 13.1   Women board directors: a global comparison

Country	Latest census figures	
Australia	8.3 %	2008
Canada	13.0 %	2007
New Zealand	8.7 %	2006
South Africa	14.3 %	2008
United Kingdom	11.0 %	2007
United States	14.8 %	2007

Source: EOWA, 2008b

Furthermore, only four Australian boards have a woman as chair of their organization (2 percent), and only four companies have a female CEO (2 percent). Just over half of the companies in the ASX 200 listing recorded that they had no women board director (51 percent), and there is a decline in the number of boards who have two or more women directors; 11.5 percent in 2008 compared with 13.5 percent in 2006. Only 6 percent of companies in the ASX 200 have 25 percent or more of women board directors, which is half the proportion who filled these roles in 2006.

A picture of "women's progress melting away" (EOWA, 2008b:2) emerges when the following data is considered. There are no women executive managers in almost half of the ASX 200 companies (45.5 percent), a rise from the 39.5 percent of companies without executive female management in 2006. Just over half (54.5 percent) of the ASX 200 companies have at least one women in the role of executive manager, and this figure is less than the 60.5 percent recorded in 2006. In addition, the proportion of ASX 200 companies with two or more women executive managers has also declined to 23.5 percent, a reduction from 30 percent in 2006. In 2008, a small number of companies (16.5 percent) stated that they had 25 percent or more women executive managers in their employ. This figure had decreased from the 18 percent recorded in 2006 (EOWA, 2008b). Unfortunately, no data is available on female (or male) Indigenous managers in the Australian workforce.

In addition to the disproportionate numbers of males and females who fill executive or senior roles, there are similar disparities observed in the numbers of men and women who hold various roles in our parliamentary system. Although Australia passed the Commonwealth Franchise Act in 1902, giving women the right to vote and stand for Parliament, it took almost 20 years before a woman was elected into a State parliament seat, and a further 20 years before women filled seats in the Commonwealth Parliament (Parliament of Australia, 2010).

However, progress has been made. As late as the 1980s, only six women filled Senate seats, and no woman was in the House of Representatives. In 2008, 33 percent of all parliamentarians are women in the Commonwealth Government, and there is a female prime minister for the first time in our history, as well as seven female ministers (out of a total of 30) and three parliamentary secretaries (out of a total of 12). Therefore, currently, 23 percent of ministerial positions, and one-fifth of all cabinet members are women (Women in Australia, 2009). In addition, 41.2 percent of parliamentarians in the Australian Capital Territory (ACT) are women, with a low of 26 percent in the Western Australian Government (Office for Women, 2008).

The following comparison illustrated in Table 13.2 outlines the progress of women in the Parliament of Australia over a 22-year-period. It will be noted that no data was available for the numbers of Indigenous women filling these roles in the Australian Parliament.

Table 13.2   **Women in the Parliament of Australia 1987–2009 (selected years)**

Year of Election	House of Representatives (Lower House)		Senate (Upper House)		Total	Percentage of total seats
	Number	Percentage	Number	Percentage		
1987*	9	6.1	17	22.4	26	11.6
1996*	23	15.5	23	30.3	46	20.5
2001*	38	25.3	23	30.2	61	27.2
2009**	40	26.6	27	35.5	67	29.6

Source:

* Women in Parliament, Statistics on House of Representatives and the Senate, Parliamentary Library, Parliament of Australia, 2001, www.aph.gov.au/library/

** Parliamentary Education Office. Parliament of Australia, 2009, www.peo.gov.au/faq

Overall, the data presented highlights the under-representation of women in management and leadership positions in Australia in the public, private and parliamentary sectors. Despite the significant research conducted into examining the barriers that have impeded women in their career progression, inequities remain.

We continue to see an enormous untapped potential as women's skills, educational qualifications, experience, and acknowledged strengths in the area of management and leadership are underutilized. In relation to Australia, factors thought to be influential are work–life balance issues and multiple roles (for example, Charlesworth, 1997; DeCeiri et al., 2005; Hudson, 2005; Pocock et al., 2001; Von Doussa, 2007) and the persistent stereotypes held about women as to their suitability to hold management roles (for example, Davidson and Cooper, 1992; Schein and Muller, 1992; Schein, 1975; 1994; 2001; 2006; Wood, 2008). The inaccessibility to networks seen as male domains (Lyness and Heilman, 2006), and lack of mentors (Morgan and Davidson, 2008) have been proposed as factors in the under-representation of women in senior management roles (Palermo, 2004); these factors are also likely to influence Australian women.

Previous research has suggested that women have lower career aspirations than men (Davidson and Cooper, 1992). However, managerial women do not necessarily have lower career aspirations than their male colleagues. Australian research reported that career aspirations between male and female middle managers were very similar in a sample of 507 managers drawn from 24 large

Australian organizations, with high proportions of male (83 percent) and female (76 percent) middle managers stating they aspired to a senior management position (Wood and Lindorff, 2001). Furthermore, it should not be assumed that all women make decisions to leave their organization for the purpose of starting a family. In the above study only 21 percent of female managers had a dependent child living at home at the time of the survey (cf. 66 percent of male managers) (Wood and Lindorff, 2001). This reflects a phenomenon that has been noted in previous research (Wood and Newton, 2006) which suggests that a proportion of women in management positions forego having children in order to further their careers (Wajcman, 1999). Whatever the causes, the "glass ceiling" remains for Australian women in management, and recognition of this reality is believed to have provided an impetus for women embarking on entrepreneurial business ventures (Still and Walker, 2006).

Women Entrepreneurs

Individual entrepreneurial activity in Australia is often seen as synonymous with small business enterprises, self-employment, small and medium enterprises (SME) and home-based businesses, and the data from each of the above areas is often drawn upon to study entrepreneurial enterprises. In Australia, the term "small business operator" refers to a business with less than 20 employees. In June 2006, 68 percent of small business operators were male and 32 percent were female (ABS, 2008d). The proportion of operators who had been in business for less than 12 months was 9.5 percent (males), compared to 11.8 percent (females). In contrast, a greater proportion of male operators had been in business for 20 years or more (23.6 percent) compared to the female cohort (16.4 percent) (ABS, 2008c). Almost all of the business operators (96 percent) stated that they would be still operating their current business in 12 months time (ABS, 2008c), indicating high degrees of confidence.

Since 2004, a third of all small businesses have been reported to be owned and operated by women (ABS, 2004); in 2007, similar proportions were reported (Weaven, Isaac and Herington, 2007). The growth in businesses owned by women had exceeded the rates of growth in enterprises owned and operated by males by 2002 (ABS, 2003), however, the early-stage business participation of females was reported to have dropped from 11 percent in 2003 to just 7.6 percent in 2005 (Frederick, Kuratko and Hodgetts, 2007). The incidence of Australian women sole-owners in franchises is much lower, with only 11 percent of women choosing this business model (Frazer and Weaven, 2004).

A profile of the self-employed female business owner and her business in contemporary Australia has been compiled in recent research by Still and Walker (2006). The benchmark profile is a woman who is well educated, married with children, and is aged 30 years and over. She is an Australian born/naturalized citizen who works full time in the business, which provides the majority of support for the household and is the only one in which she is involved. In addition, the business is a micro-business or a sole-trader operation which employs few full-time or part-time staff (typically five employees or fewer). It operates in the service sector and has been operating for more than one year.

Currently, most male and female small business operators are between 30–50 years of age (57 percent and 60 percent respectively), with 9 percent of both male and female entrepreneurs being younger than 30 years of age (ABS, 2008d). The majority of male small business operators were born in Australia (70 percent) with 30 percent being born overseas. For females, the proportions are 74 percent and 26 percent respectively (ABS, 2008d). In addition, there is a significant gender difference in the hours worked for small business operators, with more males reporting that they worked full time (80 percent cf. 39 percent of females) (ABS, 2008d).

To date, the area of Indigenous entrepreneurship is under-researched and it is difficult to ascertain an accurate picture of the involvement of Indigenous entrepreneurs (Frederick and Foley, 2006). In 1999, the estimated proportion of Indigenous self-employment in the labour force was 2.4 percent, which was one-third of that of the non-Indigenous population (Fuller et al., 1999). More recent reports confirm that Indigenous Australians continue to be much less likely to be self-employed than non-Indigenous Australians (Frederick and Foley, 2006).

Recent figures indicate that 6,800 (6 percent) of employed Indigenous people worked in their own businesses (compared to 17 percent of employed non-Indigenous Australians) (ABS, 2006b). The highest proportion of self-employed Indigenous persons were in the 35–44 age group (ABS, 2006c), with most Indigenous business owners being found in major cities (7 percent, with the lowest occurring in very remote areas (2 percent) (ABS, 2006b). A higher proportion of male Indigenous Australians are self-employed (68 percent) than Indigenous Australian females (32 percent) (ABS, 2006c), and the highest proportion of Indigenous self-employment is found in the construction industry (ABS, 2006c).

These low figures of entrepreneurial participation illustrate the enormous difficulties that continue to be faced by Indigenous peoples in contemporary Australian society (Frederick, Kuratko and Hodgetts, 2007), and it is likely that Indigenous female entrepreneurs may face even more barriers in setting up in business, ranging from socio-economic and environmental factors that affect their health and wellbeing (ABS, 2008f), to accessing credit (McDonnell, 1999).

Country Legislation

The Equal Opportunity for Women in the Workplace Act 1999 (EOWWA Act) which was formerly known as the Affirmative Action (Equal Opportunity for Women) Act, 1986 (Cth), was designed to focus on the different experiences of men and women in the workforce. In Australia, the term "affirmative action" encompasses an understanding that it is not enough to find an act of discrimination unlawful; action needs to be taken to address past and present discriminatory practices, as well as to eradicate discriminatory practices in the future (French and Strachan, 2007). However, some authors argue that there has been insufficient evaluation of the impact upon women in employment (for example, French and Strachan, 2007). Others argue that the legislation itself operates to maintain the glass ceiling experienced by many working women (for example, Fastenau, 2006).

A unique feature of the EOWWA Act was the explicit aim to overcome discrimination in the workplace by creating organizational change through recognizing barriers that may be in operation, and identifying ways to eliminate these. The EOWW Act requires private sector organizations with more than 100 employees to implement an equal opportunity programme and to report to the EOWA (the Agency) on the issues, actions and priorities across a range of employment matters and to analyze the outcomes of these initiatives (French and Strachan, 2007: 315).

Therefore, the Act was conceived to "promote the elimination of discrimination and provision of equal opportunity for women in employment" (French and Strachan, 2007:315), and within such a framework, it was envisaged that subsequent employment decisions would be merit based. In essence, seven specific areas of employment are considered in the data gathering required for these reports: "recruitment and selection; promotion and transfer;

training and development; work organization; conditions of employment; sexual harassment; and pregnancy and breastfeeding" (French and Strachan, 2007:319).

After an analysis of the data received from participating organizations, the Affirmative Action Agency has the power to bestow recognition on companies by waiving the annual requirement to report their data, or by awarding the accolade of Employer of Choice for Women (EOCFW) on "successful" organizations. A very small proportion of reporting organizations (less than 4 percent) have been awarded EOCFW status (French and Strachan, 2007).

Initiatives Supporting Women in the Workforce

Organizations covered by the Act are required to develop and implement a workplace programme with a view to ensuring that organizations identify and address any issues relevant to the career advancement of female staff. Some organizations have embraced the spirit of the legislation by going much further than an initial compliance. For example, IBM has recently been named the 2007 Employer of Choice for women in Australia, which is an unbroken record of seven consecutive years (IBM, 2007).

This organization has developed policies that have been instrumental in increasing the number of women holding executive positions, recruiting and retaining older workers, as well as enhancing possibilities for the work–life balance of their employees. IBM has been recognized for its commitment to become, and remain an employer of choice for women. The company frequently wins diversity awards in relation to the advancement of women, and the employment and inclusion of older workers, as well as disabled workers (IBM, 2007).

It is clear that some organizations are appearing to be taking equal opportunity for women seriously, and hence initiatives are being embraced and implemented into the workplace. Recently, the EOWA in Australia released a list of 111 organizations that were named as "2009 Employer of Choice for Women" (EOWA, 2009).

The exemplary organizations (see www.eowa.gov.au/EOWA_Employer_Of_Choice_For_Women) are illustrating an awareness of the importance to both attract as well as retain valued employees. However, it is obvious that many more organizations need to adopt a similar philosophy.

The Future

This chapter has outlined the numerous factors operating that appear to keep women in Australia under-represented in the workforce in general, and in roles of power, seniority or status more specifically. It may be that the legislation adopted to address these very issues is incapable of doing so.

In a recent review of the equal employment opportunity policies and practices within the Australian finance and insurance industry, French and Strachan (2007: 326) concluded that "women's advancement into leadership in this industry is not related to equal employment opportunity activities as they are currently implemented". This research further found that within this industry, relatively few organizations were taking the initiative to develop strategies that would proactively address three key areas of recruiting, promoting, and retaining women. In fact, a third of all organizations participating in this research made no mention of these key issues in their annual reports to EOWA (French and Strachan, 2007).

This finding points to the limitations in this legislation to actually "promote the elimination of discrimination and provision of equal opportunity for women in employment" (French and Strachan, 2007:315). There appears to be several reasons for this. Firstly, there is a commonly held perception that women are already treated equally in the three key areas outlined above, indicating a lack of critical analysis of the processes and systems that operate within organizations. Obviously, advances have been made in areas such as flexible work hours and job-sharing, and most recently, in paid parental leave for care givers for 18 weeks from 2011 (Symonds and Ong, 2009). However, there still remains a real need for embracing the development of female staff through appropriate career opportunities (French and Strachan, 2007).

Secondly, the legislation has not been able to protect women from a perception that they will be penalized for accessing family-friendly policies in their organizations. Almost a quarter of the sample of 2,443 professional and managerial women in an American organization, stated that there was a recognition in their workplace that women who accessed the available options would not be promoted in the future (Hewlett and Luce, 2005).

Thirdly, it appears that Equal Employment Opportunity (EEO) has become watered down in its intent; it does not deliver what it has promised in either recruitment, promotion or development (Fastenau, 2006). There is also cause for concern in the observation that some organizations are beginning to withdraw from the annual reporting process. In the 2003–2004 reporting period, from the 2,712 companies who reported that period, only 17 companies (0.6 percent) failed to comply (Fastenau, 2006). In 2008, only 12 organizations were non-compliant (0.5 percent), however 200 less organizations (2513) submitted a report in this period (EOWA, 2008c). Further problems in realizing the intent of the legislation are suggested by less than 4 percent of reporting organizations receiving the Employer of Choice for Women (EOCFW) award, which is bestowed on exemplary organizations (French and Strachan, 2007).

In addition, waived organizations (those who have been given an exemption for up to three years because they have shown that their EEO practices relating to the seven key employment areas are "on-track") within the finance and insurance industry do not appear to be doing better or even as well as companies that continue to report each year in terms of women in leadership roles (French and Strachan, 2007).

Furthermore, there has been a marked drop-out rate of Australian universities in applying for the citation of EOCFW, with several prestigious universities failing to meet the citation criterion, and openly questioning whether they would re-apply in the future. Reasons for this appear to be a frustration with the new standards introduced by the EOWA in order to "raise the bar" for organizations. Criticisms of the criteria have included: "too generic", "irrelevant or inconsistent" or "increasingly onerous to administer" (Trounson, 2009).

It seems that many organizations are addressing the stated "letter of the law" of the EEO legislation, but they are not drilling down to a level which captures *the spirit* of the legislation. Even amongst the organizations that do appear to acknowledge the barriers to women's career opportunities, they do not take the added step of specifying clear outcomes for the programmes they set in place, nor do they require that senior managers are responsible for achieving these goals (Fastenau, 2006).

All of the above issues point to the possibility that the Australian Government appear to lack a genuine commitment to dealing with these issues in a way that is likely to bring about real change. This is incongruous given the stated desire to increase the participation of women in leadership roles throughout

Australian society by the Australian Government: "...from representation in parliament, government, and senior levels in the public and private sectors, to leadership roles in communities throughout Australia" (Office for Women, 2008:2).

It appears that it may be time to go back to the drawing-board, and to recognize that there is a gendered perspective to the practice of management within many Australian organizations. Such cultures have the capacity to inhibit genuine opportunities for women in management. "This is of particular economic importance when women play an increasingly crucial role in twenty-first century organisations" (Mavin, Bryans and Waring, 2004:575), and when it is acknowledged that increasing the proportions of women in senior executive roles is likely to impact positively on the bottom line for businesses (Office for Women, 2008).

One step in this direction would be for organizations to "create strategies that increase development and advancement opportunities for women" (Catalyst, 2009:26). However, as has been outlined in this chapter, creating strategies is not enough. In order for real changes to be made to the numbers of women in Australia to fill senior roles in the private and public sector, in government representation, and to receive equal pay for their work, there has to be a level of commitment across the board, and widespread culture change, which has not yet occurred in this country. Talent has to be recognized and rewarded, on the basis of merit, regardless of the sex of the individual.

In Australia, EOWA has outlined a vision that Australians need to work together to ensure that there will be a time when women can enter the workforce without having assumptions made about what they can or cannot do *because they are women*. Such a vision encompasses that women will become an integral part of the informal networks that foster decision makers. They will not be harassed because they are women, and they will be able to have sufficient flexibility in their work to allow them to fulfill their family responsibilities. Finally, they will receive open access to significant career opportunities based on the merit principle, and of course, they will receive equal pay for the "equal work" they perform (EOWA, 2008b). This is a future for working women that I hope my daughter will experience as a reality.

References

Australian Bureau of Statistics (2003) *Women in Trade* (Canberra: Australian Government Publishing Service).

Australian Bureau of Statistics (2004) *Characteristics of Small Business*, Catalogue No. 8127.0 (Canberra: Australian Government Publishing Service).

Australian Bureau of Statistics (2006a) *Population Characteristics, Aboriginal and Torres Strait Islander Australians*, Catalogue No. 4713.0 (Canberra: Australian Government Publishing Service).

Australian Bureau of Statistics (2006b) *Census of Population and Housing* (Census Tables), Catalogue No. 2068.0 (Canberra: Australian Government Publishing Service).

Australian Bureau of Statistics (2006c) *Self-employed Aboriginal and Torres Strait Islander People, 2006*, Catalogue No. 4722.0.55.009 (Canberra: Australian Government Publishing Service).

Australian Bureau of Statistics (2007) *Australian Social Trends*, Catalogue No. 4102.0 (Canberra: Australian Government Publishing Service).

Australian Bureau of Statistics (2008a) *Education and Work*. May, 2008, Catalogue No. 6227.0 (Canberra: Australian Government Publishing Service).

Australian Bureau of Statistics (2008b) *Average Weekly Earnings*, May, 2008, Catalogue No. 6302.0 (Canberra: Australian Government Publishing Service).

Australian Bureau of Statistics (2008c) *Counts of Australian Business Operators*, October, 2008, Catalogue No. 8175.0 (Canberra: Australian Government Publishing Service).

Australian Bureau of Statistics (2008d) *Australian Small Business Operators – Findings from the 2005 and 2006 Characteristics of Small Business Surveys, 2005–06*, Catalogue 8127.0 (Canberra: Australian Government Publishing Service).

Australian Bureau of Statistics (2008e) *Labour Force Characteristics of Aboriginal and Torres Strait Islander Australians, Estimates from the Labour Force Survey, 2007*, Catalogue No. 6287.0 (Canberra: Australian Government Publishing Service).

Australian Bureau of Statistics (2008f) *The Health and Wellbeing of Aboriginal and Torres Strait Islander Women: A Snapshot, 2004–05*, Catalogue No. 4722.0.55.001 (Canberra: Australian Government Publishing Service).

Australian Bureau of Statistics (2009a) *Labour Force Australia*, Catalogue No. 6202.0, Table 01, March, 2009 (Canberra: Australian Government Publishing Service).

Australian Bureau of Statistics (2009b) *Labour Force, Australia*, Detailed Quarterly Table 07 (6291.0.55.003). Catalogue No. 6202.0. Employed persons by Occupation and Sex (Canberra: Australian Government Publishing Service).

Australian Bureau of Statistics (2009c) *Experimental Life Tables for Aboriginal and Torres Strait Islander Australians, 2005–2007*, Catalogue No. 3302.0.55.003 (Canberra: Australian Government Publishing Service).

AHRC (Australian Human Rights Commission) (2009) *Women in Leadership*, http://www.hreoc.gov.au/sex_discrimination/programs/women_leadership.html, accessed 27 May, 2009.

Bagwell, S. (1993) Why women don't make it, *Financial Review*, August 27, 1–3.

Burrows, S. (2008) New workplace laws must help women, *The Lamp*, September 11.

Catalyst (2009) *Cascading Gender Biases, Compounding Effects: An Assessment of Talent Management Systems* (New York, NY: Catalyst).

Charlesworth, S. (1997) Enterprise bargaining and women workers: the seven perils of flexibility, *Labour and Industry*, 8(2), 101–115.

Davidson, M. J. and Cooper, C. (1992) *Shattering the Glass Ceiling. The Woman Manager* (London, UK: Paul Chapman).

De Ceiri, H., Holmes, B., Abbott, J. and Pettit, T. (2005) Achievements and challenges for work/life balance strategies in Australian organisations, *International Journal of Human Resource Management*, 16,(1), 90–103.

DEST (Department of Education, Science and Training) (2008) *Summary of Students 2008 [first half year]:* Selected Higher Education Statistics, www.dest.gov.au, accessed 25 May, 2009.

Equal Opportunity for Women in the Workplace Agency (2008a) *2008 EOWA Australian Census of Women in Leadership* (Sydney: Commonwealth of Australia).

Equal Opportunity for Women in the Workplace Agency Census Media Kit (2008b) *2008 EOWA Australian Census of Women in Leadership*. Press Release, 28 October, 2008.

Equal Opportunity for Women in the Workplace Agency (2008c) *Annual Report 2007/2008* (Sydney: Commonwealth of Australia).

Equal Opportunity for Women in the Workplace Agency (2009) www.eowa.gov.au, accessed 1 May, 2009.

Fastenau, M. (2006) Explaining the persistence of the glass ceiling. In S. Charlesworth, K. Douglas, M. Fastenau and S. Cartwright (eds) *Women and Work 2005: Current RMIT University Research* (Melbourne: RMIT Publishing, pp. 61–80).

Frazer, L. and Weaven, S. (2004) *Franchising Australia 2004* (Brisbane: Griffith University).

Frederick, H. H. and Foley, D. (2006) Indigenous populations as disadvantaged entrepreneurs in Australia and New Zealand, *The International Indigenous Journal of Entrepreneurship, Advancement, Strategy and Education*, 2(2), http://www.indigenousjournal.com/IIJEASVolIIss2Frederick.pdf.

Frederick, H. H., Kuratko, D. F. and Hodgetts, R. M. (2007) *Entrepreneurship: Theory, Process and Practice* (South Melbourne, Victoria: Nelson Australia).

French, E. and Strachan, G. (2007) Equal opportunity outcomes for women in the finance industry in Australia: Evaluating the merit of EEO plans, *Asia Pacific Journal of Human Resources*, 45(3), 314–332.

Fuller, D., Dansie, P., Jones, M. and Holmes, S. (1999) Indigenous Australians and self employment, *Small Enterprise Research: The Journal of SEAANZ*, 7(2), 5–28.

Hausmann, R., Tyson, L. D. and Zahidi, S. (2008) *The Global Gender Gap Report* (Switzerland: World Economic Forum).

Hewlett, S. A. and Luce, C. B. (2005) Off-Ramps and on-ramps: keeping talented women on the road to success, *Harvard Business Review*, 83(3), March, 43–54.

Hudson Highland Group (2005) *The Case for Work/Life Balance*, 20:20 series (Auckland: Hudson Global Resources Australia Pty. Ltd).

IBM (2007) *IBM named '2007 Employer of Choice for Women*, http://www-07.ibm.com/au/diversity/awards/2007/eowa.html, accessed 21 May, 2009.

Lyness, K. and Heilman, M. (2006) When fit is fundamental: Performance evaluations and promotions of upper-level female and male managers, *Journal of Applied Psychology*, 91(4), 777–785.

Mavin, S., Bryans, P. and Waring, T. (2004) Unlearning gender blindness: new directions in management education, *Management Decision*, 42(3/4), 565–578.

McDonnell, S. (1999) *The Grameen Bank Micro-credit Model: Lessons for Australian Indigenous Economic Policy*. Discussion Paper No. 178/1999, Centre for Aboriginal Economic Policy Research (Canberra: The Australian National University).

Morgan, L. and Davidson, M. J. (2008) Sexual dynamics in mentoring relationships: A critical review, *British Journal of Management*, 19(S1), s120–s129.

Office for Women (2008). *Ensuring Women's Equal Place in Society*. Fact Sheet 5, November, 2008. (Canberra: Australian Government, Department of Families, Housing, Community Services and Indigenous Affairs).

Palermo, J. (2004) *Breaking the Cultural Mould: The Key to Women's Career Success*, Hudson 20:20 series: Hudson Global Resources and Human Capital Solutions.

Parliament of Australia: Senate (2010) *Women in the Senate*, Senate Brief No. 3, April, www.aph.gov.au/senate, accessed 8 March, 2011.

Parliamentary Education Office, Parliament of Australia (2009) *Frequently Asked Questions, Our Parliament* (House of Representatives and The Senate), http://www.peo.gov.au/faq, accessed 21 August, 2009.

Pocock, B., van Wanrooy, B., Strazzari, S. and Bridge, K. (2001) *Fifty families. What Unreasonable Hours are Doing to Australians, their Families and their Communities*, Adelaide University website, http://www.actu.org.au/public/campaigns/reasonable/files/fiftyfamilies_one.pdf, accessed 8 March, 2011.

Schein, V. E. (1975) Relationships between sex-role stereotypes and requisite management characteristics among female managers, *Journal of Applied Psychology*, 60(3), 340–344.

Schein, V. E. (1994) Managerial sex typing: A persistent and pervasive barrier to women's opportunities. In M. J. Davidson and R. J. Burke (eds) *Women in Management: Current Research Issues* (London: Paul Chapman, pp. 41–52).

Schein, V. E. (2001) A global look at psychological barriers to women's progress in management, *Journal of Social Issues*, 57(4), 675–688.

Schein, V. E. (2006) *Women in Management: Reflections and Projections*. Key-note speech presented at the 26th International Congress of Applied Psychology, Athens, Greece, 17 July, 2006.

Schein, V. E., and Mueller, R. (1992) Sex role stereotyping and requisite management characteristics: A cross cultural look, *Journal of Organizational Behaviour*, 13(5), 439–447.

Still, L. V. and Walker, E. A. (2006) The self-employed woman owner and her business: an Australian profile, *Women in Management Review*, 21(4), 294–310.

Symonds, A. and Ong, T. (2009) Primary caregivers get 18 weeks leave, *Australian Financial Review*, Monday 11 May, 2009, p. 7.

The Lamp (2007) Women the biggest losers under WorkChoices, May, p. 24.

Trounson, A. (2009) Equal opportunity too hard as Unis. Drop out, *The Australian*, 25 March, p. 30.

Von Doussa, J. (2007) It's about time: Key findings from the women, men, work and family project, *Family Matters*, 76, 48–54.

Wajcman, J. (1999) *Managing Like a Man: Women and Men in Corporate Management* (Cambridge: Polity).

Weaven, S., Isaac, J. and Herington, C. (2007) Franchising as a path to self-employment for Australian female entrepreneurs, *Journal of Management and Organization* 13(4), 345–365.

Women in Parliament, Statistics on House of Representatives and the Senate, Parliamentary Library, Parliament of Australia (2001) www.aph.gov.au/library/.

Wood, G. J. (2008) Gender stereotypical attitudes: past, present and future influences on women's career advancement, *Equal Opportunity International*, 27(7), 613–628.

Wood, G. J. and Lindorff, M. (2001) Sex differences in explanations for career progress, *Women in Management Review*, 16(4), 152–162.

Wood, G. J. and Newton, J. (2006) Childlessness and women managers: 'choice', Context and discourses, *Gender, Work and Organization*, 13(4), 338–358.

Women in Australia (2009) *Women in Australia. Department of Families, Housing, Community Services and Indigenous Affairs* (Canberra: Australian Government).

14

Women in Management in New Zealand

Judy McGregor

Introduction

When New Zealand's highest paid female senior manager, Theresa Gattung, resigned in 2007 as CEO of the telco, Telecom, the business media wrote: "Let's face it, the woman had to go, she was too honest. In today's business world, that simply won't do." (Fairfax Business Media, 2007).

The quote provides insight into the masculine managerial style that has traditionally dominated New Zealand's corporate sector. It remains to be seen if the global recession provides greater opportunities for women's representation at the top following the inevitable reassessment of corporate values. As Gattung's resignation shows, there are signs of slippage in the tiny number of women at the top in New Zealand. The previous pattern of positive incremental change, however small, appears to have stalled and in some areas is sliding backwards.

This chapter aims to report on women's status in management in New Zealand and to consider the influence of regulation and voluntarism on the progress of managerial women in the public and private sectors.

Labour Force Characteristics

Record numbers of New Zealand women have entered the workforce in the past 50 years. This phenomenal social change has occurred within two generations. The labour force participation of New Zealand women reached its highest ever in September 2008 at 62.6 percent, up from 29 percent in 1959. This compares with a labour force participation rate for men of 75 percent, and giving New Zealand a labour force participation rate overall of 68.7 percent, (2,172,000 people) the equal-highest level ever recording according to Statistics New Zealand (2008).

Just over 70 percent of all women aged between 20–64 years are in paid work, compared with 85 percent of men in these peak income-generating years. Yet despite this, women in the 25–34 years age group tend to leave the workforce in greater numbers than in other similar Organisation for Economic Co-operation and Development (OECD) countries when they have children, returning when those children get older. This prompted the then Prime Minister, Helen Clark, in 2005 "with almost Soviet-style exhortations for women" to strongly encourage mothers to join and stay in the workforce (Black, 2006).

New Zealand, like other countries, is predicting a slowdown in labour force growth largely because of population ageing. Beyond 2020 the labour market will plateau in size and around 80 percent of the current market will still be in the workforce in 2020 (Department of Labour, 2008a). A newer demographic trend, that of more older women staying in the workforce beyond 65 years of age is a consequence both of labour force ageing and of New Zealand's long established anti-age discrimination which prohibits compulsory retirement. Whether these women have to work for financial security given their average earnings are 12.5 percent lower than men's, or want to stay in work longer for social connection and personal fulfilment, requires more research in the New Zealand context.

However, the high female participation rate occurred before the recent global economic crisis which could impact in the short and medium term on labour force participation rates. Will women be disproportionately disadvantaged by increased unemployment which is predicted to rise to 7.5 percent throughout 2009–2010 from the 4.6 percent unemployment rate recorded in the December 2008 Household Labour Force Survey (Department of Labour, 2008c)? The global downturn is impacting on women's work in retail, services and professional and administrative support. Current indications are negative. Unemployment rates in the quarter to December 2008 show women lost 7,000 jobs compared with 3,000 jobs lost by men (Department of Labour, 2008b).

Women are still concentrated in a narrower range of jobs than men and are predominantly clustered in health, the service sector, education and caring industries (Department of Labour, 2008c). This occupational segregation contributes to the gender pay gap indicating that women's work continues to be under-valued in New Zealand, as it is in many other developed countries. The gender pay gap has remained at about 12 percent since 2001, with women's median hourly earnings at NZ$17.50 compared to NZ$20.00 for men (Department of Labour, 2008c).

Pay and employment equity reviews have been undertaken in 27 of the 39 public service organizations throughout the health sector including district health boards and in the compulsory school sector in recent years. In every case, gender pay gaps in median full-time equivalent earnings were recorded of between 3 to 35 percent, according to the Pay and Employment Equity Steering Group Report (Department of Labour, 2008c). In all organizations reviewed except one, women were found to be under-represented in senior management and under-represented in management overall (Department of Labour, 2008c). This is particularly significant given that larger numbers of women work in the health, education and the public sector and that in New Zealand the public sector tends to lead women's workplace progress. Furthermore, it should also be noted that the gender pay gap is also more pronounced for New Zealand's indigenous women. European Pakeha women's median hourly earnings (NZ$18.22) are significantly higher than both Maori and Pacific women (NZ$15.15 and NZ$14.75 respectively) (Department of Labour, 2008c).

Women Pursuing Education

Participation in tertiary education is an indicator of the extent to which women are currently acquiring the skills and qualifications to equip them to participate in work, society and public life. In 2007, women were slightly more likely than men to be enrolled in a tertiary qualification, 14.2 percent compared with 12.3 percent and accounted for 54 percent (241,000) of domestic students enrolled. While the proportion of both men and women enrolled in tertiary qualifications increased between 1999 and 2005 it has decreased slightly since 2005, according to the Ministry of Women's Affairs Indicators for Change report (2008). Women are more likely than men to be enrolled in higher-level than lower-level qualifications. Sixty-one percent of students who completed a tertiary qualification in 2006 were women and an estimated 50 percent of female students completed within five years compared with 40 percent of men (New Zealand University Vice-Chancellors' Committee, 2008).

Despite women's increased tertiary participation, female graduates almost immediately suffer a gender pay gap in workplaces (New Zealand University Vice-Chancellors' Committee, 2008). The financial outcomes of higher educational participation for women challenge the perceived orthodoxy that once women are better qualified the gender pay gap will shrink. The New Zealand University Vice-Chancellors Committee's annual survey of all graduates shows significantly different salary outcomes for men and women six months after graduation in 11 occupational fields (New Zealand University Vice-Chancellors' Committee, 2008) For example, in commerce and business, the median salary for male graduates is NZ$50,000 compared with NZ$43,334 for women. In health there is an NZ$11,000 median salary differential in favour of men, in social and behavioural sciences there is a NZ$5,000 difference and even in the humanities, a traditionally female domain, men are approximately NZ$2,500 better off.

Young women, too, are significantly under-represented in start-up trades training in the Modern Apprenticeship scheme. The big three industries dominating the scheme are overwhelmingly male; building and construction at 2,057 men and 9 women; motor engineering 1,629 men and 52 women; and engineering 1,634 men and 14 women. Only the recent addition of hairdressing as an occupation qualifying for funding with 266 women and 11 men has increased the number of females in trades training to 1,361 or 11.03 percent compared with 10,983 men at 88.97 percent (Modern Apprenticeships, 2008). The Modern Apprenticeship scheme has received considerable public funding at a time when financing a university qualification is increasingly user-pays. Female university student leaders have expressed concern about policies and funding of employment pathways that reinforce gender inequity (Modern Apprenticeships, 2008). It is interestingly to note that "women's only" educational scholarships were recently challenged by a men's rights researcher who asked the New Zealand Human Rights Commission whether they now contravene the Human Rights Act 1993, given the rise in women's participation and achievement in tertiary education. While discrimination on the grounds of sex is unlawful, the Human Rights Act does allow for special measures to ensure equality. Many of the organizations providing targeted funding for women, such as the Federation of Graduate Women, are constituted as charitable trusts which are exempt from anti-discrimination legislation (Human Rights Commission, 2009).

Unfortunately the "zero sum" debate continues in New Zealand with male researchers focusing on women's "privilege" in educational participation and feminist researchers referencing gender disparity in outcomes. New Zealand's economic development and social cohesion depends on *both* men and women participating fully in educational pathways, including State-subsidized trades training and tertiary education and having equal outcomes as a result. The evidence shows participation is uneven and outcomes include entrenched occupational segregation and a persistent gender pay gap disadvantaging women.

Women in Management

While there have been increasing numbers in women in management in New Zealand over the past 20 years, there is a profound difference between glacial progress in the corporate sector and the steady if unspectacular movement in the public sector. To some extent this reflects the statutory compulsion for equal employment opportunities in the public sector which stimulates progress and provides transparency through reporting and monitoring. By contrast the voluntary approach in the private sector results in less impetus and less visibility (McGregor, 2008).

In the corporate sector, women scarcely feature at the top of publicly listed companies. A tiny 1.6 percent (three) of the chief executives of the 186 companies listed in the three securities markets of the New Zealand Exchange, the New Zealand Stock Market (NZSX), the New Zealand Debt Market (NZDX) and the New Zealand Alternative market (NZAX) were women, as at October 2007 (Human Rights Commission, 2008).

The Equal Employment Opportunities (EEO) Trust in New Zealand has collected unpublished data from the marzipan layer of senior management below CEO in the top 100 companies of the NZSX. Senior management was defined by the companies themselves and included executive teams, senior management teams, leadership teams and chief executive direct reports. A total of 569 positions were identified in total, of which 80 were women representing 14 percent of the senior management of the top 100 companies. Human resources specialists dominated with 18 of the 80 women, followed by legal counsel and corporate or public relations.

As illustrated in Table 14.1, women held 8.65 percent of board directorships of the top 100 companies in 2008, up from 7.13 percent in 2006. There were 54 female directorships out of the total of 624 directorships. Sixty of the top

100 companies have no women on their boards and only 2 of the top 100 companies by market capitalization have gender parity in their boardrooms (McGregor, 2008).

Table 14.1   New Zealand Exchange companies and female directors

At October 2007	NZSX (Top 100)	NZAX	NZDX
Female-held directorships	54 (8.65%)	7 (5.07%)	16 (5.73%)
Companies with female directors	40 (40%)	6 (21.42%)	13 (24.52%)
Companies with one female director	27 (27%)	5 (17.85%)	10 (18.86%)
Companies with two or more female directors	13 (13%)	1 (3.57%)	3 (5.66%)

Source: McGregor, 2008

Moving beyond publicly listed companies and comparing men's and women's status in privately held businesses shows a distinct improvement in women's status in management. For example, women in senior management in New Zealand were reported at 27 percent ahead of Australia (23 percent), the UK (21 percent) and the US (20 percent), and behind the Philippines (47 percent) China (31 percent) and Turkey (29 percent) in an annual business survey undertaken by an accountancy company (Grant Thornton, 2009). The data from over 7,200 privately held businesses in 36 economies shows Japan at the bottom with 7 percent and that women overall still hold less than a quarter of senior management positions in privately held business globally. However, the difference in gender representation of publicly listed companies and privately held businesses reflects the number of family-owned private companies, the smaller size of much private business and the fact the female entrepreneurship generally starts in private business (McGregor, 2008).

Nevertheless, there is some evidence that indigenous women in New Zealand are better represented in the management of their own organizations. A Human Rights Commission study for the 2008 census report of Māori organizations consisting of iwi (tribal) authorities and Māori affiliated and owned businesses showed a 27.47 percent representation of Māori women in management (McGregor, 2008).

On a more positive note, comparison of the private sector figures with the public service are more encouraging. New Zealand's public service is a good measure of women's progress in managerial ranks given the high number of women employed in the State sector (59 percent) (McGregor, 2008). Equal employment opportunities are also compulsory in the public sector in New Zealand under the State Sector Act 1988 while it is largely voluntary in the private sector. Monitoring of public service women in management shows a familiar picture of small numbers and slow progress (McGregor, 2008). Less than a quarter (23 percent) of public service chief executives are women. At the next level down, in senior management, women continue to be under-represented compared with their labour force representation, with 38 percent of senior managers in the public service being women (McGregor, 2008). This is despite 24 of the 35 public service departments employing more women than men. The high numbers of women employed in the State sector reflects the relatively high number of female-dominated occupations such as social workers, case workers, clerical staff, teachers and nurses. Since 2002, the percentage of women in senior management in the core public service has fluctuated between 35.1 percent (2003) and 37.8 percent (2007) (McGregor, 2008).

Women also fare better in government appointments to statutory bodies (up 1 percent to 42 percent in 2008) than they do in private sector boardroom appointments (8.65 percent in 2008) (McGregor, 2008). However, New Zealand has only a short time to live up to promises made internationally by successive governments to reach 50 percent gender parity in government-appointed bodies by 2010 (McGregor, 2008).

Specific sectors where women and management research has been undertaken shows similar patterns of under-representation. For example, while the number of women in local government management has doubled over ten years (369 in 1996 to 837 in 2006), women still hold only 5 percent of CEO positions and 24 percent of second-tier management jobs (Drage and Johnston, 2008). Barriers identified by these authors for women in local government include:

- sexism of male mayors;

- career structures dominated by male engineers and accountants;

- lack of support from other managers to apply;

- the style of management expected;

- a long work hours culture and work–life balance issues.

Leadership and management in primary schools has also been researched in terms of succession and gender (Brooking, 2008). Brooking's (2008) results show that in 2002 women represented 82 percent of the workforce in New Zealand primary schools, but were disproportionately under-represented in leadership, occupying over 40 percent of principal positions. This meant that 60 percent of principals were appointed from a 18 percent male pool of the workforce. By 2005 it was 43.5 percent female principals and 80.5 percent of senior managers, indicating a very slow rise in the number being appointed from a stable group of senior managers. The pool of men had fallen to 14 percent yet still had the majority of principal appointments. "These facts suggest that there is a very large pool of well qualified and experienced women who may be hitting a glass ceiling," (Brooking, 2008:42). Brooking's analysis of why the equal employment opportunities gender balance principle was being subverted by school boards identified three possible reasons for male preference. These were a desire for "masculinist heroic leadership", concern about feminized schooling and the need to have male role models for boys, and the attraction of sports heroes for male team sports (Brooking, 2008).

While the statistics and findings presented above provide an adequate summary of where women are at the top in the public and private sectors, there is an urgent need to repeat the nationwide, benchmark studies of women in management that were conducted in the 1990s (Still, McGregor and Dewe, 1994) and in 2000 (McGregor, 2004). These allowed for longitudinal tracking using standardized databases, provided rigorous cross-country comparison with New Zealand's neighbour, Australia, and tracked women's progress in the hierarchy of management from junior to senior management levels.

Women Entrepreneurs

Defining entrepreneurship has been traditionally difficult. In New Zealand the problem is compounded by the micro-size of business and the fact that starting a new business has become a proxy for entrepreneurship. The Global Entrepreneurship Monitor (GEM) report claimed in 2004 that New Zealand has the highest women's entrepreneurship rate in the developed world, although the entrepreneurial gender gap is still severe with women suffering a

30 percent deficit compared to the numbers of male entrepreneurs (Acs et al., 2004). One of the report's authors said policy makers in New Zealand need to promote entrepreneurial education at all levels, encourage more women to pursue technical degrees and commercialize ideas (Frederick, 2005). However, unfortunately, New Zealand does not feature in the most recent GEM report (Bosma et al., 2008).

There was a total of 385,521 self-employed in March 2007, about 20 percent of the total labour force. About 15 percent of women in the labour force were self-employed (25 percent men) across three types of self-employment: self-employed with no staff, self-employed with staff or as unpaid workers in a family business. Clearly, indications are that the number of self-employed women is growing and the entry rate of women is higher than that of men (Massey and Harris, 2003). In this 2003 survey, of all women who were self-employed, 30 were employers, 53 were sole operators and 17 percent were unpaid in a family business (more than twice as may as men). Self-employed women were slightly younger than men, better qualified and more Maori and Pacific women were unpaid in family firms. Like other areas of the labour market, the levels of income for self-employed women are lower than they are for self-employed men and more self-employed women are more likely to be part time (Massey and Harris, 2003).

Country Legislation

Women's progress at the top in both management and governance in New Zealand is hampered by the absence of comprehensive equal employment opportunities legislation and positive duties and the lack of political will to compel the private sector to do better. The private sector is bound only by the general anti-discrimination and employment law frameworks. While many in the private sector may promote women, it is difficult to gather a reliable picture because of the absence of reporting requirements in the private sector. Data gathering is ad hoc, variable and of limited visibility.

The public sector must be a "Good employer" under the State Sector Act 1988, the Crown Entities Act 2004 (which includes all 21 district health boards) and the Local Government Act 2002. Under these statutes a good employer is an employer who operates a personnel policy containing provisions generally accepted as necessary for the fair and proper treatment of employees in all aspects of their employment. Legislative provisions require:

- good and safe working conditions;

- equal employment opportunities programmes;

- impartial selection processes;

- recognition of Māori, ethnic and minority groups, persons with disabilities and women.

Monitoring of the good employer obligations of 96 Crown entities (which include health, energy and public agencies) is undertaken by the Human Rights Commission. The State Services Commission has oversight of the core public service.

The strange distinction between the public and private sectors is unlikely to change in the near future. There is almost complete absence of public or political dialectic in New Zealand about quotas or affirmative action to redress wholesale gender imbalances in business leadership (McGregor, 2008). In a stocktake of equal employment opportunities, Mintrom and True (2004:122) urged advocates to "work towards the introduction of legislation that places stronger positive duties on all employers, starting with large organizations, to develop and implement EEO plans, and regularly report on the outcomes."

While employment and pre-employment discrimination complaints are one of the most frequent areas of complaint to the Human Rights Commission, the individual nature of the complaints makes anti-discrimination legislation a limited mechanism for women (McGregor, 2008). The process used to progress complaints is dispute resolution which can afford satisfaction to individual parties but limits strategic litigation to develop the law. The Office of Human Rights Proceedings, the litigation arm of the Commission won a landmark sex discrimination case against a major employer, *Talleys Fisheries Ltd v Caitlin Lewis and Anor HC WN* in 2002, but the case took six years to resolve.

Initiatives Supporting Women in the Workforce

The dynamic of requiring governments to periodically submit to international peer review on women's rights has particular significance in New Zealand, perhaps because of its small size and geographical isolation and the country's pride in its international human rights reputation. As Rubenstein (2008) notes, the compilation of regular compliance reports for the United Nations Convention on the Elimination of All Forms of Discrimination Against Women (CEDAW) in itself acts as a stimulus for change. For example, the issue of women in management and governance was referred to in the CEDAW committee's concluding comments (United Nations Convention on the Elimination of All Forms of Discrimination Against Women, 2007). New Zealand was urged in the next five years to establish goals and timeframes to increase the number of women in decision-making positions at the local level, in the civil service, in political parties, district health boards, statutory boards and the judiciary.

Women in management also features in the New Zealand Human Rights Commission's submission to the Universal Periodic Review (UPR) held by the United Nations Human Rights Council (UNHRC). The UPR is a significant new human rights mechanism that provides an important opportunity for states to assess and evaluate each other every four years on the basis of reliable and objective information. It looks at whether states are fulfilling human rights obligations and commitments. In its report on New Zealand's Human Rights Performance (2008) the Commission recommends that: "the government establishes targets for improving representation of women in senior management in the public service, and sets a minimum target of halving the gender pay gap by 2012 and eliminating it by 2020" (Human Rights Commission, 2008:10).

The Agenda for Change in the New Zealand Census of Women's Participation 2008 also urges the Minister of State Services to set a benchmark for the State Services Commission to achieve gender parity in chief executive appointments in five years. The State Services Commissioner was asked to make chief executives accountable through performance management processes for increased representation of women in senior management positions. For example, the 60 top 100 companies listed on the NSX without a single woman on their boards were urged to prioritize female appointments as soon as a board vacancy arose.

There are, however, no activities such as political sponsorship of quota-setting legislation (as in Norway, (Hole, 2009)), cross-company mentoring schemes (as in the UK (Sealy, Vinnicombe and Singh, 2008)) or male champions systematically providing an impetus for change. While a number of women's leaders networks have been established recently, they appear to more fulfil the function of social support rather than strategic activism.

Nevertheless, some successful sectoral initiatives are worth noting to increase the pool of women for promotion. The most notable is a pan-university women in leadership programme that now has 80 alumni from the eight New Zealand universities. The programme has increased female expectation of promotion in the tertiary system and is challenging universities to redress the low percentage of women as professors and associate professors (19.19 percent) (McGregor, 2008).

The Future

New Zealand improved its rating in the Global Gender Gap Report 2008 to fifth out of 130 countries, but it is ranked only fifteenth in the world in economic participation and opportunity in relation to the ratio of women to men as legislators, senior official and managers (Hausmann, Tyson and Zahidi, 2008).

New Zealand's problem with women's progress is that expectations for women are not matched by the reality of their representation. New Zealand was the first nation State to grant women suffrage and has enjoyed recent strong female political leadership with two consecutive female prime ministers before the current male incumbent. It has made undoubted achievements in women's education and all these indicators are closely bound up in New Zealanders' view of themselves as progressive and fair.

Complacency tinged with self-congratulation infects popular thinking about women's progress in management and governance. This comes at a time when organized women's activism is not strong and is not popular with younger women.

New Zealand needs a circuit breaker to challenge the continuing indifference to women's status in management and governance. Senior business champions, both men and women, need to be indentified as agents of change. They have a job to do to convince their peers of both the business case and social cohesion rationale to better utilize the female talent pool in a highly-skilled, global labour market.

Policy work also needs to be undertaken to test the business benefits of universal equal employment opportunities legislation that binds both the private and public sectors. Positive duties legislation could provide greater transparency of, and accountability for, the enduring problem of too few women at the top.

References

Acs, Z. J., Arenius, P., Hay, M. and Minniti, M. (2004) *Global Entrepreneurship Monitor 2004 Executive Report*, http://www.gemconsortium.org/download/1299642005137/GEM_2004_Exec_Report.pdf, accessed 21 January, 2009.

Black, J. (2006) The mother myth, *The Listener* [Online], 202(3432), http://www.listener.co.nz/issue/3432/features/5517/the_mother_myth.html, accessed 21 January, 2009.

Bosma, N., Acs, Z. J., Autio, E,. Coduras, A. and Levie, J. (2008) *Global Entrepreneurship Monitor 2008 Executive Report*, http://www.gemconsortium.org/download/1299642674762/GEM_Global_08.pdf, accessed 11 March, 2009.

Brooking, K. (2008) The future challenge of principal succession in New Zealand primary schools: implications of quality and gender, *International Studies in Educational Administration*, 36(1), 41–55.

Department of Labour (2008a) *Workforce 2020. Forces for Change in the Future Labour Market of New Zealand*, http://www.dol.govt.nz/PDFs/forces-for-change.pdf, accessed 21 January, 2009.

Department of Labour (2008b) *Household Labour Force Survey*, http://www.dol.govt.nz/publications/lmr/archive/hlfs-dec-08/lmr-hlfs-summary.asp, accessed 21 January, 2009.

Department of Labour (2008c) *Report of the Pay and Employment Equity Steering Group*, http://www.dol.govt.nz/services/PayAndEmploymentEquity/news/reports/peeu-annual-report-07-08.pdf, accessed 21 January, 2009.

Drage, J. and Johnston, K (2008) Local government management – where are the women? In J. McGregor (ed.) *New Zealand Census of Women's Participation* (Wellington: New Zealand Human Rights Commission, pp. 59–61).

Fairfax Business Media (2007) *Theresa Gattung Hangs Up*, http://blogs.reseller.co.nz/reseller/channelling/2007/02/theresa_gattung_hangs_up.html, accessed 21 January, 2009.

Frederick, H. (2005) New Zealand's women entrepreneurship rate could be better, *Scoop Independent News*, http://www.scoop.co.nz/stories/BU0503/S00084.htm, accessed 11 March, 2009.

Hausmann, R., Tyson, L. D. and Zahidi, S. (2008) *The Global Gender Gap Report 2008*, http://live.isitesoftware.co.nz/neon/documents/Global%20Gender%20Gap%202008%20report.pdf, accessed 11 March, 2009.

Hole, A. (2009) *Diversity Deployed: the Norwegian Story*, Keynote address to "Time for Action 2nd Diversity on Boards Conference, 1–3 September, 2009, Sydney.

Human Rights Commission (2008) *Report on New Zealand's Human Rights Performance*, http://www.hrc.co.nz/hrc_new/hrc/cms/files/documents/23-Feb-

2009_14-49-08_Report_on_NZs_Human_Rights_Performance.pdf, accessed 21 January, 2009.

Human Rights Commission (2009) *Clarification on Scholarships for Men and Women*, http://www.hrc.co.nz/home/hrc/newsandissues/clarificationonscholarships formenandwomen.php, accessed 21 January, 2009.

Massey, C. and Harris, C. (2003) *Discovering the Potential of Women in Small Business* Wellington, New Zealand: New Zealand Centre for SME Research, Massey University).

McGregor, J. (2004) Women in management in New Zealand. In M. J. Davidson and R. J. Burke (eds) *Women in Management Worldwide: Facts, Figures and Analysis* (Aldershot: Gower, pp. 211–224).

McGregor, J. (ed) (2008) *New Zealand Census of Women's Participation* (Wellington: Human Rights Commission).

Mintrom, M. and True, J. (2004) *Framework for the Future: Equal Employment Opportunities in New Zealand*, http://www.neon.org.nz/documents/2%20 Framework%20for%20the%20Future-full%20report%2010June04.pdf, accessed 11 March, 2009.

Ministry of Women's Affairs (2008) *Indicators for Change: Tracking Progress of New Zealand Women*, http://www.mwa.govt.nz/news-and-pubs/publications/ indicators-for-change.pdf, accessed 21 January, 2009.

Modern Apprenticeships (2008) http://www.neon.org.nz/eeoissues/modern apprenticeships/, accessed 12 March, 2011.

National Equal Opportunities Network (2008) *Modern Apprenticeships*, http:// www.neon.org.nz/eeoissues/modernapprenticeships/, accessed 21 January, 2009.

New Zealand Vice-Chancellors' Committee (2008) *NZUniGradStats*, http://www. nzvcc.ac.nz/files/u10/NZUniGradStats3.pdf, accessed 21 January, 2009.

Rubenstein, M. (2008) UN Disability Convention comes into force, *Equal Opportunities Review*, 176, 6–7.

Sealy, R., Vinnicombe, S. and Singh, V. (2008) *The Female FTSE Report 2008* (Cranfield: Cranfield University).

Statistics, New Zealand (2008) *New Zealand Household Labour Force Survey*, http://search.stats.govt.nz/search?w=household%20labour%20force%20 survey, accessed 21 January, 2009.

Still, L., McGregor, J. and Dewe, P. (1994) Room at the top? A comparison of the employment status of women in management in Australia and New Zealand, *International Journal of Employment Studies*, 2(2), 267–287.

Thornton, G. (2009) *Women Still Hold Less Than a Quarter of Senior Management*, http://www.internationalbusinessreport.com/Press-room/2009/women_in_ business.asp positions in privately held businesses, accessed 12 March, 2011.

United Nations Convention on the Elimination of All Forms of Discrimination Against Women (2007) *Concluding Comments of the Committee on the Elimination of Discrimination Against Women: New Zealand*. Thirty-ninth session 23 July, 10 August, http://daccess-dds-ny.un.org/doc/UNDOC/GEN/N06/342/12/PDF/N0634212.pdf?OpenElement, accessed 21 January, 2009.

PART V

Women in Management – Asia

15

Women in Management in China

Fang Lee Cooke

Introduction

China has a population of over 1.32 billion people, 48.5 percent of them are women and 55.6 percent are rural residents in 2007 (China Statistical Yearbook, 2008). The Chinese population is a relatively homogenous one in terms of ethnicity. The *han* ethnic group makes up over 91 percent of the population, whereas the other 55 ethnic minority groups consist of less than 9 percent of the population. Religion is not commonly practised in part due to the continuous suppression, albeit gradually relaxing, of non-communist beliefs by the State.

Since the founding of the Socialist China in 1949, significant progress has been made in achieving gender equality in education, employment and wage payment and social security provisions. This is necessarily an outcome of the strong intervention by the State. There has been a rising proportion of women participating in higher education and entering professional and managerial jobs at all levels in the last two decades (see China Statistical Yearbook, 2008). Despite this progress, discrimination against women in recruitment is worsening in part due to the marketization and the rising level of unemployment of university graduates. Once recruited, women face formidable barriers to career advancement. This is particularly the case in government and civil service organizations where the macro-political processes continue to exert salient and often decisive influences (Zhao and Zhou, 2004) and performance may be more difficult to be measured.

Two national non-government organizations (NGOs) – the All-China Women's Federation (ACWF) and the China Association of Women Entrepreneurs (CAWE) – have been set up to provide services and represent women's interests, including those of women managers and entrepreneurs. The ACWF, established in 1949, is a semi-government organization as it is funded by the Government and operates under its direction. Founded in 1985, CAWE is a group member of the ACWF and the China Enterprise Confederation (CEC), which is the only official employer association that the State recognizes at the national level as the sole representative of employers interests. What these NGOs have in common is their strong tie with the Government and the need for them to operate within its rules. As Unger and Chan (1995) observed, the State forms some kind of unequal partnerships with these organizations which often act on behalf of the State and help implement Government policies.

The assessment of achievements of and challenges to women in management in China needs to be conducted within the above political, economic and social context. This chapter provides an overview of the level of participation in employment and education by Chinese women. It outlines the patterns of their professional and managerial/entrepreneurial positions and the provisions of gender equality regulations and initiatives. Throughout the chapter, progress in these areas is summarized and challenges to gender equality in management are highlighted. The chapter concludes that whilst the level of gender equality is relatively high in China, measured by the education and employment level, there remain insurmountable barriers to women's managerial career. Moreover, gender equality achieved during the State-planned economy period is at risk of being eroded as the deepening marketization continues to dilute the level of State influence (Cooke, 2010).

Labour Force Characteristics

A distinct feature of women's labour market participation in China is that it has one of the highest women's participation rates in the world that is characterized by full-time employment. Women make up 45 percent of the labour force (The World Bank Group, 2006), with nearly 38 percent of the full-time workforce in urban units being women (China Statistical Yearbook 2008; also see Table 15.1). The majority of working women work full time throughout most of their working life, including those with child care responsibility. They tend to be interrupted only by a short period of maternity leave or by unemployment. There are several related reasons for Chinese women's high participation rate in the labour market. One is that participation in employment is seen as an important indicator of women's liberation and independence by the Chinese State. Another reason is that the socialist Government's economic policy that favoured full employment with low wage and low inflation, particularly during the State-planned economy period (1949–1978), necessitates dual wages to support a family (Cooke, 2007).

Table 15.1   Proportion (%) of female employees by ownership and sector for all employees in urban units (end of 1995 and 2007)

Item	Proportion(%) of female employment by ownership and sector in urban units							
	Total		State ownership		Collective ownership		Other ownership	
	1995	2007	1995	2007	1995	2007	1995	2007
National Total	38.6	37.8	36.1	37.1	44.6	35.4	48.3	39.0
Farming, forestry, animal Husbandry, fishery	37.6	36.9	37.8	37.1	31.9	26.2	37.2	36.6
Mining and quarrying	25.9	20.5	24.4	22.0	42.1	24.7	22.8	18.9
Manufacturing	45.2	43.1	40.9	32.8	53.1	43.3	49.7	45.1
Electricity, gas and water production and supply	31.4	29.9	31.5	30.3	32.1	31.5	28.8	29.0
Construction	19.4	13.6	20.7	15.6	17.8	14.8	14.2	12.3
Traffic, transport, storage and post	26.5	27.2	25.9	26.7	29.4	31.3	24.2	27.9
Wholesale and retail and hotels and catering*	46.3	45.1 / 54.2	44.9	37.4 / 53.8	47.5	41.4 / 58.4	56.4	51.2 / 54.1
Finance	40.0	49.5	39.3	46.7	41.9	43.4	46.0	54.5
Real estate	33.7	33.6	34.1	34.6	33.2	34.8	31.9	33.2
Social welfare**	44.1	49.7	43.0	49.0	55.1	55.3	59.0	61.7
Health care**	56.9	60.3	58.1	60.8	49.7	55.3	57.8	62.0
Education**	41.9	49.2	41.8	49.1	48.9	51.4	42.5	51.9
Culture and art**	40.1	46.0	40.2	46.2	39.2	40.7	42.6	45.1
Governmental and party agencies, social organizations	22.6	27.6	22.5	27.5	35.0	41.7	30.0	33.8

Sources: compiled from China Statistical Yearbook 1996:101–2; China Labour Statistical Yearbook 2008:20–2, China Statistical Yearbook 2008:141–143

*   Figures in 1995 were combined as one entry "Wholesale, retail andcatering", but separated in 2007 as entries under "Wholesale and retail" and "Hotels and catering".

**   Wage figures for the social welfare and health care sectors were in the same combined category in 1995 and 2004 figures. Wage figures for the education and culture and art sectors were in the same combined category in 1995 but separated in 2007.

Note: Figures contained in this table include only urban workers and not rural migrant workers working in the urban units. Gender statistics on rural migrant workers working in urban industries are not available. However, it is known that the majority of workers in the construction industry are male rural migrant workers, whereas the majority of workers in the catering industry tend to be female rural migrant workers. Women are specified by law to retire five years earlier than men of the same occupation. This partly accounts for their lower proportion in the total workforce in employment.

The accessibility to extended family support networks and low-cost childcare services further enables dual full-time working among couples with young children. The one-child policy enforced by the Government since the 1980s to control the population growth has further reduced the amount of childcare work for working couples. A third reason is that most of the working women are full-time workers because there are no established arrangements for part-time work in China to accommodate working mothers (Cooke, 2007).

It is worth noting that women's employment rate has experienced a small but steady decline since the 1990s. For example, in 1995, women consisted of 38.6 percent of the national workforce in the urban sector. This was reduced to 37.8 percent by the end of 2007 (China Statistical Yearbook, 2008). A key contributing factor to this reduction is the large-scale downsizing in the State-owned and collectively-owned enterprises since the mid-1990s where women had been disproportionately selected for redundancy (Cooke, 2005). Similar waves of downsizing also took place in recent years in the public sector and Government organizations (Cooke, 2005), although the scale has been much smaller and with less damaging effect to women employees. For a number of reasons including age, education, skill portfolio and job preference, retrenched women workers tend to encounter more difficulties, and often discrimination, than men in regaining employment (Cooke, 2005; Lu and Zhao, 2002). As a result, an increasing proportion of women are engaged in informal employment, such as hourly and temporary work, with low pay and little, if any, social security provision (Lu and Zhao, 2002).

Compared with countries where career interruptions and part-time work are key features in women's labour market participation, particularly for those with family commitment (for example, Cooke, 2010; O'Reilly and Fagan, 1998; Rubery, Smith and Fagan, 1998; Stockman, Bonney and Sheng, 1995), gender segregation is relatively less pronounced in China. While women tend to be over-represented in certain industrial sectors such as education, health care, finance, wholesale, retail and catering (in part, because these jobs are traditionally seen to be more suitable for women), they are present in all sectors and occupations in a relatively even pattern (see Table 15.1). However, it must be noted that women tend to be under-represented in certain industrial sectors and types of organizations for very different reasons. For example, women are under-represented in the mining and construction industry due to the high risk and physically demanding nature of the jobs (the employment law bans women from working in mines or in deep water). Similarly, women are under-represented in government and Party organizations where power and control continues to be dominated by men (Cooke, 2009b), as is the case in most countries. Government organizations are amongst those sectors that have the lowest proportion of women employees. The majority of women who are employed in government organizations are in administrative roles or work as officials in the lower ranks (Cooke, 2005). This is in spite of the fact that the education level of women is very close to that of men in the sector.

Women Pursuing Education

In line with the world trend, Chinese women's education level has been rising steadily in the past three decades, with increases at the tertiary education level being more dramatic than that in the primary and secondary education. In 2004, female students made up 47 percent of the students in primary and secondary schools. Fourteen percent of women of their age group were enrolled in colleges/ universities, compared to 17 percent of men of the same age group (The World Bank Group, 2006). However, it will take some more years for the educational attainment level of the female workforce as a whole to catch up with that of the male workforce because of the more significant gaps between the two amongst the older workforce. For example, in 2007, 52.7 percent of the female workforce, compared to 64.5 percent of male, had secondary school levels of education. Over 7.1 percent of the male workforce, compared to 6 percent of the female workforce, held a college or university degree qualification (China Statistical Yearbook, 2008).

A major problem encountered by women graduates is employment. The rapid expansion of the Chinese higher education sector since the early 2000s has led to a rising level of unemployment of university graduates. Increasingly, employers only hire job candidates who have at least two years of work experience. Costs of training and retention problems are the main reasons for employers' unwillingness to employ university graduates who have no work experience (Cooke, 2009a). The highly controversial Labour Contract Law enacted in 2008 further deters employers from hiring graduates to try them out, as the Law imposes a number of restrictions on employers in wage payment and termination of contract (Fu, 2008). While discrimination against women graduates in recruitment has long existed (Cooke, 2005), this problem is exacerbated by the dramatic increase of university graduates in recent years. In 2009, some 6 million students graduated from the universities, nearly six times as many as in 2000. Only about 70 percent of those graduated in 2008 found employment within a year (The Economist, 2009).

Women in Management

A comprehensive set of statistics on women in management in China, including minority figures, is not available. But what is clear is that women continue to be under-represented in organizational leadership positions. Despite their significant advancement in educational attainments and a respectable inroad into professional and technical positions, only 0.5 percent of women worked as heads of organizations in 2007, compared with 1.8 percent of men who did so (China Statistical Yearbook, 2008). In terms of women's participation in politics, women constitute less than 22 percent of all representatives of the National People's Congress (NPC) (China Statistical Yearbook, 2008). NPC is the highest organ of State powers in principle. Its main functions and powers include: formulation of laws and administrative policies, delegating authority and the supervision of other governing organs. The gross under-presence of women representatives may mean that women's voices are less heard and their issues of concerns less addressed.

To some extent, differences in education levels in the older workforce is accountable for a much smaller proportion of women than men are in leadership positions, For example, in 2007, 64.5 percent of the male workforce had a secondary school level of education, whereas 52.7 percent of women held the same education qualification. Over 7.1 percent of the male workforce held a college or university degree qualification, whereas 6 percent of the female workforce were educated to these levels (China Statistical Yearbook, 2008). However, the Chinese patriarchal cultural value and gender discrimination at workplaces that reflects societal values are far more significant factors that have led to the low presence of women in management positions. The conventional family norm is for the husband to deal with the external matters and the wife to look after home life. The husband's career also takes precedence, even though most couples are dual earners with similar educational backgrounds between husband and wife. It is not expected, or in some cases tolerated, that a wife should be more advanced in her career than her husband (Cooke, 2009b).

If the dominance of the State sector and the direct intervention from the State during the State-planned economy period had led to significant achievements in gender equality at workplaces in the urban area (Liu, Meng and Zhang, 2000), then these achievements have arguably been eroded since the 1980s. As a result of the marketization, employers are granted greater autonomy in operating their businesses and human resource management (HRM) practices (Zhou, 2000). Discriminative practices widely exist in recruitment, job allocation, training, promotion, redundancy and retirement (Cooke, 2005). Organizations that violate equal opportunity regulations either deliberately or due to ignorance are rarely punished. Few organizations have an equal opportunity policy and/or a career development policy in place as part of their HR policy. Where a clear career development and promotion policy is absent or ineffectively implemented, employees may have to rely more on the informal organizational career structure and networks outside the organization to advance their careers (Cooke, 2009b). This presents additional barriers to women due to the patriarchal structure and gender norm.

Career advancement for women in Government organizations is particularly difficult where promotion criteria may be more elastic and promotion processes less transparent, despite the existence of a standard set of promotion criteria and procedures nationwide (Cooke, 2009b). In order to increase the number of women in leadership positions in Government organizations, the Government introduced a token policy in the early 2000s which specifies that there must be at least one woman in each management team at each level (Cooke, 2009b). This does not mean that women will be lifted into the leadership position regardless of their competence. Rather, it creates a small opening for women in politics to advance their career through competition. Local government organizations typically implement the policy by the letter instead of in good spirit. In other words, only one woman is appointed in the management team, who is usually put in deputy positions. Even when women have managed to gain the same official rank as their male counterparts, they are often placed in less lucrative departments with less organizational resources allocated to the posts. This further handicaps women's ability to network to obtain political and social capital within and outside the organization needed to perform their tasks and to gain further promotions (Cooke, 2009b).

Women Entrepreneurs

The total number of women entrepreneurs in China is unclear, due to the existence of different definitions and the lack of national statistics that is publicly available. Nevertheless, according to official reports of a national study conducted in 2002, women entrepreneurs made up over 20 percent of all the entrepreneurs in China by 2002 and 41 percent of them worked in the private sector (The Embassy of the People's Republic of China in the United States of America, 2002). Over 60 percent of the enterprises registered by women emerged after 1996. Women entrepreneurs' enterprises were mainly distributed in manufacturing (13.8 percent), industries of electric power, gas and water supply (19.4 percent), wholesale and retail trade and catering (19.1 percent) and social services (14.6 percent). In particular, around 45 percent of the businesses of women entrepreneurs were in the service sector. The majority of the women entrepreneurs (80 percent) were between the age of 30 and 49. Over 96 percent of the small and medium-sized (SME) enterprises owned by women entrepreneurs were in profit in 2002 (cited on the CAWE website, accessed on 14 May, 2009).

Government support in recent years to facilitate laid-off women workers from the State-owned enterprises to regain employment has been an important factor contributing to women's entrepreneurial success (cited on Expressindia. com, accessed on 14 May, 2009). Forms of support include small loans for business start-up and training courses for business management. In addition, the growth of women entrepreneurs can be attributed to a number of economic factors as a result of China's deepening economic reform. These include: the continuing growth of the private sector, particularly self-employed businesses; the continuing restructuring of China's industrial structure, with the resultant emergence of new service industries such as community work, tourism, health care and insurance; the accelerating rate of urbanization and the emerging development of the country's vast western region. For example, in 1998, 11 percent of the country's total workforce worked in private and self-employed businesses; this was increased to 12 percent in 2007. In 1998, 26.7 percent of the total workforce worked in the tertiary sector; this was increased to 32.4 percent in 2007 (China Statistical Yearbook, 2002; 2008).

As noted earlier, the CAWE is the main official organization that organizes and represents women entrepreneurs. A registered association of the Ministry of Civil Affairs, CAWE is under the direct administration of State Asset Supervision and Administration Commission of the State Council. By 2008, it had 46 group members from various provinces, municipalities and autonomous regions and more than 10,000 individual direct and indirect members who were successful women entrepreneurs, well-known government officials, company directors and managers. The mission of CAWE is to provide services to its members, to represent Chinese women entrepreneurs and to create a bridge between women entrepreneurs and the Government and between women entrepreneurs and women from all walks of life, both within and outside China (CAWE website, accessed on 14 May, 2009). However, it is important to note that CAWE's individual membership has so far been constituted by women in leadership roles in large businesses and Government organizations.

Women in small and self-employed businesses remain largely unorganized and unrepresented. Their voice may be less heard and needs less met. Yet, it is this group of women entrepreneurs who may need more support for their personal and business development.

Country Legislation

A succession of regulations and administrative policies has been introduced by the State since 1949 when the socialist China was founded (see Cooke, 2004 for more detail). In particular, several pieces of the legislation were introduced over the last three decades when China underwent significant economic restructuring, resultant in large-scale downsizing in the State sector and the radical growth of the private sector. These regulations were intended to promote gender equality and to protect women's rights and interests in their working, family and social life. The promulgation of "The Program for the Development of Chinese Women (2001–2010)" by the State Council also provides new goals, tasks and measures concerning women's development in the new century (ACWF website, accessed on 12 May, 2009).

Initiatives Supporting Women in the Workforce

Initiatives adopted by employers to support women's career development have been limited. Instead, the ACWF and the CAWE are the two main national bodies that champion women's development through a range of initiatives, often in response to the State's direction. A number of high-profile (international) events were held in recent years to showcase Chinese women's achievements and highlight future development needs and goals. For example, the Centenary Outstanding Women's Forum on Pioneering was held in Beijing in 2001. The forum was addressed by senior politicians and economists and was attended by more than 200 outstanding women entrepreneurs from 29 provinces. The theme of the forum was to help women entrepreneurs to grow their business and improve their business strategy in the light of the internationalization, informatization and capitalization of the market and China's accession to the World Trade Organization (ACWF website, accessed on 12 May, 2009).

A nation-wide "Essays Competition on the Sustainable Development of Chinese Women Entrepreneurs" was initiated by CAWE in 2008. The initiative was supported by the US-based Women's Network for a Sustainable Future (WNSF) and the Centre for International Business Ethics (CIBE) of the China Foreign Economy and Trade University. The intention of the competition was to give women entrepreneurs a voice in the sustainability debate, to raise their awareness of corporate social responsibility and to stimulate their motivation and creativeness. During the period between March 2008 and July 2009, individual entrepreneurs (identity check applied) were invited to submit an essay of 3,000 words (in Chinese) to the CAWE online. The essay was in the format of an authentic case study of the candidate's business which reported how the sustainable development of the enterprise was achieved and what economic, social and environmental benefits it has created as a result. Winning essays (voted online by the public and overseen by an expert committee) were to be included in the Development Report of Chinese Women Entrepreneurs 2009 (CAWE website, accessed on 12 May, 2009). It must be noted that while these events create new inspirations and aspirations for women's development cause at the national level, they are largely symbolic and elitist occasions that fail to engage organizations at the local level to embed the equality culture necessary for women's career advancement on a larger scale.

In addition to occasional events to create renewed momentum for women's development cause, a number of initiatives are implemented by ACWF on a more regular basis. For example, in order to raise the number and proportion of women at top decision-making level and top administrative level, ACWF and its local branches have set up a talented women database and play a major role in training and developing women cadres and recommending outstanding women candidates to the Government departments concerned for promotion (ACWF website, accessed on 12 May, 2009). Furthermore, in order to help Chinese women to broaden their knowledge base and develop their leadership and entrepreneurial skills, ACWF organizes (often in conjunction with government organizations and CAWE branches), women cadres and entrepreneurs for site visits in different parts of the country and overseas to learn good practices. Facilitating urban unemployed women and rural women to start up their own business is another function that the ACWF branches provide. The services include, for example, disseminating Government policy, providing training to develop women's entrepreneurial skills, lobbying for business loans and facilitating business applications approval from the local government (ACWF website, accessed on 12 May, 2009).

A number of smaller women's professional associations, often as a branch of the main industry-based professional association, have been established in the last two decades to organize women professionals and facilitate their continuous professional development. These include, for example, the Chinese Women Geological Workers' Committee of the Geological Association of China (founded in 1990), the Women Mayors Chapter of China Association of Mayors (founded in 1991), the China Women Scientific and Technological Workers Association (founded in 1993) (ACWF website, accessed on 12 May, 2009). The existence of these associations may help enhance women's professional identity and provide a forum for women to communicate with and support each other. However, this kind of gender solidarity is gentle and largely formed on a professional and social basis. It is unlikely to develop into a political force to advance women's cause and certainly does not tackle, at least not directly, barriers to women's advancement within their employing organization.

The Future

It is evident from the material presented in this chapter that Chinese women today enjoy a similar level of education to their male counterparts. They have a high participation rate in the labour market. There is a relatively low level of gender segregation in industries and occupations with the exception of a couple of industries (China Statistical Yearbook, 2008). The gender pay gap is moderate compared with that in some other countries. However, these achievements have not led to a true level of gender equality in China. Women's career progression remains severely handicapped by gender norms, inaccessibility to organizational resources to gain political and social capital crucial for promotion, and persistent employer discrimination in the selection for recruitment, redundancy and promotion (Cooke, 2009b). As such, women have made little progress in mainstreaming into organizational leadership positions and political arena in the last two decades. It is worth noting that gender discrimination is perhaps at its highest in government organizations, a sector which should in principle be the leader in implementing gender equality legislation and initiatives (Cooke, 2009b). The unwillingness of the Government to harmonize the retirement age between men and women through legislative change (despite rising demands from women's pressure groups) further disadvantages women in the selection for career development and promotion and in their pension income.

Career development support for women managers comes mainly from professional associations external to the employing organizations. Women entrepreneurs remain a minority amongst business owners and the majority of their businesses are small (CAWE website, accessed on 14 May, 2009). Moreover, a new concern is that women university graduates are encountering increasing difficulties in gaining employment. Although some measures are being taken by the Government (for example, loans for university graduates to start up their business) and universities (for example, career advice and counselling for women students who are encountering employment problems) to address the problem, these measures are unlikely to tackle the roots of the cause – employers' discrimination. This problem, which is likely to persist for sometime, is going to impact on the future stock of women candidates for managerial roles. Effective policy intervention is therefore necessary to prevent present conditions from declining further and future prospects being undermined.

References

All-China Women's Federation (ACWF) http://www.women.org.cn/english/english/whatisnws/07-25-01.htm, accessed 12 May, 2009.

China Association of Women Entrepreneurs (CAWE) website, http://www.cawe.org.cn/xhjj.htm, accessed 14 May, 2009.

China Statistical Yearbook (1996, 2002, 2003 and 2008) (Beijing: China Statistics Publishing House).

Cooke, F. L. (2004) Women in management in China. In M. Davidson and R. Burke (eds) *Women in Management Worldwide: Facts, Figures and Analysis* (Aldershot: Gower Publishing, pp. 243–258).

Cooke, F. L. (2005) *HRM, Work and Employment in China* (London: Routledge).

Cooke, F. L. (2007) Husband's career first: renegotiating career and family commitment among migrant Chinese academic couples in Britain, *Work, Employment and Society*, 21(1) 47–65.

Cooke, F. L. (2009a) *Performance and Retention Management in Chinese Private Firms: Key Challenges and Emerging HR Practices*, AIRAANZ Annual Conference, Newcastle, Australia, 4–6 February.

Cooke, F. L. (2009b) The changing face of women managers in China. In C. Rowley and V. Yukondi (eds) *The Changing Face of Women Management in Asia* (London: Routledge, pp. 19–42).

Cooke, F. L. (2010), Women's participation in employment in Asia: A comparative analysis of China, India, Japan and South Korea, *International Journal of Human Resource Management*, 21(10–12), 2249–2270.

The Economist (2009) Chinese unemployment: Where will all the students go?, 8 April, 2009, http://www.economist.com/world/asia/displaystory.cfm?story_id=13446878, accessed on 12 May, 2009.

The Embassy of the People's Republic of China in the United States of America (2002) http://www.china-embassy.org/eng/zt/zgrq/t36655.htm, accessed on 14 May, 2009.

Expressindia.com (2005) Chinese Women Entrepreneurs Equal Men in Number, http://www.expressindia.com/news/fullstory.php?newsid=53734, accessed on 14 May, 2009.

Fu, Z. Y. (2008) The implementation of Labour Contract Law and employment of university graduates, *Journal of Qiongzhou University*, 15, 95–96.

Liu, P., Meng, X. and Zhang, J. (2000) Sectoral gender wage differentials and discrimination in the transitional Chinese economy, *Journal of Population Economics*, 13, 331–352.

Lu, Q. and Zhao, Y. M. (2002) Gender segregation in China since the economic reform, *Journal of Southern Yangtze University* (Humanities and Social Sciences), 1, 22–48.

O'Reilly, J. and Fagan, C. (1998) *Part-time Prospects: An International Comparison of Part-time Work in Europe, North America and the Pacific Rim* (London: Routledge).

Rubery, J., Smith, M. and Fagan, C. (1998) *Women's Employment in Europe: Trends and Prospects* (London: Routledge).

Stockman, N., Bonney, N. and Sheng, X. (1995) *Women's Work in East and West: The Dual Burden of Employment and Family Life* (London: UCL Press Ltd).

Unger, J. and Chan, A. (1995) China, corporatism, and the East Asian model, *The Australian Journal of Chinese Affairs*, 33(1), 29–53.

The World Bank Group (2006) *GenderStats Database of Gender Statistics*, http://genderstats.worldbank.org/home.asp, accessed 20 March, 2007.

Xinhua Yuebao (*Xinhua Monthly*) (1995) An outline of Chinese women's development 1995–2000, 10, 48-55.

Zhao, W. and Zhou, X. (2004) Chinese organizations in transition: Changing promotion patterns in the reform era, *Organization Science*, 15(2),186–199.

Zhou, X. (2000) Economic transformation an income inequality in urban China: Evidence from panel data, *American Journal of Sociology*, 105(4), 1135–1174.

16

Women in Management in Israel

Ronit Kark and Ronit Waismel-Manor[1]

Introduction

This chapter provides an updated profile of women in management and leadership positions in Israel and some of the challenges they face. To better understand women's advances in this domain we also analyze the broader Israeli society and context, highlighting the socio-political, historical and cultural developments that have shaped the scope and nature of women's representation in management. We begin with a description of recent trends in the women's labour force in Israel, and issues related to education. We then focus on three groups of women – managers, directors and entrepreneurs – as illustrations of the different challenges women face in the public, private and non-government organizations (NGO) spheres. The next section summarizes legislation and initiatives aimed at enhancing the role of women in the workforce. We conclude by considering the paradox of the duality of women's opportunities in management given the persistent military conflict in Israel, and the duality that arises when regional traditional–familial roles and attitudes clash with the developed and westernized culture that coexists in the country.

Labour Force Characteristics

Since the early 1980s, there has been a significant increase in the proportion of women in the civilian labour force (see Table 16.1). Women now make up close to 50 percent of the labour force in Israel and are more likely to be employed, stay employed during their lifetimes and work full time. However, women are still mostly employed in part-time positions. Work for pay has become an important facet of women's self-identity, alongside their strong commitment to family life. Israel, as well as other countries in Europe and North America,

---

1 The authors contributed equally to this paper and their names appear in alphabetical order.

is commonly defined as a "work-oriented" country; that is, a country in which people are more likely to endorse women's paid work (and even full-time paid work[2]) than are people in other countries (Treas and Widmer, 2000). Moreover, research indicates that more Israeli mothers of pre-school-aged children are in the labour force than their counterparts in many other industrialized nations (Mandel and Semyonov, 2006).

Table 16.1   Women in the labour force in Israel (1980–2008)

Percentage of women in labour force (LF)	1980	2000	2007/8
Women in LF as % of all women	36	48	51
Married women in LF	39	56	59
25–54 year old women in LF	50	69	72
Working part time (35 hrs/wk)	47	42	40
Women as % of total LF	37	46	47

Source: CBS, 2001; 2008; Women and Men in Israel, 2009

Despite its post-industrial economy and westernized lifestyle, Israeli society is known for its "familialism" (Fogiel-Bijaoui, 2002; Remennick, 2006). The family and motherhood continue to play a crucial role at both the individual and collective levels, and are among the key social values of Israeli society. This is evident in the high marriage rates, the relatively low (although growing) divorce rates, and total fertility rates, which are among the highest in the developed industrialized world. One interesting expression of this cultural ideal can be seen in the way in which motherhood and work are integrated. For example, in Israel there is an extremely limited presence of childless women in the political, economic and academic elites (Herzog, 1999; Frenkel, 2006). A list of the 50 most influential women in the Israeli economy drawn up by the prominent newspaper *Ha'aretz* in 2003 included only two childless women. A more recent list of the 50 most influential women in the Israeli economy drawn up by *Lady Globes* in 2010 included only six childless women, with an average of 2.4 children per woman. In comparison, according to Hewlett (2002), about 40 percent of the women in the top percentile of wage earners in the US do not have children (Frenkel, 2006).

---

2   In Canada and Israel, the countries voicing the strongest support for full-time work by mothers of pre-school children, only 18 percent of the respondents chose this response.

As a cultural code, familialism takes for granted an unequal gender division of labour. The Israeli woman is generally viewed as a wife and mother, whose primary responsibility is to bear children and take care of her home and family. Her paid work is widely accepted as a secondary contribution to the family's livelihood (Fogiel-Bijaoui, 2002). Thus, in the past the widespread gender contract in Israel was one that expected women to do paid labour, but not have a career. Since the 1970s, however, Israeli public discourse has changed, and the issue of equal opportunities and the opening up of professions and industrial sectors to women has become increasingly important. Nonetheless, overall there has not been a notable change in the cultural ideal that calls for the integration of motherhood and paid labour (Frenkel, 2006; Kark, 2007).

There are also significant ethnic and national differences in the numbers of women in the labour force. In 2008, among Jewish women, 65.4 percent of those born in Israel compared to 36.6 percent of those born in the countries of North Africa and the Middle East, (referred to as "Easterners"), and 49.6 percent of those originating from Europe and North and South America, (referred to as "Westerners"), were in the labour force. Comparing nationalities, 56.7 percent of the Jewish women were in the labour force compared to 21 percent of Arab-Israeli women.[3] With regards to religion, 36 percent of Arab-Israeli Christian women, 23 percent of Druze women and only 18 percent of Moslem-Israeli women were employed in the labour force (CBS, 2008). The higher representation of the Christian women in the labour force in comparison to the Moslem and Druze women is explained by their higher level of education and their more modern life style (Reches and Rodintzki, 2009).

Labour force participation among Arab women is hindered by insufficient childcare facilities, poor educational facilities, limited employment opportunities, cultural norms that object to women working outside the home and discrimination on the part of Jewish and Arab employers (Bram and Avtiasam, 1997; Izraeli, 1999). These disadvantages are at their greatest where gender and other minority identities intersect (for example, ethnicity, class, nationality). Therefore, eastern Jewish women, but much more so Arab women, may have a double disadvantage as workers and as applicants for managerial roles (Kark and Eagly, 2010).

Women constitute over 65 percent of those employed by the State, with the vast majority employed in education, health and welfare and public

---

3   Figures only include citizens of Israel and exclude foreign workers (legal and illegal) and
     Palestinian labour.

administration (Shachal-Rozenfeld and Berger, 2008). Studies have shown that women employed in the public sector are more likely than others to work when they have young children and less likely to interrupt their employment (Okun, Oliver and Khiat-Marelli, 2007; Stier and Yaish, 2008). Moreover, recent research has pointed out that women employed in the public sector appear to be subject to lower pay discrimination than other women (Yaish and Kraus, 2003). In the private sector, individual employers have greater freedom to discriminate and the salary range between the bottom and the top is much greater than in the public sector where collective agreements and public scrutiny make it harder to discriminate and set a ceiling on salary levels.

Education remains the best single predictor of women's labour force participation. For example, in 2007, out of all mothers of children aged two to four years, 82.8 percent were in the labour force compared to 91.6 percent of the same mothers with 16 years and more of formal schooling. Similarly, among mothers with three children under the age of 14, 76 percent were in the labour force, compared to 87.2 percent among the same mothers with 16 years and more of education (CBS, 2007). The growing number of women in higher education (discussed below) re-enforces their attachment to the labour market.

Women Pursuing Education

In the last two decades there has been a rapid expansion in the number of degree-granting academic institutions. Between 1990 and 2000, the number of students studying for the first (bachelor's) degree grew on average 9.3 percent a year, compared with an increase of just 6.4 percent between 2006–2007 (CBS, 2007). This increase was absorbed primarily by newly established colleges that specialize in fields closely related to the labour market such as computer science, management sciences and law. Women have continued to increase their investment in formal education as a means of improving job prospects in the labour market. In 1968 women constituted 43 percent of all university students, in 1990 they were 51 percent and by the academic year of 2007 women had surpassed men at all three academic levels and constituted 56 percent of all students in academic institutions (Women and Men in Israel, 2009). However, the numbers vary by field of study.

Table 16.2   Percentage of women in the student population by degree and field of study 2006/7

Field of study	Degree			Total
	First*	Second	Third	
Total	56	57	53	56
Humanities	63	71	60	63
Social sciences	62	56	63	61
Business administration	55	47	51	51
Law	46	52	40	47
Medicine	50	54	63	54
Para-medical studies	80	82	70	81
Mathematics, statistics & computer science**	35	30	26	NA
Biological sciences **	66	64	57	NA
Physical science**	37	38	38	NA
Engineering & architecture	25	27	29	25

Source: CBS, 2008

*   First degree is based on combined universities and academic colleges data.

**   Includes only universities.

Table 16.2 shows that women are over-represented in the humanities, social sciences, biology and para-medical studies. In 2007, women comprised almost half the students in business, management and law, occupations that lead to managerial positions. The picture for the exact sciences, technology and engineering is different, showing that in mathematics, statistics, computer science and engineering the number of women awarded different degrees is still low (Berlinski, 2005; Kark, 2007).

Despite the fact that the percentage of women graduating from doctoral programmes exceeds 50 percent, only 24 percent of university faculty members at all levels and research fields (including in the arts, humanities and social sciences) are women. Furthermore, the higher one climbs on the academic ladder the lower the number of women, and at the highest echelon (that is, full professors) the figure stands at somewhat less than 10 percent (Messner-Yaron and Kahanovitch, 2003). Therefore, despite the widely accepted theory that human capital (for example, increased formal education) contributes to enhanced opportunities for advancement, research in Israel suggests that women receive lower returns than men for their investment in education (Izraeli, 2004).

Women in Management

Although women in Israel have more access today to managerial positions than at any other period in history, equal representation remains a distant goal. Nevertheless, the increase of women in managerial roles is substantial. In 1981 women constituted less than 9 percent of all managers but over 36 percent of the labour force. By 2007 they constituted 28 percent of all managers (CBS, 2007), 47 percent of the professionals and 47 percent of the labour force (Women and Men in Israel, 2009). The significant increase in women managers is best understood within the context of the major transformation of Israeli society from a collective, protectionist and State-centred culture to a more individualist, open, neo-liberal one (Ezrahi, 1997; Shalev, 1992). Individualism has been accompanied by increased emphasis on material success and the term "career" which had been associated with self-promotion and exploitation, lost its pejorative connotation and by the 1980s became a legitimate object of aspiration (Izraeli, 2004). This cultural change, in conjunction with the expanding economy and the accompanying growth in managerial positions (from 3.7 percent of the labour force in 1981 to 7.3 percent in 2000) opened a window of opportunity for women. Since 2000 there has been a decline in the number of managerial positions which peaked at 6.5 percent in 2007 (CBS, 2007) while the economy continued to expand at a slower pace. Nevertheless, due to the overall growth in managerial positions and the figures for women, more women began moving up the organizational and occupational ladders, encouraged and supported by women's organizations and feminists working in government. However, these women are concentrated at lower and middle levels of management. Across all economic sectors, substantially more men than women occupy positions that confer major decision-making authority and the ability to influence others' pay and promotions (Smith, 2002).

Women managers in Israel adhere to the family imperative and combine family and work life. Table 16.3 shows that the proportion of women managers who are married, separated and divorced is not significantly different from the proportion among non-managers. Furthermore, women managers have on average 2.04 children and non-managers 2.27 children. The small difference in number of children may be partly explained by the fact that in Israel, religiosity is the main predictor of number of children, not occupation. Women who become managers are less likely to be orthodox (Izraeli, 2004).

Table 16.3   Marital status by gender and managerial status 2000 (%)

	Married	Separated	Divorced	Widowed	Single	Average number of children
Men managers	85.9	0.7	3.0	0.5	9.9	n/a
Women managers	71.9	1.0	9.8	2.2	14.8	2.04
Women non-managers	73.6	1.2	9.1	2.7	13.5	2.27

Source: CBS, Labour Force Survey 2001

Table 16.4 indicates that men's and women's median years of schooling was similar in the year 2000, but women were more likely to have attended an academic institution than either men managers or women non-managers. They worked on average 7.9 hours a week more than women non-managers but 8.5 hours less than men managers. Although not represented in Table 16.4 below, women managers were on average slightly younger than men managers, reflecting their recent entry into management. More than 30 percent of women managers, compared to 20 percent of men managers were 34 years old or younger in 2007 (CBS, 2007).

Table 16.4   Managers and non-managers by gender, schooling and hours worked 2007

	Median years of schooling	Academic institution*	Hours weekly
Men managers	15 yrs	47	49.9
Women managers	15 yrs	57	41.3
Women non-managers	n/a	34	33.4

Source: CBS, Labour Force Survey 2007
*   Percentage whose last school attended was an academic institution.

Women's representation in management positions is highly contingent on the sector (public, private and NGOs) and on the type of specialization and economic branch. In the public or government sector, women in Israel enjoy considerable visibility and positions of authority, whereas in the private sector women's gains have been more limited.

The overall proportion of women managers in senior positions in the civil service increased gradually from 37 percent in 1997 to 46 percent of managers in 2007. However, the figures vary considerably across ministries. In 2008, the three ministries with the greatest proportion of women in senior positions were Welfare, Justice and Health (between 64–66 percent) and the ministries with the lowest proportion of senior women managers (12 and 11 percent respectively) were Internal Security and Tourism (Shachal-Rozenfeld and Berger, 2008). Given that in 2009 only two of the 30 ministers and three of the nine deputy ministers were women, men still tipped the scale.

In 2006, the first female President of the Supreme Court was sworn in. Women constitute 51 percent of the civil judges at all levels and 30 percent of those on the Supreme Court (Raz, 2008). With regards to the Israeli governing body, the Knesset, women's representation is much lower. There were 21 women members in the 18th Knesset elected in 2008 (representing 17.5 percent of the Israeli Parliament). This was the largest number of women ever in the Knesset. Women have also been represented recently for the first time in some influential roles. A woman served as the Speaker of the 17th Knesset, and in the 18th Knesset a woman heads the largest political party after having served as Vice Prime Minister and Minister of Foreign Affairs in the 17th Knesset.

Another important component of the public sector is the Israeli Defence Forces (IDF). In Israel, service in the armed forces is mandatory. Following high school graduation, men and women are drafted when they reach the age of 18. In the last decades there has been a moderate increase in the number of women in almost every rank in the IDF. Between 25 and 30 percent of officers with the rank of captain or major are women, 12 percent of all lieutenants in the IDF are women and 4 percent of all the lieutenant colonels. Currently there are only three women with a rank of brigadier. In the higher ranks women are not represented (Integration of women in the IDF, 2009).

Thus, from the rank of lieutenant and upwards there is clearly an under-representation of women in the military and its body of commanders. The strong link between military service and citizenship in Israel extends the effect of the military on women's status not only to the period of their army service, but it also affects their status in Israeli civilian society. The advantages men in commanding positions obtain and derive from military service are converted into advantages in civilian life. Military elites shift easily into roles in civilian life (for example, political, managerial, educational and so on), thus contributing to the sustainability and reproduction of gender inequality.

As seen in other countries (Kark and Eagly, 2010), in Israel women usually have more access to power in the non-profit sector. Although there are no official figures, women are broadly represented in management and CEO positions in non-profit NGOs. For example, in 2008 most of the managers and CEOs of the "green environmental organizations" in Israel were women (Mor, 2008). This can be explained by the ideological agenda of preserving and caring for the environment, which fits the stereotypes of women's roles, the lower salaries in non-profit organizations, and certain women's opportunity to chose their workplace based on interest and ideology and not on economical considerations (since usually they are secondary bread winners).

Whereas women constitute 44.2 percent of the managers in the government/ public sector, and possibly a higher percentage in non-profit organizations, they constitute only 22.7 percent of the managers in the private/business sector which employs most of managers: 88.2 percent of all men managers and 73.4 percent of all women managers. In the private sector women are most likely to be in staff rather than line positions. They move into positions of expertise, but rarely into positions of power and control over the organization and its resources (Izraeli, 2004). For example, out of the 328 top earners for 2004, only 15 were women (Asimon, 2005). A survey conducted by MIDGAM (2008) on a representative sample of 250 industrial firms (using a broad definition of manager: "a worker responsible for the work of others") found that 66 percent of the firms surveyed had no women managers. Women managers, furthermore, earned on average 17 percent less than men managers.

There is a definite gender structure to the distribution of managers among fields of specialization and economic branches in the private sector. For example, according to a 2008 D&B survey of the 1,400 largest companies in Israel, women constituted 47.1 percent of the human resource managers, 16.6 percent of financial managers and 15.3 percent of sales and marketing managers. Women were most under-represented among managers at the senior levels of these business firms; namely as chairperson (2.2 percent) and in senior "masculine" positions such as operation managers (5.4 percent) and logistics managers (9.7 percent). In comparison to a 2006 D&B survey, there has been a notable improvement in the number of female CEOs (from 6.6 percent to 8.8 percent) and Deputy CEOs (from 11.4 percent to 15.9 percent) (Dun and Bradstreet Israel, 2009).

A recent survey of 20 leading private sector firms by a leading Israeli economic newspaper showed that although women were on the top management team of all of these firms, in most there were only one or two women and in specific professional managerial roles (for example, spokeswomen, legal adviser and HR manager) (Parnet, 2009). These advisory roles (staff versus line roles) are usually the less senior ones in the top management team and usually command lower salaries. Thus, although women's representation in these top management teams is on the rise and is significant in itself, women's minority status and limited power create a framework in which their ability to influence is restricted.

In March 1993, the Knesset passed an affirmative action amendment requiring ministers to appoint qualified women to boards of the approximately 750 Government companies in which women were not properly represented. Ministers initially did not comply with the amendment and in December 1993, the Cabinet approved the appointments of three male directors to two Government-owned companies whose boards had no women directors. The Israel Women's Network, a feminist lobby, consequently filed two petitions to the Supreme Court demanding that the Government and the relevant ministers explain why they had not appointed women directors as required by law. On November 1, 1994, the Supreme Court acting in its capacity as the High Court of Justice annulled the appointment of the men as directors and required the ministers to appoint women in their stead (High Court of Justice, 1994).

The strong position taken by the Court had an almost immediate impact on appointments to the boards of Government-owned companies. Ministers sought women candidates and more women came to see themselves as potential candidates. Between 1993 and 2000, the proportion of women directors of Government companies rose from approximately 7 percent to 38 percent, and the proportion of companies with women directors increased from 31 percent in 1993 to 78.5 percent in 1997 (Izraeli and Hillel, 2000). However, this positive development did not continue and up to 2007 the proportion of companies with women directors dropped to 67 percent in 2007. As a result, a Government decision in March 2007 ruled that, within two years, ministers must appoint women to directorates of Government companies until 50 percent representation is achieved. As a result, the proportion of women directors of Government companies reached 38.5 percent in February 2008 (The Authority for the Advancement of the Status of Women, n.d.). Although the numbers hold some promise for Jewish women, Arab women's representation increased from just over 1 percent in 2000 to just over 2 percent of the directors in 2006, once again illustrating the gap between sub-groups of women in Israeli society (Segev, 2007).

Attempts by feminist organizations to introduce affirmative actions in the private sector have met with much greater opposition on the grounds that it is not legitimate to interfere with the market economy. The President of the Publicly Traded Firms Union estimated in 2006 that women directors comprised about 15 percent of all directors in these companies (Tamir, 2007).

Women Entrepreneurs

The meaningful changes which have taken place in Israeli society in the last few decades have resulted in a considerable increase in the number of new businesses. These changes include a push towards privatization of large Government-owned sectors of the economy, and the growth of the private business sector. In addition, employers' preference to employ sub-contracted workers, and technological changes which have facilitated setting up home-based freelance work, have also increased the share of entrepreneurship. Starting a business became a more respectable occupation than it had been previously; about 65 percent of Israelis who took part in an international survey on entrepreneurial activity said setting up a new business was a desirable career track (Ben-David, 2005). In addition, in that survey, more than half of those who started a business recently indicated they were drawn into entrepreneurship by opportunity, the desire for independence and/or to increase their income, and not because they were forced into entrepreneurship out of necessity.

In the 1990s, the Government began to view entrepreneurship as an important vehicle for the economic integration of some half million immigrants from the former Soviet Union who arrived between 1988 and 1993 and encouraged them through the funding of technological incubators, the Small and Medium Enterprises Authority and a network of Centres for Promoting Entrepreneurship. Women were encouraged to take advantage of these opportunities by taking special training courses for future women entrepreneurs, seminars for businesswomen and entrepreneurs, and business clubs for women (Israel Small and Medium Enterprises Authority, n.d.). Some Centres for Promoting Entrepreneurship ran special training programmes for women from specific sectors such as Arab women and ultra-orthodox women wanting to set up home-based businesses. In 2003, 38 percent of the applications for assistance from these Centers came from women, compared to 31 percent in 2000 (Ben-David, 2005).

In 2005, only 6.4 percent of the female labour force could be classified as entrepreneurs, compared to 16.1 percent for men. Of these, 9.3 percent of the men and 4.9 percent of the women were self-employed; and 6.9 percent and 1.5 percent respectively were employers (Waismel-Manor and Nadiv, 2010). Women's businesses are concentrated in a small number of economic branches including services and retailing and are under-represented in wholesaling, manufacturing and big business in general.

A study of women's lifestyle ventures in Israel (Lerner and Almor, 2002) found that 58 percent of the firms were concentrated in the service sector (for example, childcare, graphics, advertising), 23 percent were in manufacturing (mainly fashion and cosmetics) and 19 percent were retail businesses (mainly fashion and apparel stores), and they employed an average of 15.2 persons. Moreover, 29 percent of the businesses did not employ any additional people and only 9 percent employed 55 or more employees. Flexibility and the desire to give priority to family over work were important motivators for women to open their own business. According to the 2005 Labour Force Survey, because self-employment provides greater ability to adjust work demands to family demands, self-employed women worked on average fewer hours per week than organizationally employed women (33 hours per week compared to 35 hours per week) (Waismel-Manor and Nadiv, 2010).

Among the thousands of hi-tech start-ups that mushroomed during the 1990s, only a very small proportion –less than 2 percent – were set up by women alone or in conjunction with others (Rosen-Genut, 2001). Furthermore, although Israel has one of the highest number of patents per-person in the world (Ha-Poalim Bank, 2000), the percentage of women inventors is low. Between the years of 2000 to 2005, among the patents submitted to the Registrar of Patents, less than 6 percent were submitted by women inventors (Yaniski-Ravid, 2007).

Country Legislation

Since the 1950s, Israel has been among the leading States in granting special protection to working women, and especially to working mothers. The issue of granting equal opportunity, beyond mere formal equality, however, is a more recent one that emerged only in the mid-1980s when women's groups called for legislation that would add protective measures to the concept of equal opportunity (Raday, 1995).

The 1988 Equal Opportunities in Employment Law combined the demand for formal equality with the recognition of the legitimacy of different provisions for men and women on the basis of biological differences and stipulated that such provisions do not constitute discrimination. Furthermore, the law put the onus of proof on the employer that s/he did not discriminate among employees or persons seeking employment on account of their sex or personal status in acceptance of employment, terms of employment, advancement, vocational training or dismissal. The law also recognized sexual harassment as a form of prejudice. A 2004 amendment to this law protects pregnant women against discrimination in employment.

The 2000 amendment to the Women's Equal Rights Law (1951) was a key legislative development (Halperin-Kaddari, 2004). It requires that affirmative action measures be taken to ensure equality in areas that include housing, employment, health and welfare. In 2005, the Law was amended again, making appropriate representation for women in all public bodies that determine national policy mandatory.

In 1995 the Knesset passed the Equal Pay Act which replaced earlier laws and requires equal pay and other remuneration for essentially equal, equivalent work or work of comparable worth performed for the same employer in the same workplace. The Knesset's readiness to promote equal rights for women, however, stopped short of providing budgets required for their effective implementation. There are no agencies responsible for implementation and there have been relatively few cases of discrimination claims taken to court. The Equal Employment Opportunity Commission was only set up in 2008, its goals being to ensure equality at work and to generate public awareness regarding the importance of equality. Moreover, for the first time in Israel, there is now a Governmental agency that has the authority to file civil suits in cases pertaining discrimination at work.

In recent decades, the Supreme Court acting in its capacity as the High Court of Justice has had a powerful impact on establishing the principle of gender equality (Ziv, 1999). Its impact on the ground, however, has been curtailed by resistance to the principle of equality. In 1998, despite the Supreme Court ruling obligating the Minister of Work and Welfare to search for a suitable woman candidate for the position of Associate Director of the National Insurance Institute where all nine Associate Directors were men, the Minister gave the job to a man from his political party. Similarly, in April 2009, the Supreme Court determined that the Prime Minister had to re-evaluate the pool of candidates for the position of the Director General of the Anti-Drug Authority because his decision did not incorporate the principle of equal representation. Unfortunately, the male candidate was chosen once again.

Maternal rights such as the 12-week maternity leave with full pay covered by the National Social Security Institute (extended in 2007 to 14 weeks), and up to one year leave without pay or paid leave of absence to care for a sick child, have been transformed into parental rights (for fathers as well as mothers) while preserving the mother's privileged position. Only if the mother fails to use her sick leave does the right transfer to the father. Fathers were granted the right to take up to six of the 14 weeks maternity in place of their wives provided mothers returned to work during that time. However, only several hundred fathers have availed themselves of this right to date.

Upon return, mothers can choose between public and private childcare options. The State subsidizes a national network of childcare services run by three large women's organizations, where cost is proportional to income. In addition, municipalities support childcare services and there are privately-run kindergartens. In July 2009, the Knesset passed a law giving working mothers of children aged five years or younger one tax credit point for day-care expenses. Education is compulsory and free from the age of five. It is free but not compulsory from the age of four. The short school day enforced in Israel, in which grade one ends at noon and only extends slightly during the remainder of primary school, is a major constraint for women pursuing managerial careers.

Initiatives Supporting Women in the Workforce

Two different kinds of initiatives to support the advancement of women have been taken: official initiatives sponsored by the Government, and grass roots initiatives sponsored by individual feminists or women's organizations. The most significant Government-sponsored body is the Knesset Committee for the Advancement of the Status of Women established in 1992 and granted the status of permanent Knesset Committee in 1996. In addition, a narrower mechanism, the Prime Minister's Adviser on the Status of Women, has operated since the early 1980s. The Prime Minister's Adviser coordinates local Advisers on the Status of Women in the municipalities and the local authorities. Although these advisers do not have a large budget, and their power is limited, they represent many cities, towns and regions in Israel and are able to form a country-wide network of over 230 advisers that can advance change within their organizations and in society as a whole.

The Department for the Advancement of Women within the Civil Service, established in 1996, serves as an address for complaints from women, sponsors educational programmes, and regularly collects and disseminates statistics on women's representation in the civil service. This department attempts to impact the different ministries by having a representative in each ministry who takes on an extra role as the adviser for the advancement of women in addition to her other professional duties. Here also a network of about 70 representatives has been formed that connects all the ministries and serves as a platform for actions that can lead to the advancement of women in the civil service. However, due to low funding and power resources their influence is somewhat limited.

The earliest private initiatives to promote the advancement of women include the establishment of the Senior Women Executive Forum within the Israel Management Centre (1986) and courses for training women in management (1988) and future women directors (1993). Towards the end of the 1980s forums were set up to enable each woman to acquire the "tricks of the trade" to become managers, entrepreneurs or company directors. These forums emphasize personal transformation, skill acquisition and networking among women as means to achieve goals and become independent, and economically successful women. Although quite successful, these types of programmes have been dubbed "fix the women" programmes (for example, Ely and Meyerson, 2000; Kark, 2004), since they focus on changing and "fixing" women and not on changing society or the system. Thus, while resisting the male monopoly of the business world, these women's organizations do not challenge the gender structure of power within it.

In the private sector, most companies have not initiated "family-friendly" policies or programmes to advance women. Those that have, mainly permit flexible starting and ending times to accommodate working parents and mothers who have young children and are breastfeeding. For example, about 50 percent of the 277 organizations in the public and private sector whose human resources professionals participated in an Internet-based survey, granted flexible starting and ending times and allowed vacation days without pay to attend sick relatives. However, most of the respondents also said that their organization expects them to put their work life before their family life (Alon et al., 2009). One notable initiative in the private sector is a forum for women managers in hi-tech, called "Women Managers @ Hi-Tech", that was set up in 2005. This forum aims to advance organizational cultures that promote a work–life balance and family-friendly policies.

There have also been substantial actions taken by the grass root women's organizations to advance women to management positions. One such interesting initiative was "Women Renewing Management", which took place in 2005–2007, and was a feminist, multicultural project designed to create a network of directors of social welfare services, women's organizations, feminist organizations and organizations for social change. The overall aim of the organizers was to be involved in systematic and critical learning of feminist theories and principles of management, and instil feminist principles in management within feminist organizations, as well as other types of organizations (initiated by "Shatil" and "The Voice of Women").

Thus, the different programmes run by feminist grass roots organizations in conjunction with their lobby and legislation efforts have been fruitful in pushing the agenda of women's leadership in Israel and providing political visibility. However, their ability to reshape the existing situation is restricted and is based on the strategy of small wins.

The Future

Currently women are present in management and leadership roles in Israel, however their number in higher ranks is still far from being on a par to that of men. Many of the possible explanations for the limited representation of women in management in Israel are common to other countries as well (for example, lack of role models, stereotypes concerning gender and the management fields, gender discrimination, masculine norms of management roles, and so on). However, there are also unique and particular characteristics of the Israeli context and culture that are likely to hinder women's integration into management roles (for example, social norms of familialism and the current military conflict).

It should be noted that the characteristics of Israeli society reviewed above, although they lead to the accumulation of disadvantages to women's advancement in management, also give women some advantages and privileges which are not always apparent in other countries and contexts. One of the most salient of these is the possibility to combine motherhood with a professional and managerial career, without being forced to give up one of these worlds. This situation forms what we term the "paradox of the duality" of women's opportunities and representation in management in Israel. This paradox reflects the unique Israeli context as a country in the Middle East operating in a turbulent political, economical and military environment, with strong ties nevertheless to the Western world and its norms. This duality is even sharper for various sub-groups in Israeli society (for example, Arab women living in Israel, ultra Orthodox Jewish women, and so on). Although individual women continue to excel and gain access to more senior positions, for the majority of educated and aspiring women the near future looks more promising than it did in previous years – but only to a limited extent.

The authors thank the late Dafna Izraeli who was the author of the chapter on women in Israel in the first edition of this book. Prof. Izraeli contributed enormously to the study of women in leadership and management positions in Israel and continues to inspire women today.

References

Alon, V., Harpaz, I., Tzafrir, S. and Meshoulan, Y. (2009) *Employees' Benefits and Flexible Employment Arrangements*, Center for the Study of Organizations & Human Resource Management, organizations.haifa.ac.il/html/html_eng/survey3-WLB.pdf, accessed 1 August, 2009.*

Asimon (2005) *Top-earning Women*, http://www.asimon.co.il/ArticlePage.aspx?AID=634&AcatID=63, accessed 2 August, 2009.*

Authority for the Advancement of the Status of Women (n.d.) http://www.women.gov.il/MA/yetzug/yetzug1/.*

Ben-David, L. (2005) *Update on Women's Entrepreneurship in Israel*, The Knesset's Center for Research and Information.*

Berlinski, S. (2005) *Women in Academia*, A report presented to the Council for Higher Education,Tel-Aviv, Israel.*

Bram, I. and Avtisam, I. (1997) The status of the Arab women at work. In A. Maor (ed.) *Women: The Rising Power* (Tel-Aviv, Israel: Sifriat Hapoalim Publisher, pp. 228–242). *

Central Bureau of Statistics (2001) *Statistical Abstract of Israel*, no. 52.

Central Bureau of Statistics (2007) *Statistical Abstract of Israel*, no. 58.

Central Bureau of Statistics (2008) *Statistical Abstract of Israel*, no. 59.

Dun & Bradstreet Israel (2009) D&B Report Shows Minor Improvement in Women's Representation in Managerial Positions, http://dundb.co.il/NewsShowHeb1.asp?idnum=453, accessed 2 August 2009.*

Ely, R. J. and Meyerson, D. E. (2000) Theories of gender in organizations: a new approach to organizational analysis and change, *Research in Organizational Behavior*, 22, 103–151.

Ezrahi, Y. (1997) *Rubber Bullets: Power and Conscience in Modern Israel* (New York, NY: Farrar, Straus & Giroux).

Fogiel-Bijaoui, S. (2002) Familism, postmodernity and the state: the case of Israel, *The Journal of Israeli History*, 21(1–2), 38–62.

Frenkel, M. (2006) *Reprogramming Femininity: Gender Performance in the Israeli Hi-tech Industry between Global and Local Gender Orders*, Working Paper, Jerusalem, The Hebrew University.

Halperin-Kaddari, R. (2004) *Women in Israel: A State of Their Own* (Philadelphia, PA: Pennsylvania University Press).

Ha-Poalim Bank (2000) The Israeli hi-tech: the current state of affairs, *Economical Review*, 130.*

Herzog, H. (1999) *Gendering Politics: Women in Israel* (Ann Arbor, MI: University of Michigan Press).

Hewlett, S. A. (2002) *Creating a Life: Professional Women and the Quest for Children* (New York, NY: Talk Miramax Books).

High Court of Justice (1994) 453/94, 454/94, *Israel Women's Network v. Government of Israel et al.*, PD (5) 501.*

Integration of Women in the IDF (2009) http://www.mfa.gov.il/MFA/Israel+beyond+politics/Integration_women_in_IDF-March_2009.htm, accessed 12 August, 2009.

Israel Small and Medium Enterprises Authority (n.d.) http://www.asakim.org.il/ english.php?pageid=0, accessed 12 August, 2009.

Izraeli, D. N. (1999) Women in the labour force. In D. N. Izraeli, A. Friedman, H. Herzog, S. Bijaoui, H. Naveh, H. Dahan-Kalev and M. Hassan (eds), *Sex, Gender, Politics* (Tel Aviv: Hakibbutz Hameuchad, pp. 167–216).*

Izraeli, D. N. (2004) Women in management in Israel. In M. J. Davidson and R. J. Burke (eds) *Women in Management Worldwide: Facts, Figures and Analysis* (Aldershot: Gower Publishing, pp. 294–310).

Izraeli, D. N. and Hillel, R. (2000) *Women's Representation in Boards of Government-owned Companies: 1993–97*, Unpublished Report, Ramat Gan: Bar-Ilan University. *

Kark, R. (2004) The transformational leader: who is (s)he? A Feminist perspective, *Journal of Organization Change Management*, Special issue on Transformational Leadership Research: Issues and Implications, 17(2), 160–176.

Kark, R. (2007) Women in the land of milk, honey and hi-technology: The Israeli case. In R. Burke and M. Mattis (eds), *Women and Minorities in Science, Technology, Engineering and Mathematics: Opening the Pipeline* (New York, NY: Edward Elgar, pp. 152–191).

Kark, R. and Eagly, A. (2010). Gender and leadership: Negotiating the labyrinth. In J. Chrisler and D. R. McCreary (eds) *Handbook of Gender Research and Psychology*. New York, NY: Springer, pp. 443–468.

Lerner, M. and Almor, T. (2002) Relationships among strategic capabilities and the performance of women-owned small ventures, *Journal of Small Business Management*, 40(2), 109–225.

Mandel, H. and Semyonov, M. (2006) The welfare state paradox: a comparative analysis of welfare-state policies and women's employment opportunities in 20 countries, *American Journal of Sociology*, 111(6), 1910–1949.

Messer-Yaron, H. and Kahanovitch, S. (2003, 2005) *Women in Science and Technology in Israel: State of Affairs* (The National Council for the Promotion of Women in Science and Technology).*

MIDGAM Consulting and Research Inc. (2008) *Women Managers in Industry 2008*, http://www.globes.co.il/news/article.aspx?QUID=1056,U1244283477661&did=1000432133, accessed 12 August, 2009.

Mor, R. (2008) A feminine environment. *Haaretz*, The Marker, 29 August.*

Okun, B. S., Oliver, A. L. and Khiat-Marelli, O. (2007) The public sector, family structure, and labour market behavior: Jewish mothers in Israel, *Work and Occupations* 34(2), 174–204.

Parnet, T. (2009) Women in management survey, *Calcalist*, 5 March.*

Raday, F. (1995) Women in the labour market. In F. Raday, C. Shalev and M. Liban-Kobi (eds) *The Status of Women in Society and Law* (Tel Aviv: Shoken).

Raz, H. (2008) Women to dominate the Judiciary. *Haaretz, The Marker*, 28 May, http://www.haaretz.co.il/hasite/pages/ShArtPE.jhtml?itemNo=987797&contrassID=2&subContrassID=6&sbSubContrassID=0, accessed 28 May, 2008.*

Reches, E. and Rodintzki, A (2009) The Arab Society in Israel, *The Abraham Fund Initiatives*, Israel.

Remennick, L. (2006) The quest for the perfect baby; why do Israeli women seek prenatal genetic testing? *Sociology of Health and Illness*, 28(1), 21–53.

Rosen-Genut, A. (2001) Difficult to be a woman manager, *Status*, 24–26.*

Segev, D. (2007) *Under representation of women in the public sphere*, http://www.asimon.co.il/ArticlePage.aspx?AID=3821&AcatID=42#At, accessed 30 March, 2011.*

Shachal-Rozenfeld, T. and Berger, Y. (2008) *2007 Activity Report* (Israel: Civil Service Commission).*

Shalev, M. (1992) *Labour and the Political Economy in Israel* (Oxford: Oxford University Press).

Smith, R. A. (2002) Race, gender, and authority in the workplace: theory and research, *Annual Review of Sociology*, 28, 509–542.

Stier, H. and Yaish, M. (2008) The determinants of women's employment dynamics: the case of Israeli women, *European Sociological Review*, 24(3), 363–377.

Tamir, T. (2007) *Women in Israel 2006 – Between Theory and Reality* (Ramt-Kan: Israel Women's Network).*

Treas, J. and Widmer, E. D. (2000) Married women's employment over the life course: attitudes in cross-national perspective, *Social Forces*, 78(4), 1409–1436.

Waismel-Manor, R. and Nadiv, R. (2010). Work and family among self-employed women in Israel. In V. Muhlbauer and L. Kulik (eds) *Working Families* (Rishon Letzion: Peles Publishing, pp. 223–245).*

Women and Men in Israel (2009) *Statistilite*, no. 89, http://www.cbs.gov.il/www/statistical/mw2008_h.pdf, accessed 1 August, 2009.

Yaish, M. and Kraus, V. (2003) The consequences of economic restructuring for the gender earnings gap, *Work Employment and Society*, 17(1), 5–28.

Yaniski-Ravid, S. (2007) The exclusion of female inventors in the meeting point between the field of property, patents, work and gender discourse. In D. Erez-Barak, S. Yaniski-Ravid, Y. Biton and D. Fogin (eds) *Study of Law, Gender and Feminism* (Tel Aviv: Nevo and the Academic Press).*

Ziv, N. (1999) The Disability law in Israel and the United States: a comparative perspective, *Israel Yearbook of Human Rights*, 28, 171–202.

*   In Hebrew.

17

Women in Management in Lebanon

Hayfaa Tlaiss and Saleema Kauser

Introduction

Described as the most westernized Arab nation, Lebanon is perceived as the artefact of the interaction of the western world and the Middle East. The Lebanese culture amalgamates the European, Christian and the Arab non-fundamentalist Muslim values (Neal, Finlay and Tansey 2005). Therefore, one could argue that the role of women in Lebanon has been impacted by this European-Middle Eastern interaction (Neal, Finlay and Tansey 2005). Despite the usage of a common Arabic language, differences between the religions are deep and reflected in the social and the behavioural patterns of the society. In addition, religion is critical as it is the basis of the national constitution and the allocation of power and thus interferes in the economic development of the country.

In recent years, the migration of Lebanese men to the wealthier neighbouring Arab countries (Sidani, 2005; MENA, 2007) has created a brain drain and the difficult post civil war economic conditions have paved the way for the involvement of women in the country's economic activities (Jamali, Sidani and Safieddine, 2005; Jamali, Safieddine and Daouk, 2006). Despite the increase of women in employment, women managers are grossly under-represented in Lebanese organizations at the lower, middle and senior levels (Jamali, Sidani and Safieddine, 2005). Generally, to date, there is little empirical evidence on Lebanese women managers. Studies that have attempted to inspect the status of women in management in a number of countries in the Middle Eastern region including Lebanon (Jamali, Safieddine and Daouk 2006; 2007; Jamali, Sidani and Safieddine, 2005; Tlaiss, 2009), Egypt (Kattara, 2005), United Arab Emirates (UAE) and the Gulf (Abdallah 1996; Metcalfe 2006; Salloum 2003) have shown that there is a prejudice clustering of educated and well-experienced women in the lower levels of managers across a wide range of organizations in several industries. For example, in a pioneering study that addressed more than 50 women managers, Jamali, Sidani and Safieddine (2005) found out that Lebanese women find it difficult to progress in management because of the several organizational and societal barriers that hinder their managerial advancement. Drawing on these studies, this chapter aims to look at the broader picture of Lebanese women in the workforce and also describes one of the few studies on Lebanese women in management recently carried out by the authors.

Labour Force Characteristics

The last two decades have witnessed a significant increase in the proportion of women in the labour force. In 2006, women accounted for 50.2 percent of the Lebanese's 3,755,034 population and have been an integral part of the economy since the Lebanese civil war during the 1970s. Political, economic and demographic changes helped trigger this participation in the labour force. First, as a consequence of the civil war, the extreme financial and economic adversity that the Lebanese society was confronting was perhaps the main driver that facilitated the participation of women in the workforce (Sidani, 2002). Consequently, women entered the labour force as teachers, administrative workers and nurses. Second, as a result of high unemployment levels, poor salaries and poor living conditions in Lebanon after the civil war, highly educated Lebanese males migrated to the neighbouring countries, seeking better living and employment opportunities (ILO, 2006). This migration of males created a "brain drain" and a shortage of educated people within Lebanon (Jamali, Sidani and Safieddine, 2005; Tlaiss 2009). This shortage facilitated the incursion of women into non-traditional jobs and contributed to their increased employment in several sectors including banking, hospitality and law industries (ILO, 2006; MENA, 2007).

Despite, this influx of women into the workforce, (AHDR, 2005), Lebanese women accounted for less than one-third (27.8 percent) of the economically active population in 1994. Table 17.1 presents data for the occupational structure of women's employment. The data shows that women's share in administrative and commercial occupations is larger than their share in scientific and management professions. In general, between 1975 and 2002, women's labour participation rates averaged at 30.3 percent (HDR, 2004). However, by 2007, a modest 32.4 percent was recorded revealing a very minor increase (MENA 2007; HDR, 2008), which declined again in 2009 to 29 percent (UNDP/POGAR 2009).

Finally, turning our attention to pay, women's average salaries have always been notably lower than those of men. This inequality is even more evident in higher paying jobs, where women are better educated than their male counterparts and yet are paid less for doing the same job (MENA, 2007). Moreover, despite their strong presence in the services sector (81 percent), in health and social services (63.3 percent) and education (62.2 percent), compared to trade (17 percent), agriculture (16.6 percent), and industry (16.1 percent); women continue to earn less than men in Lebanon (Bayt.com, 2007; MENA 2007; UNDP/POGAR 2009). Women's estimated earnings in 2002, were US$2,552 compared to US$8,226 for males (HDR, 2004).) Nevertheless, there were modest improvements between 2002 and 2005 as women's estimated income increased to US$2,701 in 2005 compared to US$8,585 for males (HDR, 2008). This does not come as a surprise considering most management positions continue to be occupied by men and serves as an explanation as to why women continue to be under-represented within the management hierarchy.

Table 17.1   Distribution of the labour force by gender and employment sector, 1970 and 1987 (%)

Occupation	Male		Female		Total	
	1970	1987	1970	1987	1970	1987
Agricultural workers	18.0	13.2	22.8	6.1	18.9	12.0
Technical and scientific professions	7.4	32.2	21.2	12.7	9.8	29.4
Managers and high-level employment	2.3	4.4	0.2	3.3	2.0	4.2
Administrative employees	7.9	6.9	10.3	30.5	8.3	10.8
Commercial sector and sales employees	14.2	9.1	3.2	21.0	12.3	11.0
Non-agricultural workers and drivers	37.2	18.8	19.6	11.9	34.1;	17.7
Services workers	9.4	6.1	22.5	11.8	11.7	7.0
Military and other professions	3.5	8.9	0.3	2.7	2.9	7.9
Total	100	100	100	100	100	100

Source: Central Directorate of Statistics, Labor Force; Survey, 1970; Kasparian, R., and Beaudoin. A., La population déplacée au Liban, 1975–1987, Université Saint-Joseph (Beyrouth, Liban) – Université Laval (Québec, Canada), February 1992.

Women Pursuing Education

One of the main changes that Lebanon has undergone to eradicate gender discrimination in the workplace is the education of girls which has contributed greatly towards the economic and social development of Lebanese women. A recent report by the United Nations (MENA, 2007) highlighted that education and training for women is more of a prerequisite for women to participate in the labour force than it is for men (MENA, 2007) and provides women with a competitive edge over less-educated men in the workforce (UNDP/POGAR, 2009). According to MENA (2007) 48 percent of women employees have university degrees, compared to only 33 percent of male colleagues who have degrees.

Although recent accurate data on the status of Lebanese women in education is unavailable (MENA, 2007), there is evidence to suggest that the levels of education achieved by Lebanese women has been steadily increasing since the end of the Lebanese War in 1991 (HDR, 2004). According to World Bank statistics, enrolment rates for females have increased over the past 30 years (World Bank, 2005). The Programme of Governance for the Arab Region reported (UNDP/POGAR, 2009) that adult female illiteracy decreased from 37 percent in 1980 to 19.7 percent in 2000, with 8 percent illiteracy among young females. In 1994, for example females accounted for 47.5 percent of the students enrolled in elementary schools, 49.7 percent for the intermediate level and 52.8 percent of the total enrolled at secondary level (UNDP, 1997). In 2000, these enrolment rates had increased to 102 percent for females compared to 105 percent for males, with the gross secondary female enrolment rate increasing to 83 percent compared to 76 percent for males (World Bank, 2005). As for the gross percentage of school age population, enrolment levels for females in primary school rose from 76.2 percent in 1990 to 89.4 percent in 2001 and to 79 percent in 2002 for secondary school (UNDP, 2008). Thus, school enrolment for females, as a percentage of the gross school enrolment in Lebanon had increased from 39 percent in 2000 to 50 percent in 2005 (MENA, 2007). Similarly, female enrolment rates in vocational education reached 40 percent in 2000 (UN/ESCWA Report, 2004) as the enrolment rate of females in higher education exceeded those of males (MENA, 2007) (see Table 17.2). Interestingly, in higher education, women students account for 53 percent of the student population (Association of Lebanese Banks, 2000; World Bank, 2005; UNDP/POGAR, 2009). In 2006, there were 38 universities in Lebanon with 146,961 students and 13,770 professors (Centre of Research and Teaching Development, 2006).

Table 17.2   University education distribution by sex in 2005–2006

	Students	Administrators	Teacher
Females	79,256	2,360	4,473
Males	67,705	2,197	9,297
Total	14,691	4,557	13,770

Source: Centre of Research and Teaching Development (2006)

Thus, while the level of education for Lebanese women has improved, female participation in the workforce increased by less than 1 percent between 1997 and 2004 (Living Conditions National Survey 2004).

Furthermore, Tlaiss (2009) along with the Association of Lebanese Banks (2000) reported that the number of women holding managerial posts in Lebanon is substantially lower than their education and experience would warrant.

Women in Management

Women's participation as managers and decision makers within the public sector is almost insignificant. In October 2004, for the first time, two women were appointed to the Lebanese Cabinet. Today, the number of women ministers has not changed as two female ministers were appointed in the newly formed Government in November 2009. More recent evidence has noted that prejudices and traditional attitudes namely nepotism, prevents non-political families from reaching high positions in the Lebanese political life (Tlaiss, 2009).

Within the judiciary system, women are also under-represented as judges. In 2007, only 27.5 percent of the judges in Lebanon were women (MENA, 2007). Moreover, women judges in higher courts are currently 32.7 percent of the total number of judges (UNDP, 2008). Only 19.5 percent of the judges at the State Consultative Council are women (MENA, 2007), and there are no women among the presidents or vice presidents of supreme courts and the number of women among judges of the highest level is only 18 percent of the total (Sha'rani, 2004).

In other public administration positions, Table 17.3 illustrates that the status of Lebanese women is not much better. Of the 90 posts as general director in the public sector, only one was occupied by a woman in 1994 (UNDP, 1997) which increased to 3 percent in 2000 (MENA, 2007; Sha'rani, 2004). As ambassadors, women constituted 3.3 percent (UNDP, 1997) of the total number of ambassadors in 2000 (Sha'rani, 2004). As a head of the municipal council, only two out of the 736 council heads are women. Similarly, women's participation in professional associations and labour unions does not portray a better image. Despite the increase in the number of women in professional occupations, such as doctors, engineers and lawyers, in the year 2000 there was one woman on the board of the Teacher's Union and no women on the boards of engineers and physicians (Sha'rani, 2004).

Table 17.3   Participation of Lebanese women in decision making in public life

Members of Parliament	3 women out of 128
Ambassadors	2 women out of 53
Director General	3 women out of 22
Dean in the Lebanese University	1 woman out of 13
Head of the Municipal Council	2 women out of 736
The Teachers' Union	1 woman out of 12 board members
The Secondary Teachers' Union	2 women out of 18 board members
The Engineers' Union	0 women on the union's board
The Physicians' Order	0 women on the union's board
The Pharmacists' Order	1 women was twice elected as its president
The Dentists Order	1 women was twice elected as its president
The Bar Association	2 women on the boards
Judge in the State Consultative Council	6 women out of 365 judges
Judge in the Judicial Court	66 of the 365 judges

Source: Sha'rani, 2004. Statistics cited in the National Report about the Situation of Women in Lebanon for the Year 2000

Lebanon has been described as the pioneer in the Arab region for enjoying relaxed codes regarding women's participation in economic and political activities (Sidani, 2005) and in allowing women to pursue jobs and responsibilities outside traditionally allocated roles (Sidani, 2002). Despite this, Lebanese women continue to cluster at lower and supervisory levels of management with only 8.5 percent of women in high administrative positions (Labaki 1997;

MENA 2007). Women comprise less than 5 percent of top management positions (Eid, 2002) and earn less than their male counterparts (Association of Lebanese Banks, 2000). The majority of employed women work in health and education and social services sector (62.2 percent) compared to 16.1 percent in industry (MENA, 2007). According to the Association of Lebanese Banks (2000), women constitute 90 percent of the total workforce in the banking sector yet hold less than 20 percent of management positions, with none in executive positions (UNDP/POGA, 2009). Thus, while equally educated women and men enter the labour workforce in relatively similar numbers, decision-making positions remain the preserve of men (Association of Lebanese Banks, 2000). This inequality has been attributed mainly to the patriarchal nature of the Lebanese society, which traditionally considers "breadwinning" and working outside the home as the man's role (AHDR, 2005; MENA, 2007).

However, knowledge concerning the experiences of Lebanese women managers is scant and rather contradictory. According to Jamali, Sidani and Safieddine (2005), Lebanese women managers continue to face a number of barriers within their organizations that impact the progression of their careers. The study found that both the socio-cultural environment and the corporate environment created attitudinal constraints by favouring men over women and structural constraints via excluding women from networks and denying them corporate support. However, in another study that focused on middle and senior women managers in the Lebanese banking sector, Jamali, Safieddine and Daouk (2006) described the organizational cultures as having positive attitudes towards women and being rather supportive. Thus, unlike their counterparts in the previous study, Lebanese women bankers were satisfied with their organizational practices, career development opportunities and organizational support mechanisms.

NEW STUDY OF LEBANESE WOMEN MANAGERS

Given the conflicting results and in an attempt to have a clearer understanding, the authors have recently conducted a detailed study of Lebanese women managers covering the societal, organizational and gender-based factors that impact the career advancement of women managers. The study is of primary importance since our knowledge about the extent to which women's economic and social rights in the workplace are being addressed is sparse. What also makes this study even more interesting, is the focus on the impact of the religious affiliation, given that women in this region work in an environment in which religion has a significant role.

Understanding the status of women in Lebanon is rather a complex issue as it needs to be examined from within the Lebanese socio-cultural and religious affiliation perspective. The Middle Eastern culture has always been described as favouring men, with gender stereotypes that consider women suitable for nurturing and men suitable for positions of management and leadership (AHDR, 2005; Jamali, Sidani and Safieddine, 2005; MENA, 2007; Sidani, 2005). Lebanon has somewhat relaxed codes regarding women's participation in economic and political activities (Neal, Finlay and Tansey 2005; Sidani, 2005). The religious diversity and the sub-cultures distinguish Lebanon from the rest of the Arab world. Therefore, it is rather safe to say that the general role of women in Lebanon has been impacted by this European–Middle Eastern, Christian–Muslim interaction (Neal, Finlay and Tansey 2005).

Historically, Arab Muslims and Christians have co-existed for centuries and have been impacted by the same historic events with nations developing common values and morals (Weir, 2003). Despite these common values, Muslims and Christians hold different attitudes regarding the status of women, and thus perceptions pertaining to the role of women in Lebanon also differ. For example, a recent study conducted on a sample of Lebanese Muslim and Christian university students, revealed that the perception of gender roles is highly influenced by the religious affiliation (Abouchedid, 2007). According to this study, Lebanese Muslim students were found to have a more conservative perception of women in terms of allocating roles suitable for women when compared to their Christian counterparts. Furthermore, Cunningham and Sarayah (1993) found that Christian women were more likely to socialize with men and were more comfortable working with men compared to Muslim women. According to these authors, Islam emphasizes the role of women in their homes and gives men the power over women (Cunningham and Sarayah, 1993). This however, does not negate the assumption that Islam has been exploited by the Middle Eastern patriarchy to justify discrimination against women (Kazemi, 2000) and that discriminatory practices are not justified or permitted by Islamic texts (Hamdan, 2005). Islam is inseparable from the cultures in the Middle East and governs most aspects of everyday life of every Muslim (Hutchings and Weir, 2006), including the private and public, political, social and economic aspects. What further amplifies the role of religious affiliations in Lebanon is that it is the foundation of the politics in Lebanon. Therefore, it is very important to understand the perceptions of both Muslim and Christian women managers regarding the factors that impact their career advancement.

In our study, a total of 85 in-depth, face-to-face, semi-structured interviews were conducted with women managers over a period of ten months. The 85 managers who participated in the study represented of a broad range of industries including financial services, media and telecommunication, tourism and hospitality, education and healthcare. The participants occupied junior-, middle- and senior-level positions. On the basis of past research and given the methodological challenges of collecting data (Omair, 2008), obtaining a representative sample of women managers in this region through conventional sampling was difficult. Thus, interviewees were contacted through a network of personal contacts and referrals.

The interviews covered a number of dimensions including personal and occupational demographics; family background; with a prime emphasis on gender-based, organizational and socio-cultural factors that related to the status and career experiences of women managers. The analysis of the interviews revealed that social and cultural aspects play a major role in shaping the status and the experience of women managers. Patriarchal values emphasizing the nurturing role of women as mothers and wives were found to be highly entrenched within the Lebanese society. A number of respondents stated that within this patriarchal system a woman's position within and duties toward the family, proceed over her right to a successful career. Most of the interviewees were of the opinion that the greatest obstacle to their career progression was related to patriarchal societal norms.

Although these opinions were commonly shared by the interviewees, Muslim managers were more inclined to emphasize that socio-cultural sanctions represented major obstacles to their career aspirations. This was mainly attributed to the significant value that Islam puts on marriage and having children for Muslim women. With regard to gender stereotypes, Christian managers perceived their society as having greater egalitarian gender role attitudes than their Muslim counterparts. Given the link between Islamic values and the patriarchcal nature of Arab society (Esposito 1991; Moghadam 2004) these findings would suggest that pre-Islamic cultural customs that assign women a lower status in society commanded a strong foothold among the Muslim interviewees when compared to their Christian counterparts. It is also interesting to note here that some of the women interviewed referred to the existence of inter-religious differences in social and gender-related attitudes whereby in Muslim communities females enjoyed less freedom and equality compared to their male counterparts as well as their Christian female counterparts.

Female managers, regardless of religion, age, educational background or level in the managerial hierarchy, asserted the importance of educational attainment and work experience as fostering their career advancement. They considered their level of education and professional experience, in addition to their personal characteristics including decisiveness, rationality and hard work as enhancing their career progression. They also reported that exhibiting masculine traits was not necessary for women to become more successful in their careers.

As for marital status, and work and family responsibilities, the majority of the Muslim and Christian interviewees were married with more than one child. In Middle Eastern countries marriage is a social necessity and women are pressurized by their families to get married and have children (Kausar 1995; Khattab 1996). As expected, the single managers highlighted the positive impact of their single status in comparison to their married counterparts in terms of having fewer responsibilities towards the family and more time and effort to dedicate to their careers.

Married managers, however, emphasized the importance of the family and indicated that motherhood was not a barrier to their career progression. Most women emphasized the help they received from their family, mainly parents and in-laws and especially childcare as instrumental to their success. Furthermore, although having a maid or a domestic helper has been traditionally attributed only to the affluent groups, this does not seem to be the case in Lebanon. According to the Ministry of Labour, out of the total of 107,561 work permits issued in 2006, 80,845 work permits (75.2 percent of permits) were for the maid category. Not surprisingly, almost all the interviewees had at least one domestic helper in her house and perceived the domestic helpers as crucial to their success, allowing them to dedicate more time and effort to their careers.

Regarding the organizational environment, the majority of interviewees indicated that the corporate culture and environment strongly favours men over women and is thus a hindrance to their career aspirations. This suggests that gender inequities are strongly entrenched in the organizational culture of Lebanese firms and are negatively impacting the career advancement of women managers through validating the belief that management is a male domain (Wood, 2008). A number of the women interviewees complained about the negative attitudes, perceptions and stereotypes embedded in the cultures of their organizations and found them to be unsupportive and discriminating. This salience of stereotypical attitudes was frequently mentioned as hampering their career progression. These highly masculine cultures alienated many of the women who believed that the organizatuional culture limited their ability to integrate with their male colleagues and to build networks at work.

In addition, the majority of the women managers perceived that when it came to professional development and promotions, they were being measured on the male model of career development. According to these female managers, although their male colleagues were less educated and professional, they were more likely to be promoted to middle and senior managers at a faster pace than women despite their performance not being as efficient and effective as theirs. They also reported that their male counterparts received higher salaries than women. Hence, the women managers stressed their need for more organizational support.

Nevertheless, Lebanese women managers did not support the idea of the importance of a mentor for their career development. This non-consenting attitude to the importance of mentoring suggests that mentoring as a concept appears to be non-existent in the Lebanese workplace. Therefore, the majority of women managers did not attribute their success to simply having a mentor because most of them never had one. More significant, however, was the fact that women managers did not feel isolated or undervalued at work despite their token presence. Even those who felt isolated as tokens internalized their status as a source of pride and motivation. They considered their token presence among a majority of men as a sign of differentiation and an achievement that few women accomplish.

Women Entrepreneurs

Given the problems that women face in finding paid employment in Lebanon, female entrepreneurship is negligible (Husseini, 1997). However, since the Beijing conference, the Government has been actively attempting to increase the number of women-owned businesses. A number of associations like the Lebanese Business Women Association (LBWA), the Working Women's League, and the Lebanese League for Women in Business (LLWB) have been lobbying support for female-owned businesses. A recent survey involving 230 businesswomen across Lebanon found the majority of women entrepreneurs focused on areas selling consumer and domestic goods, with 35.1 percent of women-owned businesses in trade-related areas; 31.1 percent in textiles and clothing (IFC, 2007). According to MENA (2007) 28 percent of the construction and services companies in Lebanon are owned by women.

The Economic and Social Commission for Western Asia (ESCWA) (2004) documented that in 2002 self-employment rates of women were 11.6 percent of the labour force compared to 29.6 percent for men. Pisturi, et al. (2008) estimated that only 15 percent of the total entrepreneurial activity in Lebanon is female. This is attributed to a number of reasons, including access to finance, market access together with regulatory and bureaucratic red tape. Further intensifying this state of affairs are attitudes that regard men as the head of the household (Husseini, 1997; Jamali, 2009). In Lebanon, the percentage of female borrowers is 35 percent (Asrawi, 2005). Women tend to finance their activities through corporate gains (54 percent); family and friends (20 percent) and banks (20 percent), as well as securing loans through micro-finance agencies like Ameen and Al Majmoua (USAID, 1999; Aswari 2005; IFC 2007). In addition, access to markets, in particular international markets, is difficult (Isaia, 2005) because the majority of women do not register their business (Husseini, 1997) due to regulatory and bureaucratic red tape (World Bank, 2005). Furthermore, a lack of proper infrastructure and the high cost of public services (IFC and CAWTAR, 2007) are additional obstacles to accessing markets in Lebanon (Isaia 2005). Finally, lack of opportunities for business networking for women (Jamali, 2009) which are male dominated, further limits the prospects for women-owned businesses (Husseni 1997; Sha'rani, 2004).

Country Legislation

The general status of women in the Lebanese public, social, economic and legal life has been largely determined by the Lebanese Constitution which was adopted in 1926 but has been through a series of revisions. In the general preamble of the Constitution, Lebanon is defined as a democratic country based on "equality of rights and duties among all citizens without discrimination". According to Article 7 (Equality) of the Constitution, all women have the right to participate in the political aspects of the country and were given the right to vote and elect in 1953.

The Employment Act or the Lebanese Labour Law of 1946 regulates the conditions, rights and obligations of work for all employees. The labour law defines an employee as "any man or woman working for an employer for a wage" and has provisions that apply exclusively to women – Part II (*Du Travial des Enfants et des Femmes*) – Sections 26, 27, 28 and 29 under the title of *Du Travail des Femmes*.

Section 26 emphasizes the idea of equality under the employment law. According to this section (revised on 26 May, 2000), it is forbidden on the part of any employer to discriminate between employees based on their gender in any area of work. As for Section 27, it prohibits women in the industrial sector. Section 28 (revised on 26 May, 2000) stipulates that all working women are entitled to maternity leave for a period of seven weeks. This period includes the time before and after delivery. However, this leave will only be granted upon the submission of pregnant women of a medical report that states the estimated date of delivery. Furthermore, Section 29 also revised on 26 May, 2000 documents that women are entitled to full salary during their maternity leave. It also prohibits the employers from firing the women or giving them any warnings during their maternity leave unless it can be proven that she was recruited by another employer during her maternity leave.

In addition to these sections in the Labour law, Lebanese women are entitled to the Provident Fund Ordinance in the same manner as their male counterparts. However, it is critical to mention that despite legislation to the contrary, employers pay women less than their male counterparts for the same work.

Initiatives Supporting Women in the Workforce

Middle Eastern governments have only recently addressed gender and employment as important aspects of development (World Bank, 2005). Overall, governments have not taken serious measures to improve female participation in economic activities. Their policies do not ensure equal employment opportunities or promotion of women into management and decision-making positions (Lopez-Claros and Schwab, 2005).

The Future

The current reality is that organizational practices in Lebanon lack training and development opportunities; lack performance appraisals; offer poorer salaries and so on, and are heavily structured against women's promotion and career progression. This, coupled with the economic and political situation, as well as the social reality, provides little in the way of change. In 2008 Lebanon's national debt was US$45.65 billion dollars and the cost of servicing this debt has allowed employers to exploit the labour market. Hence, women find themselves obliged to preserve their source of income, even at their own expense of not being promoted and granted the training and development opportunities that they have earned. Israel's attacks on Lebanon in 2006 further damaged the economy through destroying the country's infrastructure resulting in the fleeing of foreign investments. Along with the internal political conflict between the different religious and political groups, the Government is rather focused on preserving the Lebanese economy and civil peace, rather than enforcing non-discriminatory laws of employment. Thus, there appears to be little hope in the development of national policies and initiations aimed at encouraging the empowerment of women in the workplace.

The paucity of data on Lebanese women managers and the increase of women's professional development highlight the urgency for more research in this area. Future research on women managers in the Middle Eastern region is not only important and significant, to the development of these nations. It will also help generate answers to the many problems that both men and women face in the organizational and socio-cultural settings.

References

Abdallah, I. A. (1996) Attitudes towards women in the Arabian Gulf region, *Women in Management Review*, 11(1), 29–39.

Abouchedid, K. E. (2007) Correlates of religious affiliation, religiosity and gender role attitudes among Lebanese Christian and Muslim college students, *Equal Opportunities International*, 25(3), 193–208.

AHDR (Arab Human Development Report) (2005) *Towards the Rise of Women in the Arab World* (United Nations Development Program: Regional Bureau for Arab States. Jordan: National Press).

Asrawi, F. (2005) *Microfinance in Lebanon: Case Study CHF International' Ameen 2005*. Gender Entrepreneurship Markets (GEM)/International Finance Corporation (IFC). GEM Country Brief- Lebanon 2007, http://www.ifc.org/ifcext/gempepmena.nsf/AttachmentsByTitle/Lebanon_GEM_Country_Brief/$FILE/Lebanon+GEM+Country+Brief+Feb+2007.pdf, accessed February, 2010.

Association of Lebanese Banks (2000) *The Stakes and Challenges for Women in Lebanese Banking* (Beirut: Lebanon: Association of Lebanese Banks).

Bayt.com. (2007) *The Rising Ranks of Women in the Middle East Workplace.*

Centre of Research and Teaching Development (2006) *Education in Lebanon Report.*

Cunnigham, R. B. and Sarayah, Y. K. (1993) *Wasta: The Hidden Force in the Middle Eastern Society* (Westport, CT: Praeger).

Eid, F. (2002) Daunting hurdles slow career progress of Lebanese women, *Khaleej Times*, 1 March, 2008, www.khaleejtimes.co.ae/ktarchive/100502/editor.html, accessed February 2010.

ESCWA (Economic and Social Commission for Western Asia) (2004) *Where do Arab Women Stand in the Development Process: A Gender-Based Statistical Analysis* (New York, NY: United Nations).

Esposito, J. (1991) *Islam: the Straight Path* (Oxford, UK: Oxford University Press).

GEM Country Brief – Lebanon (2007) (Washington, DC: International Finance Corporation, World Bank Group).

Hamdan, A. (2005) Women and education in Saudi Arabia: challenges and achievement, *International Education Journal*, 6(1), 42–64.

HDR (Human Development Report) (2008) *Gender Related Development Index* (New York, NY: United Nations Development Program).

HDR (Human Development Report) (2004) *Cultural Liberty in Today's Diverse World* (New York, NY: United Nations Development Program).

Husseini, R. (1997) Promoting women entrepreneurs in Lebanon: the experience of UNIFEM, *Gender and Development*, 5(1), 49–53.

Hutchings, K. and Weir, D. (2006) Guanxi and Wasta: a comparison, *Thunderbird International Business Review*, 48(1), 141–156.

IFC (International Finance Corporation) (2007) *Gender Entrepreneurship Markets (GEM).*

IFC and CAWTAR (International Finance Corporation & Centre of Arab Women for Training and Research) (2007) *Women Entrepreneurs in the Middle East and North Africa: Characteristics, Contributions and Challenges* (Washington, DC: International Finance Corporation, World Bank Group).

ILO (International Labor Organization) (2006) *An ILO Post Conflict: Decent Work Programme for Lebanon* (Lebanon: Regional Office for Arab States).

Isaia, E. (2005) *The Micro Credit Sector in Lebanon: Al Majmoua Experience*. Gender Entrepreneurship Markets (GEM)/International Finance Corporation (IFC), GEM Country Brief – Lebanon, 2007, http://www.ifc.org/ifcext/gempepmena.nsf/AttachmentsByTitle/Lebanon_GEM_Country_Brief/$FILE/Lebanon+GEM+Country+Brief+Feb+2007.pdf, accessed February, 2010.

Jamali, D. (2009) Constraints and opportunities facing women entrepreneurs in developing countries: a relational perspective, *Gender in Management: An International Review*, 24(4), 232–251.

Jamali, D., Safieddine, A. and Daouk, M (2006) The glass ceiling: some positive trends from the Lebanese banking sector, *Women in Management Review*, 21(8), 625–642.

Jamali, D., Safeddine, A. and Daouk, M. (2007) Corporate governance and women: an empirical study of top and middle women managers in the Lebanese sector, *Corporate Governance*, 7(5), 574–585.

Jamali, D., Sidani, Y. and Safieddine, A. (2005) Constraints facing working women in Lebanon: an insider view, *Women in Management Review*, 20(8), 581–594.

Kattara, H. (2005) Career challenges for female managers in Egyptian hotels, *International Journal of Contemporary Hospitality Management*, 17(3), 238–251.

Kausar, Z. (1995) Women in feminism and politics: new directions towards Islamization. In A. Omar and M. J. Davidson (2001), Women in management: a comparative cross-cultural overview, *Cross Cultural Management*, 8(3/4), 35–67.

Kazemi, F. (2000) Gender, Islam and politics, *Social Research*, 67(2), 453–474.

Khattab, H. (1996) *The Muslim Woman's Handbook* (London: TA-HA Publishers).

Labaki, H. N. (1997) Perceived acceptance of women business leaders in Lebanon. In D. Jamali, Y. Sidani and A. Safieddine (2005), Constraints facing working women in Lebanon: an insider view, *Women in Management Review*, 20(8), 581–594.

Lopez-Claros, A. and Schwab, K. (2005) *The Arab World Competitiveness Report 2005* (New York, NY: Palgrave Macmillan).

MENA (Middle East and North Africa Gender Overview) (2007) The World Bank.

Metcalfe, B. D. (2006) Exploring cultural dimensions of gender and management in the Middle East, *Thunderbird International Business Review*, 48(1), 93–107.

Moghadam, V. (2004) Patriarchy in transition: women and the changing family in the Middle East, *Journal of Comparative Family Studies*, 35(2), 137–152.

National Survey of Household Living Conditions, Lebanon (2004) *Central Administration for Statistics, Beirut – Lebanon*, http://www.cas.gov.lb/index.php?option=com_content&view=frontpage&Itemid=28, accessed February, 2010.

Neal, M., Finlay, J. and Tansey, R. (2005) My father knows the minister: a comparative study of Arab women's attitudes towards leadership authority, *Women in Management Review*, 20(7), 478–497.

Omair, K. (2008) Women in management in the Arab context, *Education, Business and Society: Contemporary Middle Eastern Issues*, 1(2), 107–123.

Pistrui, D., Fahed-Sreih, J., Huang, W. and Welsch, H. (2008) *Entrepreneurial led family business development in post-war Lebanon*, USASBE 2008 Proceedings, pp. 847–862.

Salloum, H. (2003) Women in the United Arab Emirates, *Contemporary Review*, 283, 101–104.

Sha'rani, A. (2004) *The Lebanese women: reality and aspirations*, 15 May, 2006, www.nclw.org.lb/lebanesemid.cfm, accessed February, 2010.

Sidani, Y. (2002) Management in Lebanon. In M. Warner (ed.) *International Encyclopedia of Business and Management*, 2nd ed. (London: Thomson Learning, pp. 3797–3802).

Sidani, Y. (2005) Women, work, and Islam in Arab societies, *Women in Management Review*, 20(7), 498–512.

Tlaiss, H. (2009) *Managerial Progression: The Case of Lebanon*, Unpublished PhD thesis, Manchester Business School, University of Manchester.

UNDP (United National Development Program) (1997) *A Profile of Sustainable Human Development in Lebanon*, Centre for Public Sector Projects and Studies, http://www.undp.org.lb/programme/governance/advocacy/nhdr/nhdr97/contents.pdf, accessed February, 2010.

UNDP (United National Development Program) (2008) *What we do: The Millennium Development Goals for Lebanon*, http://www.undp.org.lb/WhatWeDo/MDGs.cfm, accessed February, 2010.

UN/ESCWA (United Nations and Economic and Social Commission for Western Asia) (2004) *Summary Report on the Status of Women in Arab Countries for the Arab Regional Conference: 10 Years after Beijing*, July 2004.

UNDP/POGAR (United Nations Development Program/Program on Governance in the Arab Region) (2009).

US AID (1999) *Gender Integration in USAID/Lebanon's Program: A Preliminary Assessment*. Gender Entrepreneurship Markets (GEM)/International Finanace Corporation (IFC). GEM Country Brief – Lebanon 2007, http://www.ifc.org/ifcext/gempepmena.nsf/AttachmentsByTitle/Lebanon_GEM_Country_Brief/$FILE/Lebanon+GEM+Country+Brief+Feb+2007.pdf, accessed February, 2010.

Weir, D. T. (2003) Human resource development in the Arab Middle East: a fourth paradigm. In M. Lee (ed.) *HRD in a Complex World* (London: Routledge, pp. 69–82).

Wood, J. (2008) *Gendered Lives: Communication, Gender, and Culture*, 8th edition (Boston, MA: Wadsworth Cengage Learning).

World Bank (2005) *The Status and Progress of Women in the Middle East and North Africa* (World Bank Middle East and North Africa Socio-Economic Development Group, Washington, DC: World Bank Publications).

18

Women in Management in Turkey

Hayat Kabasakal, Zeynep Aycan, Fahri Karakaş and Ceyda Maden

Introduction

The Republic of Turkey is located mainly in Anatolia (west Asia) and partly in the Balkans (southeast Europe). It had 71.5 million inhabitants at the end of 2008 and 75 percent of the population lived in urban areas (TurkStat, 2009a). The country has been a convenient bridge between east and west throughout history. The analysis of women in society and in management positions conveys the simultaneous influence of eastern and western cultures in the Turkish context.

The Republic of Turkey has been established upon the demise of the Ottoman Empire. After the defeat of the Ottoman Empire in the First World War, under the leadership of Mustafa Kemal Atatürk, Turks won the independence war and established the new republic in 1923. As the President of the new republic, Atatürk guided a series of reforms in social, political, linguistic and economic areas, which were later referred to as Kemalist principles. The Kemalist principles, which constituted the dominant State ideology, had important implications for the modernization and emancipation of Turkish women (Arat, 1999).

The reforms of the republic carried the values of secularism, nationalism and modernism which incorporated westernization into society. Women were assigned an important role in this modernization project and their progress was interpreted as a significant measure of success in reaching modernity, westernization and development of the nation (Arat, 1994; 1999). This State ideology upheld the value of gender equality in employment and elimination of discriminatory policies from the formal processes of public employment.

The cornerstones of emancipation of women in the Turkish Republic were widely distributed through education, legislative and administrative reforms, political rights, public visibility and professionalism. The impact of the reforms was significant among middle- and upper-class families, while their influence was only partial among lower socio-economic groups and in rural areas. In the post-1980 period, however, two types of changes emerged in the direction of weakening the ideology of "State feminism" (that is, advocacy of women's movement demands inside the State by women's policy agencies; Kantola and Squires, 2008) that dominated the early republican era (Healy, Özbilgin and Aliefendioğlu, 2005). Firstly, change was related to the neo-liberal economic programme that had been applied since the 1980s and resulted in the weakening of the Government labour market regulation. "This has diluted the traditional sex equality discourse of the republican ideology pursued by the state in all sectors" (Healy, Özbilgin and Aliefendioğlu, 2005:254). Secondly, newly emerging political parties and economic institutions advocated gender segregation, which is considered to be against the principle of secularism. In contemporary Turkish society, these trends created a duality between secularism on the one hand and religiousness and patriarchal Middle Eastern values on the other hand.

The changes in the post-1980 period have created some variations in social attitudes regarding the image of Turkish women: "The image of republican Turkish women, expected to 'self-sacrifice' and 'pioneer' for the advancement of the nation, has lost its influence on a new generation of young women graduates" (Healy, Özbilgin and Aliefendioğlu, 2005:254). Like women in other developed nations of the world, Turkish women started to perceive their careers from a standpoint of individualistic motivation rather than a collectivist sense of fulfilling a national duty.

In summary, despite the significant attempts at modernization of women as dominant State ideology in the early republican era, some conflicting and traditional roles are simultaneously present in Turkish society, even among middle and upper classes which have internalized these principles. With the changes that have emerged since 1980s, "state feminism" has weakened and attitudes favouring gender segregation have gained momentum. Traditional roles that are prevalent in parts of society and the current right-wing

Government, in power since 2003, promote segregation of gender roles, the role of women as mothers and wives and traits that are considered to be feminine. This chapter provides an analysis of the existing gender segregation in Turkish society. It aims to portray women's general standing in society in terms of their contribution to the labour force as well as their position in specific areas, including management, politics and entrepreneurship. This chapter will also examine women's general well-being in terms of their income, educational and legal standing and attitudes towards them in society. It will summarize with positive initiatives that aim to support women and prospects about future.

Labour Force Characteristics

The Turkish labour force has been experiencing major changes since the 1950s (Özar, 1994). First, as a consequence of massive mechanization in agriculture, there has been significant migration from rural to urban areas, leading to an increase in the urban labour force. Second, industrial and services sectors grew rapidly after the 1960s. As a result of these two trends, the agricultural labour force dropped significantly and the non-agricultural labour force portrayed an upward trend. Parallel with the fall in the agricultural labour force, women's percentage in the total labour force steadily dropped. While women constituted 43.1 percent of the total labour force in 1955, this ratio declined to 26.2 percent in 2007. Parallel with this trend, men's share in the labour force increased from 56.9 percent in 1955 to 73.8 percent in 2007.

Effects of migration placed women's labour in a much more disadvantageous position since a significant difference has emerged between labour force participation of urban women and men. Women's overall participation in the labour force decreased from 34.2 percent in 1990 to 24.8 percent in 2007. In the same period, their participation increased slightly in urban areas, from 17.1 percent to 20.2 percent, whereas in rural areas it decreased from 52.0 to 32.7 percent. Although there is a slight increase in the participation of women in the labour force in urban areas, it is still small with only one in five women being a part of this labour force (TurkStat, 2007). The urban–rural percentages reveal that living in urban places does not provide enough "job opportunities" to those women who migrated from rural areas (Tan et al., 2008).

When one looks at the distribution of women's labour in different sectors over the years, one sees a continuous decrease in the share of women's labour in agriculture, and an increase in the industrial and services sectors. As seen in Table 18.1, women's share in agriculture dropped from 53.3 percent in 1955 to 46.7 percent in 2007. In parallel, in 1955 women constituted 12.3 percent of industrial workers and 6 percent of service employees, while these figures gradually increased to 15.1 percent in industry and to 20.6 percent in the services sector in 2007 (TurkStat, 2007).

Table 18.1   Distribution of employment by economic sector and gender

	1955			1990			2007		
	Female %	Male %	Total %	Female %	Male %	Total %	Female %	Male %	Total %
Agriculture	53.3	46.7	77.4	55.0	45.0	53.7	46.7	53.3	26.4
Industry	12.3	87.7	28.2	13.8	86.2	17.9	15.1	84.9	25.5
Services	6.0	94.0	14.4	14.0	86.0	28.4	20.6	79.4	48.1
Total	43.1	56.9	100.0	36.0	64.0	100.0	26.2	73.8	100.0

Source: TurkStat, Household Labour Force Survey Results, 2007

Household Labour Force Survey results revealed that in 2007, 47.3 percent of economically active women were employed in the agricultural sector, 37.9 percent were employed in the services sector and 14.8 percent were employed in industry. While the agricultural sector still continues to be the main source of employment for Turkish women, the services sector has been the fastest growing employment area for women in recent years as the percentage of women employed in services increased by 11.6 percent from 2000 to 2007 (TurkStat, 2007).

In urban areas, women also engage in various economic activities that are not reflected in formal market statistics (Özbay, 1994). Studies on women's labour in the informal sector show that waged domestic labour is very common among urban women from lower socio-economic groups (Kalaycıoğlu and Rittersberger, 1998; Zeytinoğlu et al., 1997). Further, the small-scale firms which are in sub-contracting arrangements are often able to survive with the help of family members and women's contribution to the production process (which is largely unpaid or very low paid) (Dedeoğlu, 2004). Several studies showed that only a very few of the women labourers in metropolitan areas were covered by the social security system and even a smaller percentage were union members (Eyüboğlu, Özar and Tufan-Tanrıöver, 1998; İlkkaracan, 1998). They work under undesirable environmental conditions and have low levels of job satisfaction (Eraydın, 1998).

In Turkey, there are two major wage-related concerns about compensation of women's labour. First of all, employment opportunities which are available for women are generally concentrated in those sectors paying low wage rates. Turkish women are mainly concentrated in labour-intensive and low-paying jobs, like textile and ready-made garment industries. Secondly, in a given sector and employment status, women in general earn less than men.

The World Bank's Turkey Labour Market Study Report (2006) drew attention to the growing earning differentials between men and women in urban areas from 1988 to 2002. Male–female earning gaps have expanded between 1988 and 2002, considering both "all wage and salary earners" and "full-time wage and salary earners". The 2002 estimates reflect that women earn between 78 and 83 percent of men's income, depending on whether all wage and salary earners are considered or only the full-time earners are taken into account (World Bank, 2006). Examination of recent statistics regarding the wage gap between men and women at different occupational categories reveals that without any sector differentiation, in most of the occupational categories, men earn higher wages than women. As reflected in Table 18.2, the gap is wider in some particular categories like craft and related trades workers and plant/machine operators–assemblers. One interesting observation is that when compared on the basis of their average monthly wage rates, female legislators, senior officials and managers earn 2.5 percent more than their male colleagues (TurkStat, 2006).

Table 18.2   Average monthly (gross) wage rate based on gender and occupation and wage gap ratio

	Men (New Turkish Liras)	Women (New Turkish Liras)	Wage gap ratio*
Legislators, senior, officials and managers	2,723	2,790	102.5
Professionals	1,982	1,685	85.9
Clerks	1,226	1,056	86.1
Service workers and shop market sales workers	804	750	93.3
Skilled agricultural, and fishery workers	851	691	81.2
Craft and related trades workers	893	692	77.5
Plant and machine operators and assemblers	901	693	76.9
Elementary occupations	751	656	87.4

Source: TurkStat, Earnings Structure Questionnaire Results, 2006
*   Calculated as mean female monthly wages divided by mean male wages.

The studies on wage differentials between men and women in Turkey present significant results regarding the disadvantageous position of women. Selim and İlkkaracan (2006) found that in the private sector, wages of women stand for 37.7 percent of the wages they earn in the public sector and this ratio is 53.9 percent for men. The authors also found that in the public sector men earn 5.8 percent more than women after controlling for other variables that may contribute to wage differences. Dayıoğlu and Kasnakoğlu (1997) propose that in patriarchal societies, paying low wages to women is deemed to be normal since women's earnings are not recognized as a part of a family's budget but only as a minor contribution to it. However, "education" is a significant factor which balances the prevalent disparity between men and women given the fact that as the education level of women increases from primary school to high school level, their annual earnings increase and correspond to 93 percent of men's earnings at high school level (TurkStat, 2006).

Women Pursuing Education

Education of women and men is one of the major problems in the way of social development and modernization of Turkey. After the proclamation of the Republic of Turkey, Kemalist principles and State ideology that aims to improve women's position in society achieved some success in providing widespread education to Turkish women. Primary education is compulsory for both girls and boys and parents who do not send their children to school are liable to imprisonment.

In the early years of the Republic, the rate of literacy was very low among women and over the years there has been a significant increase in the rate of literate women. In 1990, 67.4 percent of women and 89.8 percent of men were literate, by 2006 the literacy rate increased gradually both for women and men, reaching 80.4 percent and 96.0 percent, respectively in 2006.

By a law enacted in 1997, compulsory education was raised from five to eight years, by combining primary and junior-high school education. Accordingly, the rights of girls to receive junior-high school education were put under State guarantee. In the 1997/98 educational year, the schooling ratio for women was 78.9 percent for primary education and 34.1 percent for secondary education. Over ten years, for women, the schooling ratio in primary education reached 90.1 percent whereas the same ratio increased to 52.1 and 18.6 for secondary and higher education, respectively. This situation can be associated with the rise of private and public initiatives and campaigns that promote equal education opportunity for women (more information on these initiatives and campaigns are provided later in this chapter).

Despite the improvements in women's education, there are a few points that need to be addressed. Although primary education is compulsory for both girls and boys, the discrepancy in their literacy and schooling ratios, particularly before 1997, shows that boys are more advantageous in continuing their education. This is related to the dominant patriarchal values in society, which perceive women's role as restricted to duties and roles at home rather than achievement in the public arena. Particularly in rural areas, due to the fall of agricultural sector and emerging poverty after the 1980s, a significant group of girls cannot continue their education. When a family's income is restricted, the scarce resource that is to be spent on sending children to school is likely to be allocated to boys rather than girls. In the 2006/07 education year, 60 percent of children who were at the primary school level but did not continue their education were girls (Rankin and Aytaç, 2006; Tan et al., 2008).

Representing the cultural norms prevalent in society, gender roles are apparent in both vocational schools and university education, as there are distinct differences between the concentration areas of female and male students. Girls are placed in vocational schools that teach subjects which can be considered to be a part of the female role, such as home economics, child rearing and sewing, and boys are placed in schools that train them for jobs with a higher market value, such as electricians and carpenters (Ministry of National Education, 2006–2007). At universities, female students constitute more than half of the students studying in non-technical areas such as language and literature (66.5 percent) and art (51.4 percent). Furthermore, their enrolment percentage portrays a gradual increase in the social sciences and applied social sciences and males' dominance in technical sciences is still prevalent (ÖSYM, 2007). In general, the employment of women with vocational school and higher education has increased significantly in the recent years and as a general trend, it can be stated that "education" plays a primary role in improving women's position by increasing their employability in better paid jobs with social security (Tan et al., 2008).

Women in Management

As part of the modernization project of the Republic, professionalization of women carried a significant importance. Beginning with the early years of the republic, middle- and upper-class families placed a high importance on the education of their daughters in highly prestigious professions. During the 1980s, Turkish women started to perceive their careers with a more individualistic motivation rather than as a duty for national development (Healy, Özbilgin and Aliefendioğlu, 2005) and continued to pursue education and careers in highly prominent professions.

The percentage of Turkish women in high-status professions can be considered to be of a high ratio, even in comparison to many other industrialized western countries. In relation to some of the prestigious professions, for example, 60 percent of pharmacists, 19 percent of physicians, 30 percent of dentists, 34 percent of lawyers and 23 percent of professors were women in Turkey in the 1990s and early 2000s (Gürüz 2001; Koray 1991).

As Table 18.3 shows, in 2007, there were 61 women per 100 men in professional jobs and 41 women per 100 men in technical/associate professions (TurkStat, 2007). In urban areas, 28.5 percent of employed women were regarded as professionals, technicians and associate professionals (TurkStat, 2007), and this is an area where women are most concentrated (Tan et al., 2008).

Table 18.3   Percentage of employed population by occupation (2007), population over 15 years of age

	Male	Female	Female per 100 male
Legislators, senior, officials and managers	10.7	2.7	9
Professionals	5.1	8.9	61
Clerks	6.2	7.1	41
Technicians and associated professionals	4.8	9.4	70
Service workers and shop market sales workers	12.9	9.0	25
Skilled agricultural and fishery workers	16.8	36.4	76
Craft and related trades workers	17.4	4.9	10
Plant and machine operators and assemblers	13.2	3.9	11
Elementary occupations	13.0	17.7	48

Source: TurkStat, Household Labour Force Survey Results, 2007

Nevertheless, the success of women in prestigious professional occupations is not reflected in the same proportions to decision-making positions. There are only nine women per 100 men in administrative and managerial positions, accounting for only 9.6 percent of all such positions (see Table 18.4) (TurkStat, 2007) and there are no statistics available on demographic characteristics of these women managers or on minority women managers. While women frequently work in high-skill and technical professions, their representation drops sharply in high-level managerial positions (Kabasakal 1998; 1999). The same situation is not observed for men. In 2007, 11.3 percent of employed men worked in professional occupations and 10.7 percent of them were regarded as legislators, senior, officials and managers (TurkStat, 2007).

Table 18.4   **Percentage of men and women in managerial and professional jobs (2007), population over 15 years of age**

	Legislators, senior officials and managers	Professionals	Technicians and associated professionals
Male	90.4	61.2	70.0
Female	9.6	38.8	30.0

Source: TurkStat, Household Labour Force Survey Results, 2007

The trend is similar in the education sector where women have high representation rates. Although women made up 44 percent of the teachers employed by the Ministry of Education, only 7 percent of school principals were women (Kadınlar, 1990). Women are not represented at decisional and discretionary power positions in labour unions despite the fact that labour unions are institutions that examine the problems of female workers, propose strategies to eliminate discrimination, encourage participation of women in decision-making positions, and promote equal opportunities (KSGM,[1] 2008). In 2008, there were no female managers on the board of directors of workers' confederations and only five of the chairs of the 91 labour unions (5.4 percent), and 32 of the 481 board of directors (6.6 percent) were women. Labour unions in the public sector portrayed a relatively better situation; five of the chairpersons of the 51 labour unions (9.8 percent) and 26 of the 325 centre managers (8.0 percent) were women (KSGM, 2008).

---

1   Prime Ministry General Directorate on the Status of Women.

WOMEN MANAGERS IN THE PUBLIC SECTOR

In Turkish bureaucracy, women in managerial positions constitute 17.9 percent of all bureaucrats in similar positions. The representation of women at managerial ranks decreases sharply as they go up in the hierarchy from supervisory and middle levels to upper executive positions. While women constituted 27.3 percent of deputy managers, 25 percent of assistant secretary generals and 30 percent of secretary generals, this ratio dropped to 6.8 percent among presidents as of April 2007. Further, they had a significantly smaller share of 3.6 percent in under secretary, governor and director general positions and were not even represented at under secretary and governor levels (KSGM, 2008).

Table 18.5   Women in managerial positions in some occupations in the public sector, 2007

	Women	Total	Women %
Ambassador	15	166	9.0
Consul General	2	58	3.4
Governor and Deputy Governor	5	563	0.9
Rector	5	93	5.3
Dean	82	648	12.6

Source: Prime Ministry General Directorate on the Status of Women, *Women in Power and Decision Making*, 2008

Table 18.5 illustrates the percentage and number of women holding some managerial positions in foreign affairs, public administration and education sectors in 2007. At the level of ambassadors, there were 15 women out of 166 (9.0 percent), while the ratio of women consul generals decreased to 3.4 percent. Women's representation in provincial public administration was almost non-existent as there were only five women assigned to the position of governors and deputy governors (KSGM, 2008). In 93 Turkish universities, 12.6 percent of all the deans and only 5.3 percent of rectors were women (KSGM, 2008).

WOMEN MANAGERS IN THE PRIVATE SECTOR

Although there is no census data that portrays the percentage of Turkish women managers in the private sector, there are some international reports which provide country comparisons regarding the situation of women in leadership positions. One of the prominent reports about worldwide gender equality was "The Global Gender Gap 2006 Report", which was submitted to the World Economic Forum 2006. In this report, it was stated that women in Turkey have greater opportunities to be promoted to leadership positions in various enterprises when compared to many European (EU) and Organisation for Economic Co-operation and Development (OECD) countries.[2] In the international ranking developed based on the opportunities provided to women to attain managerial positions, Turkey ranked 57th of 115 countries, surpassing numerous EU members (TISK, 2008).

Recent studies (Nalbant 2002; Örücü, Kılıç and Kılıç, 2007) showed that factors related with low levels of women's representation in senior management positions reflected gender–role stereotypes. In general, there is a perceived incongruity in society between the qualities associated with women and successful managers (Sümer, 2006). Sümer's study showed that women were perceived to be lower on task-orientation and emotional stability than both men and successful managers, and these attributions maybe among the factors that act as barriers to women's advancement to executive and strategic decision-making positions.

As part of the conflicting roles of women professionals, the role of mother and wife conflicts with career roles. A study compared 20 female and 20 male Turkish white-collar workers and found that marriage had a negative affect on women's careers (Kabasakal 1998; 1999). Similar findings were reported by Aycan (2004) which suggested that men had more negative attitudes towards women in management (that is, believing that they are not suitable for managerial jobs) due to women's family-related roles and responsibilities. In her study among male and female managers working in several business organizations, Aycan (2004) found that societal attitudes towards women in management were slightly positive. Both male and female respondents were moderate in their beliefs about women's competencies to carry out work and family responsibilities with success and had doubts about women's assertiveness, intelligence and willingness to become successful business

---

2   Prime Ministry General Directorate on the Status of Women, *Women in Power and Decision Making*, 2008.

leaders. In addition, Aycan's study (2004) pointed to a discrepancy between the actual and the ideal, in such a way that while respondents doubted the competencies of women, they thought that women's status in work life and their advancement opportunities should be improved. This can be explained by the System Justification Theory (Jost and Banaji, 1994) which suggests that women internalize societal values that disadvantage them to justify their low status.

For Turkish women in managerial and highly prestigious professions, the conflicting roles of wife, mother and career result in these women facing different dynamics compared to women in unskilled or semi-skilled jobs or to other career women in more developed countries. Turkish women in high-status jobs, and who come from a privileged background, are in a more advantageous position in reconciling the conflicting demands of their career and home duties by delegating the housework and child-rearing responsibilities to low-paid domestics. Given the fact that wages paid to domestics in developing countries are relatively low, professional women with a high socio-economic background can easily employ at least one domestic at home. In addition, Turkish society is characterized by high levels of family collectivism (Kabasakal and Bodur, 2002; 2007), where there is high interdependence between members of large families, and it is common practice that grandmothers and aunts take on part of the housework and child-rearing responsibilities.

In her study based on a series of in-depth interviews with top and middle level managers, Aycan (2004) indicated that respondents did not report any particular barriers (nor support) in their organizations because of their gender. Yet they indicated that they had "to convince 'themselves' first that it was okay not to personally fulfill domestic duties, but instead to get assistance from family or paid help" (Aycan 2004:473). One of the most serious difficulties they faced in their organizations was in getting into social and communication networks in male-oriented organizational contexts. Studies on the characteristics of the few women who were able to move up to senior managerial positions show that senior women managers come from a privileged background (Arbak et al., 1998; Kabasakal 1998; 1999). It is likely that the elite background of women helps in overcoming the lower status associated with femaleness and provides the prestige that is required for the execution of power and influence in executive positions (Kabasakal 1998; 1999). That may be why women in executive positions do report that they experience no major barriers in organizational contexts despite the fact that they experience many difficulties in getting into networks and convincing themselves and others that they can balance their work and home responsibilities (Aycan, 2004).

WOMEN IN POLITICS

Turkey is one of the first countries to grant women the right to vote and to be voted for. Women were given political rights in the 1930s – the right to vote and to run in municipal elections in 1930 and in national elections in 1934. Turkish women were granted these rights much earlier than their counterparts in many industrialized western countries. However, parallel with the above arguments that women are scarce in executive positions, the proportion of women elected to the Turkish Parliament has been very low. In the 2007 elections, women's representation in the Parliament reached 9.1 percent, the highest figure up to now.

Women parliamentarians in Turkey carry mainly an "elite" background. This may be why they were not keen to attend issues concerning women's rights, but inclined more towards policies and activities to promote modernization and westernization (Güneş-Ayata, 1994). An elite background is also common amongst women ministers who took posts in cabinets. The first women minister was assigned in 1971. There are no women presidents in the history of the Turkish Republic yet, whereas there is only one prime minister, Tansu Çiller, who served in this post in the mid-1990s. In the 2000s, the last two cabinets included only one women minister, who was responsible for issues concerning women and family (TurkStat, 2009b). Currently there are two women ministers in the Cabinet.

Although political parties in Turkey nominated more female candidates for the 2009 local elections, there has been little progress because of several factors such as huge expenses of standing as a candidate, male domination in politics, and the prevailing cultural image of local administration as a "man's business". Another reason is that politics is associated with images in women's minds, such as lies (28 percent), unfulfilled promises (27.3) and corruption (12.6 percent), according to a recent survey conducted in Ankara (Özerkmen, 2008).

Women Entrepreneurs

Figures in Table 18.6, regarding the distribution of men and women by type of employment, reflect a positive change in women's engagement in economic and entrepreneurial activities. The ratio of women who work as unpaid family workers decreased from 69.2 in 1990 to 38.2 percent in 2007. On the other hand, the ratio of women working as regular and casual employees increased from 21.7 to 48.5 percent in the same period. The number of women who are sole traders reflect a minor increase from 8.7 to 12.0 percent and women in employer status increased from a negligible 0.4 percent to 1.3 percent from 1990 to 2007. (TurkStat, 2007) Although the ratio of women employees increased significantly, the number of women entrepreneurs still remains too low compared to their male counterparts. Actually, "entrepreneurship" seems to be the employment category where women have the lowest representation.

Table 18.6   Type of employment (15 years and older)

	Regular and casual employee		Employer		Sole trader worker		Unpaid family worker	
	Women %	Men %	Women %	Men %	Women %	Men %	Women %	Men %
1990	21.7	46.5	0.4	6.3	8.7	34.2	69.2	13.0
2000	35.3	53.5	0.7	6.8	11.8	29.4	52.1	10.4
2007	48.5	61.5	1.3	7.0	12.0	25.9	38.2	5.6

Source: TurkStat, Household Labour Force Survey Results, 2007

Given the fact that women are not able to find paid jobs as easily as their male counterparts, it would be expected that they would engage more in starting a new venture, which would provide them with the opportunity to work in exchange for economic gain. However, compared to many other countries, entrepreneurship is still a rare activity among Turkish women.

The low levels of entrepreneurship among women may be related to the dominant patriarchal relationships in society and family. Because women's main role is perceived as being restricted to inside the house, many entrepreneurial activities that family members engage in are considered to be under the ownership of men. A study carried out on 220 women entrepreneurs in the capital city, Ankara, showed that entrepreneurship carries serious difficulties for women (Özgen and Ufuk, 2000). The most important problems that arose during the start-up of their businesses were provision of capital, bureaucratic procedures and having no experience (Ufuk and Özgen, 2001). 71.4 percent of women entrepreneurs in the sample experienced conflict between their entrepreneurship roles and family roles as wife, mother and housewife; and faced difficulties in balancing their work and family lives. In another study on 463 dual-career family members with preschool children, Aycan and Eskin (2005) found that women experienced significantly more work–family conflict compared to men.

Some public and non-profit institutions, including the Women Entrepreneurs Association of Turkey (KAGIDER), Union of Chambers and Commodity Exchanges in Turkey (TOBB), Directorate General on Status of Women (KSGM), Women Entrepreneurs Business Development Center, and Foundation for the Support of Women's Work (KEDV) have recently started a number of projects to increase and support women's entrepreneurship in Turkey, such as supporting the opening of food stores, handicraft and weaving businesses, promoting income-generating skills for women, establishing women's entrepreneurship training and support centres, and providing micro-credits for women entrepreneurs (Ecevit, 2007). The Small and Medium Size Industry Development Organisation (KOSGEB), for example, operates and supports 39 women's enterprises in its business development centres (Ecevit, 2007). Within the framework of the Social Risk Mitigating Project, 1246 micro-income generating projects were started in 2006 to benefit women (Ecevit, 2007). Similarly, Grameenbank Diyarbakır Project provided 2,330 poor women micro-credits in 2005 to support them in starting up their own businesses (Adaman and Bulut, 2007). Although these programmes and initiatives have helped to create a positive momentum for women entrepreneurs in Turkey, there have not been integrative frameworks, policies and coordination across these programmes to support and empower women entrepreneurs in a sustainable and systematic manner.

Country Legislation

Turkish women have enjoyed extensive social and political rights since the beginning of the Turkish Republic. The principle of the equality of women and men has been adopted in the Constitution and in the early laws of Turkey.

In the last decade, it has been realized that laws in practice are insufficient for ensuring social and political rights of women in Turkey. Accordingly, there have been recent legal changes introduced to improve the social status of women in Turkey. Significant legal changes regarding women's equality took place in the Turkish Civil Code in 2002 and in the Turkish Penal Code in 2005 (Özden, 2006) to increase women's equal participation in social, economic and political life. Reforms to the Turkish Civil Code have granted women and men equal rights in marriage, divorce and property ownership. The amendments in the Constitution make up the most important part of the reforms directed towards women.

In addition to the laws that influence the general status of women in society, there are two sets of laws that cover the employment-related issues of individuals in Turkish society (Zeytinoğlu et al., 2001): The Constitution and the Labour Law. According to the latest Turkish Constitution, which was accepted in 1982, all individuals are equal before law, irrespective of language, race, colour, gender, political opinion, belief, religion and sect, or any such consideration. Under the Constitution, every individual has the right and duty to work and no one shall be required to perform work unsuitable for her/his age, gender or capacity. Minors, women and persons with disabilities shall enjoy special protection with regard to working conditions. Every individual has the right to work in public service and no criteria other than merit shall be taken into consideration for employment in the public sector.

Turkey has recently taken the equal opportunities for women in employment issue under legal guarantee by incorporating provisions regarding equal participation of women into the Labour Act. In the New Labour Act, effective as of 2003, employers must not make any discrimination, either directly or indirectly, against an employee in the conditions of her employment contract due to the employee's gender or maternity; and gender, marital status, family responsibilities and pregnancy shall not constitute a valid reason for termination of the contract (KSGM, 2009). As well, provisions regarding sexual harassment in the workplace and part-time work are also included in the Law for the first time. However, despite significant legal improvements, it is not possible to say that gender equality has been reflected completely in employment practices in accordance with these changes.

Initiatives Supporting Women in the Workforce

In the last two decades, there have been a number of Governmental, non-governmental and professional initiatives to support women in the areas of education, employment and entrepreneurship.

Turkey has recently participated in many international conferences and has signed many international agreements to support women in the field of education. Some of the objectives regarding women are to increase the ratio of literacy among women to 100 percent, to decrease the maternal–child mortality by 50 percent, and to remove the reservations included in the Charter for the Elimination of Discrimination against Women (CEDAW). Turkey, by increasing compulsory education to a total of eight years, has taken a significant step to resolve girls' access problems in education; targeting to make the schooling rate reach 100 percent for girls and boys. Since 2003, there has been a series of new initiatives and national campaigns by non-government organizations (NGOs) and these have been very successful in boosting the enrolment of girls. (KGSM, 2009).

Since the 1980s there has been an increase in the number of voluntary women institutions established in Turkey. Through the mobilization of the general public, these women's institutions have played a significant part in consciousness-raising endeavours on women's problems, opening more centres for helping women who were victims of violence or abuse. The Foundation for the Advancement and Recognition of Turkish Women, The Women's Shelter Foundation of Purple Roof, The Flying Broom, the Association of Women's Rights Protection, Women's Solidarity Foundation, the Association for the Support and Training of Women Candidates are just a few names among more than 150 voluntary women's organizations working nationwide. The number of Women's Studies Centres set up in universities has reached 13 and a Woman's Library was founded. Finally, a number of projects were put into practice by governmental and NGOs to support professional and entrepreneurial skill development for women including Project Supporting Women Entrepreneurship, Professional Development and Employment Project for Girls and Women, Women's Professional Empowerment Project, and Microcredit Project for Women Entrepreneurs (KSGM, 2009).

Although these Governmental and non-governmental initiatives have been quite effective in supporting women's labour, women in the private sector still need to overcome gender barriers in order to prove themselves successful in a male-oriented business culture. In order to understand if private organizations in Turkey apply any policies to enhance the status of their women employees, interviews with managers of two management consulting firms were conducted by the authors of this chapter in 2002 (Kabasakal, Aycan and Karakaş, 2004). These two consulting firms have a wide customer-base and provide services in human resources applications. As reported by the interviewed managers, no firm among their customers was identified as providing any initiatives to enhance the status of women in management. Therefore, introducing positive discrimination policies to advance women to managerial positions seems a viable option for corporations to overcome gender barriers and the glass ceiling phenomenon in business.

The Future

Looking into the future, in order to improve the status of women in all segments of Turkish society, there is a need to improve their education level and close the gap between the two sexes in terms of their education. While primary education is mandatory for both girls and boys, the Turkish State needs to strictly enforce this legislation on families, particularly in the case of girls. The increase in primary education from five to eight years seems to make a significant improvement in the education level in society, particularly among girls. In addition, further increasing compulsory education to 12 years (high school) would improve the social and economic status of women. In order to overcome inequality in the schooling ratio for men and women and to enhance educational opportunities for girls, a higher education budget is needed. Tan et al. (2008) emphasized that, in Turkey, the share of education, which was 4.3 percent in 2007, is still below the OECD average though it has increased by 100 percent compared with the figure in 1995.

In general, laws that influence the general status and employment-related issues of women are gender-neutral. Many recent changes have been made in the constitution, civil law and labour law in order to provide equal opportunities to women. Furthermore, there have been several Governmental, non-governmental and professional initiatives to support women in the areas of education, employment, politics and entrepreneurship. NGOs have been very successful in national campaigns geared towards improving the education levels of girls. More progress aiming at 100 percent schooling needs to be the target.

Governmental organizations, NGOs, as well as private organizations, need to be more active in promoting women's status in economic areas. Although some banks provide special credits targeted at women entrepreneurs, more advertising, less bureaucracy and improved conditions would help in extending credit to women entrepreneurs. Further, organizations can develop human resource practices targeted for employing and promoting more women under equal payment conditions. Private sector performance has been sub-standard in this matter and needs to be actively involved as a social responsibility project. Improving the status of Turkish women in all areas of life would contribute greatly to the well-being of society and would pay back with maximum returns.

References

Adaman, F. and Bulut, T. (2007) *Diyarbakır'dan İstanbul'a 500 Milyonluk Umut Hikayeleri: Mikrokredi Maceraları [500 Million Worth Hope Stories from Diyarbakır to İstanbul: Microcredit Adventures]* (İstanbul: İletişim Yayınları).

Arat, Z. (1994) Liberation or indoctrination: women's education in Turkey, *Boğaziçi Journal: Review of Social, Economic and Administrative Studies,* 8(1–2), 83–105.

Arat, Z. (1999) *Deconstructing Images of the Turkish Woman* (New York, NY: Palgrave).

Arbak, Y., Kabasakal, H., Katrinli A. E., Timurcanday, O. and Zeytinoğlu, I. U. (1998) Women managers in Turkey: the impact of leadership styles and personality, *The Journal of Management Systems,* 10(1), 53–60.

Aycan, Z. (2004) Key success factors for women in management in Turkey, *Applied Psychology: An International Review,* 53(3), 453–477.

Aycan, Z. and Eskin, M. (2005) Childcare, spousal, and organizational support in predicting work-family conflict for females and males in dual-earner families with preschool children. *Sex Roles,* 53(7), 453–471.

Dayıoğlu, M. and Kasnakoğlu, Z. (1997) Kentsel kesimde kadın ve erkeklerin işgücüne katılımları ve kazanç farklılıkları [Differences in participation in labourforce and earnings between men and women in urban areas], *METU Studies in Development,* 24(3), 329–361.

Dedeoğlu, S. (2004) *Working for Family: The Role of Women's Informal Lobor in the Survival of Family-Owned Garment Ateliers in İstanbul, Turkey,* http://www.wid.msu.edu/resources/papers/pdf/WP281.pdf, accessed 2 March, 2009.

Ecevit, Y. (2007) *A Critical Approach to Women's Entrepreneurship in Turkey* (Ankara: International Labour Office).

Eraydın, A. (1998) Dış pazarlara açılan konfeksiyon sanayinde yeni üretim süreçleri ve bu sektörde çalışan kadınlar [New production processes in the ready made garments industry and the role of women], *İktisat Dergisi,* 377(March), 44–53.

Eyüboğlu, A., Özar Ş. and Tufan-Tanrıöver, H. (1998) Kentli kadınların çalışma koşulları ve çalışma yaşamını terk nedenleri [Working conditions of urban women and the reasons for leaving work] *İktisat Dergisi,* 377, 37–43.

Güneş-Ayata, A. (1994) Women in the legislature, *Boğaziçi Journal: Review of Social*, Economic and Administrative Studies, 8(1–2), 107–120.

Gürüz, K. (2001) Dünyada ve Türkiye'de Yükseköğretim: Tarihçe ve Bugünkü Sevk ve İdare Sistemleri [Higher Education in Turkey and the World: History and Administration Systems] (Ankara: ÖSYM Publications).

Healy, G., Özbilgin, M. and Aliefendioğlu, H. (2005) Academic employment and gender: a Turkish challenge to vertical sex segregation, *European Journal of Industrial Relations*, 11(2), 247–264.

İlkkaracan, İ. (1998) Kentli kadınlar ve çalışma yaşamı [Women living in cities and business life]. In A. B. Mirzaoğlu (ed) *75 Yılda Kadınlar ve Erkekler [Women and Men in 75 Years]* (İstanbul, Turkey: Tarih Vakfı, pp. 285–302).

Jost, J. T. and Banaji, M. (1994) The role of stereotyping in system justification and the production of false consciousness, *British Journal of Social Psychology*, 33(1), 1–27.

Kabasakal, H. (1998) Top women managers in Turkey. A. B. Mirzaoğlu (ed.) *75 Yılda Kadınlar ve Erkekler [Women and Men in 75 Years]* (İstanbul: Tarih Vakfı, pp. 303–312.

Kabasakal, H. (1999) A profile of top women managers in Turkey. In Z. F. Arat (ed) *Deconstructing Images of the Turkish Women* (New York, NY: Palgrave, pp. 225–240.

Kabasakal, H., Aycan, Z. and Karakaş, F. (2004) Women in management in Turkey. In M. J. Davidson and R. J. Burke (eds) *Women in Management Worldwide: Facts, Figures and Analysis* (Aldershot: Gower Publishing).

Kabasakal, H. and Bodur, M. (2002) Arabic cluster: a bridge between east and west, *Journal of World Business*, 37(1), 40–54.

Kabasakal, H. and Bodur, M. (2007) Leadership and culture in Turkey: A multifaceted phenomenon. In J. S. Chokar, F. C. Brodbeck and R. J. House (eds) *Culture and Leadership in Across the World, The GLOBE Book of In-Depth Studies of 25 Societies* (Mahwah, NJ: Lawrence Albaum Associates, Inc., pp. 835–874).

Kadınlar (Women). (1990) *Cumhuriyet Gazetesi*, September 15, 7.

Kalaycıoğlu, S. and Rittersberger-Tılıç, H. (1998). İş ilişkilerine kadınca bir bakış: Ev hizmetinde çalışan kadınlar [A woman prospect on business relationships: Women who work for home service]. In A. B. Mirzaoğlu (ed.) *75 Yılda Kadınlar ve Erkekler [Women and Men in 75 Years]* (İstanbul: Tarih Vakfı, pp. 225–235).

Kantola, J. and Squires; J. (2008) *From State Feminism to Market Feminism?* Paper presented at the International Studies Association Annual International Convention, San Francisco, CA, March 26–29.

Koray, M. (1991) *Günümüzdeki Yaklaşımlar Işığında Kadın ve Siyaset [Women and Politics in the Light of Current Approaches]* (İstanbul: Türkiye Sosyal Ekonomik Araştırmalar Vakfı).

KSGM (Kadının Statüsü Genel Müdürlüğü) (2008) *Women in Power and Decision-Making Policy Document*, Directorate General on Status of Women, http://www.ksgm.gov.tr/Pdf/kararalma_ing.pdf, accessed 18 March, 2009.

KSGM (Kadının Statüsü Genel Müdürlüğü) (2009) *Labor Act, Directorate General on Status of Women*, http://www.ksgm.gov.tr/kanun_4857_iskanunu.php, accessed 2 March, 2009.

Ministry of National Education (2006–2007) *National Education Statistics*, http://sgb.meb.gov.tr/istatistik/meb_istatistikleri_orgun_egitim_2006_2007.pdf, accessed 18 March, 2009.

Nalbant, M. (2002) *Kamu Çalışanlarının Kadın Yöneticilerde Liderlik Davranışlarını Algılamaları ve Bir Anket Çalısması [Perceptions of Public Employees in Understanding Leadership Behaviors in Women Managers and A Survey Study]*. Basılmamıs Yüksek Lisans Tezi, Unpublished Master Thesis, Ankara: Gazi Üniversitesi Sosyal Bilimler Enstitüsü.

Örücü, E., Kılıç, R. and Kılıç, T. (2007) Cam tavan sendromu ve kadınların üst düzey yönetici pozisyonuna yükselmelerindeki engeller: Balıkesir ili örnegi [Glass ceiling syndrome and obstacles which impede women's progress towards senior management levels], *Yönetim ve Ekonomi*, 14(2), 117–135.

ÖSYM (2007) *2006–2007 Higher Education Statistics*, Higher Education Council Student Selection and Placement Center, http://www.osym.gov.tr/BelgeGoster.aspx?F6E10F8892433CFFA91171E62F0FF1533D26410A22C2CA34, accessed 18 March, 2009.

Özar, Ş. (1994) Some observations on the position of women in the labor market in the development process of Turkey, *Boğaziçi Journal: Review of Social, Economic and Administrative Studies*, 8(1–2), 21–43.

Özbay, F. (1994) Women's labor in rural and urban settings, *Boğaziçi Journal: Review of Social, Economic and Administrative Studies*, 8 (1–2), 5–19.

Özden, Ö. T. (2006) *Women in Turkey and Turkish Civil Code*, http://www.allacademic.com/meta/p_mla_apa_research_citation/1/2/1/1/9/p121196_index.html, accessed 24 April, 2009.

Özerkmen, N. (2008) Siyaset erkek işi midir? [Is politics a man's business?]. *Cumhuriyet*, 18 December, http://kitapdergi.cumhuriyet.com.tr/?im=yhs&kid=20&hn=24122, accessed 26 March, 2008.

Özgen, Ö. and Ufuk, H. (2000) *Kırsal Kesimde Kadın Egitimi [Education of Women in Rural Areas]* (Ankara: TMMOB Ziraat Mühendisleri Odası Yayınları).

Rankin, B. and Aytaç, I. (2006) Gender inequality in schooling: the case of Turkey, *Sociology of Education*, 79(1), 25–43.

Selim, R. and İlkkaracan, İ. (2006) Kamu sektöründe kadın-erkek farklılıkları [Differences of women and men in public sector]. In D. Bayraktar, F. Çebi and B. Bolat (eds) *Sıtkı Gözlü'ye Armağan [A Gift to Sıtkı Gözlü]* (İstanbul: İstanbul Üniversitesi İşletme Fakültesi Yayınları, pp. 293–306).

SIS (State Institute of Statistics, Prime Ministry, Republic of Turkey) (1995) *Women in Statistics 1927–1992* (Ankara: DIE Press).

Sümer, H. C. (2006) Women in management: Still waiting to be full members of the club, *Sex Roles*, 55(1–2), 63–72.

Tan, M., Ecevit, Y., Sancar-Üşür S. and Acuner, S. (2008) *Türkiye'de Toplumsal Cinsiyet Eşitsizliği: Sorunlar, Öncelikler ve Çözüm Önerileri [Social Gender Inequality in Turkey: Problems, Priorities and Suggestions]*, http://www.tusiad. org/tusiad_cms.nsf/LHome/30328AE15A0B0A61C225748700382F70/$FILE/ KADINRAPOR.pdf, accessed 3 March, 2009.

TISK (Turkish Confederation of Employer Associations) (2008) *OECD Ülkelerinde Kadınlar ve Erkekler [Men and Women in OECD Countries]* (Ankara: Türkiye İşveren Sendikaları Konfederasyonu Yayınları).

TurkStat (2006) *Population and Development Indicators*, Turkish Statistical Institute, http://nkg.tuik.gov.tr/goster.asp?aile=3, accessed 18 March, 2009.

TurkStat (2007) *Household Labour Force Survey Results*, Turkish Statistical Institute, http://www.tuik.gov.tr/isgucu/basla1.do, accessed 18 March, 2009.

TurkStat (2009a) *Address Based Population Registration Results*, Turkish Statistical Institute, http://www.tuik.gov.tr/VeriBilgi.do?tb_id=39&ust_id=11, accessed 2 March, 2009.

TurkStat (2009b) *Population, Demography, Housing and Gender, Political Life*, Turkish Statistical Institute. http://www.turkstat.gov.tr/VeriBilgi.do?tb_ id=41&ust_id=11, accessed 2 March, 2009.

Ufuk, H. and Özgen, Ö. (2001) The profile of women entrepreneurs: a sample from Turkey, *International Journal of Consumer Studies*, 25(4), 299–308.

World Bank (2006) *Turkey Labor Market Study*, http://siteresources.worldbank.org/ INTTURKEY/Resources/361616-1144320150009/Labor_Study.pdf, accessed 6 March, 2009.

Zeytinoğlu, I. U., Özmen, Ö. T., Katrinli, A. E., Kabasakal, H. and Arbak, Y. (1997) Invisible employment: Women as waged domestic workers in Turkey. In B. Fitzpatrick (ed) *Bargaining in Diversity: Colour, Gender, and Ethnicity*, Vol. 6 of the Official Proceedings of the Fifth IIRA European Regional Industrial Relations Congress, Dublin, pp. 59–75.

Zeytinoğlu, I. U., Özmen, Ö. T., Katrinli, A. E., Kabasakal, H. and Arbak, Y. (2001) Factors affecting women managers' careers in Turkey. In M. Cinar (ed.) *The Economics of Women and Work in the Middle East and North Africa (Research in Middle East Economics, Volume 4)*, (Stanford, CT: JAI Press Inc., pp. 225–245)

PART VI

Women in Management – South America

19

Women in Management in Argentina

Roberto Kertész and Haydée Kravetz

Introduction

The City Hall of Buenos Aires, instituted in 1973, annually called for nominations known as the "Illustrious Citizen" but by 2005, of 194 nominations, only 25 were for women (18 percent), However, for the first time in Argentine history, a woman, Cristina Fernández, was elected as President in 2007.

After the severe financial crisis of 2001–2002, a new feminine leadership has developed in Argentina. This might be attributed to the failure of many previous prejudices and to the rise of diversity as a new cultural value. Today we can witness more women than men in public gyms, including participation in the martial arts, which was inconceivable 50 years ago.

According to Heller (2009) women tend to lead with a more horizontal, inclusive style, encouraging teamwork, strengthening the participation of subordinates and bring traditional social skills from their roles at home into the workplace. In younger women in particular, these include more open communication, flexibility, expression and acceptance of emotions, empathy, systemic thinking and faster adaptation to change (Heller, 2009). Moreover, recently the well-known French sociologist, Alain Touraine, affirmed in 2006 in Chile during the election of Michelle Bachelet as President, that: "Women need to be aware that now is their opportunity to transform society… without the need of a feministic approach." Nevertheless, at the same time, whilst women are increasingly entering leadership and managerial positions, they still face home–work conflicts despite men assuming greater responsibilities as fathers and helping with domestic tasks in the home (Heller, 2009). Even so, single mothers who run their homes alone represent a severe unresolved problem in Argentina, especially in the northern provinces and a significant part of the greater province of Buenos Aires (Novik, Rojo and Castillo, 2007). It is also relevant to mention the improvement in the ranking of the Index of Human Development (UN Report, 2003), as Argentina progressed from position 39 to 34 (2003), placing them in top rankings out of 177 countries (UN Report, 2003, see Table 19.1).

Table 19.1   Composition of the Index of Human Development

Index	Longevity	Education	Decent standard of living
Index of Human Development	Life expectancy at birth	Adults alphabetization Combined matriculation	Adjusted by income per capita in parity of Acquisitive Power
Index of Development by Genre	Feminine and masculine expectancy of life at birth	Feminine and masculine rates of adult alphabetization Combined feminine and masculine Relationship of combined matriculation	Adjusted by the income per capita in parity of Acquisitive Power in US$, based on the feminine and masculine participation in the income produced by remuneration

Source: United Nations Report on Human Development, 2003

Labour Force Characteristics

Regarding the labour force characteristics in Argentina, women represent 41.1 percent of the total labour force with around 30 percent of managerial positions, but only 1–2 percent of senior ones. Participation of men and women in the economically active population, employment rate and private registered employment in 2006 are illustrated in Figure 19.1 (Novik, Rojo and Castillo, 2007). Although women represent a 52 percent proportion of the total population, their employment rate is significantly less with only 30.5 percent in private sector employment.

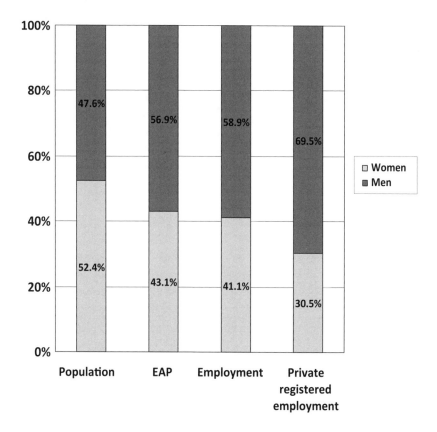

Figure 19.1   Percentage participation of men and women in the
               Economically Active population (EAP), employment and
               private registered employment, 2006

Source: Novik et al (2007)

Table 19.2 highlights how the percentage of women working in manufacturing, commerce and the services have actually decreased since 1996 (Novik, Rojo and Costillo, 2007). What is clear is that there is massive gender segregation in the Argentine workforce, with 75 percent of Latin American women working in the service sectors (ILO, 2008) (see Table 19.3).

Table 19.2   Rate of female employment by sector, every two years and during the decade

Sector	Feminity rate					Differences			
	1996	1998	2001	2004	2006	1996–1998	1999–2001	2001–2006	1996–2006
Manufacturing industries	17.9	18.2	18.7	18.3	18.4	0.3	0.5	-0.3	0.5
Commerce and repairing	28.5	29.5	31.4	31.4	32.4	1.2	1.7	1.1	4
Services	40.4	40.3	42.4	41.9	41.7	-0.1	2.1	-0.8	1.3

Source: Novik, Rojo and Castillo, 2007

Table 19.3   Percentage of women's employment by sector

Branch of activity	Percentage of women working in the branch
Domestic service	94.9
Teaching	76. 4
Social services	63.2
Hotels and restaurants	46.8
Community services	39.5
Public administration and defence	38.8
Commerce	36.8
Financial services	33.5
Manufacture industry	29.3
Transportation and storing	15
Primary activities	11.7
Other branches	19.1

Source: Ministry of Work Report, 2007

Certainly, home and family responsibilities have been shown to influence Argentine women's choices about types of employment (Kertész, Atalaya and Kertész, 2003). A study by Calvo (2006) revealed that four million women were working in Argentina but they were earning 30 percent less than their male counterparts. Furthermore, according to the Ministry of Labour, Employment and Social Security, these active women are 29 percent more likely to lose their jobs compared to men and only one-third reached supervisory/management position.

For many women with children, one of the ways to enter the labour market is through domestic service. According to the Observatorio de la Maternidad (Maternity Observatory, 2009), 20.4 percent of working mothers secure these jobs. Furthermore, almost seven out of ten single mothers are employed in these types of low-pay jobs compared to less than five out of ten married or unmarried women living with their children's father. Finally, this report revealed that 55.2 percent of divorced or separated mothers had unregistered work positions.

It should be noted that low educational levels also act as a strong disadvantage and 42 percent of mothers working in domestic service did not complete high school, indicating the need to promote their education and the prevention of early pregnancies. Undoubtedly, the majority of these women get trapped in the "poverty trap" with little hope of change.

Another study by the Latin American Foundation of Economic Research (FIEL), on the economic trends of Argentine women from 1998 to 2006, showed an increment in their inclusion in the work market. Facilitating factors were a greater family income per capita, smaller number of children and greater investment in education. By 2005, the participation of women in the labour market had risen to 56 percent against 81 percent for men, but both exponents (men and women) with higher-education degrees reached 67.3 percent (Cristini and Bermudez, 2007).

Those women enjoying high and medium income levels can hire domestic help and other employees. However, those women on low incomes still assume the responsibility for running their home as well. According to the INDEC (National Institute of Statistics and Census, 2006), in 1991 women still carried out most of the work in 23 percent of homes; this situation grew to a 32 percent in 2006, but female unemployment fluctuated between 30–40 percent, much greater than in men. Undoubtedly, women's jobs are less stable and easier to eliminate during critical times of the economy and Cristini and Bermudez (2007) found female unemployment was more prevalent in businesses with low profits and in the service and commerce areas.

At the same time, Heller (2009) asserts that: "Time is a scarce resource for everybody, but much more for women. Positions implicating decisions demand around 10–12 hours daily. Paradoxically, most women at high levels are married and with children, which is not common in the United States or Europe, and keeps showing that the new reality demands postgraduate studies as well as travelling abroad, specialized training and job transfers, generating roles conflicts within the family." The report prepared by FIEL (Cristini and Bermudez, 2007) also mentioned the lack of enough career advice available to women as a factor hindering career success. Nevertheless, despite these data, a recent INDEC (2009) report showed that between the third trimester of 2003 and the second of 2009, female salaries had quadrupled from an average of 300 Argentine pesos monthly to 1,200 (taking into account a high inflation rate during this period). Men, on the other hand, only increased 3.55 times, from 450 to 1,600. The International Labour Organization (2008) also reported that women's participation in the Great Buenos Aires area (the zone of the Buenos Aires Province surrounding the capital city) represented 52.3 percent of the total working population, descending in poorer regions such as the northeast and northwest to 45.7 percent.

Table 19.4 illustrates that, by 2007, the pay differential between men and women in Argentina was 0.54 percent compared to 0.8 percent in Sweden and 0.39 percent in Peru (Ministry of Work, 2007).

Table 19.4   Pay differentials in different countries

Country	Pay differential between men and women: relative percentage earned by women
Sweden	0.8
Brazil	0.58
Argentina	0.54
Chile	0.40
Peru	0.39

Source: Ministry of Work Report, 2007

Kliksberg (2009), an internationally well-known economist, stated that not only are social security benefits inferior for women, but women also dedicate much more time to home chores (four hours per day on average compared to half an hour for their partners), as well as to childcare (between one to two hours against a half an hour by the fathers). Another study by ADECCO (2009) Consulting in Human Resources and the Di Tella University on the Latin American Work Index predicted that during 2009 the worldwide employment rate would descend more due to the economic crisis, but on the other hand, more women would be actually looking for employment. They also predicted a change in the so-called Corporate Social Responsibility as organizations are applying work models that reconcile family life and labour, for instance, through special facilities for mothers.

Women Pursuing Education

Similar to other countries, a higher percentage of university (55 percent) and tertiary (75 percent) students in Argentina are women (INDEC, 2006; Fontdevila, 2006) and their academic performance is better than that observed in males. No discrimination exists in relation to the acceptance of female students or teachers in Argentine universities. However, women still predominate in the humanistic and service fields and more men choose hard sciences. Moreover, in certain academic disciplines, some paradoxes can still be observed. For instance, in disciplines such as psychology, with an overwhelming predominance of female students, over 90 percent of professors are men at the Buenos Aires University (Fontdevila, 2006). A similar situation occurs in the school of medicine at the same university, despite the proportion of women studying increasing from approximately 20 percent in 1958 to 60 percent in 2009 (Kertész, personal observation, 2010). This might be related to the current low pay of medical doctors, steering male students to better remunerated careers, such as computing sciences or engineering. However, certain subjects such as engineering persist as "masculine" and teaching, mental health and humanistic studies, as "feminine" (Fontdevila, 2006).

In the University of Flores, as a result of the strong equalitarian approach (depicted in its statute), women head 50 percent of the six schools, and hold two vice-presidencies and three of the five Secretariats: Academic, Finance and Extension (Flores University Organization Chart, 2009).

The amount of women in presidential positions in private universities is only three out of 57 and seven out of 48 in State universities and total only 10 percent.(Ministry of Education, 2009) Nevertheless, the number of women who are deans of schools is higher. We don't have reliable data on this, we estimate this to be a figure of 30 percent, again mostly in social and artistic areas.

Presently there is a governmental project to make secondary education obligatory, similar to Japan. If it progresses, a significant number of girls and also older women might achieve this level of education, increasing their chances of obtaining qualified jobs. It is interesting to note, however, in some occupations women reach their retirement age at 55 (teaching positions in the provinces, for instance) and others at 60 and, as their children are not living in their home, a fair amount of them pursue a university career as mature students, mostly in the social sciences (Flores University student statistics, 1995–2009).

Women in Management

Although women represent 41.1 percent of the workforce, as we mentioned previously, only 1–2 percent of CEOs are women in Argentine firms (Novik, Rojo and Castillo, 2007) and they occupy managerial positions in only 40 percent of all firms (Heller, 2009). In the Argentine Government there is only one CEO, in the Mortgage Bank, Clarisa Estol. According to Heller (2009), women were traditionally accused of insufficient experience and skills to be able to lead at the highest level. Furthermore, Argentine women earn between 30–35 percent less than men in similar positions (International Labour Organization, 2008) and according to the World Economic Forum they occupy the fifty-fourth place in an international list of 58 with regard to salary equality.

Grant Thornton International (2008) reported that only 17 percent of managerial jobs were occupied by women. Indeed, this is quite a low percentage even when compared to other countries of this region: Brazil 39 percent, Mexico 31 percent, Chile 24 percent (Grant Thornton International, 2008). Pregnancy is still considered a limitation to career development and after childbirth mothers tend to reduce their participation in the workforce. In 47 percent of local companies, no women were found in managerial jobs, 29 percent had one woman at a high level, 12 percent had two women and another 14 percent three or more in senior management (Grant Thornton International, 2009).

In synthesis, female presence in the labour market is reduced as they climb up the hierarchy. The highest proportion of women managers are concentrated in the health and financial services, where they occupied 59 percent of managerial posts, 38 percent of section leaders and 10 percent of directors (Heller, 2009). Conversely, the energy sector has the lowest proportion of women in leadership positions, with 20 percent being area heads, 17 percent directors and 15 percent as vice presidents or presidents (Heller, 2009). Moreover, the percentage of women in management decreases even more in operations, production, systems engineering and communications; hence, men predominate in "hard" occupations and women in "soft" ones, particularly those linked to care and social skills (Heller, 2009).

Regarding the "glass ceiling" (discrimination of women in organizations) the National Council for Women (2006) proposed a *vertical_*one, referring to discrimination and prejudice in relation to promoting women into senior positions with higher pay. They also considered *horizontal segmentation,* in which women are segregated into typically female jobs in the service industries and men in traditionally masculine occupations related to production, sciences and advanced technologies. Videla (2009), an executive of Manpower Argentina, stated that besides the glass ceiling, there is also a *cement* one: the self-imposed limitations to ambition and power as well as the fear of taking advantage of flexible working time due to concerns linked to the risk of limiting the chances of promotion.

Videla (2009) also noted that in Latin America, women hold between 25 and 35 percent of leadership positions but in Argentina the figures are even lower, with women holding only 20 percent of managerial jobs and 7 percent of top management positions. In addition to the many obstacles facing women, Videla (2009) also stresses the importance of training and the access to male informal networks. In 2009, the National Institute for Discrimination of Xenophobia and Racism (INADI) supported by the World Bank Group, launched a programme for certification of companies with genre equality .This is a way of fighting the maternity leave prejudice, although research demonstrated that in Argentina the labour costs of maternity paid by Social Security represents only 0.05 percent and that absenteeism for this motive is a fallacy (INADI, 2009).

Now, one needs to question whether increasing the mere quantity of women in management is enough or is their leadership style more important? Maria Rigat-Pflaum, Director of Genre Projects of the Friedrich Ebert German Foundation of Argentina, considers that *both* are important. This author also observed that, in spite of the relatively high proportion of female legislators (38.3 percent), the number of female province governors, majors or ministers in Argentina is very low compared to Brazil, Chile or Colombia (Di Marco, 2005). Furthermore, Polack (2009) reported that only 26 (17 percent) of the 126 most important political posts were occupied by women.

Women also occupy senior posts in the Armed Forces and it is significant that for the first time in Argentine history, the Minister of Defence is a woman, Nilda Garre. Also for the first time in history, two women were designated as

Commissary Inspectors of the Federal Police. One of them, Mabel Franco, a lawyer, was distinguished as an "outstanding personality" by the American Embassy in Argentina, in recognition for promoting the rights of women. Franco is also Chief of the Department of Judicial Support and Social Protection and she teaches at the School of Criminology Sciences of the Federal Police, where 80 percent of students are female, as they consider that this area offers important career opportunities, as well as helping to fight violence and drug addictions. They also stated that their appointments open new avenues for women in the police force. When the women were asked about their ambitions about becoming chief of police, they did not view this as a possibility for them at the moment, but stated that: "If there is a female President, why not have some day a female Chief of Police?" Since 2006, four women have been appointed Commissary Majors in the Buenos Aires Province (Reina, 2009).

Women Entrepreneurs

Between 2007 and 2008, the rate of their female entrepreneurs in Argentina increased from 11.3 percent to 15.8 percent, according to the Global Entrepreneurship Monitor (Torres Carbonell, 2009). Obviously this growth was also influenced by the whirlwind of the international recession: "More than a half of this increase was motivated by financial needs and the deterioration of the financial situation of Argentina in June 2008, when this survey was performed" (Torres Martorell, in Sarelagui, 2009)... "the most popular new businesses included education, clothing, beauty, design, home issues, gastronomy, tourism and services and many female entrepreneurs work from home (with the aid of computers) and are able to balance child care and work more easily" (Torres Martorell, 2009).

In her article on May 26, 2009 in the *Nacion* newspaper, entitled "Argentina has more and more entrepreneur women", Mercedes Bartelt noted that this country progressed from fourteenth to eighth position in two years, according to a worldwide ranking of quality of life and independence (Bartelt, 2009). The first place was awarded to Peru and the second to Thailand, with a Rate of Entreprenurship Activity (REA) of 26.06 percent and 25.95 percent respectively. At the bottom of the ratings were Latvia, Russia and Austria. Other Latin American countries included in the top ten were Brazil (seventh) and Chile (ninth) (Bartelt, 2009). Bartelt (2009) maintained that, between 2005 and 2007, the businesses owned by women in Argentina increased from 7.2 percent to 13.34 percent and nowadays almost 16 percent of the adult female population is related to a self- owned business. These women entrepreneurs tend to be more conservative than their male counterparts but, on average, still work an 18-hour working day. "The gap between masculine and feminine projects is diminishing, as ladies see more opportunities and realized that as entrepreneurs they can harmonize their professional and personal life" (Bartelt, 2009).

On the other hand, Vivot (2006) in her graduation paper at the administration school on "The profile of the entrepreneur women: are they really different form their male peers?", stated in her summary that: "In the last decade, there was a growth in the number of female enterprises, combined with many studies concentrating on their organizational aspects but failing to consider gender differences in their profiles." Comparative research was, therefore, conducted, with a male and a female group of entrepreneurs (15 members each) in the services sector.

Similarities as well as differences were found. The former related to similar objectives, organization structure and development problems for both men and women. The latter depicted a more participative, human and holistic style in women who tended to network and to adapt more easily to environmental changes. Meanwhile, men tended more towards long-range planning and to apply their previous experiences in larger organizations (Vivot, 2006).

Country Legislation

In the Argentine Government, women constitute 48 percent of employees and 11 percent of the highest posts in the ministries. They were first allowed to vote in 1951 and after that date, legislation related to marital rights have changed considerably, allowing similar rights to both parties, overcoming a strong "machista" (discriminate) orientation, and present legislation regarding matrimonial disputes is egalitarian. We must take into account that an overwhelming majority of European immigrants to Argentina arrived from the south of Italy and areas of Spain which underwent nearly 1,000 years of Muslim occupation, which might explain the roots of that prejudiced attitude.

The Law of Female Quotas "specifying at least 30 percent of political parties' proposals for legislative positions are to be women" was approved during the Menem Government in 1991. On the website of the National Council for Women it is stated that "this allowed dealing with long dated hidden agendas, such as violence and sexual aggression towards women, responsible procreation, alimony…" (National Council for Women, 2006; Noticias Breves, 2006).

It is also important to mention that in 2009 the Legislature of the Buenos Aires City Government was declared as "The Year of Women's Political Rights" (law 2715/2008), to be acted upon by means of cultural and teaching meetings, public shows, conferences on historical and political debates and other related activities. This law was remitted to the Women's General Office, a branch of the Ministry of Social Development. Regarding justice, the Supreme Court has two women amongst its nine members. Beatriz Kohen, a member of the Latin American Team of Gender and Justice (ELA), (oriented to improve the situation of women in the Justice), in an interview with journalist Sandra Chaher commented that:

> To have two female members in the Supreme Court of Justice is not the end of discrimination in the field, but it helps as many lawyers of our sex might consider themselves as possible judges. And women are not represented in this area as they should be. They are a majority in the Law Schools and are almost 50 percent of the lawyers. But their access to decision positions does not assure that they have a gender outlook... and this might include their sentences.
>
> (Kohen, 2004a)

Initiatives Supporting Women in the Workforce

According to Faur (2008), the Argentine Senate is made up of 41.6 percent women and 35 female deputies (35 percent), surpassing the minimum quota of 30 percent. In 2008, the Legislature of the Capital City Government (Buenos Aries) was made up of 35 percent women (equal to the National Parliament): in 2007, 33 percent; in 2003, 40 percent; and only 10 percent in 1983, showing important growth (General Direction of Statistics and Census, 2008). At the Executive level in the city, only 18 percent are female, 79 percent are male (with an unoccupied 3 percent), showing once more the limited decision-making power conferred to women (Direccion General de Estadisticas y Censos, 2008).

Regarding the population over 60 years of age, in 2008 63 percent were female and 37 percent males with female life expectancy in 2005 being 80.2 years and males only 72.6 years. These data point to the importance of achieving economic support in old age, particularly for the high number of women (Direccion General de Estadisticas y Censos, 2009).

Recently three women were designated ministerial posts, two in traditionally male ministries – Defence and Economy – and the third in Public Health. Furthermore, two women recently entered the Supreme Court of Justice, but perhaps the most important issue concerns the growing public awareness of cases of gender discrimination, such as the violation of rights. Moreover, the parity of sexes in the legislative bodies is supposed to be achieved internationally around the year 2040 (Faur, 2008).

A recent development is related to the Information and Communication Technologies (ITC) projects with gender perspectives. Argentina, as part of Latin America, suffers from the scarcity of resources for their financing and the difficulties in reaching the cooperation agencies with these funds (Ocampo, 2008). Garcia (2008) has confirmed this, stressing the need to overcome bureaucratic obstacles to obtain economic help for this purposes and stating that in general "we are not empowered to fill these eternal and complicated forms".

Finally, the UNIFEM (United Nations Fund for the Development of Women) held its first Meeting at Cordoba city, Argentina (UNIFEM, 2009), entitled "Where is the money for women's rights?" Its main objectives coincide strongly with the title of this section (initiatives supporting women in the workforce):

- to end the different expressions of violence against women;

- to strengthen the democratic governability, promoting the equality between genders in public management;

- to reduce poverty, inequality and exclusion of women;

- to reduce the dissemination of HIV/AIDS among women and girls.

The Future

It is very important to note that, presently, the quota systems exists only for political positions, stipulating that women occupy 30 percent of posts. However, the Women in Equality Foundation (MEI) published on their website (MEI, 2009) the following document, with requirements for the future, countersigned by the Association of Women Judges of Argentina (AMJA, 2010), which we summarize below:

"What political reform do we want?"

- We want a reform which guarantees the equality of rights between citizens of both sexes.

- The Quota Law is a key factor regarding political representation. Internationally, we occupy fifth place with 41.6 percent of women holding positions in the Parliament, after Rwanda (56.3 percent), Sweden (47.3 percent), South Africa,(43 percent) and Iceland (42. 9 percent), according to the International Institute for Democracy end Electoral Assistance (IDEA, 2009).

- We look forward to a 50 percent representation, to be extended to the Executive (Presidency) and Judicial Power.

- Both sexes need permanent training for political jobs.

- Most political parties have to reform their charters allowing decision power to women.

With the advent of new technology and availability of the Internet, today's women fluctuate between their individual development and childbearing and family commitments. Gitelman's (2009) research on Argentine women from 25 to 45 years of age, concerning their values, indicated that the future trend would be for women to be more self-centered and to enjoy satisfaction from their own achievements, instead of indirectly as "the wife of" or "the mother of successful women".

This new image and role for women inevitably affects male roles, with men increasingly assuming responsibilities for children and home care in a much more balanced way. During times of unemployment, we witnessed in many cases a role inversion, as the wife had the only job to bring money home and the husband had to perform customarily feminine chores such as shopping, cooking, cleaning and looking after the children.

Also the longer life expectancy (48 years in 1900 compared with 80 years in 2005) brings new challenges for "retired" women. As the retirement age usually coincides with the "empty nest" many women with "banal life scripts" (Dusay, 1974) from 55 on, face an existence without purpose. But this can and will be changed.

In the last few years in Argentina, multiple opportunities have arisen for better personal fulfilment of women, including special academic courses, collaboration in non-profit organizations, entrepreneurship, generation of social networks with shared interests, access to entertainment and tourism. Furthermore, despite the economic crisis and educational deficits, we have experienced small increases in female rights. Access for women into higher education continues despite the continued gender segregation in both subject choice and types of careers. Unfortunately, in the foreseeable future, we predict that restrictions to women's access to the higher managerial jobs will persist, in both the private and public spheres. The same goes for their almost complete exclusion from leadership positions in trade unions.

Compared to other Latin American counties, regarding the Opening Dimension for access to work, Argentina is placed second after Brazil. This is especially valuable as it shows that Argentina is surpassing countries with relatively more stable economies, such as Columbia and Chile. Although the percentage of female tertiary and university students is greater than the percentage of males, females currently hold relatively few higher managerial posts in these institutions, and this situation is unlikely to change for some time

The number of female entrepreneurs has undoubtedly increased in the last few years, mainly as a result of the international recession as well as their growing tendency to become more proactive (alone or together as part of a couple). Finally, in relation to country legislation, promoting women's rights issues to gain vote share at forthcoming elections will offer examples of important female role models who "have made it" – these women will serve as inspiration for their peers.

References

ADECCO and Di Tella University-Indice Laboral de América Latina (ILAM) (2009) *Latin American Work Index*, www.adecco.com, accessed 15 October, 2009.

AMJA (Association of Women Jodges of Argentina) (2010) www.amja.org.ar, accessed 13 January, 2010.

Bárcena, A. (2008) *Economic Commission for Latin America and the Caribbean Report*, Executive Secretary, CEPAL, accessed 19 December, 2009.

Bartelt, M. (2009) Argentina tiene más y más emprendedoras [Argentina has more and more women entrepreneurs], *La Nacion*, 26 May 2009.

Berne, E. (1972) *What Do You Say After You Say Hello?* (New York, NY: Grove Press).

Bonder, G. (2009) Regional Chair of UNESCO of Women, Science and Technology in Latin America Clarin, 30 December, p. 50.

Buenos Aires City Government (2008) *2009 as The Year of Women´s Political Rights* (Law 2715/2008), Official Bulletin.

Calvo, P. (2006) www.clarin.com/suplementos/zona/2006/08/20/z-03215.htm, accessed 17 October, 2009.

Consejo Nacional de la Mujer [National Council for Women] (2006) www.cnm. gov.ar/actividades/Actividades2006_Ene_Feb.htm, accessed 16 September, 2009. Cristini, M. and Bermudez, G. (2007) *El Mapa Económico de las m Ujeres Argentinas, 1998–2006 [The Economic Map of Argentine Women, 1998–2006)*, Work Document No. 93, FIEL (Foundation of Latin American Economics Research).

Di Marco, L. (2005) www.lanacion.com.ar/nota.asp?nota_id=761830, 4 December, accessed 16 September, 2009.

Direccion General de Estadisticas y Censos [General Direction of Statistics and Census] (2008) *Buenos Aires City Government*, www.buenosaires.gob.ar, accessed 18 October, 2009.

Direccion General de Estadistica y Censos [General Direction of Statistics and Census] (2009) *Gênero y Ciudad Report*, Buenos Aires City Government, 8 March.

Dusay, K. (1974) *Personal Communication*, San Francisco.

Faur, E. (2008) *Desafíos Para la igualdad de Género en la Argentina, PNUD [Challenges for the Equality of Genres in Argentina]* 1st edition, Buenos Aires, PNUD, www.degeneroweb.pdf, accessed 21 October, 2009.

Flores University (1995–2009) *Student Statistics,* Annual reports to the Ministry of Education of Argentina, 2005–2009, accessed 10 April, 2010.

Flores University (2009) *Organization Chart*, www.uflo.edu.ar, accessed 10 April, 2010.

Fontdevila, E. (2006) *Noticias Breves [News Briefs]*, www.foro.gentelink.com/index.php?action=printpage, accessed 10 October, 2009.

Garcia, D. (2008) *Red Nosotras*, www.ticyep.blogspot.com/2008_03_01_archive. html, accessed 2 November, 2009.

Gitelman, Natalia (2009) *Mujeres a la Conquista de un Espacio Privado [Women in the Conquest of a Private Space]*, www.mujeressinfronteras.com, accessed 28 June, 2010

Grant Thornton International Business Report (2008) in Saralegui, R. Una pared de crystal [A glass wall], *La Nacion*, 8 March, 2009, pp. 1–2.

Heller, Lidia Consulting (2008) International Labour Organization Report, *La Nacion*, 8 March, 2009, www.lanacion.com.ar/nota.asp?nota_id=1106486.

IDEA (International Institute for Democracy end Electoral Assistance) (2009) www.quotaproject.org, accessed 14 January, 2009.

ILO (International Labour Organization) (2008) *Report on Work and Family*, 24 November, www.oit.org.ar/pagina.php?pagina=705, accessed 8 March, 2009.

INADI (National Institute for Discrimination of Xenophobia and Racism) (2009) www.lubertino.org.ar/lubertino/images/.../Informe_Trianual.pdf, accessed 2 December, 2009.

INDEC (National Institute of Statistics and Census, 2006), *La Nacion*, August 9, 2009

INDEC (National Institute of Statistics and Census, 2009) *Permanent Home Survey 2003–2009*, www.indec.gov.ar/nuevaweb/cuadros/74/pob_tot_1sem09.pdf, accessed 2 January, 2010.

Kertész, R. (2010) Personal observation.

Kertész, R., Atalaya, C. and Kertész, A. (2003) *Análisis Transaccional Integrado*, 3rd Edition, Buenos Aires, University of Flores.

Kliksberg, B. (2009) A las Mujeres no les va bien en América Latina [Women don't do well in Latin America], *Clarin Newspaper*, 20 May, p. 25.

Kohen, B. (2004a) Interview with Sandra Chaher, *Pagina 12*, 18 June 2004

Martínez Jiménez, R. (2009) Research on women in family firms. Current status and future directions, *Family Business Review*, 22(1), 53–64.

MEI (Mujeres en Igualdad) [Women in Equality] (2009) www.sdh.gba.gov.ar/comunicacion/links.php, accessed 13 January, 2009.

Ministry of Education of Argentina (2009) www.me.gov.ar, accessed 2 January, 2010.

Ministry of Work Report (2007) *Percentages of Women According to Branch of Activity*, www.trabajo.gov.ar/.../estadisticas/.../Capitulo%203_%20Gestion%20productiva%20y%20diferenciales%20en%20la%2, accessed 30 October, 2009.

Noticias Breves (Brief News) (2006) *Publication of the School of Exact and Natural Sciences*, Buenos Aires University, 22 August, www.fcen.uba.ar/prensa/noticias72006/noticias_22ago:2006.html, accessed 21 October, 2009.

Novik, M., Rojo, S. and Castillo, V. (2007) *El Trabajo Femenino en la Post-Convertibilidad Argentina 2003–2007 [The Feminine Work During the Argentine Post-Convertibility 2003–2007]*, Permanent Survey of Homes, Observatory of Employment and Enterprise Dynamics and CEPAL/GTZ Program, Modernization of the State, Public Administration and Economic Development, Ministry of Work, Employment and Social Security.

Observatorio de la Maternidad [Maternity Observatory] Newsletter Nº 17 (2009), www.o-maternidad.org.ar/.../Newsletter%20del%20observatorio%20 n17.pdf, accessed 8 November, 2009.

Ocampo, I. (2008) *Entre lo Pedido y lo Obtenido, un Delicado Equilibrio [Between the Requested and the Achieved: A Delicate Balance]*, www.enredando.org.ar/ imprimir.shtml, 25 March, accessed 12 June, 2009.

Polack, M. E. (2009) Scarce genre politics, *La Nacion*, promoting women's rights issues to gain vote share at forthcoming elections will offer examples of important female role models who "have made it" – these women will serve as inspiration for their peers.

Ponsowy, M. and Niebieskikwiat, N. (2009) *Mujeres Politicas y Argentinas [Women and Argentine Policy]* (Buenos Aires: Del Nuevo Extremo).

Raggio, J. E. (2009) ADECCO Consulting Group and Di Tella Finances Research Center Report (2008), *La Nacion*, 7 June, www.adecco.com.ar, accessed 30 September, 2009.

Reina, L. (2009) Two women achieved the Commissary Inspector positions in the police, *La Nacion*, 30 December.

Torres Carbonell, S. (2009) *Emprendedoras [Entrepreneurs]*, www.lanacion.com. ar/nota.asp?nota_id=1106486, p. 3, 8 March, accessed 3 November, 2009.

Torres Martorell, S. (2009) *El Techo de Cristal in Emprendedoras [The Glass Ceiling in Entrepreneurship]*, www.lanacion.com.ar/nota.asp?nota_id=1106486, p. 3, 8 March, accessed 3 November, 2009.

UNIFEM (United Nations Development Fund for Women) (2009) *Where is the Money for Women's Rights?* First Encounter, Southern Women Fund, Cordoba, 25 and 26 September, Cordoba, Argentina.

United Nations Report on Human Development (2003).

Videla, M. A. (2009) *Una Pared de Crystal [A Glass Wall]*, www.lanacion.com.ar/ nota.asp?nota_id=1108486, p. 2, accessed 5 November, 2009.

Vivot, M. (2009 *El Perfil de la Mujer Emprendedora: Son Realmente Diferentes de sus Pares Masculinos? [The Profile of the Female Entrepreneur: Are They Really Different from their Masculine Peers?]* Student graduation paper, San Andres University, Argentina, 26 August.

PART VII

Women in Management – Africa

20

Women in Management in South Africa

Babita Mathur-Helm

Introduction

This chapter discusses the changing status of women in management in South Africa. It builds on the conclusions in the 2004 edition of *Women in Management Worldwide* (Mathur-Helm, 2004), and describes the persisting marginalization of women in South Africa as a result of racial, rather than purely gender issues.

First, this chapter provides an overview of South African labour force characteristics, indicating the roles of women and men – which reveal a gendered division of labour, where men are regarded as leaders and women as followers (Pandor, 2005). Women's attitudes towards work are changing, thus allowing them to keep pace with global trends and to manage their work and personal lives more effectively. The following section explores the representation of women among those pursuing education by examining South Africa's educational progress in general, and draws comparisons by referring to a wide range of literature covering various factors affecting the education of women. This is gleaned from discussions over the past 10 to 20 years and the historic changes around women in management. While significant attention has been afforded to foster and utilize the women workforce effectively as leaders and managers through recognition of their talents and skills, the gender gap remains in the corporate workplace, at universities and in society at large. The chapter discusses some of the main barriers for women in career progression and advancement into positions of executive leadership. Next, the focus moves to women entrepreneurs, who are supported through significant small business development initiatives by the South African Government. The chapter then outlines and analyses the country's legislation and organizational initiatives supporting the advancement of women in the workplace. The chapter concludes with recommendations regarding future directions.

Despite the daunting challenges reflected in this introduction, South Africa presently recognizes that women have a crucial role to play in stimulating economic growth, value addition and wealth creation. Furthermore, several financial institutions are trying to align structures and policies with legislative requirements through funding, employment and procurement activities, to meet the aspirations of the country's women.

Labour Force Characteristics

Women account for only a third of the country's labour force (Mathur-Helm, 2005). In mid-2007, the country's population stood at some 47.9 million, up from the 2001 census count of 44.8 million (Statistics South Africa, 2007). While women make up 52.1 percent of the adult (15–65 years) population, only 41.3 percent are employed (Labour Force Survey, 2007). Hence women's labour force participation relative to the adult population does not correspond meaningfully (Industrial Development Corporation (IDC) Annual Report, 2006/07).

Prior to 1994, the apartheid acts curbed the participation of all women, more so the black women, in various aspects of life. Almost one-quarter of African (black) women continue to work in "elementary" occupations like office cleaning and domestic work (Maziya, 2006), and many rely on the wages of their migrant–labourer husbands, working in the mines. Today, black women are the worst off, with an unemployment rate of 52.8 percent (Labour Force Survey, 2006) and are predominantly employed as teachers and nurses (DTI Report, 2008).

Coloured women, in particular, worked in factories in the food and clothing industries. White women were excluded from most formal employment, except secretarial and clerical work. Although this exclusion was not legislated, many white women were denied access to employment by conservative ideas within Afrikaans and English communities about women's place in society (Msimang, 2001).

The year 1999 saw a rise in the numbers of women joining the labour force, due to the emergence of the informal sector which would seem to be basic survival activity, creating little in the way of employment or wealth (Ntoula,

1989) through entrepreneurship. This led to more than half of the female self-employment growth rate between 1995 and 1999 (Klasen and Woolard, 2000).

The Labour Force Survey (2005) reported a rise in the unemployment rates of women at 31.7 percent, higher than the unemployment rates of men at 22.6 percent during the same period. In 2006, a similar pattern was evident in the absorption (which refers to the percentage of the employed population within the working age, Statistics South Africa, 2007) of women at 34.1 percent and men at 49.3 percent, with participation rates of women at 49.9 percent and men at 63.7 percent (Labour Force Survey, 2006). In 2007, the employment was partially stable due to higher unemployment rates, so much so that the labour force participation rate for both women and men remained unchanged since 2006 (Labour Force Survey, 2007).

Another relevant trend regarding gender wage differences and ethnicity found traces of race-specific gender discrimination among women. Most black and coloured women work in the informal sectors and are concentrated in low-paying jobs, and earn less than men for the same jobs (Hinks, 2002). Standing, Sender and Weeks (1996) found huge wage discrepancy related to race and gender, wherein white women not only earned more than the black men's equivalent, but also received far higher wages in the same job compared to black women (Hinks, 2002). Similarly, Hinks (2002) indicated a lower average female wage rate in the technician and associate professional clerk sectors than the equivalent male figures.

In the IT sector, women are underrepresented, which corresponds with the current reality for women across the globe. It should be noted that in South Africa, the lower representation of women in certain high-tech jobs has as much to do with race as it does with gender (Gender Initiative Institute, 2004).

Women Pursuing Education

Although, 61 percent of the total population of 5 million uneducated adults are women in South Africa (James, 2000; Chigona and Chetty, 2007), their education status has certainly improved since the 1994 transition. Historically in South Africa access to both tertiary and high school education has been the domain of the privileged minority. The decision about who would be educated 10 to 15 years ago is impacting on the current selection pool of potential management and executive candidates (April, Dreyer and Blass, 2007).

Some of the indicators of improvement in women's educational status are the implementation of the African National Congress Policy Framework for Education and Training (1994) and the National Gender Summit (2001) largely neglected in the process of transformation (Chigona and Chetty, 2007). Today, South Africa has the highest levels of female education in Africa, more girls enrolling for primary, secondary and tertiary education (Global Gender Gap Report, 2008), as well as a much larger percentage of women participation in the economy (40 percent).

Although girls at the primary levels achieve at an equal level with boys, however, their performance in secondary schools begins to falter (Hallman, 2004). Approximately, 35 percent of girls have had school delays compared to 45 percent of boys between the ages of 14 to 15 years. The school delays for girls are reported to be pregnancy-related (adolescent childbearing in South Africa is high), causing huge hindrances to the girls' educational success (Chigona and Chetty, 2007).

Present-day South Africa finds more women being educated in the fields of business and commerce (Makosana, 2001). Although, they still constitute, on average, less than 30 percent of MBA students, and the faculty of business schools remains predominantly male (Grobler, 2006). Between 2006 and 2008, there were 71 percent male and 29 percent female enrolments in the MBA programme in South Africa. The numbers of women on the MBA programme have, however, grown from 20 percent in 2000 (Mathur-Helm, 2004) to 30 percent presently.

The impact of gender discrimination on women was filtered through a rigid system of race discrimination – so that white women would have been negatively affected, but black women would have been subjected to the combined negative impact of both gender and race discrimination (De la Rey and Duncan, 2003). Higher education was stratified along racial lines with different institutions for each racial group. The repercussions of that are even felt to this day, as young black graduates acquire their qualifications quite late at the postgraduate and master's levels.

In addition, economic pressures also hindered black women's ability to acquire higher education (Makosana, 2001; Yamatoni, 1995). Makosana (2001) found strong parental contributions at the undergraduate levels, followed by scholarships at the graduate level, and women's own contributions, spousal benefits and combinations of other sources to be the other alternatives, as sources of funding for higher education. Makosana (2001) indicates sometimes black women had to shoulder the full financial burden for their education; however, a strong belief in the value of education, developed through their families, helped those who dropped out to come back and finish their degrees and to secure high-ranking positions within the South African education system.

Today, the schools are becoming more multicultural in enrolling students across racial lines; hence, several historically disadvantaged children have the opportunity to enrol at private and semi-private schools to acquire quality education, since today their parents can afford it.

Women in Management

South Africa faces key challenges in the development and retention of their women from middle to senior/executive and top management levels. Women's development is often submerged in the overall talent management strategy, as predominantly male, senior executives overlook their development (Babb, 2006). According to Babb (2006) three people (one woman and two men) from a particular bank were, for example, accepted for enrolment on an MBA programme, but the bank paid for the men's studies only, and refused to pay the woman's fees. Needless to say she soon left the bank and sought employment elsewhere. Hence, South Africa's businesses are overlooking opportunities to attract, retain and develop their women managers (Babb, 2006).

Besides several dynamics, South African women's biggest challenge is in becoming their families' sole breadwinners, as many husbands are losing jobs (Mathur-Helm, 2006). Not understanding that families can sometimes become the barrier to their career, women often reject a challenging career or a high-paying position for fear of getting caught with extra burdens. They hence continue working at lower-level positions in order to keep both their home and work worlds going (Mathur-Helm, 2006). Powell and Butterfield (2003) and O'Connor (2001) suggest that more women than men do not wish to occupy senior management positions or are less interested than men in reaching the senior management ranks. Perhaps this is the case because they have different aspirations to men (O'Connor, 2001).

Some researchers (for example, Rosener, 1995) have suggested that women have a more relational, cooperative and compassionate style of leadership, as opposed to men. This leadership style clashes with the general commanding and controlling style of management and leadership that most South African organizations still practice. They firmly believe that women do not show leadership potential and behave differently from conventional male leaders in ways that could be detrimental to themselves and to the organizations (Mathur-Helm, 2004).

These organizations fail to see women as an integral part of decision making in sectors where major economic and financial matters are involved (Mathur-Helm, 2006), hence, women's access to decision-making positions is restricted. April, Dreyer and Blass (2007) refer to Pile (2004) who stated: "Where women are being advanced, it is because of regulatory requirements and not because it is seen as a competitive advantage."

While the work environment in South Africa is highly regulated by legislation, leading to greater equity in the workplace (Mathur-Helm, 2004), most corporate organizations claim to have eliminated discrimination by changing their educational parity and social attitudes towards women (Mathur-Helm, 2006). However, the South African Women in Corporate Leadership Census (2006) takes a brief look at some of the company-specific targets for 2008, which clearly indicate that not many women, particularly the non-whites, have managed to reach the top management and corporate board-level positions yet.

In 1998, white males constituted 89 percent of senior management in South Africa, with 6 percent being black males and the remaining 5 percent being either from the coloured or the Indian population. The 2006 census indicates some rise and some decline in the representation of women corporate leaders (women directors and women executive managers). Women's directorship has increased from 10.7 percent in the previous annual census to 11.5 percent in 2006 (Grobler, 2006). In conjunction, there was a decrease in the numbers of women senior/executive managers from 19.8 percent to 16.8 percent, despite a significant increase in the numbers of executive managers from 5,558 in 2005 to 7,890 in 2006, thus indicating a much larger male selection for the positions than females, which is a concern. In all management levels black women are in the minority, and account for only 11.4 percent of managerial positions, 1.2 percent top management positions and 0.5 percent occupancy as directors in major South African companies while white women account for 18.4 percent (CASE, 2006). Lack of education, societal perceptions, the glass ceiling, the queen bee syndrome and work–life balance issues are some of the main barriers to career progression and advancement of black women to positions of executive leadership (April, Dreyer and Blass, 2007; Thompson, 2006; Van der Boom, 2003).

Burke and McKeen (1994) indicate that access to executive opportunities is heavily dependent upon an individual's level of education. Similarly, Muiruri-Mwagiry (2006) suggests that entry to equal opportunities in leadership begins with access to education and the acquisition of the right qualifications. The biggest reported threat posed to the advancement of women to positions of executive leadership in this country is a lack of access to quality high school and tertiary education (April, Dreyer and Blass, 2007). While qualification levels, which are objective merits likely to enhance credibility, are more beneficial to women than to men, who have less difficulty assuming a managerial role (Melamed, 1996), qualification levels can also be a vehicle for helping women to break through the glass ceiling (Leeming and Baruch, 1998; Mathur-Helm, 2006).

Although women are entering management positions in increasing numbers, their access to senior leadership positions is limited (April, Dreyer and Blass, 2007). According to Mathur-Helm (2006) several social, cultural and structural barriers emerging from societal perceptions account for this. Given that South African organizations have failed to see their women managers in the role of senior leaders, possibly the very few women who have managed successfully to reach the top levels have done so by displaying the male-oriented commanding and controlling leadership traits, while the rest who have remained unsuccessful in reaching the top levels have possibly clashed with the existing male leadership models, owing to their less commanding and controlling styles.

Mathur-Helm (2006) found the glass ceiling to be an invisible barrier preventing women from moving up the corporate ladder; thus, indicating its existence in South African corporate environments. Perhaps, an additional challenge for them would be to maintain a balance between career and family – the latter duty dictated by societal pressures around women's role in child-rearing (April, Dreyer and Blass, 2007; Booysen, 2007). Women in South Africa are aware that balancing personal/family life with a corporate career may be too demanding for them and will require many sacrifices. On one hand, there are women who have to take professional roles seriously as they are increasingly becoming sole breadwinners (Mathur-Helm, 2006), but they are having to reject high-paying positions in order to be able to provide full care as well as emotional and psychological support to their families. On the other hand, a set of women is emerging which is becoming less and less involved with family affairs, by reducing family burdens and remaining single or delaying partnerships and having children (Mathur-Helm, 2006). Both situations are bringing women face-to-face with various dilemmas, impelling them to make complex personal choices (Mathur-Helm, 2006). However, in all of this the men's roles are also changing as many of them are losing their jobs and becoming secondary breadwinners or household husbands.

Finally, the existence of the queen bee syndrome could be another barrier to career progress of women executives, not only in South Africa, but worldwide (Davidson and Cooper, 1992). April, Dreyer and Blass (2007) describe a queen bee as an executive woman who is unhelpful to other women, partly because of a desire to remain unique in an organization. Thus, it is an attitude of reluctance by executive women to risk their own careers by promoting other women (April, Dreyer and Blass, 2007; Staines, Travis and Hayagrante 1973). No South African study has as yet indicated the existence of the queen bee syndrome in the country's corporate organizations. However, the attitudes and behaviours of some women board directors make one ponder whether this is indeed evidence of the queen bee mode.

The present government has streamlined its policy to include women at all levels of society; thus clearly indicating a significant change in women's role and place in the government. The presence of a critical mass of women parliamentarians has been very important in the adoption of legislation that is not gender sensitive (Pandor, 2005). 2005 saw a dramatic change in government with the appointment of South Africa's first female deputy president (Top Women in Business and Government, 2006). Currently in South Africa up to 37 percent of all parliamentary seats and 43 percent of the national cabinet are held by women, with the majority being black women (Myakayaka-Manzini, 2002). Most State municipalities are now pushing for greater reforms in the gender composition of the political and administrative structures by appointing nearly 50 percent of women in senior management positions and mayoral committees.

Women Entrepreneurs

The South African Women Entrepreneurs' Network (SAWEN) was established to assist aspiring and existing women in business. The network advocates policy changes and capacity building, and facilitates the access of women to business resources and information (Top Women in Business and Government, 2006). It is supported by the National Department of Trade and Industry, along with JSE Limited (formerly the JSE Securities Exchange South Africa). It has implemented strategies to train women entrepreneurs in the working of stocks, commodity and bond markets, and also how to engage with markets (Top Women in Business and Government, 2006).

From construction to manufacturing and from medical research to textile design, women and women-owned companies are making their mark in every sphere of business and industry in South Africa (Industrial Development Corporation (IDC) Annual Report 2006/07). Out of an estimated 1.7 million non-VAT registered businesses in the country, approximately 91 percent were owned by Black Africans, and 33 percent of the existing businesses are women owned (Scarborough and Zimmerer, 2000). Black women predominantly run the largest single self-employed segment and small business segment, with low participation in value-adding business opportunities (Labour Force Survey, 2005). Comparatively, the white women entrepreneurs are better placed compared to their black counterparts. For example, they are more qualified and skilled with 8.9 percent of white women in semi-skilled positions compared to 27.7 percent representation of black women (Altman, 2005; Labour Force Survey, 2006).

Entrepreneurship offers women the opportunity to use their skills and experience, but also allows them to opt out of the rat race (April, Dreyer and Blass, 2007). Hence, one of the primary motivations for women to choose entrepreneurship over a corporate career is to have quality of life (April, Dreyer and Blass, 2007). But, while women find empowerment and flexibility through entrepreneurship, several barriers still exist for them to fully participate as entrepreneurs. One of these is the very real entry barrier, as reflected in the uneven distribution of business ownership between women and men entrepreneurs. Female entrepreneurs avoiding the male-dominated business sectors, for instance, have insufficient access to finance and credit facilities, no collateral, no or poor credit history, no business track record and lack of legal status (Mathur-Helm, 2008; O'Neill & Viljoen, 2001). This is combined with the psychological hindrances embedded in cultural norms, obstacles in employment legislation and policy, and lack of information, training, finance, markets, technology and business infrastructure (Mathur-Helm, 2008). Additionally, absence of infrastructure for skills development and capacity-building, and a fragmented approach to identifying issues and developing strategies to influence policy affecting business and government interventions (DTI, 2006), are further barriers to women's growth as entrepreneurs.

Country Legislation

A broad turf of legislative support presented to women in the decade 1999–2008, included: the rewriting of the tax tables in 1995, the Liberation of Abortion Act in 1996, the Customary Marriage and Domestic Violence Acts in 1998, the Maternity Provisions and Breast-Feeding Code in 1997, the Basic Conditions of Employment Act in 1996 and the Sexual Harassment Code in the Labour Relations Act of 1996 (Haffajee, 1999; Mathur-Helm, 2004), along with attention to reproductive health and nutrition, equality in education and employment, childcare and related policies. Additionally, the Government authorized the international Convention on the Elimination of All Forms of Discrimination against Women (CEDAW), by passing the Gender Policy Framework (GPF) in 1996 and the Employment Equity Act of 1998 have made women legal equals of men in the workplace, by increasing their representation from 41 percent in 2000 (Labour Force Survey, 2002) to 49.9 percent in 2006.

The legislation is supported by numerous government initiatives. These include a National Women's Empowerment Policy, the signing of a number of United Nations Conventions on Women, the Joint Standing Committee on the Improvement of the Quality of Life and Status of Women, the Commission on Gender Equality, the Women's Charter for Effective Equality (1993), the Interim Constitution of the Republic of South Africa (1993), the Reconstruction and Development Programme (1994), the National Report of the Status of Women in South Africa prepared for the World Conference on Women held in Beijing in 1995, and South African Women on the Road to Development, Equality and Peace (Beijing Conference Plan of Action, 1995), for increasing women's participation in the policy and decision-making processes.

Initiatives Supporting Women in the Workforce

In the past few years, job advertisements are becoming more and more inviting to women (Mathur-Helm, 2004), by informing the masses about the importance of valuing and utilizing the female workforce. Generally, job advertisements mention clearly that only an affirmative-action candidate need apply, which indicates female or a non-white candidates. Hence, suitably qualified women have an opportunity to apply.

Previously, white women's aspirations and opportunities were limited by the policies of banks that would not let married women take out loans or open accounts without the permission of their husbands; by employers who fired women when they got pregnant; and by an educational system that encouraged women to take courses in nursing or teaching at school level rather than in dentistry or higher education (Msimang, 2001). This began to shift towards the 1980s as university enrolment evened out for white women and men, and as career opportunities began to open up in a number of non-traditional disciplines (Msimang, 2001). The Basic Conditions of Employment Act of 1997 (BCEA) and the Labour Relations Act of 1995 (LRA) have influenced the style and parameters within which workers can be employed and organized as it sets out clear-cut rules about overtime, working hours and remuneration, while the LRA allows legal strikes and industrial action for all workers (Msimang, 2001).

The Future

South Africa is an upper-middle income country, but is a country of stark contrasts. The extreme inequality evident in its society means that one sees destitution, hunger and overcrowding side-by-side with affluence (Woolard, 2002). Many women are still trapped in these debilitating circumstances and will only be freed when socio-political transformation finally becomes a reality for the poorest of the poor. Despite various efforts to equalise society by the Government, the private sector and individuals since 1994, the attainment of an equitable society, also for women, faces seemingly insurmountable hurdles of every kind and is not yet in sight.

In the more affluent strata of South African society, barriers and challenges remain deep-seated for women of all races embarking on executive careers. While the handicaps imposed by the race-related discriminatory policies of the past still present serious obstacles, many other factors stand in the way of women's progress. With South Africa's tradition-based society, cultural and social values and expectations also play a huge role in defining the gender roles and identities for people at large. The barriers in reaching executive and leadership positions are constructed largely from the stereotypes of female roles, and often even empowered women do not know how exactly to break free from these. Indeed, getting to the top of the leadership ladder takes more than qualifications, experience and tenacity. Without the right support structure in place, women who are also mothers will find it seemingly impossible to succeed in the top echelons of business.

References

Altman, M. (2005) Wage trends and Dynamics in SA, HSRC Report.

April, K., Dreyer, S. and Blass, E. (2007) Gender impediments to the South African executive boardroom, *South African Journal of Labour Relations*, 31(2), 51–65.

Babb, S. (2006) 'The skills challenge: Attracting, retaining and skilling women', *Top Women in Business and Government*, 3rd Edition, TOPCO Publishers, Cape Town.

Booysen, L. (2007) Social identity challenges: Challenges facing leadership. In K. April and M. Shokley (eds) *Diversity in Africa: The Coming of Age of a Continent* (Basingstoke: Palgrave Macmillan).

Burke, R. and McKeen, C. (1994) Career development among managerial and professional women. In M. Davidson and R. Burke (eds) *Women in Management: Current Research Issues* (London: Paul Chapman).

Chigona, A. and Chetty, R. (2007) Girls' education in South Africa: special consideration to teen mothers as learners, *Journal of Education for International Development*, 3(1).

Community Agency for Social Enquiry (CASE) (2006) *Management Employment in South Africa: a Review and Some Projections*, Government publishers, South Africa.

Davidson, M. and Cooper, C. (1992) Shattering the Glass ceiling: The Woman Manager (London: Paul Chapman).

De la Rey, C. and Duncan, N. (2003). Racism: A socio-psychological perspective. In K. Ratele and K. Duncan (eds) *Social Psychology and Inter-group Relations in South Africa* (Cape Town: Press/Juta & Co., pp. 45–66).

DTI Report (2006) Department of Trade and Industry, Republic of South Africa.

Gender Initiatives Institute Report (2004) Cisco Learning Institute, South Africa.

Global Gender Gap Report (2008) World Economic Forum, Geneva, Switzerland.

Grobler, J. (2006) So where to for South African women in corporate leadership?, *Top Women in Business and Government*, 3rd Edition, TOPCO Publishers, Cape Town.

Haffajee, F. (1999) Who will cook for the women MPs?, *Mail & Guardian*, 25 February.

Hallman, K. (2004) Orphanhood, Poverty and HIV Risk Behaviours among Adolescents in KwaZulu-Natal, South Africa, Population Council, New York.

Hinks, T. (2002) Gender wage differentials and discrimination in the new South Africa, *Applied Economics*, 34, 2043–2052.

Industrial Development Corporation (IDC) *Annual Report 2006/07*, Parliamentary Monitoring Group, South Africa.

James, W. (2000) *Values, Education and Democracy*, Report of Working Group on Values in Education, South Africa.

Klasen, S. and Woolard, I. (2000) Surviving Unemployment without State Support: Unemployment and Household Formation in South Africa, Sonderforschungsbereich 386, Institute of Statistic Publication.

Labour Force Survey (2000) Statistics South Africa.

Labour Force Survey (2002) Statistics South Africa.

Labour Force Survey (2005) Statistics South Africa.

Labour Force Survey (2006) Statistics South Africa.

Labour Force Survey (2007) Statistics South Africa.

Leeming, A. and Baruch, Y. (1998) The MBA as a bridge over the troubled waters of discrimination, *Women in Management Review*, 13(3), 95–104.

Makosana, N. Z. (2001) Accessing higher education in Apartheid South Africa: a gender perspective, *Jenda: A Journal of Culture and African Women Studies*, 1(1).

Mathur-Helm, B. (2004) Women in management in South Africa. In M. J. Davidson and R. J. Burke (eds) *Women in Management Worldwide: Facts, Figures and Analysis* (Aldershot: Gower Publishing).

Mathur-Helm, B. (2005) Equal opportunity and affirmative action for South African women: a benefit or barrier?, *Women in Management Review*, 20(1 and 2).

Mathur-Helm, B. (2006) Women and the glass ceiling in South African banks: an illusion or reality?, *Women in Management Review*, 1(4).

Mathur-Helm, B. (2008) Women entrepreneurs in South Africa. In S. Fielden, M. Davidson and R. Burke (eds) *International Handbook of Women and Small Business Entrepreneurship* (Cheltenham: Edward Elgar).

Maziya, M. (2006) Employment equity and the labour market. In D. Gqubule (ed.) *Making Mistakes Righting Wrongs* (South Africa: Jonathan Ball Publishers).

Melamed, T. (1996) Career success: An assessment of a gender specific model, *Journal of Occupational and Organisational Psychology*, 69(3), 217–242.

Msimang, S. (2001) Affirmative action in the new South Africa: the politics of representation, law and equity, *Women in Action*, 2.

Muiruri-Mwagiry, W. (2006) *Gender and Empowerment in the Context of African Leadership in a Changing world*, Communication, Learning and Leadership Lecture Series, Graduate School of Business, UCT.

Myakayaka-Manzini, M. (2002) *Women Empowered: Women in Parliament in South Africa*, International IDEA handbook (South Africa: IDEA).

Ntoula, R. (1989) Spaza Shops: backbone of the informal sector, *African Business & Chamber of Commerce Review*, 16(6).

O'Connor, V. J. (2001) Women and men in senior management – a "different needs" hypothesis, *Women in Management Review*, 16(8), 400–404.

O'Neill, R. C. and Viljoen, L. (2001) Support for female entrepreneurs in South Africa: Improvement or decline, *Journal of Family Ecology and Consumer Sciences*, 29.

Pandor, N. (2005) Address by the Minister of Education at the Women Creating Wealth Conference, Gauteng, South Africa.

Pile, J. (2004), *A Fair Opinion*, http://www.bwasa.co.za.

Powell, G. and Butterfireld, A. (2003) Gender, gender identity, and aspirations to top management, *Women in Management Review*, 18(1/2), 88–96.

Rosener, J. B. (1995) America's Competitive Secret: Women Managers (New York, NY: Oxford University Press).

Rospabe, S. (1999) The Role of South African Trade Unions on Discrimination against African Workers, Mimeo, University of Auvergne.

Scarborough, N. M. and Zimmerer, T. (2000) *Effective Small Business Management: An Entrepreneurial Approach* (Englewood Cliffs, NJ: Prentice Hall).

South African National Census (2006) Statistics South Africa.

Staines, G., Tavris, C. and Hayagrante, T. (1973) The queen bee syndrome. In Tavris, C. (ed.) *The Female Experience* (Del Mar, CA: CRM Books).

Standing, G., Sender, J. and Weeks, J. (1996) *Restructuring the Labour Market: The South African challenge*, An ILO Country Review, International Labour Organisation, Geneva.

Statistics South Africa (2001) South African Population Census.

Statistics South Africa (2006) South African Population Census.

Statistics South Africa (2007) South African Population Census.

Thompson, T. (2006) *South African Women in Corporate Leadership: Census 2006*, Businesswomen's Association, http://www.bwasa.co.za.

Top Women in Business and Government (2006) 3rd Edition, Cape Town.

Unterhalter, E. (2004) Gender Equality and Education in South Africa: Measurements, Scores and Strategies, Paper delivered at British Council, HSRC Conference, Cape Town.

Van der Boom, M. (2003) Women in international management: An international perspective on women's ways of leadership, *Women in Management Review*, 18(3), 132–146.

Woolard, I. D. (2002) *An Overview of Poverty and Inequality in South Africa*, Working paper, Human Science Research Council, South Africa.

Yamatoni, H. (1995) Consequences of academic fund shortage for low income black students: the needs study, *Journal of Education*, 64(Spring), 154–161.

Index